Paul's Way
of Knowing

Paul's Way of Knowing

Story, Experience, and the Spirit

Ian W. Scott

Baker Academic
a division of Baker Publishing Group
Grand Rapids, Michigan

© 2006 by Mohr Siebeck, Tübingen, Germany

Published in 2009 by Baker Academic
a division of Baker Publishing Group
P.O. Box 6287, Grand Rapids, MI 49516-6287
www.bakeracademic.com

Originally published in 2006 in Tübingen, Germany, by Mohr Siebeck GmbH & C. KG Tübingen as
Implicit Epistemology in the Letters of Paul

Printed in the United States of America

Library of Congress Cataloging-in-Publication Data is on file at the Library of Congress, Washington,
DC

ISBN 978-0-8010-3609-5

Contents

Part Two: The Structure of Paul's Knowledge

Preface

This book represents a revised version of my Ph.D. dissertation, completed at McMaster University. I owe a debt of gratitude to my doctoral supervisor, Prof. Stephen Westerholm. Though I have, at times, winced at his trenchant criticisms, his relentless attention to detail has saved me from writing a much poorer piece of work. I cannot now talk about Paul, or any other writer for that matter, without hearing Prof. Westerholm's refrain in my ears: "Where is it in the text?" Perhaps even more important, he has taught me to be rigorously honest about the object of my study and to recognize the subtle signs that my own ideas are beginning to run roughshod over what Paul has written. Beyond all of this, however, I am grateful for his friendship and his encouragement when the road was difficult.

I must also thank my other professors at McMaster University, in particular professors Eileen Schuller, Adele Reinhartz, Alan Mendelson, and Graeme MacQueene. I am deeply grateful both for the chance to learn from their rich understanding of the first-century world and for the way they have treated me from the beginning as a colleague and friend. I regret not having had the time to take seminars with Prof. Peter Widdicombe and Prof. Travis Kroeker, but their friendship, advice, and conversation also helped to make my years at McMaster, and my work on this book, both richer and easier to bear. One's intellectual life does not begin, of course, at the start of Ph.D. studies, and I would be remiss if I did not acknowledge the role of my earlier teachers. In particular, Prof. Iain Provan and Prof. Rikki Watts both helped to ignite my fascination with early Christianity and Judaism, and both have continued to offer welcome encouragement and advice.

Thanks are also due to my fellow graduate students at McMaster. I now realize that the community we enjoyed in the basement of University Hall was a rare thing. I am especially grateful for the friendship of David Vuyadinov, Ken Penner, David Miller, Derek Melanson, and Scott Dunham, all of whom helped in different ways to spur this work on. Nor can I forget the communities at Church of the Resurrection, Anglican, and St. John the

Evangelist Anglican Church in Hamilton, who provided my spiritual nourishment.

I was foolish enough to ignore the gentle advice of my professors and to take up a full-time faculty position before this thesis was finished. I only wish, however, that all of my poor decisions would turn out as well as this one has. My completing of the thesis, and now its publication in the present form, is due in large part to the patient support and warm encouragement of my colleagues at King's University College at The University of Western Ontario.

I am grateful to Prof. Jörg Frey and the other editors for including this volume in the *Wissenschaftliche Untersuchungen zum Neuen Testament*, and to Mr. Matthias Spitzner for his patient help in preparing the manuscript. I also appreciate the useful comments of the several people who read the manuscript in various stages of revision, and I am especially grateful to Dr. David Miller for taking the time during a busy summer to read the penultimate draft. My tireless research assistant, Ian Koiter, also saved me much needed time chasing down some of the last few references and checking the indices.

Finally, I must thank my wife, Susan, and my children, Emmett, Elizabeth, and Kathryn. Without their loving support the long evenings and weekends in the library and the office would have been impossible. It is the time spent with them which has helped me to remember that I am a human being first and a scholar second. I only hope that I can offer as much in return.

London, Ontario   August 2005

Abbreviations

1. Bible and Apocrypha

Books not listed here are cited with the full form of their names.

Gen	Genesis	Esth	Esther
Exod	Exodus	Neh	Nehemiah
Lev	Leviticus	2 Esdr	2 Esdras (LXX)
Deut	Deuteronomy	Ps	Psalms
Josh	Joshua	Prov	Proverbs
Judg	Judges	Isa	Isaiah
1 Sam	1 Samuel	Jer	Jeremiah
1 Kgs	1 Kings	Ezek	Ezekiel
2 Kgs	2 Kings	Dan	Daniel
3 Kdms	3 Kingdoms (LXX)	Hos	Hosea
4 Kdms	4 Kingdoms (LXX)	Mic	Micah
1 Chr	1 Chronicles	Nah	Nahum
2 Chr	2 Chronicles	Hab	Habakkuk
Bar	Baruch	2 Macc	2 Maccabees
Bel	Bel and the Dragon (in additions to Daniel)	3 Macc	3 Maccabees
		4 Macc	4 Maccabees
Jdt	Judith	Sir	Ben Sira
1 Esd	1 Esdras		(Ecclesiasticus)
Add Esth	Additions to Esther	Tob	Tobit
4 Ezra	*4 Ezra*	Wis	Wisdom of Solomon
Matt	Matthew	2 Thess	2 Thessalonians
Rom	Romans	1 Tim	1 Timothy
1 Cor	1 Corinthians	2 Tim	2 Timothy
2 Cor	2 Corinthians	Phlm	Philemon
Gal	Galatians	Heb	Hebrews
Eph	Ephesians	Jas	James
Phil	Philippians	1 Pet	1 Peter
Col	Colossians	2 Pet	2 Peter
1 Thess	1 Thessalonians		

2. Other Ancient Authors, Writings, and Collections

1 En.	*1 Enoch*
1QapGen	*Genesis Apocryphon*
1QH	*Hodayot* (*Thanksgiving Hymns*)
1QM	*Milḥamah* (*War Scroll*)
1QpHab	*Pesher Habakkuk*
1QS	*Rule of the Community* (*Serek Hayaḥad*)
2 Bar.	*2 Baruch*
2 En.	*2 Enoch*
2 Bar.	*2 Baruch*
4QFlor	*Florilegium* (*Midrash on Eschatology*[a])
4QMMT	*Miqṣat Ma'aśê ha-Torah*
4QpNah	*Pesher Nahum*
11QT	*Temple Scroll*
A.J.	Flavius Josephus, *Antiquitates judaicae* (*Jewish Antiquities*)
Abr.	*De Abrahamo* (*On the Life of Abraham*)
Adol. poet. aud.	Plutarch, *Quomodo adolescens poetas audire debeat*
Aet.	Philo, *De aeternitate mundi* (*On the Eternity of the World*)
Agr.	Philo, *De agricultura* (*On Agriculture*)
Am.	(Pseudo-)Lucian of Samosata, *Amores* (*Affairs of the Heart*)
Ant. rom.	Dionysius of Halicarnassus, *Antiquitates romanae*
Ap. Const.	*The Apostolic Constitutions*
Apoc. Ab.	*Apocalypse of Abraham*
Athen.	Athenaeus
b. Ber.	*Babylonian Talmud*, tractate *Berakhot*
B.J.	Flavius Josephus, *Bellum judaicum* (*Jewish War*)
BGU	*Ägyptische Urkunden aus den königlichen* (later *Staatlichen*) *Museen zu Berlin: Griechische Urkunden*. Berlin: Widmann, 1895–.
C. Ap.	Flavius Josephus, *Contra Apionem* (*Against Apion*)
CD	Cairo Genizah copy of the *Damascus Document*
CH	*Corpus Hermeticum*
Cher.	Philo, *De cherubim* (*On the Cherubim*)
Cic.	Plutarch, *Cicero*
Conf.	Philo, *De confusione linguarum* (*On the Confusion of Tongues*)
Congr.	Philo, *De congressu eruditionis gratia* (*On the Preliminary Studies*)
Contempl.	Philo, *De vita contemplativa* (*On the Contemplative Life*)
Cor.	Demosthenes, *De corona* (*On the Crown*)
Cyr.	Xenophon, *Cyropaedia*
Decal.	Philo, *De decalogo* (*On the Decalogue*)
De esu	Plutarch, *De esu carnium*
Deipn.	Athenaeus, *Deipnosophistae*
Dem.	Dionysius of Halicarnassus, *De Demosthene* (*On Demosthenes*)

Det.	Philo, *Quod deterius potiori insidari soleat* (*That the Worse Attacks the Better*)
Deus	Philo, *Quod Deus sit immutabilis* (*That God is Unchangeable*)
Dio Chrys.	Dio Chrysostom
Diod. Sic.	Diodorus Siculus
Diog. L.	Diogenes Laertius
Dion. Hal.	Dionysius of Halicarnassus
Diss.	Epictetus, *Dissertationes*
Epict.	Epictetus
Eth. nic.	Aristotle, *Ethica Nichomachea* (*Nichomachean Ethics*)
Euseb.	Eusebius
Exod. Rab.	*Exodus Rabbah*
Fr.	*Fragments*
Fug.	Philo, *De fuga et inventione* (*On Flight and Finding*)
Gen. Rab.	*Genesis Rabbah*
Geogr.	Strabo, *Geographica*
Haer.	Irenaeus, *Adversus Haereses* (*Against Heresies*)
Her.	Philo, *Quis rerum divinarum heres sit* (*Who Is the Heir?*)
Is. Os.	Plutarch, *De Iside et Osiride*
Jos.	Flavius Josephus
Jos. Asen.	*Joseph and Aseneth*
Jub.	*Jubilees*
Leg.	Philo, *Legum allegoriae* (*Allegorical Interpretation*)
Legat.	Philo, *Legatio ad Gaium* (*On the Embassy to Gaius*)
Let. Arist.	*Letter of Aristeas*
Lib. Ed.	(Pseudo-)Plutarch, *De liberis educandis*
Lys.	Plato, *Lysis*
m. Avot	*Mishnah*, tractate *Avot*
m. Sanh.	*Mishnah*, tractate *Sanhedrin*
Math.	Sextus Empiricus, *Adversus Mathematicos* (*Against the Mathematicians*)
Mek. Exod.	*Mekilta Exodus*
Mem.	Xenophon, *Memorabilia*
Mer.	Plautus, *Mercator* (*The Merchant*)
Metam.	Ovid, *Metamorphoses*
Migr.	Philo, *De migratione Abrahami* (*On the Migration of Abraham*)
Mos.	Philo, *De vita Mosis* (*On the Life of Moses*)
Mut.	Philo, *De mutatione nominum* (*On the Change of Names*)
Nat. fac.	Galen, *De naturalibus facultatibus* (*On the Natural Faculties*)
Num.	Plutarch, *Numa*
Odes Sol.	*The Odes of Solomon*
OGIS	Dittenberger, Wilhelm, ed. *Orientis Graeci Inscriptiones Selectae*. 2 vols. Leipzig: S. Herzel, 1903–1905.
Opif.	Philo, *De opificio mundi* (*On the Creation of the World*)
Or.	*Orationes* (*Speeches*)

P. Hal. I	Graeca Halensis, ed. *Dikaiomata*. Berlin: Weidmann, 1913.
P. Hib.	Grenfell, B. P., A. Hunt, E. Turner, and M. Lenger, eds. *The Hibeh Papyri*. 2 vols. Graeco-Roman Memoirs 7, 32. London: Egypt Exploration Society, 1906, 1955.
P. Lond.	Kenyon, F. G., and H. I. Bell, eds. *Greek Papyri in the British Museum*. 5 vols. London: British Museum, 1893–1917.
P. Oxy.	Grenfell, B. P., A. Hunt, and H. I. Bell, eds. *The Oxyrhynchus Papyri*. 17 vols. London: Egypt Exploration Society, 1898–1927.
P. Tebt.	Grenfell, B. P., A. Hunt, and J. Gilbart Smyly, eds. *The Tebtunis Papyri*. 4 vols. London: Frowde, 1902–.
Pesiq. R.	*Pesiqta Rabbati*
Phaedr.	Plato, *Phaedrus*
Phileb.	Plato, *Philebus*
Pirqe R. El.	*Pirqe Rabbi Eliezer*
Plant.	Philo, *De plantatione* (*On Planting*)
Plut.	Plutarch
Pol.	Aristotle, *Politica* (*Politics*)
Polyb.	Polybius
Pomp.	Dionysius of Halicarnassus, *Epistula ad Pompeium Geminum*
Post.	Philo, *De posteritate Caini* (*On the Posterity of Cain*)
Praem.	Philo, *De praemiis et poenis* (*On Rewards and Punishments*)
Praep. ev.	Eusebius, *Praeparatio evangelica* (*Preparation for the Gospel*)
Pss. Sol.	*Psalms of Solomon*
Pyr.	Sextus Empiricus, *Pyrrhoniae Hypotyposes* (*Outlines of Pyrrhonism*)
Pyth.	Pindar, *Pythionikai* (*Pythian Odes*)
Pyth. orac.	Plutarch, *De Pythiae oraculis*
QG	Philo, *Quaestiones et solutiones in Genesin*
Resp.	Plato, *Republic*
Rhet.	Aristotle, *Rhetorica* (*Rhetoric*)
Sacr.	Philo, *De sacrificiis Abelis et Caini* (*On the Sacrifices of Cain and Abel*)
Sext. Emp.	Sextus Empiricus
Sept.	Aeschylus, *Septem contra Thebas* (*Seven Against Thebes*)
Sib. Or.	*The Sibylline Oracles*
Somn.	Philo, *De somniis* (*On Dreams*)
Spec.	Philo, *De specialibus legibus* (*On the Special Laws*)
SVF	Arnim, Hans Friedrich August von, ed. *Stoicorum veterum fragmenta*. 4 vols. Leipzig: B. G. Tübner, 1903–1924.
T. 12 Patr.	*Testaments of the Twelve Patriarchs*
T. Asher	*Testament of Asher* (*Testaments of the Twelve Patriarchs*)
T. Dan	*Testament of Dan* (*Testaments of the Twelve Patriarchs*)
T. Iss.	*Testament of Issachar* (*Testaments of the Twelve Patriarchs*)
T. Job	*Testament of Job*
T. Jos.	*Testament of Joseph* (*Testaments of the Twelve Patriarchs*)
T. Jud.	*Testament of Judah* (*Testaments of the Twelve Patriarchs*)
T. Levi	*Testament of Lev* (*Testaments of the Twelve Patriarchs*)
T. Mos.	*Testament of Moses*

T. Naph.	*Testament of Naphtali* (*Testaments of the Twelve Patriarchs*)
T. Reu.	*Testament of Reuben* (*Testaments of the Twelve Patriarchs*)
T. Zeb.	*Testament of Zebulun* (*Testaments of the Twelve Patriarchs*)
t. Soṭah	*Tosefta*, tractate *Soṭah*
Tg. Onq. Gen	*Targum Onqelos on Genesis*
Tg. Ps.-J.	*Targum Pseudo-Jonathan*
Tim.	Plato, *Timaeus*
Tusc.	Cicero, *Tusculanae disputationes* (*Tusculan Disputations*)
Virt.	Philo, *De virtutibus* (*On the Virtues*)
Xenoph.	Xenophon

3. Journals, Series, and Modern Works

AB	The Anchor Bible
AGJU	Arbeiten zur Geschichte des Antiken Judentums und des Urchristentums
AnBib	Analecta Biblica
AThANT	Abhandlungen zur Theologie des Alten und Neuen Testaments
BDAG	Danker, F. W., ed. *A Greek-English Lexicon of the New Testament and Other Early Christian Literature.* 3rd ed. Chicago and London: University of Chicago Press, 2000.
BDF	Blass, F., and A. Debrunner. *A Greek Grammar of the New Testament and Other Early Christian Literature.* Translated and revised by Robert W. Funk. Chicago and London: University of Chicago Press, 1961.
BECNT	Baker Exegetical Commentary on the New Testament
BET	Beiträge zur evangelischen Theologie
BNTC	Black's New Testament Commentary
CBQ	*Catholic Biblical Quarterly*
DSD	*Dead Sea Discoveries*
ExpTim	*Expository Times*
EKK	Evangelisch-Katholischer Kommentar zum Neuen Testament
EQ	*Evangelical Quarterly*
EstBib	*Estudios Biblicos*
ETL	*Ephemerides Theologicae Lovanienses*
HALOT	Koehler, Ludwig, and Walter Baumgartner. *The Hebrew and Aramaic Lexicon of the Old Testament.* Study Edition. 2 vols. Revised by Walter Baumgartner and Johann Jakob Stamm. Edited by M. E. J. Richardson. Leiden: E. J. Brill, 2001.
HTK	Herders theologischer Kommentar zum Neuen Testament
HTR	*Harvard Theological Review*
ICC	The International Critical Commentary
Int	*Interpretation*
Interpretation	Interpretation: A Bible Commentary for Teaching and Preaching
JBL	*Journal of Biblical Literature*
JETS	*Journal of the Evangelical Theological Society*

JSNT	*Journal for the Study of the New Testament*
JSNTSup	Journal for the Study of the New Testament: Supplement Series
KEK	Kritisch-exegetischer Kommentar über das Neue Testament (Meyer)
LCL	The Loeb Classical Library
L-N	Louw, Johannes P., and Eugene A. Nida. *Greek-English Lexicon of the New Testament Based on Semantic Domains*. 2 vols. New York: United Bible Societies, 1988.
LSJ	Liddell, Henry George, and Robert Scott. *A Greek-English Lexicon*. 9th ed. Revised by Henry Stuart Jones and Roderick McKenzie. Oxford: Clarendon Press, 1940.
M-M	Moulton, James Hope, and George Milligan. *The Vocabulary of the Greek Testament Illustrated from the Papyri and Other Non-literary Sources*. Grand Rapids: Wm. B. Eerdmans, 1930.
Moffat	The Moffat New Testament Commentary
NCBC	The New Century Bible Commentary
NIBC	New International Biblical Commentary
NICNT	The New International Commentary on the New Testament
NIDNTT	*The New International Dictionary of New Testament Theology*
NIGTC	New International Greek Testament Commentary
NIV	New International Version
NovT	*Novum Testamentum*
NovTSup	*Supplements to Novum Testamentum*
NPNF	Schaff, Philip, ed. *A Select Library of the Nicene and Post-Nicene Fathers of the Christian Church*. Grand Rapids: Eerdmans, 1989.
NRSV	New Revised Standard Version
NTS	*New Testament Studies*
OCD	Hornblower, S. and A. Spawforth, eds. *Oxford Classical Dictionary*. 3rd edition. Oxford: Oxford University Press, 1996.
OTL	The Old Testament Library
PVTG	Pseudepigrapha Veteris Testamenti Graeci
RTR	*Reformed Theological Review*
SP	Sacra Pagina
SBLDS	Society of Biblical Literature Dissertation Series
SNTSMS	Society for New Testament Studies Monograph Series
SEÅ	*Svensk Exegetisk Årsbok*
SJT	*Scottish Journal of Theology*
SPhA	*The Studia Philonica Annual*
TDNT	Kittel, G., and G. Friedrich, eds. *Theological Dictionary of the New Testament*. Translated by G. W. Bromiley. 10 vols. Grand Rapids, 1964–76.
THKNT	*Theologischer Handkommentar zum Neuen Testament*
TLG	Pantelia, Maria, director. *Thesaurus Linguae Graecae*. No pages. Online: http://www.tlg.uci.edu.
TS	*Theological Studies*
TSK	*Theologische Studien und Kritiken*
VC	*Vigiliae christianae*

VT	*Vetus Testamentum*
WBC	Word Biblical Commentary
WTJ	*Westminster Theological Journal*
WUNT	*Wissenschaftliche Untersuchungen zum Neuen Testament*
ZNW	*Zeitschrift für die neutestamentliche Wissenschaft*
ZST	*Zeitschrift für systematische Theologie*

4. General Abbreviations

BCE	Before the Common Era (= BC)
CE	Common Era (= AD)
LXX	Septuagint
MT	Masoretic Text (of the Old Testament)
NT	New Testament
OT	Old Testament

Introduction

A Dilemma, a Question, and a Sketch of the Answer

1. The Dilemma

If anything is clear about the early Christian movement it is that the first believers in Christ were not technical philosophers. In *The Passing of Peregrinus* the second-century satirist Lucian of Samosata (b. ca. 120 CE) unleashes his wit on the gullible Christians who were so easily duped by the charlatan Peregrinus Proteus. One can detect behind Lucian's sarcasm a genuine amazement that anyone would reject the Greek pantheon of gods, only to worship a crucified Jew from the backwater province of Palestine. What seems to stir up Lucian's derision even more than the content of these beliefs, however, is the lack of critical thought which the Christians apply to their doctrines. "All this," he explains, "they take quite on trust," with the effect that the Christians are perfect targets for a con artist such as Peregrinus: "Now an adroit, unscrupulous fellow, who has seen the world, has only to get among these simple souls, and his fortune is pretty soon made; he plays with them."[1] Not only does Lucian's attitude betray the wide intellectual gulf which lay between the Roman elites and most early Christians, but it also echoes a criticism which has been repeated innumerable times in the centuries since the dawning of the "Age of Reason." Despite occasional attempts to dress itself up in the trappings of philosophical respectability, Christianity has never been able to escape its reputation for encouraging a less than rational belief in traditional doctrines. Somewhere at its roots the Christian movement seems to have been shaped by a kind of thinking very unlike the rationalisms which characterized Lucian's Roman philosophy and modern European thought after Descartes.

Before we add our assent to Lucian's judgement on the early Christians, however, we must observe that the past century witnessed a disturbing

---

[1] Lucian, *Peregrinus*, 11–13 (quotation from 13).

erosion of our confidence in the powers of human reason. This post-modern insecurity is captured by Umberto Eco in his novel *Foucault's Pendulum* when the enigmatic Belbo describes to Casaubon the epiphany which he experienced as he gazed at the enormous pendulum which hangs in the Conservatoire des arts et métiers in Paris:

> ". . . then last year, when I saw the Pendulum, I understood everything."
> "Everything?"
> "Almost everything. You see, Casaubon, even the Pendulum is a false prophet. You look at it, you think it's the only fixed point in the cosmos, but if you detach it from the ceiling of the Conservatoire and hang it in a brothel, it works just the same. And there are other pendulums: there's one in New York, in the UN building, there's one in the science museum in San Francisco, and God knows how many others. Wherever you put it, Foucault's Pendulum swings from a motionless point while the earth rotates beneath it. Every point of the universe is a fixed point: all you have to do is hang the Pendulum from it."
> "God is everywhere?"
> "In a sense, yes. That's why the Pendulum disturbs me. It promises the infinite, but where to put the infinite is left to me."[2]

What makes Belbo's anxiety so poignant for many contemporary readers is that we share his sense of loss. We too have become aware that the cherished beliefs, the unquestioned assumptions which once formed the bedrock of reality, seem now to float rootless. There seems no way to find the absolute centre of things, and so every circle we inscribe at the boundary of our world appears arbitrary. Yet, like Belbo, most of us cannot celebrate this sense of epistemic dislocation. Rather it overwhelms us like seasickness, a pervasive *nausée* which we learn to tolerate but for which we cannot help wishing we could find a cure. Our minds recoil at the thought that we are as absurd as Beckett's characters as they wait for Godot, their world constricted to the ugly banalities of boots, sore feet, and cruelty. We crave a myth to live by as we need air, but even more we have a need to *believe* the myth. We want its world to be real. We want the anchor point of that pendulum to really *be* the centre of the world, a fixed point from which we can measure our place. Hence the search for a centre has not died. Richard Rorty's pragmatic relativism, the communitarianism of Habermas, Wittgenstein's rooting of language games in a "form of life," Quine's redefinition of philosophy as the servant of science, Levinas' absolute ethical responsibility in the gaze of the

---

[2] Eco, *Foucault's Pendulum*, 201.

"other," each represents in its own way a rebellion against Beckett's vision of absurdity. Even Derrida, whose flag was often waved on this side of the Atlantic as the champion who would put an end to all settled meaningfulness, began to talk later in his life of real ethical meaning in concepts such as "hospitality." It is still unclear, however, just how that meaningful centre for thought and life can be trusted, how we can really come to believe a myth again. Lucian's smug confidence in the power of reason has given way in many of us to Belbo's tragic uncertainty.

In this context we see more and more thinkers looking back in order to look forward. In Continental philosophy we can perceive a "religious turn" which seems to involve the conviction that there are important sources for meaning which were excluded, fatally, by the secularism of the Enlightenment. In theology too we see a shift away from the classical liberal project of reconstructing religion on the grounds of secular reason, away from Bultmann's demythologization, and toward a more humble engagement with the pre-modern past. In the post-liberalism of Hans Frei, George Lindbeck, and Thomas Oden or in the work of the "Radical Orthodoxy" group we see a hope that Aquinas, Augustine, Athanasius, and Paul may not have been so naive in their belief. Suddenly the early Christians do not look quite as foolish for their refusal to play Lucian's rationalist game. Could it be, we wonder, that they stood in living contact with ways of grounding belief and meaning which we have forgotten, approaches which are vitally important now if we are to escape the death throes of modernity?

2. The Question

Enter Paul. The present project is conceived as another contribution to this exploration of the epistemological resources of our Western past and, for theology, of our Christian past. The question which we will pursue is how Paul, as the most influential Christian thinker in the first century, assumed he could know about God. It is clear that the Apostle did not ask how knowledge was possible in the sense that we do now after Descartes and Kant. Nor was he concerned with the self-conscious logic of the Stoics or with the arguments of the Skeptics. In part this is because, whatever exposure he may have had to the philosophical street-preachers in his native Tarsus, Paul did not belong to the social elite to whom the details of Hellenistic philosophy were for the most part restricted. In part Paul was not overtly concerned about epistemology because he was a Jew and, prior to his experience on the Damascus road, a fairly traditional one. Yet it is this very *lack* of interest in theorizing about knowledge which makes him so valuable as the object of our study. For in reading the letters of this Apostle to the Gentiles we step outside of the technical epistemological tradition stretching from Plato, through Descartes and Kant, to the philosophy departments of our universities. This is not to say that Paul was entirely unaffected by popular Hellenistic philosophy. He betrays no interest, however, in the kind of epistemological debates and self-conscious logic which were a staple of elite philosophical discourse. In Paul we have the opportunity to see how someone approached religious knowledge who was at one and the same time foundational in the development of Western culture and yet relatively untouched by the epistemological currents which so many now suspect are bankrupt. What assumptions did such a thinker make about human knowledge of God? More specifically, what kind of logic did Paul employ when he tried to lead human beings from comparative ignorance into greater knowledge, and how does that logic presume we should understand human knowing?

3. The Strategy of this Study

In the first part of this study I will explore Paul's attitudes towards reason and rationality. I will begin by examining the two passages where Paul seems to address most directly the human epistemic situation: Rom 1:18–32 and 1 Cor 1:17–2:16. I will then broaden my focus to survey the evidence for Paul's attitude towards human rationality throughout his letters, and to ask what kind of rationality the Apostle seems to regard as legitimate. Finally, I will turn to survey the trend in contemporary Pauline studies which recognizes the importance of interpretive rationality in Paul's thought and argument. We will see that the Apostle seems to have a much more positive attitude towards reason than many might assume. The Spirit is, for Paul, an indispensable factor in this acquisition of knowledge, but that Spirit's role is one of facilitating proper reasoning rather than displacing human intellectual activity. Even in the believer's initial conversion to faith in Christ, I will argue, the Apostle does not understand God's sovereignty to totally eclipse human reasoning. We will also see how Paul treats the Christ event and certain other experiences as interpretive keys which, in the context of a Jewish framework of thought, will allow human beings to interpret themselves and their world properly.

In the second part we will examine Paul's claims to knowledge and ask what kind of logical structure his knowledge exhibits when it is taken as a whole. This will involve collecting all of the passages in Paul's undisputed letters[3] in which the Apostle describes human beings (himself or someone else) as knowing something. My focus will fall on the kinds of object which this knowledge grasps, so I will look at all those passages in which 1) verbs of knowing occur with an identifiable object, or 2) nouns denoting knowledge are employed and the content of that knowledge is identifiable from context. It will soon become clear that there is a narrative structure to the Apostle's knowledge. Moreover, we will see here further evidence of Paul's emphasis on hermeneutical reasoning, for the Apostle's ethical knowledge seems to arise out of this narrative as individual people are "emplotted" within the story. Finally, we will observe that this narrative knowledge is not, for Paul, an end in itself. Rather, all of the Apostle's knowing is geared to bring believers to that "knowledge of God" which includes a committed relational connection with God and Christ, a knowledge which itself constitutes salvation.

The third and largest part of this study aims to provide a clearer picture of the narrative, hermeneutical logic which Paul seems to assume is a reliable path to religious knowledge. Taking the letter to the Galatians as a sample of Paul's argumentation, I will try to uncover the logic by which that argument proceeds. My approach in this section will be similar in some ways to rhetorical analyses of Galatians. My focus, however, remains essentially different. Most rhetorical readings are concerned with identifying recognized features of ancient rhetoric in Paul's writing. While this is an important question, I am not interested here in isolating parallels with the surface structures of the Apostle's speech. Rather, I want to uncover the

---

[3] I will restrict my analysis for the most part to those letters for which there is a fair consensus that Paul is the author: Romans, 1 and 2 Corinthians, Galatians, Philippians, 1 Thessalonians, and Philemon. I also regard Colossians and 2 Thessalonians as genuine, and so I will refer to these letters as well. Neither letter, however, offers decisive or distinctive evidence for this study, so their inclusion should not skew the outcome even if they are pseudonymous.

argumentative logic which lies implicit beneath that surface.[4]

Why choose Galatians as a test site? Unlike Ephesians, Colossians, 2 Thessalonians, and the Pastoral Letters, the Pauline authorship of Galatians has not been seriously challenged. Likewise, unlike 2 Corinthians and Philippians (and in some circles 1 Thessalonians), there has never been serious debate about the integrity of the letter. This is important for our purposes, because we will be tracing the logic of Paul's argument from beginning to end. In order to do so, we need to be confident that what we are reading was, in fact, written as a single sustained argument. This leaves us with Romans, 1 Corinthians, Galatians, and perhaps 1 Thessalonians. The ongoing debate over the nature of the Corinthian situation makes 1 Corinthians a difficult letter to use as a test site. Its loose structure, in which Paul deals with a series of apparently distinct issues, also means that 1 Corinthians lacks good examples of an extended argument.[5] Likewise, the ongoing controversy over the argument of Romans would make any reconstruction of the logic in Romans as a whole very controversial. To what extent was Romans an occasional letter? If it was, what kind of situation does Paul address? How does his discussion of the Jews in chapters 9–11 fit into this argumentative setting? At present there is little consensus over any of

---

[4] The difference is clearly illustrated by a glance at Siegert's work *Argumentation bei Paulus*. The observation that Paul often uses syllogistic or enthymematic argument (*Argumentation*, 191–5) does not tell us why the Apostle selects the premises which he does or the nature of the logic by which he moves from premise to conclusion. The observation that Paul sometimes employs familiar *topoi* (*Argumentation*, 199–202) does not tell us why he selects those and not others, what he is going to say about them, or why he thinks his audience should believe him. Siegert also focusses on the symbolic and typological connections which Paul often draws, but without providing insight into the logic by which these connections (and not others) are justified (*Argumentation*, 209–24). In contrast, Siegert begins to describe the underlying logic of Paul's argumentation when he observes that Paul often focusses not only on prior causes, but also (in typical Aristotelian and Stoic fashion) on the ends of things as causes (*Argumentation,* 207; see Rom 4:16, 18; 5:20f.; 7:13; 8:15, 17; 1 Cor 1:27–31; 11:19; 2 Cor 7:9; 12:7–9; Gal 3:14, 19, 22; 4:5; Phil 1:25f.). Siegert adds: "Meist ist vom Heilsplan Gottes die Rede, auch vom Zweck der Tora und vom Zweck des Todes Jesu" (*Argumentation*, 207). See also Siegert's observation that Paul often evaluates things based on their consequences (*Argumentation*, 207).

[5] Some attempts have been made, of course, to outline an underlying argumentative unity which holds Paul's treatment of these diverse issues together (see, e.g., Mitchell, *Rhetoric of Reconciliation*). There is, however, little consensus at present about the success of such attempts.

these questions. This is not to say that the interpretation of Galatians is a simple task, and some readers will doubtless find reason to challenge my own interpretation of the letter. There is, however, broader agreement about the setting and purpose of Galatians. Moreover, the sheer length of Romans makes it less manageable as the focus of a detailed analysis. On the other hand, the very brief note from Paul to Philemon is simply not substantial enough for our purposes.[6] Left with a choice between 1 Thessalonians and Galatians, the latter emerges as the obvious candidate. On the one hand, Galatians is a much more focussed letter than is 1 Thessalonians. Throughout, Paul directs his attention to one basic issue, allowing us to see a sustained example of his reasoning.[7] On the other hand, although Paul's intention in 1 Thessalonians does include some (new?) instruction (see, for example, 4:13–5:11), the bulk of the letter either rehearses Paul's history with the community in order to strengthen their bond with him (1:2–3:13)[8] or repeats ethical injunctions which are already familiar to the audience (4:1–12; 5:12–22). This means that most of the letter either is not argumentative or simply alludes to arguments which have been presented before. In Galatians, however, we have Paul addressing a new problem with a community, and so we have an opportunity to examine his argument without having to reconstruct so much of his teaching on prior occasions. It is thus to Galatians that we can most profitably look to explore the epistemological assumptions which drive his argumentation.

This analysis will begin with the assumption that Paul intends, by means of his Galatian letter, to influence his audience. This influence is in large part aimed at their behaviour; he wants to move them to act differently. At the same time, however, the primary way in which he can influence this behaviour is via their thoughts. If he can convince them that a certain way of thinking is true, then this way of thinking will (as all preachers and

---

[6] Paul's rhetoric in Philemon is also highly allusive and depends heavily on non-discursive modes of persuasion.

[7] Betz (*Galatians*, 30) does not overstate the case when he writes that the body of the letter "contains nothing but one strictly rational argument."

[8] There may be some argumentative function in this description of their relationship. It has been suggested, for example, that the Apostle may be actively differentiating himself from common orators, in much the same way that some philosophical writers do (see Winter, *Philo and Paul*, 150–55). See also Malherbe, "Gentle as a Nurse."

politicians hope) lead them to a new way of acting.[9] To the extent that Paul himself believes in the ideas which he wants to inculcate in Galatia, Paul's purpose in the letter is largely to bring his audience from relative ignorance (belief in false ideas) to a new knowledge (belief in certain true ideas).

The method of analysis will be relatively simple. I will move sequentially through the letter, asking at each stage of Paul's argument how the Apostle is trying to influence his audience's thinking. Not all of his strategies will be rational, but our focus will be on those parts and aspects of the argument which *do* appeal to the audience as rational, thinking persons.[10] I will concentrate on the ways in which the Apostle invites his audience to follow him through a series of inferences. This does not mean simply describing what Paul actually says. It means, rather, isolating Paul's assertions in the argument and describing the logical relationships between those assertions. In this way my method will be not unlike the approach of transformational-generative (T-G) grammar. Paul's specific word choice, word order, phrasing, etc. are the "surface structure" of his argument, corresponding to the surface structure or "performance" of a sentence. Beneath the specific wording of a sentence, however, T-G grammar identifies a "deep structure" of semantic relationships between ideas. A given deep structure can be expressed by means of several different surface structures. At the same time, the deep structure of a sentence can be inferred from its surface structure. In a similar way, we will be looking to infer from the surface structure of Paul's discourse the deep structure of logical relationships which it expresses. To the extent that the Apostle's argument appeals to the reason of his audience, it is this deep structure which is the real instrument of communication and of influencing their thought.[11]

---

[9] Thurén (*Derhetorizing*, 25) rightly observes that while every act of communication is at the same time an attempt to influence the receiver, this need not reduce Paul's theology to a means of *practical* influence, since "[h]is goal may well also be to affect the theology of the addressees. Even such 'theoretical' goals are possible."

[10] As Thurén points out, while studies of the context in which Paul's thoughts arise may help us to understand why the Apostle chooses one idea over another, such studies "are of little help for *understanding the thoughts* of the apostle" (*Derhetorizing*, 13; italics original). If we are to understand Paul's ideas we must still grapple with that level of his discourse as an autonomous system.

[11] There is at least a superficial similarity here to D. Patte's structuralist distinction between Paul's "convictional logic" and his "argumentative logic," between "faith" and

In places the surface structure of Paul's argument is highly enthymematic, leaving unstated one or more premises or (particularly in his ethical instruction) even whole steps which belong to the deep structure of the argument. At these points the only option will be to try to reconstruct the missing links in Paul's inferential chain, and my analysis will become correspondingly more speculative. The criterion with which we will control this reconstruction, however, will be the same one with which we decipher such enthymematic performances in ordinary speech: the ability of the reconstructed deep structure to account for the elements of the argument which *are* explicit in the performance of the letter. Coherence will be our watchword.

Once we have outlined the deep structure of Paul's argument in Galatians, we can proceed to ask what *kind* of logical relationships it involves. In other words, we will be asking what kind of reasoning Paul employs when he guides his audience through a process of rational inference. It is at this point that we can glimpse the epistemological assumptions which underlie Paul's argument. For the Apostle will likely lead his audience through rational processes which he himself thinks are reliable ones. In other words, the kind of reasoning which Paul encourages in the members of his communities is likely the kind of reasoning which Paul believes will actually lead reliably to knowledge.[12]

"theology" (see Patte, *Paul's Faith*). After all, T-G grammar is itself a kind of linguistic structuralism. The problem with Patte's approach for our purposes, however, is his insistence that the "convictional logic" of Paul's basic symbols and concepts is distinct from (even detachable from) the logic apparent in his actual speech. This ends up locating the "real" meaning of Paul's speech very far from the ideas as the Apostle presents them, re-formulating them in a form which Paul himself would be hard-pressed to recognize. The relative autonomy of Patte's "convictional logic" also raises questions about what controls are operative on his reconstruction of that deeper meaning. On the other hand, the point of T-G grammar is that there *is* a direct link between surface structure of speech and the deep structure which it is geared to communicate. One discerns the syntax (or logic) of the deep structure precisely by studying the syntax (or logic) of the surface structure. So too in this study we will explore the underlying logic of Paul's reasoning with his audience by taking seriously the surface level of his argument and asking about the logic by which it progresses.

[12] I assume here that, as a general rule, Paul's arguments are composed in good faith and are not deliberately manipulative. There remains, of course, the possibility that Paul is deliberately deceptive or employs rhetorical arguments whose logic he himself does not

This examination of Galatians will confirm the tentative conclusions reached in Part Two about the nature of Paul's ethical knowledge. We will see that, for the Apostle, it does in fact arise from the emplotment of one's life in the theological narrative. I will also show that Paul's narrative is not simply imposed on the world. Rather, it remains open to new events which can drastically change the story's shape, and as one's construal of the narrative changes so too Paul insists that the ethical conclusions which flow from that story will also change. In all of this, Paul is simply assuming the truth of the traditional Jewish narrative which forms his overall hermeneutical framework. His argumentation tells us much about how the Apostle believes he can proceed from this starting point, but it reveals little about Paul's reasons for choosing (or retaining) this particular story. I will pause for a moment, however, in the conclusion to this study and ask whether the narrative logic which Paul assumes in his argumentation might allow us to extrapolate a way in which the story as a whole could be grounded or justified. These parting suggestions will also afford us the opportunity to ask again how Paul's use of reason in leading his audience to knowledge might be reconciled with his insistence that knowledge of God is the work of God's own Spirit.[13]

4. Caveats

Before we begin, three caveats are necessary. First, this is not a comparative investigation. It would be desirable to set Paul's own patterns of reasoning in contrast with those of his contemporaries, both elite philosophers and more humble thinkers. That comparison is, however, simply too large to be undertaken here. We may find, moreover, that this necessity turns out to be a virtue. For in our overriding concern to locate Paul in his cultural and

---

believe is valid. This possibility has been highlighted recently by, e.g., Thurén in *Derhetorizing* and Given in *True Rhetoric*. Unless we are going to accept a global hermeneutic of suspicion in relation to Paul, however, we can evaluate this possibility only on a case-by-case basis.

[13] The relationship between our reconstruction and Paul's own thought must, of course, remain tentative. We are inferring Paul's thoughts from his words, and this is always an uncertain business. As Leander Keck has observed, "[t]o touch [Paul's thinking] we must rely on inference" ("Paul as Thinker," 28).

intellectual context, it is all too easy to impose on his thought interests which are not really his own. There may be real value in trying first to understand Paul's thinking in its own right. It is my hope that this study will furnish an understanding of Paul's approach to religious knowing on the basis of which fruitful comparisons might be made down the road. At this point such comparisons would simply be premature.

Second, this study is not intended to uncover Paul's *conscious thinking*, but rather the assumptions and logical structures (perhaps never articulated in Paul's own mind) which are evident in his attempts to persuade. The difference here is similar to the difference between a description of a speaker's linguistic competence – the rules and patterns which govern that speaker's crafting of a sentence – and someone's conscious thoughts while they are speaking. Most Greek speakers never thought consciously about making their adjectives agree in gender with the nouns which they modified. Even if they did, they might have described in different ways that pattern in their language. Yet we can still observe patterns in their speech and infer from them certain grammatical and semantic relationships which seem (unconsciously) to have governed the speaker's formulation of sentences. In the same way we can infer from Paul's argument assumptions about what for him constituted valid reasons for belief, about how someone could rationally move from ignorance to knowledge, assumptions which the Apostle himself may never have brought to full consciousness.

Finally, my purpose in what follows is not to reconstruct Paul's own process of discovery. Keck rightly points out that

> arguments adduced to persuade others are not to be confused with the persuader's own thinking about the subject matter the arguments reflect. To recognize this distinction is not to accuse Paul of thinking one thing and saying another but rather to acknowledge the difference between cognition and persuasion. The track along which Paul sought to move his readers' thinking is not necessarily the same track along which his own thinking had already moved.[14]

My goal in the study which follows is thus not to uncover the path by which Paul came to his own understanding of the Gospel. The aim is, rather, to bring to the surface his tacit assumptions about how people in general can come to knowledge. Paul may in fact have followed a different track in his own discovery. Our purpose, however, is not to reconstruct that historical

---

[14] Keck, "Paul as Thinker," 27.

process, but to reconstruct Paul's assumptions about the kind of rational process which *should* take place in his audience's minds. With these cautions in mind, we turn now to our survey of Paul's attitude towards rational inquiry.

Part One

Human Reason in Paul's Letters

Chapter One

Paul's Explicit Statements about Human Reasoning

1. Romans 1:18–32

1.1. A Brief History of Interpretation

Although he did not pose the question in terms of formal philosophy, the question of human knowledge of God was not entirely foreign to Paul. Two passages in particular have been recognized for centuries as having strong epistemological implications: Romans 1:18–32 and 1 Corinthians 1:17–2:16.[1] In the first passage, Romans 1:18–32, Paul recounts the descent of humanity from an original knowledge of God to blind ignorance and immorality. The Apostle describes how "what may be known about God" has been revealed to human beings "through the things he has made" (1:19, 20).[2] Despite this knowledge of God, however, Paul says that human beings "did not honor him as God or give thanks to him," and as a result their intellectual powers were corrupted, "they became futile in their thinking, and their senseless minds were darkened" (1:21). This refusal to worship God, and the ensuing ignorance, are most evident in the pervasive idolatry in which humanity confuses the created order with the creator (1:23), and it triggers a moral decline which is in turn the basis for the divine judgement which hangs over the human race (1:24–32).

Aquinas famously took this passage as a justification for natural theology. Paul's description of human beings knowing God through the created order was interpreted by the theologian as teaching that the existence of God as "the first cause of all things" was knowable by "both good and bad" through

---

[1] Already, at the end of the fourth century CE, John Chrysostom saw a connection between these passages (*Romans*, "Homily III," on 1:23; See also his *First Corinthians*, "Homily V," on 1:29).

[2] All English biblical quotations are from the NRSV unless otherwise stated.

the operations of unaided reason.[3] Since, in 1:32, the Apostle describes
human beings as knowing that the vices of verses 29–31 deserve judgement,
Aquinas also held that Paul's vision of unaided natural knowledge included
an awareness of God's eternal law.[4] Apart from the authors of Thomistic
textbooks, however, the vast majority of interpreters have understood that
Paul's point in 1:18–32 is not to affirm humanity's intellectual powers, but to
emphasize how much humanity has *lost*.[5] So Barrett understands Paul to say
that "[o]nce man had fallen from his true relation with God, he was no longer
capable of truly rational thought about him."[6] Barrett is, moreover,
representative of most commentators when he suggests that for the Apostle
this is now "the universal state of mankind."[7] Likewise, Käsemann sees in
this passage a vision of a present humanity whose whole existence is
characterized by the "vanity" which the Old Testament associates with idols;
human beings have become "incapable of discriminating perception" and
have lost "any grasp of reality."[8] Even worse, Käsemann understands Paul to
say that, having once descended into this folly, humanity "can no longer

---

[3] Aquinas, *Summa Theologica*, I, Q. 12, A. 12 (Dominican Fathers, p. 1.58–9). Hence the
existence of God and other such natural truths "are not articles of faith, but are preambles to
the articles" (*Summa Theologica*, I, Q. 2, A. 2 [Dominican Fathers, p. 1.12]). Aquinas also
points out that this passage gives the created order a positive role in leading human beings
to God. The material world does not of itself exert a corrupting effect on the intellect
(*Summa Theologica*, I, Q. 65, A. 1 [Dominican Fathers, p. 325]). Yet we must not caricature
Aquinas' reading of Paul on this point. The theologian always insisted that sacred theology,
based on revelation, could attain a kind of knowledge of God which is impossible for the
unaided reason. Hence Aquinas understood Rom 1:19 as describing a knowledge of God
which extends only "so far as He can be known through creatures" (*Summa Theologica*, I,
Q. 1, A. 6 [Dominican Fathers, p. 1.4]). This natural knowledge, leading us only as far as
the senses can lead, does not include "the essence of God," for "the sensible effects of God
do not equal the power of God as their cause" and so his "whole power" is not knowable by
rational inference (*Summa Theologica*, I, Q. 12, A. 12 [Dominican Fathers, p. 1.58]). In
light of the revealed knowledge which is only accessible through faith, natural reason itself
can in turn be "strengthened" supernaturally and, in this case, "so much higher an
intelligible truth can be elicited from the species derived from creatures" (*Summa
Theologica*, I, Q. 111, A. 1 [Dominican Fathers, p. 1.543]).

[4] Aquinas, *Summa Theologica*, I.2, Q. 93, A. 2 (Dominican Fathers, p. 1.1004).

[5] So, e.g., Dupont, *Gnosis*, 24; Lührmann, *Offenbarungsverständnis*, 21–26.

[6] Barrett, *Romans*, 37.

[7] Barrett, *Romans*, 36. So, emphatically, Calvin, *Romans*, on 1:22.

[8] Käsemann, *Romans*, 44.

diagnose its own situation" and continues to "boast about itself" despite its hopeless ignorance of God.[9] In the present reality, then, "only the mighty revelation of righteousness, which establishes God's just claim, can reverse the spell."[10]

There continue, of course, to be significant debates about the interpretation of Romans 1:18–32. When in 1:20 Paul talks about God revealing himself through "the things which were made/done" (τοῖς ποιήμασιν), is he thinking merely of the created order as the vehicle of revelation[11] or also of the Creator's acts in history?[12] Did God's revelation offer to human beings a real possibility of knowledge[13] or did the Creator reveal himself simply in order to (εἰς τὸ εἶναι, 1:20) render human beings "without excuse" in the face of divine judgement?[14] Nor is there agreement about whether the knowledge of God is envisioned in 1:19–21 as arising from simple rational inference,[15] from an existential confrontation and recognition,[16] or from a more active kind of divine revelation.[17] Some understand Paul to be depicting a primordial state of innocence in which natural knowledge of God was a real human experience,[18] while others insist that in Paul's mind it was only ever potential.[19] Some understand this knowledge as a mere theoretical recognition

---

[9] Käsemann, *Romans*, 44. See Rom 1:22: φάσκοντες εἶναι σοφοὶ ἐμωράνθησαν.

[10] Käsemann, *Romans*, 42. See also Cranfield, *Romans*, 1.117, 118, 128; Byrne, *Romans*, 68, 71; Moo, *Romans*, 107, 118.

[11] Barrett, *Romans*, 35; Coffey, "Natural Knowledge," 675; Dodd, *Romans*, 24; Dupont, *Gnosis*, 23–24; Schreiner, *Romans*, 86.

[12] So Michel, *Römer*, 54, and, tentatively, Moo, *Romans*, 105.

[13] So Cranfield, *Romans*, 1.116; Dunn, *Romans*, 1.59.

[14] So Michel, *Römer*, 56; Moo, *Romans*, 106.

[15] So Achtemeier, *Romans*, 38; Byrne, *Romans*, 66–7; Cranfield, *Romans*, 1.116; Dodd, *Romans*, 24; Dunn, *Romans*, 1.58; Dupont, *Gnosis*, 29.

[16] For Barth the knowledge of God in 1:19–21 is the existential awareness of our own finiteness and limitation in the face of an Other who is neither finite nor limited and who appears as the boundary of our own existence (Barth, *Romans*, 45–6). See also Baillie, *Knowledge*, 126; Dupont, *Gnosis*, 30; Käsemann, *Romans*, 42–3; Michel, *Römer*, 54; Schreiner, *Romans*, 86.

[17] So Coffey, "Natural Knowledge," 675–6, 680; Moo, *Romans*, 104.

[18] Coffey, "Natural Knowledge," 675–6, 678. Several commentators see a connection between this intellectual "fall" and Genesis 3. See Achtemeier, *Romans*, 39; Bell, *No-one Seeks*, 90–102; Dunn, *Romans*, 1.57, 60–61; Hooker, "Adam."

[19] So Barth, *Romans*, 45–6; Cranfield, *Romans*, 1.114, 117; Dupont, *Gnosis*, 30–31; Michel, *Römer*, 56, 60; Moo, *Romans*, 109–10; Schreiner, *Romans*, 86.

of God's existence and attributes,[20] while others argue that for Paul it included a fuller recognition and worship of the Creator.[21] Likewise, there is little consensus about whether this knowledge is merely knowledge of God's existence and properties[22] or whether it includes an awareness of God's moral demand[23] and perhaps even a relational knowledge of the Deity as a Person.[24]

What has emerged clearly from the exegetical tradition, however, is the consensus that (Aquinas notwithstanding) Paul was *not* in Rom 1:18–32 trying to lay the groundwork for a contemporary natural theology. "[N]or," says Barrett, "does he create one unintentionally."[25] His purpose is not, as in Hellenistic natural theology, "to make man feel at home in a threatening universe," but rather to launch an accusation against humanity for a culpable *lack* of knowledge.[26] If Paul establishes anything unintentionally it is an epistemic proposal that human reason is, at least in the present state of things, constitutionally unable to reach the truth about God.[27] The Creator has made

---

[20] Moo, *Romans*, 117; Coffey, "Natural Knowledge," 675.

[21] So Byrne, *Romans*, 71, and, implicitly, Michel, *Römer*, 60. Cranfield is unusual in distinguishing between the (purely theoretical) knowledge which human beings possessed in 1:20–21 and the knowledge refused by humanity in 1:28, which he sees as involving worship, thanks, and acknowledgement of God in one's life (*Romans*, 1.128).

[22] So Calvin, *Romans*, on 1:20; Cranfield, *Romans*, 1.113, 117; Moo, *Romans*, 107.

[23] Coffey, "Natural Knowledge," 681; Dunn, *Romans*, 1.69; Käsemann, *Romans*, 41.

[24] So Bell, *No-one Seeks*, 90–102; Dupont, *Gnosis*, 30; Käsemann, *Romans*, 41; contra Schreiner, *Romans*, 85–6.

[25] Barrett, *Romans*, 35.

[26] Barrett, *Romans*, 35.

[27] Even the *Dogmatic Constitution on the Catholic Faith*, issued by the First Vatican Council in 1870, shifted away from Aquinas on this point. The constitution affirms on the basis of Rom 1:20 that "God, the source and end of all things, can be known with certainty from the consideration of created things, by the natural power of human reason (*naturali humanae rationis lumine e rebus creatis certo cognosci posse*)" (*Constitutio dogmatica de fide catholica*, chapter 2 [in Tanner, *Decrees*, 2.806]). Yet in the same breath the document adds that "the present state of the human race" in some way hampers the use of reason for attaining knowledge of God, and that this limitation makes supernatural revelation all the more necessary for contemporary people, even if *in theory* those people could know some of its content through unaided reason. Moreover, when in chapter 3 the subject of faith and its relationship to reason is raised, natural knowledge of God is not mentioned at all and the discussion seems to envision only one kind of knowledge of God, a kind in which proper reasoning must be preceded by faith. This seems to confirm that the framers did not see natural knowledge, unaided by revelation (and hence by faith), as a possibility in the present order of things (in Tanner, *Decrees*, 806–7; cf. Coffey, "Natural Knowledge," 683).

the thinking of the creatures futile (1:21 – ἐματαιώθησαν ἐν τοῖς διαλογισμοῖς αὐτῶν) and has spread the darkness of folly over human thought (ἐσκοτίσθη ἡ ἀσύνετος αὐτῶν καρδία).[28] In the present order of things, no human being can come to knowledge of God based on the universal revelation which is offered.[29]

1.2. Morality and Knowing

We must observe here, though, that the root problem in Rom 1:18–32 is not an intellectual one. It is a *moral* problem. Paul does not say here that human beings fail to know God because they are intellectually unfit or because they fail to reason properly. Rather, they fail to respond appropriately to the God they know (1:21). Their knowledge does not move them to appropriate action. Instead, they worship idols (1:23, 25). If there was nothing lacking in their initial knowledge, why did they not respond appropriately? The answer can only be that human beings failed to make the necessary moral effort to respond. Such a reading also fits with the fact that human idolatry is depicted here, as in many Jewish writings, as a moral problem.[30] The worship of idols is a vice for which human beings are held morally responsible. Hence this idolatry brings on God's punishment (1:26–27). The decisive moment in religious knowing is thus the moral struggle to respond rightly to the truth

---

[28] What is less clear is how far-reaching Paul understands this intellectual paralysis to be. Calvin believed Paul to be saying that once God had rendered human thinking "vain," the reason "could understand nothing aright" (*Romans*, on 1:21; cf. on 1:28). For Barth, on the other hand, it is the *meaning* of things in the world which we fail to recognize, "for our life in this world has meaning only in its relation to the true God" (*Romans*, 48). Even when, as a result of this disorientation, "reason itself becomes irrational," the result is a *moral* chaos (*Romans*, 53; cf. Dunn, *Romans*, 1.60; Michel, *Römer*, 60).

[29] Some have tried to read Paul as targeting a specific group of people, usually philosophers of some variety, so that the futile intellect is not universal to humanity. Chrysostom already read Rom 1:18–32 as directed specifically towards Greco-Roman philosophy. Dodd, on the other hand, defends "Greek philosophy in its higher forms," with which Paul "had no direct acquaintance." Rather, Dodd suggests that Paul is objecting to the fact that in practice popular philosophy "easily came to terms with the grossest forms of superstition and immorality" (Dodd, *Romans*, 25). All of Paul's statements here, however, seem to refer to humanity in general, without qualification.

[30] See, e.g., the account of Abram's rejection of idolatry in *Jub.* 11:14–17; 12:1–14. In Wisdom of Solomon the Gentiles are unable to recognize God in the natural order, and so stoop to idolatry, because of their "foolishness" (Wis 13:1–19). Yet this foolishness is itself treated as morally culpable (see Wis 13:8–9).

about God.[31] It is this moral effort which, Paul says, human beings are no longer able to exert, and this moral failure which blinds them to religious truth.

Why would moral effort be so determinative in the knowing process? Paul seems to depict that effort as affecting how one is able to reason. First, he says, human beings failed to make the moral effort to honour God appropriately (1:21). The consequence of this moral failure was that "they were made futile in their thinking (ἐματαιώθησαν ἐν τοῖς διαλογισμοῖς αὐτῶν), and their senseless minds were darkened (ἐσκοτίσθη ἡ ἀσύνετος αὐτῶν καρδία)" (1:21). With their thinking thus perverted, human beings then engaged in explicit idolatry (1:23).[32] Notice that up to this point God has not been actively involved in the human descent. Although the verbs describing the frustration of human thought are passive, they should probably not be regarded as divine passives, for Paul emphasizes God's role quite explicitly when he becomes involved in 1:24 and 1:26. It seems, rather, that Paul understands the moral failure to honour God to bring about by itself the corruption of human thinking which then issues in explicit idolatry. The human "thoughts" (διαλογισμοῖς) are thus not, in Paul's understanding, an autonomous faculty. Rather, the reasoning process is influenced by the reasoner's moral character.

Can we make sense of this idea that the strength and direction of our moral will could influence our reasoning? It does seem *prima facie* plausible that if one is unwilling to perform some action, one is less likely to embrace an understanding which would demand that one take that action. If I am leading

---

[31] So Dodd, *Romans*, 25; Käsemann, *Romans*, 41. In this sense Byrne can legitimately say that Paul "has no concept of a sincere atheism" (*Romans*, 67).

[32] It is not immediately clear whether the failure to give God honour and the subsequent mental "darkening" in 1:21 are to be understood as *prior to* the idolatry and moral descent of 1:23–24 or whether these two passages describe the same event in different terms. On closer examination it would seem that Paul intends two sequential stages of moral and intellectual degradation. On the one hand, nothing is mentioned in 1:21 about explicit idolatry, so that the actions of 1:23 seem to be a further development of the passive refusal to honour God in 1:21. On the other hand, the consequences of each failure are different. In 1:21 the consequence is purely intellectual, a darkening of the mind. In 1:24, however, the consequence is homosexual activity. Finally, the idolatry of 1:23 seems to be a consequence of the fact that human beings have been made foolish (ἐμωράνθησαν) in 1:22. Yet this mental degradation came about only as a *consequence* of the failure to honour God in 1:21.

a sedentary life and have not had the will to begin a regimen of physical exercise, I am more likely to embrace an understanding of my health which allows me to continue being sedentary. Of course, in many cases the bias introduced by our failures of moral will can be overcome by the sheer weight of evidence. If my doctor warns me often enough about my cholesterol levels, supporting her admonishments with a sheaf of clinical studies, I am likely to admit that my sedentary lifestyle is dangerous, in spite of my lack of will to change it. In many fields of thought, however, we do not have access to such clear and incontrovertible evidence. In cases in which the evidence requires a large degree of interpretation, or admits of several different interpretations, there is less likelihood that one will accept an interpretation which would require a shift in one's basic moral decisions. It might not be too difficult to convince me that my lack of exercise is endangering my health. It would be more difficult to convince me that there is (or is not) a personal God. The equivocal nature of the evidence allows my prior commitments to exercise a powerful influence over my ongoing thought. What is more, this kind of moral bias against a particular idea is likely to become stronger in relation to the strength of my aversion to the actions which that idea would suggest I ought to take. I may have an aversion to animal sacrifice, but that aversion is not so strong that it could not be overcome if I were given sufficient reasons for adopting a world view which required such sacrifice. It would be much, much more difficult to convince me of a world view which required *child* sacrifice. My strong bias against the latter religious perspective would arise not necessarily because of the position's inconsistency or irrationality, but simply because I am loath to accept its horrific implications for my life. Paul does not explore the nature of the morality/rationality relationship in this kind of detail. It is, nonetheless, this kind of model which he seems to presume. As Cranfield puts it, reason is not in Paul's view an "impartial arbiter capable of standing outside the influence of the ego and returning a perfectly objective judgment."[33] Instead, the strength and direction of one's moral will seems to determine, for Paul, the range of ideas which one is willing to accept.

Specifically, the Apostle suggests in these verses that human religious thought is corrupted by a chronic and powerful aversion to giving our Creator appropriate honour and worship (1:21). What is it about such worship which human beings resist so strongly? In general scholars have tended to suggest

---

[33] Cranfield, *Romans*, 1.118.

that Paul sees in human beings an illegitimate desire for independence and autonomy from God, a refusal to accept our status as created beings beneath our Creator.[34] Often it is suggested that one aspect of this desire for autonomy is an intellectual arrogance which demands that God be entirely comprehensible, intellectually controllable, and is not content with "what can be known about God" by his creatures.[35] Both of these positions would fit with Paul's statements here, although the Apostle does not elaborate on the human problem to this extent. He is content simply to say that human beings share a deep-seated aversion to acknowledging God for who he is, and that this flaw in our moral constitution corrupts all of our thinking about the Deity.

Ironically, this whole model of knowing in Rom 1:18–32 seems to leave open a surprisingly positive role for human reason in religious knowing. Many exegetes have observed that, for all its limitations, human reason is presented in these verses as a faculty which is, in principle, capable of attaining truth about God. It is simply crippled by the idolatrous tendencies of the human moral will. By implication, this would suggest that if one's moral faculties were repaired, one's reason might be free to operate as it was first intended. Hence Paul's call in Rom 12:2 for believers to allow the "renewing of your minds" so that their restored reason can make reliable ethical judgements.[36] Moreover, as Coffey suggests, this innate potential of human reason opens up the possibility that, at least to a "renewed" mind, the truths of the Gospel might well be compatible with the fruits of rational inquiry.[37] Paul might even allow that a kind of natural theology is possible for one who has been restored to intellectual wholeness by Christ.[38] This positive role for human reason in religious knowing would, however, become possible only if the endemic human resistance to God were somehow overcome.

---

[34] E.g., Achtemeier, *Romans*, 37–9; Käsemann, *Romans*, 43.

[35] So Barth, *Romans*, 44, 46; Käsemann, *Romans*, 42. Chrysostom refers specifically to Greek philosophy as a prime example of this corrupt intellectual activity in which human beings will not "bear with the limits given them" (*Romans*, "Homily III," on 1:23). Cf. Chrysostom, *First Corinthians*, "Homily V," on 1:29.

[36] So Byrne, *Romans*, 67.

[37] Coffey, "Natural Knowledge," 682–3.

[38] So Bell, *No-one Seeks*, 118, n. 250, though Bell believes that even the renewed mind of Rom 12:1–2 would not uncover much more from the created order than was already grasped in faith.

If Paul betrays some underlying optimism about human "reason," what precisely is this intellectual faculty or activity in which he perceives some promise as a path to knowledge about God? So far we have been working with the vague, undefined notion of "reason" which belongs to our contemporary categories of thought. In its broadest outlines, this "reasoning" could be defined as some sort of ordered thought which brings new insights out of existing ideas, beliefs, and perceptions. While our naïve notion does not seem too far removed from the kind of inference which Paul seems to presuppose in Romans 1:20, these vague notions will need further definition in Chapter II below.[39] First, though, we must look at another passage in which which the Apostle addresses explicitly the potential of human thought and inquiry.

2. 1 Corinthians 1:17–2:16

2.1. The "Wisdom of the World" in 1 Corinthians 1:17–31

The second passage which has shaped the understanding of Paul's epistemology is 1 Cor 1:17–2:16. There is broad agreement among exegetes that Paul is, in these verses, defending himself against the criticism of (some of) the Corinthians, while at the same time trying to address the factionalism within the community at Corinth. Paul hopes to achieve these two goals in one blow by correcting the Corinthians' understanding of "wisdom" (σοφία). For, on the one hand, it is the Apostle's apparent lack of wisdom which seems to have sparked the criticisms of some members of the community, while on the other hand it is this same competitive focus on a certain kind of wisdom which seems to have given rise to the divisions at Corinth.[40]

The Apostle begins by emphasizing that his proclamation in Corinth was not based on "eloquent wisdom (σοφία λόγου)," precisely because, had he relied on such wisdom, his message would have been "emptied of its power (κενωθῇ)" (1:17). The "message about the cross," Paul explains, appears as foolishness to those who are usually considered wise, but their judgement is faulty and they are actually "perishing." Those "who are being saved," on the

---

[39] See pp. 68–73 below.

[40] So, e.g., Bockmuehl, *Revelation and Mystery*, 157; Gillespie, "Interpreting," 151–2; Gooch, *Partial Knowledge*, 20, 23–8; Stowers, "Reason," 256.

other hand, recognize that "the wisdom of the world (τὴν σοφίαν τοῦ κόσμου)" is in fact the real foolishness because it fails to recognize this message which constitutes "the power of God (δύναμις θεοῦ)" (1:18–21). Paul's main tactic here is to draw a sharp opposition between "the wisdom of the world" and the Gospel message. His point seems to be that the kind of wisdom which most people (including at least some of the Corinthians) value so highly is actually of no use in the quest for salvation. That salvation is only effected by the Gospel message of Christ's cross – the very message which ordinary wisdom dismisses as "foolishness." In the words of Robertson and Plummer, Paul here declares "the failure of worldly cleverness in dealing with the things of God."[41] Ordinary thought and discourse cannot recognize in the Gospel their own salvation because, as Fee writes, "the cross stands in absolute, uncompromising contradiction to human wisdom."[42]

This failure of ordinary wisdom means that the tables are turned, and that such wisdom can be seen for the folly which in reality it has become, while the Gospel (for all its apparent foolishness) is revealed as God's wisdom. The message which "the world holds to be folly" is the very message which saves, so that the world's wisdom is by this very fact "refuted." Its "self-stultification" is brought to light.[43] As Barrett puts it, "What God has done in Christ crucified is a direct contradiction of human ideas of wisdom and power, yet it achieved what human wisdom and power fail to achieve."[44] The world's wisdom may remain quite competent in the sphere of ordinary affairs, but God has so arranged things that such wisdom cannot discern what is true of humanity's relationship with the Creator.[45] The effective, saving power of the (apparently foolish) Gospel forces a reconsideration of all ordinary standards of reasonableness, and in so doing it "incapacitates,

---

[41] Robertson and Plummer, *1 Corinthians*, 18.

[42] Fee, *1 Corinthians*, 66.

[43] Robertson and Plummer, *1 Corinthians*, 20.

[44] Barrett, *1 Corinthians*, 56. Cf. Fee, *1 Corinthians*, 76.

[45] Hence Wilckens emphasizes (*Weisheit*, 26–7) that in 1:20 Paul does not deny that the "wisdom" of the "wise" is genuine. He does not yet call it folly, but rather portrays God as *making* it foolish, arranging the possibilities for human salvation in such a way that ordinary wisdom cannot recognize them. Nor is the world's estimate of the gospel entirely false. Christ as the crucified one "ist in der Tat schwach," and insofar as God's action in crucifying Christ occurred as an act in the world, that divine act *is foolish.* "Der Inhalt des Kerygma," Wilckens writes, "*ist Torheit!*" (Wilckens, *Weisheit*, 37 [emphasis original]).

reverses, even turns upside down the values of this world."[46] God's way of acting has, Soards says, "dismissed [ordinary human] standards and made their logic irrelevant."[47]

What is more, this situation is precisely what God intended. It is God who *makes* the wisdom of the world foolish (ἐμώρανεν ὁ θεὸς τὴν σοφίαν τοῦ κόσμου) (1:20). He has *decided* (εὐδόκησεν) to save "those who believe" through an apparently foolish proclamation (1:21).[48] God seems intent on demonstrating his own superiority to wise humanity, demonstrating that "God's foolishness is wiser than human wisdom, and God's weakness is stronger than human strength" (1:25). In fact, this power is illustrated in the very existence of the Corinthian congregation, for God's determination to humble humanity by using "foolish" instruments is confirmed by their own social makeup (1:26–31). By painting this portrait of worldly wisdom and the powerful Gospel, the Apostle at once deflates the pretensions of those who are making factional claims to some superior wisdom and also counters the criticism from those same quarters that he himself is none too wise.[49]

Yet why does God need to assert his superiority over such worldly wisdom? What is it that, in Paul's understanding, is faulty about "the wisdom of this world"? A few interpreters have tried to suggest that Paul's focus in 1:18–2:5 is set narrowly on rhetorical skill (that is, the form of speech) or on prophetic abilities,[50] so that the Apostle is not really talking about reason or thought in general.[51] The large majority, however, understand Paul's reference to "human wisdom" to be quite broad, for Paul himself makes it encompass both the expectations of the Jewish tradition ("Jews demand signs") and the rational machinations of Greek sophists and philosophers

---

[46] Soards, *1 Corinthians*, 39.

[47] Soards, *1 Corinthians*, 41.

[48] So Calvin, *Corinthians*, on 1 Cor 1:19; Soards, *1 Corinthians*, 47.

[49] Cf. 2 Cor 1:12, where we again find Paul denying that he and Timothy acted "by fleshly wisdom (ἐν σοφίᾳ σαρκικῇ)" and opposing this wisdom to "the grace of God."

[50] So Hunt (*Inspired Body*, 76) sees Paul focussing on "spiritual wisdom."

[51] Along similar lines, Aquinas (*Summa Theologica*, I, Q. 12, A. 13 [Dominican Fathers, p. 1.59]) understood the passage to be focussed primarily on the philosophers, and not on ordinary thinking.

("Greeks desire wisdom") (1:22).[52] So what is it about ordinary human thought and discourse that incapacitates them in the religious sphere? Many exegetes see Paul emphasizing that God's action in Christ assumes a different set of intellectual and moral standards from those which human beings normally employ.[53] Gillespie, for example, understands the Apostle to imply that both the "Greek" and the "Jew" expect God's action to be characterized by "power," not weakness, so that they find the message of a crucified saviour incredible.[54] This might be understood to imply that the weakness of human wisdom is merely situational, that a different society might encourage a more successful kind of wisdom.[55] Yet most interpreters, to a greater or

---

[52] So, e.g., Wilckens, *Weisheit*, 27–8. Robertson and Plummer (*1 Corinthians*, 21) are almost certainly correct that the Jew and Greek in 1:22 are meant to encompass all of Paul's contemporary society. Cf. Gooch, *Partial Knowledge*, 32–5.

[53] It is, after all, the message of "Christ crucified" (Χριστὸν ἐσταυρωμένον) which is "a stumbling block to Jews and foolishness to Gentiles" (1:23). In other words, there is something about this event which does not fit Jewish or Greek expectations about divine action.

[54] Gillespie, "Interpreting," 154.

[55] Stowers ("Reason," 258) seems to suggest this when he insists that Paul critiques only "certain traditions of rationality"; Stowers understands the "moral and epistemic vices" which mark "worldly wisdom" to be nothing more than "conceit, arrogance, and bragging" ("Reason," 258). This would imply that the problems with ordinary reason could be solved simply by kindness and humility within the community. Such love and harmony are, in the short term, certainly what Paul wants to see in Corinth, and Stowers is correct that in 3:3–4 Paul identifies the Corinthians' factionalism as the indicator that they are pursuing inappropriate kinds of wisdom ("Reason", 258; cf. 1:11–13; 3:18–22).

Yet we must not fall into the trap of treating Paul's words *merely* as pragmatic tools used to influence his audience. In the course of influencing them he is also laying out a broad picture of the world in which the Corinthian situation is one example or symptom of a more universal problem. While Stowers takes the reference to Jew and Greek in 1:22 restrictively, to indicate that Paul is concerned only with specific social traditions of reasoning, these terms are much more likely intended by Paul to be comprehensive. "Jew and Greek" represent the two basic categories of the humanity which Paul knew. Note too that in 1:21 we are told that "the world" somehow failed to know God "through wisdom," giving rise to God's strategy of revelation through foolishness (cf. Gooch, *Partial Knowledge*, 32–5). Several exegetes see here in seed form the same idea that is expressed more fully in Rom 1:18–32 (so, e.g., Conzelmann, *1 Corinthians*, 44–5; Dupont, *Gnosis*, 25; Fee, *1 Corinthians*, 72). Even if we do not accept that connection, however, the identification of ὁ κόσμος as the subject involved in 1:21 certainly suggests a universal situation. Likewise, Dupont points out that Paul cites in 1:19–20 and 3:19–20 scriptural claims that human wisdom and reasoning *in general* are unable to reach true knowledge

lesser extent, go further, to emphasize that for Paul *no* ordinary wisdom is capable of recognizing religious truth in the Gospel. What most commentators identify as the problem here is the underlying expectation that God will submit his action to human standards of authentication, standards which arise from within human frames of reference. Wilckens sees Paul as attacking in human beings the demand "daß das Kerygma sich der Norm und dem Kriterium dessen, was in ihrem Sinn Weisheit ist, auszuliefern und zu unterwerfen habe."[56] Likewise, for Conzelmann the problem is not merely that some apply certain wrong criteria in evaluating God's actions; rather, God's wisdom "does not subject itself to human criteria, but confounds *all* such criteria."[57] In answer to this demand that truth be authenticated on our own terms, Paul and his companions "present a message of weakness that is offensive. . . . To the longing for reason, they present an outright absurdity."[58] God chooses to act in ways which will appear absurd, which will frustrate ordinary human expectations about the divine, in order to force human beings to let go of their usual frames of reference and adopt a new vantage point.[59]

Yet if this is what Paul believes God is doing when he frustrates "the wisdom of the world," the question still remains *why* God wants to frustrate these ordinary criteria for reasonableness in religious discourse. Some suggest that, for Paul, the core of the problem with human wisdom is the *hubris* involved when it tries to comprehend God.[60] These exegetes argue that

---

(Ps 94:11 [LXX 93:11]; Job 5:12; Isa 19:11–12; 29:14; see Dupont, *Gnosis*, 25).

[56] Wilckens, *Weisheit*, 34.

[57] Conzelmann, *1 Corinthians*, 55 (italics mine). See also Soards, *1 Corinthians*, 42.

[58] Soards, *1 Corinthians*, 42.

[59] Thiselton (*1 Corinthians*, 158–9) describes the message of the cross here as something which is not laid open for the audience to judge and evaluate, but instead confronts and judges the audience.

Gärtner ("Pauline and Johannine," 217–20) understands Paul to teach (like many Hellenistic thinkers) that the heavenly and the earthly are ontologically incompatible, so that human beings cannot understand God's wisdom, simply because they are human and not divine. Yet this reading overlooks Paul's emphasis on God's deliberately choosing to frustrate human wisdom. The epistemic futility of human wisdom is not a necessary situation, but rather is part of God's strategy in the restoration and judgement of the world. Along similar lines see P. Ciholas, "Knowledge and Faith."

[60] So Conzelmann, *1 Corinthians*, 42, 47; cf. Robertson and Plummer, *1 Corinthians*, 17.

any attempt to understand God's action is irredeemably flawed, so that the Gospel constitutes not a new "wisdom" or "knowledge" but an outside force – Christ – which the believer experiences without grasping it by means of reason.[61] In commenting on 1:24, Conzelmann insists that believers "do not advance beyond the situation of hearing and believing."[62] Bultmann likewise regards Pauline faith as a radical decision in the face of God's confronting Word, a decision which, if it is to remain authentic, must not devolve into the construction of a new world view.[63] There are difficulties with this reading, however, not the least of which is the fact that Paul employs reasoned arguments even in 1 Cor 1–2. If Paul appeals here to his audience's reason, if he tries to help them understand and think through the divine/human relationship, then either his practice is hopelessly out of touch with his theory or his target in 1 Cor 1:18ff. is not the attempt to understand *per se*. Moreover, nowhere in these verses does the Apostle actually condemn reason or understanding. It is "the wisdom *of the world* (τὴν σοφίαν τοῦ κόσμου)" which he says is made futile, not wisdom in and of itself.[64]

So what is it about the thinking of "the world" that, in Paul's view, God has designed the Gospel to frustrate? Many locate the problem not in an attempt to understand the ineffable, but in the unwillingness to accept the limits of human autonomy. Human beings want complete control over their own existence, and so resist the inevitable need to trust God for their security.[65] From this perspective, the Gospel need not be inherently

---

[61] Hence Conzelmann argues that the preaching of the cross is "not the propagating of a *Weltanschauung*, but the destruction of every attempt to regard a *Weltanschauung* as the way of salvation" (*1 Corinthians*, 47). See also Wilckens, *Weisheit*, 39–40.

[62] Conzelmann, *1 Corinthians*, 48.

[63] Bultmann argues that for Paul God's action in the cross "cannot in any way be *comprehended* as a possibility of salvation" ("Karl Barth," 69).

[64] So Bornkamm, *Paul*, 119, 132; Gooch, *Partial Knowledge*, 42; Soards, *1 Corinthians*, 40; Stowers, "Reason," 258.

[65] For Barrett (*1 Corinthians*, 70) this "attempt to secure [one's] position over against the Creator" is inherently idolatrous. See also Fee, *1 Corinthians*, 68; Calvin, *Corinthians*, on 1 Cor 1:17, 1:19–20.

Gooch is thus on the right track when he says that Paul's emphasis falls on "the cognitive modesty appropriate to all human intellectual activity" (*Partial Knowledge*, 42; cf. Thiselton, *1 Corinthians*, 167). We should be clear, however, that Paul is probably not concerned primarily with the limits of human reason *per se*, but rather with the corrupt

incomprehensible. Instead it is obviously designed to frustrate any attempt at confirmation from within the realm of human experience and values, so that in order to accept it one is forced to adopt a whole new frame of reference. Instead of being incomprehensible, the Gospel is unjustifiable in terms of other human systems of evaluation and plausibility.[66] Hence an acceptance of the Gospel would combat the desire for an impossible human autonomy by requiring that believers depend on God for the framework of their intellectual life. At the same time, there are for Paul other moral failures endemic to fallen humanity which, many suggest, inevitably corrupt the values and standards of reasonableness within which human wisdom operates. So, for Barrett, human wisdom is incorrigibly egocentric,[67] so that "there is no manifestation of God that man's essentially self-regarding wisdom does not twist until it has made God in its own image."[68] However we construe the moral failings which corrupt ordinary standards of reasonableness, Stowers is likely right that Paul does not reject wisdom itself, but rather "any wisdom characterized by certain moral and epistemic vices."[69] The message of the cross is thus not anti-rational. It is, rather, calculated to subvert the essentially idolatrous tendencies which pervert all fallen human thought, by forcing the believer to abandon his or her usual standards of evaluation.[70] As

---

drive for autonomy which prompts human beings to try to understand God within the terms of ordinary human experience and values.

[66] So Barrett, *1 Corinthians*, 54–5; Calvin, *Corinthians*, on 1 Cor 1:20; Chrysostom, *First Corinthians*, "Homily III," on 1:17; Gooch, *Partial Knowledge*, 40–41. See also Fee, *1 Corinthians*, 68, though Fee too suggests that in this sense the Gospel is not a new σοφία.

[67] Barrett, *1 Corinthians*, 52.

[68] Barrett, *1 Corinthians*, 54. See also Fee, *1 Corinthians*, 73–4. Thiselton (*1 Corinthians*, 166) argues that Paul attacks reason only insofar as it operates outside its proper limits and as an instrument of "manipulation and self-deception." See also Aquinas, who in commenting on 1 Cor 1:20 suggests that the wisdom of the world is foolish "because what is impossible to nature, it judges to be impossible to God" (*Summa Theologica*, I, Q. 25, A. 3 [Dominican Fathers, p. 1.139, cf. p. 137]).

[69] Stowers, "Reason," 258 (though Stowers himself describes these vices too narrowly; see above, pp. 26–7, n. 55). See also Bornkamm, "Faith and Reason," 30; Thiselton, *1 Corinthians*, 166.

[70] In somewhat different terms, Thiselton argues that Paul's gospel appears as folly in part because it represents, in M. Mitchell's words, a "paradigm of self-effacement" which runs counter to the concerns for power and control that lie beneath the Corinthian factionalism (*1 Corinthians*, 174). Thiselton also characterizes human wisdom as "short-term" and "self-absorbed" (*1 Corinthians*, 169) and the world which is constructed on the

Gillespie suggests, the *kerygma* is thus foolishness to the perishing "not because it is unintelligible, but because it all too intelligibly calls for a reversal of the human standard . . . that determines what counts as 'wisdom.'"[71] As in Romans 1, so here it is human moral weakness, a weakness of which our standards of evaluation are a symptom, which for Paul is the real problem, not reason itself.[72]

2.2. The "Demonstration of the Spirit" in 1 Corinthians 2:1–5

Paul goes on to underline in 2:1–5 that his simple presentation of the Gospel was in fact a deliberate strategy, geared to ensure that his preaching did not undermine the Gospel's subversion of that corrupt wisdom. Here, as in 1:17, Paul insists that his proclamation came not "with plausible words of wisdom (πειθοῖς σοφίας λόγοις), but with a demonstration of the Spirit and of power (ἀποδείξει πνεύματος καὶ δυνάμεως), so that your faith might rest not on human wisdom but on the power of God" (2:4–5). The majority of exegetes have understood Paul to be saying that he chose deliberately not to use eloquent rhetoric or sophisticated reasoning, but instead relied on a straightforward proclamation of the Gospel, to be accepted or rejected.[73] There has been some suggestion that when Paul confesses to having arrived in Corinth "in weakness and in fear and in much trembling" (2:3) he is referring not simply to a literal illness and anxiety,[74] nor merely to the Apostle's sense of holy fear as he carries out his divine commission, but also to his lack of "*pneumatische* δύναμις."[75] Few have been convinced, however,

---

basis of such wisdom as shot through with "structural self-centeredness, status-seeking, and supposed self-sufficiency" (*1 Corinthians*, 165).

[71] Gillespie, "Interpreting," 156. Gillespie identifies this standard as "power."

[72] See also 1 Cor 3:18–20, where Paul introduces two OT quotations concerning God's opposition to the wise by warning the audience: "Do not deceive yourselves. If you think that you are wise in this age, you should become fools so that you may become wise. For the wisdom of this world is foolishness with God." Here again the concern is not with rational thought, but with a particular kind of faulty wisdom which characterizes the present order. Moreover, Paul's point in saying this is to prepare for his injunction in 3:21–23 to avoid boasting about human leaders. This may well indicate that part of the problem with this worldly wisdom is its association with boasting.

[73] So Calvin, *Corinthians*, on 1 Cor 1:17; Robertson and Plummer, *1 Corinthians*, 31–2; Soards, *1 Corinthians*, 52–3.

[74] Robertson and Plummer, *1 Corinthians*, 31.

[75] Wilckens, *Weisheit*, 47 (though Wilckens accepts that the phrase ἐν φόβῳ καὶ ἐν

that Paul's primary focus in 2:1–5 is anything other than the justification of his lack of impressive speech and reasoning when he preached to the Corinthians. Indeed, this pattern of voluntary intellectual weakness is often seen as Paul's imitation of the pattern of God's action in Christ, who conquered by becoming weak in his shameful death.[76]

If it was not his own rhetorical force which Paul believes convinced the Corinthians, what was it? Paul explains that instead of "plausible words of wisdom (πειθοῖς σοφίας λόγοις)" he came with "a demonstration of the Spirit and of power (ἀποδείξει πνεύματος καὶ δυνάμεως)" (2:4). Here again commentators generally agree that Paul envisions some direct activity of the Holy Spirit which works on the hearer to produce belief in Paul's message.[77] Even Aquinas insists that the human capacity for natural theology is not sufficient to produce faith in Paul's Gospel on the basis of reason. Rather, "the intellect assents to the truth of faith, not as convinced by the reason, but as commanded by the will," and Aquinas points precisely to 1 Cor 2:4 when he argues that "[i]n this respect faith comes from God alone."[78] The impetus

---

τρόμῳ which follows does refer to a sense of standing under God's judgement). Gillespie argues along similar lines that the issue here cannot be simple rhetorical mastery, because of the religious context of the conversation: "It is more appropriate to infer that the power manifested in and through the interaction of wisdom and speech is considered divine in its origin and redemptive in its purpose" ("Interpreting," 155). Hence he argues that the speech καθ' ὑπεροχὴν λόγου which Paul rejects in 2:1 is speech which exhibits certain enthusiastic marks of prophetic inspiration. Yet the reference in 2:4 to words which are πειθοῖς certainly fits better with a discussion of rhetorical and logical skill than with teaching about ecstatic inspiration. When in 14:1–19 Paul discusses the ecstatic glossolalia with which the Corinthians seem to be enamoured, his point is precisely that such manifestations are often not intelligible. They do not convince the mind of anything.

[76] So Gillespie, "Interpreting," 155; Thiselton, *1 Corinthians*, 156; Wilckens, *Weisheit*, 48.

[77] So Barrett, *1 Corinthians*, 65–6; Calvin, *Corinthians*, on 1 Cor 1:20, on 2:5, and on 2:1; Chrysostom, *First Corinthians*, "Homily VI," on 2:5; Robertson and Plummer, *1 Corinthians*, 33; Gärtner, "Pauline and Johannine," 217; Soards, *1 Corinthians*, 54. Gillespie identifies the phrase πνεύματος καὶ δυνάμεως as a hendiadys ("Interpreting," 155). Indeed, Chrysostom argues that the whole problem with ordinary human reasoning is its claim to be autonomous, to function independent of the aid of God's Spirit (*First Corinthians*, "Homily VII," on 2:6; cf. Wilckens, *Weisheit*, 51).

[78] Aquinas, *Summa Theologica*, I, Q. 111, A. 1 (Dominican Fathers, p. 1.543).

to believe the Apostle's preaching arises from the direct activity of God in the hearer.[79]

This observation raises questions, though, about the relationship between the Spirit's activity and human reason. Chrysostom took 1 Cor 1:17ff. to teach that rational discussion is of no use in bringing people to knowledge of the Gospel. In discussing the passage he advised his congregation not to combat pagan thought by mounting educated arguments, but rather to fight with the example of a changed way of life.[80] Those who will not believe are compared to the insane, whose minds are perverted by illness. Such people, Chrysostom says,

> you cannot convince by human wisdom. Nay, if you want so to convince them, you do but the contrary. For the things which transcend reasoning require faith alone. Thus, should we set about convincing men by reasonings, how God became man, and entered into the Virgin's womb, and not commit the matter unto faith, they will but deride the more. Therefore they who inquire by reasonings, it is they who perish.[81]

Recognition of the truth is compared by Chrysostom to direct vision, for which one needs not to argue but simply to open one's eyes. Likewise, this faith, not reason, is the proper "organ" for perception of God's truth, just as the eye, and not the ear, is the proper organ for visual perception.[82] Yet

---

[79] Note that for Aquinas these truths of faith can be "confirmed" by rational arguments once they are apprehended by faith, though "the confirmation of what is above reason rests on what is proper to the Divine power," whether miraculous acts which only God can cause or prophetic predictions of things which only God can know (*Summa Theologica*, I.2, Q. 111, A. 4 [Dominican Fathers, p. 1138–9]).

It is not clear from this passage whether Paul understands this activity of the Spirit to override the individual will entirely (so Barrett, *1 Corinthians*, 55–6; Conzelmann, *1 Corinthians*, 42, 47; and, apparently, Fee, *1 Corinthians*, 77) or whether it becomes effective in those who already show some positive response. Paul does seem to imagine, however, that the Spirit's conviction is a stronger one than that normally produced by human reason (so Robertson and Plummer, *1 Corinthians*, 34), though it is not clear that such Spirit-induced belief is thus "above all risk of doubt" (Calvin, *Corinthians*, on 1 Cor 2:12).

[80] Chrysostom, *First Corinthians*, "Homily III," on 1:17.

[81] Chrysostom, *First Corinthians*, "Homily IV," on 1:19.

[82] Chrysostom, *First Corinthians*, "Homily IV," on 1:19. See also on 1:20–21. Cf. Calvin, *Corinthians*, on 1 Cor 1:20–21. Even Aquinas argues in connection with 1 Cor 2:6–7 that revealed truths such as the trinity of God cannot be grounded on rational argument: "Whoever, then, tries to prove the trinity of persons by natural reason, derogates from faith in two ways. Firstly, as regards the dignity of faith itself, which consists in its being

Chrysostom's reading of the passage seems to equate the speech ἐν σοφίᾳ λόγου of 1:17, the ὑπεροχὴν λόγου of 2:1, and the πειθοὶ σοφίας λόγοι of 2:4 with rational discussion itself. We saw above, however, that the "worldly wisdom" which Paul describes in 1:18–31 as futile need not be reason *per se*, but may well be reason *as it is directed by human vices* such as the idolatrous desire for complete autonomy. Paul says that he refused to frame his preaching within the values and standards of reasonableness which characterize other systems of thought. His preaching required a leap into a new system of values and a new understanding of what is plausible for God. This does not mean, however, that Paul claims to have abandoned all strategic rhetoric or rational discussion.[83] He simply repudiates the kind of oratory which some of the Corinthians seem to have craved, an oratory which made its case by appeal to ordinary human frameworks of value and reasonableness.[84] To frame this in more modern terms, Paul says that he avoided arguments which build on commonly accepted premises, but his denial still leaves room for him to have pursued an argument from coherence, in which the Gospel is presented as rationally consistent within its own terms of reference.

What does Paul mean, then, when he says that his preaching relied on "a demonstration of the Spirit and of power" for its persuasive force (2:4)? He probably does not mean, as Chrysostom assumed, that he abandoned any attempt to present the Gospel as a rational system of thought. The Apostle likely did not intend to set up the Spirit's influence as an alternative to

---

concerned with invisible things, that exceed human reason . . . . Secondly, as regards the utility of drawing others to the faith. For when anyone in the endeavor to prove the faith brings forward reasons which are not cogent, he falls under the ridicule of the unbelievers: since they suppose that we stand upon such reasons, and that we believe upon such grounds" (*Summa Theologica*, I, Q. 32, A. 1 [Dominican Fathers, p. 1.169]). Unlike the basic awareness of the Creator which may be inferred from the created order, the truths revealed by God "are held by means of a Divine light," by faith (*Summa Theologica*, I.2, Q. 62, A. 3 [Dominican Fathers, p. 1.852]).

[83] He does not claim (contra Thurén, *Derhetorizing*, 40) "not to be an orator at all".

[84] So, e.g., Siegert, *Argumentation*, 250; Gooch, *Partial Knowledge*, 47–9; Barrett, *1 Corinthians*, 68; Fee, *1 Corinthians*, 96–7; Calvin, *Corinthians*, on 1 Cor 1:17. We see the same distinction in the prologue of Epictetus, *Diss.*, where the editor confesses that the recorded lectures which follow are not polished writing, but nevertheless maintains that Epictetus' motive as he spoke was "to incite (κινῆσαι) the minds of his hearers to the best things," to produce an effect (τοῦτό γε αὐτὸ διαπράττοιντο) on the audience.

rationality, since his concern in these verses is not with rationality *per se* but with certain corrupt tendencies in the exercise of reason. At the same time, Paul seems to have realized that a rationally coherent presentation of God's action in Christ would not necessarily convince on its own, since it did not satisfy the morally corrupt urges which plague human beings.[85] So the Spirit's influence is necessary, not as a substitute for rationality in the presentation of the Gospel, but as a cure for the moral vices which usually determine what kind of divine action human beings are willing to accept as plausible and persuasive. In Paul's presentation the Spirit does not override human rationality, producing a belief in a truly irrational message. Rather, that Spirit is involved here primarily in reorienting the moral life of those who are "chosen" (1:24), so that the message which would normally appear foolish can be seen and understood as wisdom. Here we see the solution to the epistemic problem which Paul outlined in Romans 1. Human rationality may be corrupted by endemic moral failures so that the human mind consistently resists interpreting the world in the terms which the Gospel requires. Yet the Spirit of God offers Paul's audience a powerful demonstration, a "proof" of the Gospel's truth by strengthening and reorienting the listeners' moral will and allowing them to accept an interpretation of the world which they would otherwise have rejected, regardless of its internal consistency and its ability to account for human experience.

2.3. The "Wisdom of God" in 1 Corinthians 2:6–16

Although my reading here pushes beyond most exegetical explorations of 1:17–2:5, it rests on a fair consensus about the outlines of Paul's thought in

---

[85] This is most likely Paul's point in 2:5. It is usually assumed that Paul's concern in this verse is that reasoned arguments are not a solid enough ground for faith in the Gospel, so that he looks for a supernaturally produced conviction as an alternative. He explains that his preaching avoided "plausible words of wisdom" in order that "your faith might rest not on human wisdom (ἐν σοφίᾳ ἀνθρώπων) but on the power of God." Notice, however, that Paul says nothing in these verses about the instability or unreliability of reasoned arguments. Moreover, it is *human* wisdom which Paul does not want to serve as the foundation of his audience's conviction. If this human wisdom is identified with the "wisdom of the world" under discussion in 1:18–31, then it would seem that Paul's concern is not with the inherent instability of rational persuasion, but rather with the distorting and corrupting influence of worldly wisdom when it is taken as the framework for persuasion.

those verses. In contrast, we find sharp disagreement over the interpretation of the last section of this passage, 2:6–16. Already, in 1:30, Paul identified Christ as a "wisdom from God" (σοφία . . . ἀπὸ θεοῦ). Starting in 2:6, Paul turns from his rejection of human wisdom to describe a "wisdom of God" (θεοῦ σοφίαν), which is the subject of his speech (2:7). This new wisdom is unlike the "wisdom of this age" (οὐ τοῦ αἰῶνος τούτου) and has remained "secret and hidden" (ἐν μυστηρίῳ τὴν ἀποκεκρυμμένην) (2:6–7). This wisdom is revealed by the Spirit only to "the mature" (τοῖς τελείοις) (2:6), and here the Apostle compares the privileged access to divine truths which the Spirit has to the privileged access of the individual human spirit to that person's own thoughts (2:10–11). It is because the mature possess the Spirit that they too gain access to this secret wisdom of God, and it is because the "unspiritual" (ψυχικὸς δὲ ἄνθρωπος) lack this help that such divine wisdom remains "foolishness" and beyond their understanding (2:14–15).[86]

While there was broad agreement about the nature of the "worldly

---

[86] This summary assumes that all of the "spiritual" are recipients of the Spirit's revelations. Bockmuehl (*Revelation and Mystery*, 164–5) has argued for identifying the first-person plural subject of 2:1–16, and particularly the ἡμῖν of 2:10, with the apostles and prophets, and not with mature believers in general. This would make the apostles and prophets the recipients of the Spirit's revelation, while others would be dependent on the preaching of these apostolic messengers. The Spirit's role for the rest of the mature would simply be to prompt the hearer's recognition of this message as truth. The problem with this view, however, is that in 2:10–12 the reception of this revelation is based on the simple possession of the divine Spirit, not endowment with specific charismata. Paul writes: "Now we have received not the spirit of the world, but the Spirit that is from God, so that we may understand the gifts bestowed on us by God" (2:12). What is more, Thiselton points out that the most natural referent for ἡμῖν in 2:10 is τοῖς ἀγαπῶσιν αὐτόν immediately before, at the end of 2:9 (*1 Corinthians*, 255; so Fee, *1 Corinthians*, 109, n. 51; Robertson & Plummer, *1 Corinthians*, 43; Soards, *1 Corinthians*, 60). The special insight which the Spirit provides is also closely associated with the "mind of Christ" which this same "we" is said to possess in 2:16, but here the "we" is clearly inclusive of all the mature/spiritual. So, while one might plausibly limit the inspired speech of 2:13 to prophets and apostles, it is difficult to equate the inspiration of 2:10–12 with either of those restrictive charismata.

Moreover, the distinction which Bockmuehl draws between the Spirit's revelations in 2:10–12 and the Spirit's aid in understanding in 2:14–15 is highly artificial. On the one hand, it is not at all clear that by the Spirit's revelations Paul means ecstatic or visionary experiences; such revelations may well be mediated by rational or discursive activity. On the other hand, if one can grasp this wisdom only when the Spirit opens one's eyes, then this grasp would itself constitute a kind of revelation.

wisdom" in 1:17–2:5, here there has been fierce debate over the background of Paul's talk about "wisdom," "the perfect," and "mystery." Reitzenstein[87] and Bousset[88] located the source of this language in the mystery religions, and Bultmann followed their lead in depicting Paul as here addressing the followers of different "mystagogues" who offer knowledge and sacraments which furnish salvation.[89] In a slightly different sense, Wilckens argued that Paul's talk about "wisdom" and "mystery" in 2:6–16 reflects gnostic ideas circulating in Corinth.[90] Moreover, Wilckens argued that in borrowing this gnostic technical language, Paul could not keep it from colouring the thought of these verses. Hence the ideas in 2:6–16 do not reflect Paul's own thought, but rather an (only partially successful) attempt to subvert his opponents' language.[91] The vast majority of more recent commentators, however, have agreed that Bultmann and Wilckens were led down a blind alley. The evidence on which they based their model of the Corinthian theology was tenuous at best.[92] The supposed conflicts between this section and the

---

[87] Reitzenstein, *Mystery Religions*, 358.

[88] Bousset, *Kyrios Christos*, 84.

[89] Bultmann, "Karl Barth," 69.

[90] Wilckens (*Weisheit*, 19–20) argued that behind the factionalism in Corinth stands a controversy over a gnostic Christology in which Christ is identified as the σοφία of God. He suggested that this Christology also entailed a soteriology in which one participates (through baptism) with the resurrected Christ, but in which the crucifixion plays no role, either as a saving event or as a pattern for ethics (*Weisheit*, 53–60). Paul sees reflected in 2:8ff. the gnostic "Erlösermythos" in which this secret wisdom, as a *person*, enters the world in a "spiritual" form in order to reveal salvific knowledge to the "mature," so that they too can become "spiritual" and escape this existence (*Weisheit*, 71–3).

Wilckens saw this gnostic Christology behind Paul's opposition to "wisdom" in 1:17ff. as well. In fact, it is primarily because in 2:2 σοφία is set over against the Christological title (?) Χριστὸς ἐσταυρωμένος that Wilckens thought σοφία must have been "ein christologischer Titel des erhöhten Christus" in Corinth (*Weisheit*, 68–71). Note that this hypothetical gnostic background to the "wisdom" debate did not substantially affect Wilckens's reading of 1:17–2:5 because he recognized that Paul's polemic there, whatever its immediate target, is deliberately couched in broader terms (*Weisheit*, 268–70).

[91] See Wilckens, *Weisheit*, 52, 85. So Lührmann, *Offenbarungsverständnis*, 113. Martin Widmann has even suggested that the passage is an anti-Pauline interpolation ("1 Kor. 2:6–16").

[92] See, e.g., the discussion in Dupont, *Gnosis*, 151–80. Hunt (*Inspired Body*, 80) rightly emphasizes that the language which is supposed to present parallels to gnostic or mystery teaching is precisely the language which appears in a broad variety of philosophical and religious contexts. For example, Wilckens describes the opposition between the ψυχικὸς

preceding one arise not from a conflict in Paul's thought, but from an overly rigid reading of 1:18–2:5.[93] In fact, Conzelmann characterizes 2:6–16 as an example of the kind of very Pauline thinking which gave rise to the

ἄνθρωπος and the πνευματικός in 2:14–15 as typically gnostic (*Weisheit*, 88–9). Yet Paul frequently describes believers as possessing the Spirit, and in Gal 6:1 he designates the Galatian believers as οἱ πνευματικοί. While the adjective ψυχικός is used by Paul only in 1 Cor, the opposition between those with the Spirit and those without it is hardly uncharacteristic of Paul, and the adjective ψυχικός would not have been recognized in the first century as technical vocabulary (see LSJ, 2027–28). Moreover, when Paul employs the expression in 1 Cor 15:44–45 to describe all human bodies prior to the resurrection, he draws an explicit parallel with the LXX of Gen 2:7, where Adam is said to be created as ψυχὴν ζῶσαν. Wilckens recognized that in 2:12 Paul does not make the (usual?) "gnostic" declaration that the believer becomes spiritual, but asserts a radically ungnostic distance between God and the believer. Yet instead of being led to question a gnostic reading of Paul's other language, Wilckens suggested that Paul is here backtracking and trying to insure against a straightforwardly gnostic reading of what he has just written (*Weisheit*, 86; cf. 88–9).

Lührmann provides a detailed reconstruction of the way in which Paul here quotes, with isolated corrections, the Corinthian theology (*Offenbarungsverständnis*, 124–34). Conzelmann, however, argues that the apparent breaks which Lührmann notices are better understood as "polemical highlights" which Paul adds to his own wisdom teaching (*1 Corinthians*, 59). Moreover, Lührmann bases his reconstruction on the idea that a certain "Revelationschema" appears here which is inimical to Paul's theology. Yet he admits that this same "schema" appears also in passages such as Col 1:26f.; Eph 3:4f., 9f.; and Rom 16:25f. Lührmann believes that none of these passages were authored by Paul, but even if this is so, one wonders why Paul's successors so consistently warped his theology in the same (obviously unPauline?) direction. In the end, Lührmann's argument is really based on the sense that the sentiments expressed in 2:6–16 "muten im Mund des Paulus fremd an" (*Offenbarungsverständnis*, 134).

[93] Bultmann, for example, sees the description of the Gospel as "wisdom" in 2:6–16 as unPauline because he has read 1:17–2:5 as a condemnation of any and all comprehensible wisdom about God ("Karl Barth," 71). If we do not follow Bultmann's reading of the earlier passage, however, the tension disappears.

Similarly, Wilckens argued that in 2:8 Paul understands Christ to be the "lord of glory" already, even prior to his crucifixion. Yet elsewhere, he says, Paul envisions the apocalyptic exaltation of Christ as occurring only after the resurrection. This suggests to Wilckens that Paul is here talking in terms of the gnostic redeemer myth, in which a spiritual being, full of the "glory" of the spiritual realm, comes to enlighten others with his glory (*Weisheit*, 74). It is, however, quite possible that Paul refers to Christ as the "lord of glory" simply because that is how the Apostle understands him in the present, not because it was necessarily a fitting title at the time of the events Paul describes. See further Kovacs, "Archons."

Corinthians' enthusiastic excesses.[94] Hence, in a dramatic about-face, Wilckens himself eventually penned a subsequent article in which he roundly rejected his former gnostic reading of the passage.[95]

Thus the broad consensus now understands 2:6–16 as a natural extension of Paul's argument in 1:17–2:5. The "wisdom of this age" which is opposed to divine wisdom in 2:6, and whose representatives fail to recognize Christ in 2:8, is the same human wisdom which Paul has just finished rejecting at length. It thus includes both ordinary standards for rational verification and the rhetorical flair which was expected if those arguments were to carry force.[96] Paul's point in 2:6–16 is, at least in part, the same point he has been making all along: that such ordinary standards for evaluating the truth or falsehood of a message break down and become counter-productive when they encounter the Gospel. This Gospel is a "mystery" (2:7) in the Jewish apocalyptic sense of a salvific act of God which remains hidden, prepared in heaven, until its eschatological revelation, and which is known ahead of time only to God's elect.[97] Moreover, the emphasis on the Spirit as the mediator of religious knowledge has already been introduced in 2:1–5.[98] Hence, while

---

[94] Conzelmann, *1 Corinthians*, 57–60.

[95] Wilckens, "Zu 1 Kor 2.1–16."

[96] So, e.g., Fee, *1 Corinthians*, 65. This position is compatible with Hunt's suggestion that the language in 2:6–16 reflects a broad tradition of Hellenistic talk about "the human search for the divine mind" (using ἐρευνάω/ἐραυνάω and ζητέω). According to Hunt, this tradition emphasizes "the need for divine initiative," which associates the process with the "perfecting" (τέλος and cognates) of the inquirer, and which tends to talk about such knowledge as σοφία (*Inspired Body*, 10–11, 15–61), although, according to Hunt's own survey of the evidence, this pattern of usage is not as firmly attested as his summary statements would suggest (see, e.g., *Inspired Body*, 27, 39, 53). The closest parallels are restricted to Philo (*Inspired Body*, 45; cf. 39–50).

[97] See Gillespie, "Interpreting," 157. Bockmuehl (*Revelation and Mystery*, 161) plausibly compares Paul's Greek phrase σοφίαν ἐν μυστηρίῳ to the Hebrew חכמה ברז, which denotes God's "wisdom displayed in His saving design." See the use of this or an equivalent phrase in *1QH* IX 23; XII 13; *1QS* IV 18; *1QpHab* VII 15.

Most put the emphasis on the message having been unknown and being unknowable apart from the Spirit's revelation (so Robertson and Plummer, *1 Corinthians*, 37; Gillespie, "Interpreting," 157; Thiselton, *1 Corinthians*, 241). Barrett also suggests that the wisdom of the gospel is "hidden" in contrast to the worldly wisdom which "intends to be openly convincing" (*1 Corinthians*, 71; so Chrysostom, *First Corinthians*, "Homily VII," on 2:7). Both of these emphases are combined by Soards, *1 Corinthians*, 59.

[98] So Gillespie, "Interpreting," 158.

Paul's focus on "wisdom" and his use of terms such as "the mature" may arise in response to emphases in Corinth, we should read this passage primarily as a continuation of the argument outlined in 1:17–2:5.[99]

There remain, however, two interrelated questions which are less easily resolved, both of which will have a significant impact on how we understand Paul's epistemology in 1 Corinthians. The first question concerns the identity of "the mature" in 2:6. Does Paul intend this term to include all believers?[100] Or is he establishing a more restricted group within the Corinthian community who are more spiritually advanced than the rest?[101] This question is important for our purposes because if it is only a select group who receive this spiritual revelation, then the epistemic situation which Paul describes in

---

[99] Hunt (*Inspired Body*, 80) is most insistent that even the language of the passage is Paul's own, not the Corinthians'. Thiselton (*1 Corinthians*, 224–5, 241, 252) is more representative in his suggestion that Paul takes over the vocabulary of his opponents in order to reshape it – and that he does so successfully. There is also nearly universal agreement that Paul's analogy between the human πνεῦμα and the divine πνεῦμα in 2:10–11 does not imply any ontological parallel between the two kinds of "spirit" or any "divinization" of the human spirit (see Robertson and Plummer, *1 Corinthians*, 44; Fee, *1 Corinthians*, 111–12; Soards, *1 Corinthians*, 60–61; Thiselton, *1 Corinthians*, 257–8; Gärtner, "Pauline and Johannine," 220; contra Wilckens, *Weisheit*, 81, and [less clearly] Conzelmann, *1 Corinthians*, 65).

[100] So Fee, *1 Corinthians*, 102; Hunt, *Inspired Body*, 11, 67; Gärtner, "Pauline and Johannine," 220; Du Plessis, *Teleios*, 176–205; Yu, "Pneumatic Epistemology," 56–9; and (essentially) Thiselton, *1 Corinthians*, 231–3.

[101] Robertson and Plummer (*1 Corinthians*, 35) point to the contrast between the τέλειοι of 2:6 and the νήπιοι of 3:1. Likewise they equate the ψυχικοί of 2:14 with the σάρκινοι/σαρκικοί mentioned later (3:1ff.), a group which clearly includes Paul's Corinthian audience (*1 Corinthians*, 36). Wilckens (*Weisheit*, 53) agrees, but argues that the ἡμεῖς in 2:12 is not (as in 2:7, 10) identified with these τέλειοι. This is, he argues, an example of Paul's own theology protruding through his adopted gnostic schema (*Weisheit*, 87). Bultmann recognizes that Paul would not usually talk of a smaller group as those who possess the Spirit, but concludes that "the perfect" must possess the Spirit in a way that is different from other believers ("Karl Barth," 72). Bockmuehl (*Revelation and Mystery*, 160, n. 16) also observes that Paul does not include a recognition of the Corinthians' σοφία in the thanksgiving of 1:1–9 and that only some receive the λόγος σοφίας in 12:8. See also Bockmuehl's references to the הַתְּמִימִם at Qumran (*1QS* IV 22; VIII 10–12, 15–18) – full members who were given access to the mysteries of deeper knowledge – and to Philo's references (*Leg.* 3.100; *Sacr.* 60) to the τέλειοι, initiates into the divine mysteries (*Revelation and Mystery*, 159).

2:6–16 may apply only to the quest for certain esoteric teachings. It may not reflect, for instance, the situation of a person who responds to the Gospel preaching with faith. The majority of commentators, however, opt for a mediating position between these two identifications of the mature. It is true that Paul seems in 3:1–2 to exclude the Corinthian believers from the circle of the mature. They are mere "infants (νήπιοι)" who are not prepared for this full wisdom, and can only be given "milk." This makes a simple identification of the mature with all believers difficult.[102] On the other hand, it seems highly unlikely that Paul would describe any class of believers in the way he describes the "unspiritual person (ψυχικὸς . . . ἄνθρωπος)" in 2:14 as entirely lacking the Spirit.[103] This means that the Corinthians also cannot be simply equated with those who are *not* "mature." Hence Conzelmann writes that for Paul "perfection is not only the goal, but also the status of every believer," but that this status is "dialectically understood." The Corinthians cannot be treated as mature because they "do not conform to the true status conferred upon them (3:1ff)."[104] Likewise, Fee suggests that the Corinthians are, in their factional quarrels, acting out of keeping with their real status.[105]

---

[102] Fee points out, however, that Paul does not simply call the Corinthians ψυχικοί in 3:1, but rather uses the term σάρκινοι (*1 Corinthians*, 116). The Apostle thus seems deliberately to avoid equating the Corinthian audience with those who in 2:6–16 are contrasted with the mature. Less convincing is Hunt's suggestion that since Paul's statement in 3:1 about being unable to give the Corinthians the full teaching (speak to them as "spiritual") is in the aorist, it describes the situation only before their conversion (*Inspired Body*, 93).

[103] Fee points out that the ψυχικοί of 2:14 are "people who are not now, nor have they ever been, believers." They are depicted as never having received the Spirit (*1 Corinthians*, 116). So Hunt, *Inspired Body*, 82–3. Hunt points to 3:16, where "the corporate Corinthian body is a temple in which God's Spirit dwells," and to 12:13, where all believers have been "made to drink of the one Spirit" (ibid., 86). Robertson and Plummer (*1 Corinthians*, 49) try to explain this in terms of the "spiritual" person being one "in whom πνεῦμα has its rightful predominance." Yet this does not explain why the spiritual are contrasted with those who *lack* the Spirit.

Hunt also points out how "rhetorically unlikely" it is that Paul would distinguish between different ranks of believers "in a letter in which his primary aim is to appeal for the cessation of factionalism" (*Inspired Body*, 89).

[104] Conzelmann, *1 Corinthians*, 59; note, though, that Conzelmann himself does identify the ψυχικὸς ἄνθρωπος of 2:14 with the Corinthians and as an inferior class of believers (*1 Corinthians*, 71).

[105] Fee, *1 Corinthians*, 99–100, n. 8. Barrett writes that "[a]ll Christians are potentially

Paul locates the Corinthians in an ambiguous position – not really "unspiritual," but also not "mature" – in order to motivate them to overcome their factionalism and play the role of the mature.[106]

The question of the identity of the mature cannot, however, be resolved without also asking about the content of the "wisdom of God" which the Spirit imparts to them through the apostolic speech. If one understands the mature as a restricted inner circle of believers, then this wisdom cannot be the Gospel itself. It must be a set of more esoteric teachings which are not suited for everyone's ears.[107] There is, moreover, some force to this suggestion, since Paul's talk in 3:1 about withholding the "solid food" from the Corinthians who are mere "infants" does suggest that Paul has not yet shared this wisdom with them.[108] Yet he clearly *has* preached the message of Christ to them, and they are treated elsewhere in the letter as full believers.[109] This would imply, again, that the epistemic situation which Paul outlines here might apply only to the apprehension of such secondary teaching, and not to the salvific reception of the Gospel.[110] Yet Paul's description of the wisdom's content in 2:12 as an understanding of "the gifts bestowed on us by God (τὰ ὑπὸ τοῦ θεοῦ χαρισθέντα ἡμῖν)" does not sound particularly esoteric.[111]

---

perfect or *mature* in Christ (Col. i. 28), though only some are actually what all ought to be" (*1 Corinthians*, 69). So Hunt, *Inspired Body*, 102–4, and (less clearly) Soards, *1 Corinthians*, 57–8.

[106] So Fee, *1 Corinthians*, 98–9; Hunt, *Inspired Body*, 94–5.

[107] Not surprisingly, it is primarily the proponents of the gnostic interpretation of this passage who have identified the σοφία as such esoteric teaching (so Bultmann, "Karl Barth," 71). Note, however, Bockmuehl, *Revelation and Mystery*, 162–4; Gooch, *Partial Knowledge*, 44; Stowers, "Reason," 261. Gärtner is unusual in identifying the mature with all believers but still regarding this wisdom as deeper esoteric teaching, emphasizing Paul's statement that the Spirit searches "the depths of God" and knows "the things of God" (2:10–11) ("Pauline and Johannine," 219). Yet Paul does not say that the "spiritual" person shares in this complete knowledge. He says only that, by virtue of the Spirit's complete knowledge, that Spirit can share with the "spiritual" an understanding of "the gifts bestowed on us by God" (2:12).

[108] Bultmann, "Karl Barth," 71; Gooch, *Partial Knowledge*, 44.

[109] So Stowers, "Reason," 262.

[110] Stowers ("Reason," 261) argues that this revelation "is apparently unessential to their Christian life."

[111] Hence Bultmann ("Karl Barth," 71) is forced to conclude that the content of this σοφία has changed since 2:6–9, as have its recipients, so that "Paul is no longer thinking of the 'perfect' but of Christians in general." Yet Gillespie ("Interpreting," 160) rightly

Moreover, it was the crucified Christ who was identified in 1:30 as "wisdom from God (σοφία . . . ἀπὸ θεοῦ)" and in 2:1–5 as the sole content of Paul's preaching. So, when Paul says in 2:6–7 that he speaks a "wisdom" which is foreign to this age but which is "of God," the audience would most naturally assume that he is still referring to the message of the redemptive act of God through the cross.[112] Here again a solution becomes possible when we understand Paul's rhetorical situation. The wisdom which the mature can grasp is not a further esoteric doctrine, but the Gospel itself.[113] This the Corinthian audience has obviously accepted, since they have become believers in Christ. But their desire for some deeper or more sophisticated wisdom, the root of their factionalism, calls into question whether they have really understood the full implications of that Gospel. The "solid food" which Paul could not give the Corinthians is precisely the radical reorientation of one's former world view and values which the Gospel requires.[114] This is the

---

observes that Paul's grammar strongly implies a continuity of subject through from 2:6 to 2:12. The phrase τὰ ὑπὸ τοῦ θεοῦ χαρισθέντα ἡμῖν in 2:12 looks back to τὰ τοῦ θεοῦ in 2:11. These "things of God" in turn look back to the ἅ of 2:9 and hence to the "hidden wisdom" of 2:7. It is, again, this same message which the Spirit brings to speech in 2:13 and which in 2:14–15 the ψυχικοί are unable to grasp.

Conzelmann interprets Paul's description in 2:12 to mean that "the content of knowledge is the spirit – through the spirit," an unmediated "self-knowledge" (*1 Corinthians*, 60), though he later speculates that its content might be "insight into the cosmic background of the crucifixion" (*1 Corinthians*, 63). Bockmuehl suggests that Paul's phrase in 2:12 refers to "a deeper knowledge of the inheritance which is in store for those who love God" (*Revelation and Mystery*, 164, cf. 162). See, similarly, Gooch, *Partial Knowledge*, 44.

[112] So Robertson and Plummer, *1 Corinthians*, 35; Calvin, *Corinthians*, on 1 Cor 2:10; Barrett, *1 Corinthians*, 69; Fee, *1 Corinthians*, 112; Gillespie, "Interpreting," 156. Gillespie also points out that Paul has already identified the Gospel as τὸ μυστήριον τοῦ θεοῦ in 2:1 ("Interpreting," 157).

[113] Cf. 1 Cor 4:1, where Paul describes himself and Sosthenes as "stewards of God's mysteries" and where these mysteries seem to be identical with their Gospel preaching. Likewise, in Col 1:26–27 Paul describes how God has revealed "the mystery that has been hidden throughout the ages and generations" to "his saints." The mystery is "Christ in you, the hope of glory," and in 1:25 and 1:28 it seems to be identified with Paul's own proclamation. These passages confirm that Paul could at least speak of his Gospel message in terms similar to those which he employs in 1 Cor 2:7.

[114] Fee argues that the "milk" and "solid food" which Paul contrasts in 3:1–4 are not substantially different kinds of teaching. Both are simply "the good news of salvation." What Paul is highlighting, however, is that because the Corinthians regarded his teaching

true wisdom, which cannot be understood without the Spirit's help within. Hence, as with his positioning of the Corinthians in the ambiguous space between the mature and the unspiritual, here too Paul's talk about wisdom is designed to push the Corinthians into the realization that their whole quest for wisdom marks them as fools and casts a shadow of ambiguity over their status as Spirit-led believers.[115]

The epistemological model which emerges from this interpretation of 1 Cor 2:6–16 is thus one in which the Spirit plays a central role in the ability of all believers to grasp the implications of the Gospel for life. Just as one's initial acceptance of the Gospel comes as a result of the Spirit's moral influence (2:1–5), so one's deepening grasp of the implications of that message depends on the Spirit's ongoing "revelation" (2:6–16).[116] Barrett rightly emphasizes that, for Paul, those who lack the Spirit simply "cannot apprehend spiritual truths," no matter how acute their rational powers.[117] The Gospel and its radical reinterpretation of the world remain to such people simple folly. The Spirit is thus a key factor in the successful attainment of knowledge.[118]

---

as merely the initial, preparatory material, they were not able to recognize in it the profound content of divine wisdom (Fee, *1 Corinthians*, 124–5). Thiselton understands this wisdom from God as the willingness "to reappropriate the message of the cross in your innermost being" (*1 Corinthians*, 259). It is what the proclamation becomes for one who grasps a more profound consciousness of the way in which that proclamation breaks open the world's structures of thought and value (*1 Corinthians*, 260, 262). See also Robertson and Plummer, *1 Corinthians*, 39, and Soards, *1 Corinthians*, 57, though these commentators miss some of the rhetorical ambiguity which Paul creates here.

If this general understanding of the "wisdom of God" in 2:6–16 is correct, then this would explain why 1) Paul here avoids the language of evangelistic preaching, e.g., the verbs κηρύσσω and καταγγέλλω (so Hunt, ibid., 90–91), even though 2) the general epistemic situation seems to be the same as that described in 1:17–2:5, where such evangelistic language was prominent. Similar spiritual aid is needed both for the initial acceptance of the Gospel and for the ongoing appropriation of its implications.

[115] Fee, *1 Corinthians*, 98–9, 102–3.

[116] So Barrett, *1 Corinthians*, 74.

[117] Barrett, *1 Corinthians*, 77. So Dupont, *Gnosis*, 152.

[118] Gillespie points to a cluster of terms which 2:6–16 shares with chapters 12–14: ἀποκαλύπτειν (2:10; 14:30); πνευματικοί (2:13; 12:1; cf. 2:15; 14:37); πνεῦμα (2:10–14; 12:3, 4, 7–9, 11); σοφία (2:6, 7; 12:8); and τέλειοι (2:6; 14:20). Likewise, in both passages inspired speech is denoted by the verb λαλεῖν rather than κηρύσσειν (as in 1:23). The wisdom of God is hidden ἐν μυστηρίῳ in 2:7 and προφητεία allows one to know τὰ

Does this mean that Paul is an extreme fideist for whom the Spirit *displaces* the activity of reason? Several commentators seem to think it does. Fee writes that salvation is, according to these verses, only for those who "believe," who "will take the risk and put their whole trust in God to save in this way."[119] This leaves humanity with an "awful risk: trust God and be saved by his wise folly, or keep up our pretensions and perish."[120] Barrett emphasizes that, for Paul, no human being can discover the truth of the Gospel "by any achievement of his own."[121] The upshot of the passage is thus that "[t]he Spirit and the truths about God are not grasped and possessed by humans, rather, they themselves grasp humanity and direct persons toward others as the agents of God's saving work."[122] We have already seen, however, that there is reason to think that Paul's target in the preceding sections was not reason in and of itself, but reason which has been hijacked by human vices. The Spirit's role in 2:1–5 seems to be a moral restoration of believers which allows them to move into a new system of values within which the Gospel is rational and plausible. Here too there is reason to believe that Paul understood the Spirit to *renew* human reason, rather than to displace it. Barrett points to Paul's statement in 2:15 that the spiritual "discern all things" and suggests that Paul understands the believer to gain a new ability to "consider and appraise" things in the world, because the Gospel has

---

μυστήρια πάντα in 13:2 ("Interpreting," 161; cf. Dautzenberg, "Botschaft und Bedeutung," 142–3). While it is unlikely that this indicates a narrow focus on prophecy in 2:6–16, it does suggest that the Spirit is understood as active in the Apostle's preaching, much as in prophetic activity.

It is, however, less clear whether this understanding of the Spirit's role in producing faith necessarily entails divine predestination of those who are to be saved (so Calvin, *Corinthians*, on 1 Cor 2:14; apparently, Gärtner, "Pauline and Johannine," 217), or whether Paul assumes some room for human decision to either hold on to one's corrupt moral will or release it and perceive the world in light of the Gospel (so, clearly, Chrysostom, *First Corinthians*, "Homily VII," on 2:14; Thiselton, *1 Corinthians*, 270–71).

[119] Fee, *1 Corinthians*, 74.

[120] Fee, *1 Corinthians*, 77. See also Robertson and Plummer, *1 Corinthians*, 21.

[121] Barrett, *1 Corinthians*, 74. Hunt suggests that Paul is emphasizing the passivity of human beings in relation to divine wisdom in order to neutralize any individual claims to a superior access to knowledge (*Inspired Body*, 80). See also Chrysostom, *First Corinthians*, "Homily VII," on 2:7; Conzelmann, *1 Corinthians*, 65; Soards, *1 Corinthians*, 61; Thiselton, *1 Corinthians*, 263.

[122] Soards, *1 Corinthians*, 61.

provided "a moral standard by which all things may be measured."[123] Gillespie goes further and points out the consistent reference to cognitive activities in 2:6–16. The apprehension of divine wisdom does not seem to suppress rational thought, but rather involves "understanding" (εἰδέναι, 2:12) and enables the mature to "interpret" (συγκρίνειν, 2:13) and "judge" (ἀνακρίνεσθαι, 2:14, 15).[124] At the end of the passage the "spiritual" believer is left with "the mind of Christ (νοῦς Χριστοῦ)," a new way of thinking and reasoning.[125] This seems to confirm at least that the Gospel is itself comprehensible (even if some cannot accept it)[126] and that the one who, under the Spirit's impulse, has accepted that message gains a new ability to reason about the world.

This observation once again prompts questions about precisely how in Paul's thought the Spirit's ongoing revelatory activity is related to human reason. Is the revelation of the Spirit in 2:10ff. a matter of his supernaturally implanting ideas in the believer's mind, effectively bypassing the rational faculties? This is a tempting interpretation, but the prominence of human rational, interpretive activities in the passage mitigates against it. Such an irrationalist interpretation of the Spirit's revelation also assumes that the Spirit's role here

---

[123] Barrett, *1 Corinthians*, 77. This also explains, for Barrett, why the spiritual "are themselves subject to no one else's scrutiny" (2:15), for the standards which others would apply in evaluating them are not the true standards of the Gospel (*1 Corinthians*, 78).

[124] Gillespie, "Interpreting," 156. See also Gooch, who emphasizes that the Spirit's revelation retains a cognitive content ("wisdom" in 2:6, 7) which can be expressed by human language (2:7, 13), and that the words "taught by the Spirit" are "words serving interpretation (v. 13) and investigation (v. 14) rather than expressing nonrational ecstasy" (*Partial Knowledge*, 37). Cf. Hunt, *Inspired Body*, 84–6.

[125] Wilckens suggests that the wisdom of God brings with it a radically different "Wertungssystem" which the believer applies in interpreting the world (*Weisheit*, 36), while Thiselton defines the "mind of Christ" (borrowing a phrase from Weiss) as a "mode of thought" or "mind-set" (*1 Corinthians*, 275).

[126] Notice that in describing the response of the "unspiritual" to this divine wisdom (v. 14) Paul does not say they cannot understand it. He says, rather, that it is folly to them (μωρία γὰρ αὐτῷ ἐστιν) and that they are not able to "know" it (οὐ δύναται γνῶναι). The verb γινώσκω here probably means not "understand" but "acknowledge." Hence Paul goes on to say not that the Spirit's help is necessary in order to understand the message, but rather that the Spirit's aid allows one to form proper *judgements* about it (ὅτι πνευματικῶς ἀνακρίνεται). See further p. 47, n. 129 below.

is to provide new cognitive *content*.[127] The epistemic problem in 2:6–16, however, is not the *discovery* of truth about God, but the *recognition* of truth when it is presented. Paul is not assimilating the believer's whole growth in religious understanding to the model of prophetic inspiration, in which the Spirit's role is to convey a message directly.[128] It is taken for granted that a wisdom has already been made available to the world, a wisdom which is "not of this age" (οὐ τοῦ αἰῶνος τούτου) but which is "from God" (θεοῦ) (2:6–7). Access to a presentation of this wisdom does not require the Spirit's help. When Paul says in 2:14 that the "unspiritual person" is not able to "know" this wisdom (οὐ δύναται γνῶναι), he almost certainly means that

---

[127] See, e.g., Yu, "Pneumatic Epistemology," 60–61, 74–8; and Gooch, *Partial Knowledge*, 36 (though Gooch holds that 2:6–16 apply only to a limited, esoteric kind of knowledge).

[128] Contra Hunt and Gillespie, both of whom point out parallels in language between 1 Cor 2:6–16 and the discussions of charismata in chapters 12 and 14 (see above, pp. 43–44, n. 118). Gillespie understands Paul to be narrowly focussed on prophecy in 2:6–16 ("Interpreting," 151, 160), though Gillespie argues (based on the discussion of prophecy in 1 Cor 14) that this prophetic speech is inspired interpretation of the basic *kerygma* ("Interpreting," 165). As Hunt observes, however, the broader context of 1:17–2:5 makes it very difficult to understand 2:6–16 as a highly focussed discussion of prophecy (*Inspired Body*, 90). Hunt himself holds that Paul is depicting all intra-group teaching and learning as a charismatic activity analogous to prophecy, and emphasizes the community's corporate role in distinguishing between valid and invalid inspiration. See also the similar suggestions in Dupont, *Gnosis*.

The parallels to which they point are real enough. Hunt observes (*Inspired Body*, 128) that it is in emphasizing the importance of charismatic manifestations serving a constructive role in the community (and in relation to visitors) that the Apostle reintroduces language about being τέλειοι rather than νήπιοι and παιδία (14:20) (so Hunt, *Inspired Body*, 121–5). Both writers also point to Paul's use of λαλέω in 2:6–7, 13, instead of κηρύσσω or καταγγέλλω. This may suggest that Paul understands at least some teaching to be inspired by the Spirit – hence his claim in 2:13 that "we" speak God's wisdom in words which are διδακτοῖς πνεύματος. This idea is further reinforced by Dupont's observation that prophecy and teaching are closely aligned in 1 Cor 14 (*Gnosis*, 213). Even if teaching is understood as a prophetic activity, however, this does not necessarily mean that the successful *reception* of that teaching (Paul's focus in 2:6–16) is likewise analogous to prophetic inspiration. We must admit that γνῶσις is included, alongside prophecy, among the charismata in 1 Cor 12 and 14 (cf. 13:2; see Dupont, *Gnosis*, 187–8, 201–3, 213; cf. pp. 33, 214, 224–5 re. Col 3:9–10, 16). Most commentators would agree, however, that this charismatic γνῶσις is a phenomenon distinct from the knowledge which Paul usually denotes by the verbs γινώσκω and οἶδα.

such people fail to *recognize* it as wisdom, as true. For the problem facing the unspiritual here is not a problem of access to the true wisdom, but a lack of *acceptance* of the truth when they do hear it (οὐ δέχεται τὰ τοῦ πνεύματος).[129] The Spirit appears in these verses not as one who uncovers hidden content, but as one who allows believers to recognize the (openly presented) message as true.[130] The Spirit's "revelation," his "uncovering," is thus a matter of opening human eyes to the truth of the message when they encounter it.[131]

How does the Spirit open the eyes of the mature? If my reading of 1:17–2:5 is correct and the epistemic problem which Paul envisions is primarily a moral problem, then here again Paul most likely imagines the Spirit to open human eyes to the truth by healing the believers' moral constitution. Just as the initial acceptance of the Gospel required that endemic human vices be alleviated, so too the ongoing and deepening grasp of the Gospel's implications requires that the Spirit continue his moral restoration of believers. For if the Gospel is deliberately geared to be incompatible with endemic human vices and the systems of value and plausibility which those

---

[129] See also p. 45, n. 126 above. The situation is more ambiguous in 2:8, where Paul describes the ἀρχόντοι τοῦ αἰῶνος τούτου as not having "known" (ἔγνωκεν) God's hidden wisdom. Here the Apostle may well mean that these powers were completely unaware of its content, particularly since the situation envisaged precedes the crucifixion and the subsequent proclamation of the Gospel.

[130] It is true that in 2:10–11 Paul emphasizes the Spirit's privileged access to heavenly information. Notice, however, that Paul does not say that the spiritual are informed of "the depths of God," of all that the Spirit knows. That which the Spirit reveals to believers is more modest (2:12). Moreover, in 2:12 Paul does not say that the mature have received anything directly *from* the Spirit, but only that they have received the Spirit *in order that* they might know (recognize?) the truth: ἐλάβομεν ἀλλὰ τὸ πνεῦμα τὸ ἐκ τοῦ θεοῦ, ἵνα εἰδῶμεν τὰ ὑπὸ τοῦ θεοῦ χαρισθέντα ἡμῖν. Why, then, does Paul emphasize that the Spirit has privileged access to divine truth? He likely wants to characterize the Spirit as a uniquely reliable epistemic guide, one who is in a position to give human beings right standards of evaluation.

[131] This is the same problem of recognition or evaluation (rather than access) which was Paul's focus in 1:17–2:5. The process is also very much like the one which Paul envisions in 2 Cor 3:12–18, where a "veil" lies over the minds of Jews so that they cannot recognize the truth in the Scriptures, but this veil is removed for those in Christ. Note too that in 3:17 this unveiling of the mind is associated with the activity of the Spirit. See also Phil 3:15, where Paul says to the audience, "[I]f you think differently about anything, this too God will reveal to you (ὑμῖν ἀποκαλύψει)."

vices spawn, then these vices will make human beings resistant not just to the broad outlines of the message but also (and perhaps even more so) to the ongoing re-evaluation of life which that Gospel demands. This is precisely why, for Paul, the selfish rivalry and factionalism at Corinth calls into question the Corinthians' status as spiritual. For, although their initial acceptance of his preaching was an indication that the Spirit had begun his restorative work within them, their behaviour displays the fact that they are still operating (at least in part) within the world of corrupt values which the Gospel was designed by God to subvert. The Spirit has, for whatever reason, not continued to bring about the moral restoration of the Corinthian believers which would allow them to recognize and adopt the new world of values within which the Gospel makes sense.

What we must recognize in all of this is that, for Paul, the Spirit's activity does not provide a licence for irrationality. The Spirit's revelatory activity does not remove the need for rational consideration of the Gospel and its implications. On the contrary, the Spirit's moral restoration of the "chosen" is intended precisely to facilitate unobstructed rational activity. It is the Spirit's correction of the believers' deep-seated vices which allows them to recognize that the Gospel, despite its difference from "worldly wisdom," presents a rationally coherent way of interpreting the world. It is the moral influence of that same Spirit which allows believers to continue the rational interpretive task of re-evaluating all of life and reality in light of the new framework provided by the Gospel. Hence Soards argues that

> Paul is not decrying the value of sensible reflection; rather, he is insisting that humans cannot discern the reality of God through their reason based only upon their own experience. God's self-revelation in the cross is the key to comprehending God, it is the necessary starting point for valid comprehension of the divine, and without the cross we are bound to misunderstand God.[132]

The Spirit can be understood to restore and empower human reason by allowing human minds to reason within the one framework which allows true interpretations of existence.

---

[132] Soards, *1 Corinthians*, 40.

Chapter Two

Paul and Rationality: The Broader Picture

The model of knowing which has emerged from both Romans 1:18–32 and 1 Corinthians 1:17–2:16 cannot be called fideistic if by that term we mean an appeal to "faith" as an alternative to rational thought. In both passages the Apostle does affirm that, given the present state of humanity, rational inquiry cannot on its own achieve reliable knowledge of God. What is more, God has chosen to act in such a way that ordinary human inquiry will always mistake the truth about God's action for nonsense. Human beings will somehow have to transcend their ordinary framework of values in order to achieve true knowledge about God and his ways. The Gospel will force those who accept it to abandon ordinary human wisdom, as they allow the message of "Christ crucified" to redefine what counts as plausible and valuable. Paul gives no indication that the message is rationally incoherent or that his presentation avoids rational explanation. His hearers cannot comprehend its rationality, however, unless they first overcome certain moral vices which are endemic to contemporary humanity, since it is those vices which consistently distort human intellectual standards. It is the Spirit who plays the key role in this epistemic process, by healing the human moral constitution so that the internal coherence and rational implications of the Gospel can be recognized. Hence Paul affirms in 1 Cor 12:3 that "no one can say 'Jesus is Lord' except by the Holy Spirit."[1]

---

[1] Given his insistence in the section immediately following (12:4ff.) that only some members of the community are endowed with prophetic gifts, the Apostle's point here is likely not that "all Christians, at least potentially, have the capacity for inspired speech, even if it comes only in the form of a simple confession" (contra Hunt, *Inspired Body*, 110–11). The Spirit's role in this confession is likely not the role of inspiring an ecstatic utterance, but rather the role which we saw above in our exegesis of 1:17–2:16 – the Spirit influences one's fallen moral constitution so as to allow the acceptance of the Gospel. The Apostle's rhetorical point is not that all are (potential) prophets, but rather that all are endowed with the Spirit, whether they prophesy or not.

Yet these two passages, Rom 1:18–32 and 1 Cor 1:17–2:16, are not the only places where Paul makes statements with epistemological implications. It is thus necessary to ask whether my reading of these passages is in keeping with the Apostle's statements elsewhere. After all, some scholars have offered very different models of Paul's approach to human reason. Hans Leisegang, for example, in his 1923 monograph *Der Apostel Paulus als Denker*, painted a portrait of Paul's thought as a kind of irrational vision which "nicht erdacht, sondern auf einer anderen Ebene des Bewußtseins erschaut und erlebt ist."[2] For Leisegang the Apostle's mind was dominated by polar oppositions which are dealt with only by means of unresolved paradox.[3] Hence Leisegang finds in Paul a profound irrationalism in which one simply allows oneself to be overwhelmed by and enveloped in a powerful vision of reality.[4] If this is the kind of Paul which we find elsewhere in his letters, then we would have to ask some hard questions about the exegesis that I have offered above.

1. Reason in Ethical Deliberation

Space does not permit a full treatment of the subject of human reason in Paul's letters. A brief survey of other passages, however, reveals that (despite Leisegang) the whole body of the Apostle's writings attests to Paul's view that human reason is central to achieving all religious knowledge. Just as we found in 1 Cor 1:17–2:16 evidence that the Spirit-led believer continues to employ reason in understanding the world, so elsewhere we see the

---

[2] Leisegang, *Der Apostel*, 9. For Leisegang this also means that Paul's holistic vision of reality is not subject to doubt but is driven by "einer untrüglichen Gewißheit" (*Der Apostel*, 9–10).

[3] Leisegang, *Der Apostel*, 17. Cf. J. A. Fischer's suggestion that Paul's thinking stands in the "wisdom" tradition which focussed on the observation of the world's realities but tended to understand those realities in terms of paradox and irony ("Literary Forms"). Siegert also observes that Paul's argument often depends on his setting up antitheses and polar opposites, but he rightly argues that these are formal structures which need not reflect the deep structure of Paul's thought (*Argumentation*, 184).

[4] Leisegang (*Der Apostel*, 16) likens Paul's experience to that of Augustine, who is said to have moved from a critical, rational reading of the Scriptures to one in which he "mit hingebender Liebe in diese Texte versenkte" and so found in them "die wunderbarsten Aufschlüsse . . . eine sein Denken befriedigende, gewaltige Philosophie."

expectation that believers must think rationally. In 1 Corinthians 14, for example, Paul clearly favours prophetic speech over glossolalia, precisely because it is rationally comprehensible.[5] It engages the mind (νοῦς) and allows the message to be understood.[6] Why is such comprehensible speech better? Because it is such speech which "builds up (οἰκοδομεῖ)" the hearers, while incomprehensible speech remains ineffective (14:3–5, 12, 17). The implication is that moral edification of the believers takes place through intellectual activity, as they comprehend the truth with their reason.[7]

It is thus no surprise to find that the Apostle often depicts the believer's ethical decisions as flowing from a process of rational judgement. When Paul wants to urge the Philippians to follow the ethical pattern displayed by Christ, he urges them to "[l]et the same mind be in you that was in Christ Jesus (τοῦτο φρονεῖτε ἐν ὑμῖν ὃ καὶ ἐν Χριστῷ ᾽Ιησοῦ)" (2:5). It seems to be presumed that in order for the Philippians to act differently they must *think* differently. On the other hand, those who "live as enemies of the cross of Christ" think about "earthly things (τὰ ἐπίγεια φρονοῦντες)" (Phil 3:18–19).[8] Moreover, this seems to be a kind of thinking which leads to new, substantive ethical conclusions. For Paul prays that knowledge will increase among the Philippians, a knowledge with which they can "determine (δοκιμάζειν) what is best, so that in the day of Christ you may be pure and blameless" (Phil 1:9–10).[9] Similarly, in Rom 12:1–2 Paul urges the Romans to "present your bodies as a living sacrifice" to God. Yet this offering, which clearly amounts to ethical obedience, seems to be associated with the *mind* when Paul calls it

---

[5] So Bornkamm, "Faith and Reason," 36.

[6] In 14:9 Paul asks πῶς γνωσθήσεται τὸ λαλούμενον if they do not speak in comprehensible language (ἐὰν μὴ εὔσημον λόγον δῶτε). In 14:14 Paul worries that when one prays in glossolalia one's mind is "unfruitful" (ὁ δὲ νοῦς μου ἄκαρπός ἐστιν).

[7] So Lührmann, *Offenbarungsverständnis*, 37–8. Note too how even prayer and worship are productive activities for Paul only when they are engaged in not only "with the spirit (τῷ πνεύματι)" but also "with the mind (τῷ νοΐ)" (1 Cor 14:15). Cf. 14:19.

[8] See also Col 3:9–10, where the Colossians' moral renewal is described in terms of their having "stripped off the old self with its practices" and having "clothed yourselves with the new self, which is being renewed in knowledge (τὸν ἀνακαινούμενον εἰς ἐπίγνωσιν) according to the image of its creator." It is thus an intellectual renewal which lies at the root of their ethical change.

[9] So Bultmann, *Theology*, 1.326. Hence the differences in actual attainment of knowledge evident in 1 Cor 8:7 (cf. 1 Cor 8:1).

their "rational worship (λογικὴν λατρείαν)."[10] However we read that verse, Paul's following statements are clear. The Romans are to avoid "being conformed to" the ethical pattern of "this world," but are to "be transformed." Here again the transformation is to stem from "the renewing of your minds (τῇ ἀνακαινώσει τοῦ νοός),[11] so that you may discern (δοκιμάζειν) what is the will of God." Changed ethical behaviour arises from changed ways of

---

[10] Although the adjective λογική is often translated "reasonable" (so NRSV) or even "spiritual" (so NIV), Danker rightly recognizes that the emphasis of the term is on *cognitive* activity or ability (BDAG, 598). Prominent in philosophical (esp. Stoic) discourse (see, e.g., Epict., *Diss.* 1.16.20–21; cf. *Ap. Const.* 7.38.5; 8.9.8; 8.15.7; 8.41.4), the term often denotes what is non-physical within a framework of thought/matter dualism (see, e.g., Philo, *Opif.* 119; *Leg.* 1.41; *Det.* 82–83). In Philo, *Leg.* 1.70–72, the λογικός part of the human being is the seat of reason and exercises "prudence (φρόνησιν)," judgement about "the things we ought to do and of the things we ought not." The same role is played by the renewed νοῦς in Rom 12:2 (cf. *Ap. Const.* 8.12.17). In *Spec.* 1.277 Philo explains that in sacrifice what matters is the purity of the worshipper's "rational spirit (πνεῦμα λογικόν)," echoing Paul's metaphorical connection between cult and moral deliberation in Rom 12:1 (cf. *Ap. Const.* 7.35.10), and Philo's emphasis here is on pure *rationality* as what satisfies the creator (contra Moo, *Romans*, 752). The connection between the νοῦς and what is λογικός in Rom 12:1–2 is also standard among philosophical writers (e.g., Philo, *Leg.*, 2.22–23; *Spec.* 1.201; *Ap. Const.* 7.34.6).

Admittedly, in *T. Levi* 3:6 the angels' heavenly sacrifices are λογικός primarily in that they are bloodless (non-physical), rather than being particularly "rational." Yet other proposed examples of a non-cognitive sense for λογικός are far less clear (see, e.g., *CH* 1.31; 13.18, 21). Moreover, Paul cannot primarily mean in Rom 12:1–2 that the worship is (as in *T. Levi*) non-physical or inward, since it is manifested in the ethical actions of τὰ σώματα (so Cranfield, *Romans*, 2.604; contra Barrett, *Romans*, 213). Wilckens (*Römer*, 3.4–6) argues that the adjective in Rom 12 differentiates between a genuine cult and a false one, but λογικός usually designates something as "genuine" only in the sense that it is *rational* and thus appropriate to human beings (cf. Dunn, *Romans*, 2.712; C. F. Evans, "Rom 12:1–2"). Käsemann finds the closest analogy to Rom 12:1–2 in 1 Pet 2:2, 5, where new Christians drink τὸ λογικὸν ἄδολον γάλα and can then offer πνευματικὰς θυσίας. Käsemann argues on this basis that λογικός and πνευματικός were "interchangeable" (*Romans*, 329). Yet in 1 Pet the two adjectives modify referents which are deliberately distinguished (so Schreiner, *Romans*, 645). Cf. *Odes Sol.* 20.1–3. Hence in Rom 12:1 Paul most likely intends to depict the believer's moral effort as a sacrifice offered *by the reasoning mind*. Such an offering is not simply in keeping with reason (contra Schreiner, *Romans*, 645), it involves the rational activity of the believer's mind (cf. H. D. Betz, "Foundations of Christian Ethics," 63–5; Moo, *Romans*, 753).

[11] The dative τῇ ἀνακαινώσει almost certainly describes the means by which the transformation (μεταμορφοῦσθε) is effected (so Cranfield, *Romans*, 2.608).

thinking, and the use of the verb δοκιμάζειν presumes that this new pattern of thought issues in rational judgements about what one ought to do.[12] Hence in Romans 14 Paul describes the believers' ethical deliberation about the sanctity of certain days as an activity of *judgement* (κρίνω) (14:5).[13] Likewise, in 2 Cor 13:5 Paul urges the Corinthians: "Examine yourselves (ἑαυτοὺς πειράζετε) to see whether you are living in the faith." In each case the Apostle seems to presume that the believers' ethical decisions flow from a process of rational deliberation.

In keeping with this focus on rational judgement, several scholars have observed that Paul's ethical teaching is often supported by reasoned argument.[14] Stowers notes how in 1 Corinthians as a whole Paul does not

---

[12] So Bornkamm, *Paul*, 132; Dodd, *Romans*, 192. Notice too that this intellectual renewal is something which must be exhorted. Hence the imperative verbs μὴ συσχηματίζεσθε and μεταμορφοῦσθε. Believers are not to wait passively for God to renew their faculty of moral judgement. They are to begin thinking differently so that they can judge properly. Paul would certainly say that the Spirit is involved in the process (so Dunn, *Romans*, 2.714), but it is not clear that the believer's role is simply a matter of "yielding himself freely to the Spirit's leading" (Cranfield, *Romans*, 2.609).

[13] Note too how Paul describes their reaching a conclusion about the matter in terms of their being "fully convinced in their own minds (ἐν τῷ ἰδίῳ νοΐ πληροφορείσθω)." In Rom 14:22b–23 Paul continues to talk about ethical decisions in similar terms: "Blessed is the one who has no reason to condemn himself (κρίνων ἑαυτὸν) because of what he approves (δοκιμάζει). But the one who has doubts (ὁ δὲ διακρινόμενος) is condemned (κατακέκριται) if he eats, because he does not act from faith." Bultmann (*Theology*, 1.326) also draws attention to how the Apostle insists that the "weak" must be allowed to reach that knowledge on their own. This seems to confirm that the growth in knowledge which the Apostle envisions is a genuine process of intellectual discovery.

[14] Yu observes that Paul's ethical injunctions in 1 Thess 4:1–12 are not bolstered with any sort of reasoned argument ("Pneumatic Epistemology," 98–9), but 4:1 makes it clear that Paul is simply reminding the Thessalonians of teaching which they received earlier (καθὼς παρελάβετε παρ' ἡμῶν). Paul's statement in 1 Thess 4:2 that the former instructions were given "through the Lord Jesus (διὰ τοῦ κυρίου Ἰησοῦ)" *may* mean that Paul regards his teaching as mediating the instructions of the risen Lord (so Yu, "Pneumatic Epistemology," 100–103; Holtz, *1. Thessalonicher*, 154; Morris, *Thessalonians*, 120; tentatively, Best, *Thessalonians*, 158). Yet, based on Paul's practice elsewhere, this does not mean the Apostle expected them to accept his instruction without question. Moreover, Paul's distinction between himself and the Lord in 1 Cor 7 should cause us to hesitate about this interpretation of 1 Thess 4:2. Paul's claim in 1 Thess 4:1 to give instructions ἐν κυρίῳ Ἰησοῦ simply points to Christ as the common bond between Paul and his audience and the common basis of their ethical commitment (so Best,

simply issue authoritative commands, but reasons with the Corinthians as "responsible moral agents" who must employ their own rational powers to decide on the right path of action.[15] Bornkamm had already made a similar point in his article "Faith and Reason in Paul." The Apostle could, Bornkamm insists, have offered his Gospel in the form of "revelation-speeches" or prophetic words which admitted of no discussion. Such forms of preaching were, after all, not unknown in the Hellenistic world.[16] Nor does he parade charismatic or miraculous feats in order to overawe his hearers and induce them to accept his declarations.[17] Instead, Bornkamm emphasizes, Paul engages in rational argument, trying to convince his hearers at an intellectual level. In 1 Cor 6:12, for example, Paul responds to what seems to

---

Thessalonians, 156; Holtz, *1. Thessalonicher*, 152; contra Yu, "Pneumatic Epistemology," 100–103). Likewise, though in 1 Thess 4:8 Paul equates rejection of his own teaching with rejection of God's command, this is not because people are obligated to accept Paul's word without question, but because he believes that the ethic he teaches does in fact reflect God's will.

[15] Stowers, "Reason," 265; cf. Siegert, *Argumentation*, 246–7. Stowers points to 7:37 where Paul says that moral decisions are not to be made under constraint (ἀνάγκη), but (in Stowers words) "out of his or her own free will and with due deliberation." Indeed, Stowers may well be right that Paul's open approach to what he considered non-essential issues drew the criticism of the "super-apostles" who came to Corinth ("Reason," 271–2).

[16] Bornkamm, "Faith and Reason," 36; *Paul*, 119. Even in 1 Cor 9:8, where Paul emphasizes that his statement of apostolic rights in 9:1–7 is not based "on human authority (κατὰ ἄνθρωπον)," the statement is grounded not in Paul's own inspiration or apostolic status, but from the scriptural passage upon which the instruction is based.

Paul seems to appeal to direct inspiration in 1 Cor 14:37: "Anyone who claims to be a prophet, or to have spiritual powers, must acknowledge that what I am writing to you is a command of the Lord." Barrett suggests that Paul here assumes Christ's authority for his own reasoned position (*1 Corinthians*, 334). Yet this comment comes on the heels of his confrontation with the Corinthian "pneumatics." His point is not to emphasize his own authority, but to put the "spiritual" in Corinth in the position of having to accept his teaching about their use of the charismata (so Fee, *1 Corinthians*, 712; Garland, *1 Corinthians*, 674). The Apostle's clear distinction in 7:10, 12 between his own instructions and the Lord's command is likely more typical (so Soards, *1 Corinthians*, 310).

[17] Bornkamm, "Faith and Reason," 37. We could also add that Paul does not treat his Damascus road experience as if it lends him special teaching authority (contra Yu, "Pneumatic Epistemology," 207). When he does report that experience it is either to ground his claim to have a message independent of the Jerusalem group (as in Gal 1:11–17) or as evidence for the Christ's resurrection (as in 1 Cor 15:3–8). He does not rely on that experience to convince his audience that his message is true.

be a Corinthian slogan – "All things are lawful for me" – by adding the qualification that "not all things are beneficial." This response, however, seems to presume that the audience can and should derive their ethics by thinking critically about what is beneficial. Indeed, he goes on in 6:13–20 to offer some reasoned grounds for distinguishing the beneficial from the harmful. In 1 Cor 11:13, when Paul's argument for female head coverings seems to run out of steam, he calls on the audience to "judge for yourselves (ἐν ὑμῖν αὐτοῖς κρίνατε): is it proper for a woman to pray to God with her head unveiled?" What follows again is an appeal to the natural order which seems geared to help the audience make the right rational judgement.[18] Even earlier, Bultmann pointed out that when Paul asks, as he often does, whether his audience "does not know" some basic truth of the *kerygma*, the Apostle is inviting the audience to draw out the rational implication of the *kerygma* for their immediate situation.[19] So Paul's actual interactions with his communities confirm the impression that he expects believers to reach ethical decisions by way of rational deliberation.

2. Reason in Theological Inquiry and Conversion

Nor is Paul's rational argument limited to ethical issues.[20] Bultmann notes how at times what Paul claims to know is not merely the bare *kerygma*, but further "truths which 'faith'-ful reflection must draw as consequences" from

---

[18] Bornkamm remarks on "the variety of and differences in the apostle's argumentation in each case" and the absence of "set form or clichés." Paul's arguments are, Bornkamm writes, "in the best sense of the term 'motivations,' reasons for 'moving'" (*Paul*, 204). In 1 Cor 7:17–24, for example, the Apostle does not simply issue commands on the subjects of marriage and celibacy, slavery and freedom, but calls on believers to rethink their situation on the basis of Christ (Bornkamm, "Faith and Reason," 38). The only place in the ethical teaching of chapter 7 in which the instruction is cast in terms of commanding (παραγγέλλω) is 7:10, where Paul also specifies that the command comes from "the Lord" and not from himself. Even here Paul seems to feel free to make concessions when there seems to be rational justification for them (7:15). The Spirit's influence seems simply to encourage such rational thought in his statement about widows: "in my judgment (κατὰ τὴν ἐμὴν γνώμην) she is more blessed if she remains as she is. And I think that I too have the Spirit of God" (7:40).

[19] Bultmann, *Theology*, 1.326. See, e.g., Rom 6:3.

[20] Contra Yu, "Pneumatic Epistemology," 78–84.

that preached message.[21] On Bultmann's reading, Paul envisions the believers moving into deeper knowledge "of the mysteries of the history of salvation or of the eschatological occurrence."[22] Bultmann depends here in part on a questionable reading of 1 Cor 2:6–16, but he can also point to passages such as Rom 11:25ff. and 1 Cor 15:51ff. in which Paul seeks to expand the audience's understanding of saving events.[23] Drawing on Bultmann's pioneering work on Paul's use of rhetoric,[24] Bornkamm goes further to point out that in the "theological" sections of his letters Paul often seems to make use of the "diatribe," a rhetorical form which engages the hearer in rational argument, introducing possible objections in order to refute them.[25] This is not to deny that Paul's rhetoric sometimes depends as much on *pathos* and *ethos* for its persuasive force as it does on the *logos* of rational thought. Yet even in these cases the non-rational appeals tend to be introduced in support of a rational argument. The analysis of Galatians which occupies Part Three of this study will simply confirm this impression that Paul's theology is very often supported on rational grounds.

Does this mean that Paul regarded conversion itself, one's basic faith in the Gospel, as the product of rational deliberation? Many interpreters follow Bultmann in his emphatic "no" to this possibility.[26] Faith is said to spring entirely from a non-rational encounter with God, whether that encounter is

---

[21] Bultmann (*Theology*, 1.318) points to Rom 8:28; 13:11; 14:14; 1 Cor 3:16; 6:2f., 9; 15:58.

[22] Bultmann, *Theology*, 1.327.

[23] Note too how in 2 Cor 12:12 Paul expects that the Corinthians should have been able to interpret the evidence of his divine calling, the miraculous "signs of a true apostle." This seems to be a response to the Corinthian desire for "proof (δοκιμήν)" of Paul's apostleship, to which he alludes in 13:3.

[24] See Bultmann, *Der Stil*, and cf. Malherbe, "*Mê Genoito*"; Stowers, *The Diatribe*.

[25] Bornkamm, "Faith and Reason," 36. Even Yu, whose unpublished dissertation generally adopts an anti-rationalist reading of Paul, remarks on Paul's use of "fiery 'human' arguments" in Galatians and Romans ("Pneumatic Epistemology," 220).

[26] Bultmann emphasizes that the believers' initial deposit of knowledge is identical with the content of their "faith," a faith which comes as "a gift of the spirit" (*Theology*, 1.326). Hence Bultmann argues that Paul often appeals simply to "dogma," which is ungrounded in rational thought (*Theology*, 1.318; see 1 Thess 5:2; Rom 6:3; 2 Cor 5:1; 8:9). Bornkamm likewise considers it "self-evident" that "Paul does not derive the message of salvation in Jesus Christ from what man already knows by virtue of his reason. Here it can only be the resounding proclamation of what God has done in his grace" ("Faith and Reason," 35).

understood as the believer's existential moment of decision or as God's sovereign creation of faith in those whom he calls. Indeed, in many passages Paul can emphasize God's active role – through the Spirit – in bringing people to belief in the Gospel. In 2 Cor 4:4, for example, we are told that it is "the god of this world" who has "blinded the minds of the unbelievers, to keep them from seeing the light of the gospel of the glory of Christ." In the face of this blindness, the God who created light is said to have "shone in our hearts to give the light of the knowledge of the glory of God in the face of Jesus Christ" (4:6). Similarly, in 1 Cor 3:6 Paul responds to factional enthusiasm for various leaders by downplaying their role in the Corinthians' conversion: "I planted, Apollos watered, but God gave the growth."[27] Here the divine agent who produces this faith seems, as in 1 Cor 2:1–16, to be the Spirit. Likewise, in 2 Cor 3:12–18 Paul describes a metaphorical "veil" which lies over the minds of Jewish people, preventing them from understanding the truth in the Scriptures (3:14–15). "Only in Christ," we are told, "is it set aside" (3:14). It is only "when one turns to the Lord" that "the veil is removed" (3:16), and Paul goes out of his way to say that the God who performs this intellectual renewal is the Spirit (3:17).[28]

It is important to emphasize that Paul tends to speak of the Spirit's activity in the hearers of the Gospel, not of the message's own inherent power. It has been popular, in the wake of Barth, to depict *the Gospel preaching itself* as an overwhelming power which calls forth faith in those whom God has chosen.[29] Yet Paul never describes the Gospel unambiguously in these terms. True, for

---

[27] See also 2 Cor 2:14–16, where the crowd observing the proclamation of Christ is divided into two groups: those who are being saved and those who are perishing. The "aroma" of the message is "to the one a fragrance from death to death, to the other a fragrance from life to life" (2:16). Similarly, Paul says in Phil 1:28b–29 that the Philippians' perseverance and salvation are "God's doing. For he has graciously granted you the privilege not only of believing in Christ, but of suffering for him as well."

[28] So Yu, "Pneumatic Epistemology," 150–53. See also 1 Thess 1:4–5, where Paul writes: "For we know, brothers and sisters beloved by God, that he has chosen you, because (ὅτι) our message of the gospel came to you not in word only, but also in power and in the Holy Spirit and with full conviction (ἐν δυνάμει καὶ ἐν πνεύματι ἁγίῳ καὶ ἐν πληροφορίᾳ πολλῇ)." The sense of the ὅτι at the opening of v. 5 is ambiguous, so that the audience's reception of the Gospel may be the evidence of God's election or the substance of that election itself. See further p. 125, n. 14, below. In either case, however, it is the Spirit who appears to be responsible for their "full conviction."

[29] See, e.g., Hofius, "Wort Gottes," 170–71; Ridderbos, *Theology*, 234–5.

Paul the Gospel message is "the power of God" (1 Cor 1:18, 24; Rom 1:16). This does not necessarily mean that the message itself somehow contains the power to create faith.[30] Rather, the Apostle may well understand the Gospel to be God's "power" in the sense that it is the locus in which the divine power takes effect. It is when human beings believe this message that God's powerful salvation becomes effective in their lives. This need not mean that the Gospel is also responsible for *producing* faith in itself. Ridderbos also points out that in Rom 10:17 faith is said to come "from hearing" the message about Christ (ἡ πίστις ἐξ ἀκοῆς). Here again, however, it is far from clear that Paul means the mere hearing of the Gospel to be understood as the cause of the hearer's faith. The Apostle may simply mean that the Gospel preaching provides the *occasion* for faith to arise. It is when one hears the message that one has the opportunity to believe it. Yet another passage which is often introduced in support of the idea that the Gospel preaching produces faith is 1 Thess 2:13, where Paul gives thanks that when the Thessalonians received their Gospel preaching they accepted it "not as a human word but as what it really is, God's word." All that Paul actually says here, however, is that the audience accepted the Gospel message as truth from God. Granted, the fact that Paul gives thanks for their belief suggests that he understands God to have had a hand in producing this response.[31] Still, the Apostle does not specify how God influenced the Thessalonians, and he certainly does not say that the message itself exercised its own faith-producing power. The same may be said about the other passages in which God is pictured as producing the faith of the believers, or where those who respond to the Gospel are already "called" by God (e.g., Rom 1:6, 7; 4:17; 9:11, 25; 1 Cor 1:2, 24; 1 Thess 5:24). Paul does not specify in any of these cases that the Gospel message carries *within itself* this divine influence.[32] Instead, when Paul speaks explicitly about God's influence on the audience's reception of his preaching, he talks about the activity of the *Spirit*.

The question still remains whether Paul leaves any room for human reason in the process of conversion to faith in the Gospel message. It may seem, at

---

[30] Contra Ridderbos, *Theology*, 235.

[31] See also, e.g., Rom 1:8.

[32] Ridderbos provides 1 Cor 15:11 as a further example of the power of the Gospel (*Paul*, 234), but this passage simply affirms that Paul's message is identical to the message which the Corinthians came to believe.

first glance, that Paul treats the believer's basic faith in the Gospel message as a product of the Spirit's influence, plain and simple. Yet even where Paul emphasizes the Spirit's activity in producing belief, that Spirit's activity often promotes the believers' use of their own rational faculties. God's Spirit renews the convert's intellect and facilitates a new kind of reasoning by removing the veil which stifles the mind (2 Cor 3:12–18), overcoming the mind's blindness (2 Cor 4:4).[33] Such passages would suggest that the Spirit produces faith, not by inducing an irrational belief, but rather by allowing the believer to become truly rational.[34]

There are, moreover, other passages which seem to imply that God's responsibility for the believers' faith does not in Paul's mind totally eclipse the rational thought which contributes to that decision. We must notice, first, that in places the Spirit is depicted as responsible not just for the believers' initial conversion, but also for their ongoing growth in ethical knowledge.[35] Yet we saw above that, both in theory and in practice, Paul usually treats such ethical knowledge as the product of rational deliberation. This apparent tension suggests that when Paul made statements attributing the responsibility for faith or knowledge to God, he did not necessarily mean to exclude the idea that such faith or knowledge was *also* the product of the believer's reason. So in 2 Cor 5:11 Paul does cast his ministry as a matter of trying to "persuade" (πείθομεν) others of the Gospel, implying that their conversion is an intellectual process.[36] Then in 2 Cor 5:14–15 the Apostle seems to

---

[33] See also 2 Cor 5:17–18, where Paul follows up his statements about having come to comprehend Christ differently (a new kind of rational activity) with the affirmation that "new creation" is present where this interpretive shift has taken place. He then goes on to affirm that "All this is from God, who reconciled us to himself through Christ."

[34] There are again some hints that the Spirit's role is primarily to bring a moral restoration, which frees the intellect for healthy thought. Paul says in 2 Thess 2:13–14 that God chose the Thessalonians "through sanctification by the Spirit and through belief in the truth (ἐν ἁγιασμῷ πνεύματος καὶ πίστει ἀληθείας). For this purpose he called you through our proclamation of the good news (διὰ τοῦ εὐαγγελίου ἡμῶν), so that you may obtain the glory of our Lord Jesus Christ." The juxtaposition of the Spirit's moral restorative activity (ἐν ἁγιασμῷ πνεύματος) and the believer's faith is suggestive, though not conclusive.

[35] See Col 1:9–10; 2 Thess 1:3; and cf. Rom 12:3. This was also the case in 1 Cor 2:6–16, though in that passage the knowledge is less clearly restricted to the ethical sphere.

[36] Thrall (*2 Corinthians*, 1.402) is right that Paul's description of the objects of his persuasion as "human beings (ἀνθρώπους)" suggests that he is thinking of his apostolic ministry in general and not simply his responses to critics (so Furnish, *2 Corinthians*, 322;

represent his conviction that the Gospel is true as the fruit of rational judgement: "we have judged this to be true (κρίναντας τοῦτο), that one has died for all, so that those who live might live no longer for themselves, but for him who died and was raised for them."[37] Similarly, Paul lays emphasis in Phil 1:7 on the "defense and confirmation (τῇ ἀπολογίᾳ καὶ βεβαιώσει) of the gospel," an activity in which the Philippians share with Paul. Yet "defense" of a message is both a rational activity and one which is directed toward outsiders. On the other hand, the Apostle's emphasis here on confirmation reminds us that while Paul can sometimes express confidence that God will preserve the audience's faith, he can also express anxiety that rational arguments might lead believers away from the Gospel.[38] Notice too the

---

Martin, *2 Corinthians*, 121). Because this is not Paul's usual way of talking about his preaching, Thrall downplays the idea of rational discourse implied by πείθω and suggests that he is turning the language of his accusers to his own uses (*2 Corinthians*, 1.402–3; so Bultmann, *2 Corinthians*, 147). Yet even if Paul is taking over the language of his opponents, we still must deal with his willingness to use such a term for his evangelistic activity.

[37] I have here adjusted the NRSV translation, which renders κρίναντας τοῦτο as "we are convinced." That translation does not capture the idea of active, rational judgement which is conveyed by the adverbial participle κρίναντας. Thrall describes the activity denoted by κρίναντας here as "a decision taken in the past . . . concerning the significance of Christ's death" (*2 Corinthians*, 1.409; so Furnish, *2 Corinthians*, 310). Martin speaks more accurately of "a judgment formed in the past," since the sense of κρίνω here (followed by a ὅτι clause) is less volitional than cognitive. Martin and Thrall separate this judgement from Paul's conversion, making it a subsequent insight. It is, however, hard to see how Paul could have accepted the Christian Gospel without in the same moment accepting this perception of Christ's death, which (for Paul at least) was its substance and which Furnish rightly points out is presented here as a universal Christian conviction (*2 Corinthians*, 310; so Barrett, *2 Corinthians*, 168).

Note that it is in light of this judgement that Paul says: "From now on, therefore, we regard (οἴδαμεν) no one from a human point of view (κατὰ σάρκα); even though we once knew (ἐγνώκαμεν) Christ from a human point of view (κατὰ σάρκα), we know him no longer in that way" (2 Cor 5:16). In other words, the hermeneutical shift which involved Paul's new understanding of Christ came as a result of rational thinking.

[38] Paul worries in 2 Cor 11:3–4 that the false teachers are preaching "another Jesus than the one we proclaimed." His fear is that "as the serpent deceived Eve by its cunning (ἐξηπάτησεν Εὔαν ἐν τῇ πανουργίᾳ αὐτοῦ), your thoughts (τὰ νοήματα ὑμῶν) will be led astray (φθαρῇ) from a sincere and pure devotion to Christ." Similarly, in 1 Cor 3:17 Paul warns: "If anyone destroys God's temple, God will destroy that person. For God's temple is holy, and you are that temple." The context suggests that the prospect of this destruction

prominent role of reason in 1 Cor 14:25, where Paul gives us a rare glimpse of the actual process of conversion as he understands it. Paul describes the reaction of an outsider upon hearing a prophetic word delivered in the context of a Christian gathering: "After the secrets of the unbeliever's heart are disclosed, that person will bow down before God and worship him, declaring, 'God is really among you.'" While we might focus on the fact that the Spirit is the author of the prophetic gift here, notice that the outsider's reaction is actually the result of a rational inference *based on* the prophetic message which is treated as an observable event. It is because the visitor finds a stranger reciting his most intimate secrets that he is forced, by inference, to admit that a divine power is active in the group. So while we cannot deny that the Apostle sometimes depicts conversion as the result of the Spirit's power, we also should not minimize the indications that he sees conversion as resulting in part from rational thought.[39]

This dynamic tension in Paul's thought between God's sovereignty over the faith of believers and the importance of human reason is captured well in 2 Cor 10:3–5. "Indeed," Paul writes, "we live as human beings, but we do not

---

emerges from the discourse of those who claim "wisdom" (3:18–19) or from preachers whose role is analogous with Paul's activity (3:10–15).

It is because of this danger that Paul urges the Colossians in Col 1:23 to "continue (ἐπιμένετε) securely established and steadfast in the faith, without shifting (μὴ μετακινούμενοι) from the hope promised by the gospel that you heard . . ." This is in a context in which Paul has described their state prior to conversion as being "estranged and hostile in mind (τῇ διανοίᾳ)" (1:21). Hence their intellectual attitude towards God and the Gospel seems to be depicted here as something which they must actively maintain. See also 2 Thess 2:15, where Paul urges the Thessalonians to "stand firm and hold fast to the traditions that you were taught by us." Here it is less clear that the danger is false teaching, but Paul clearly does not assume God's sovereignty to guarantee that the believers' faith will endure.

Likewise, Paul urges the Colossians in 2:4 to strengthen their knowledge (by means of love) "so that no one may deceive you with plausible arguments (ὑμᾶς παραλογίζηται ἐν πιθανολογίᾳ)."

[39] See also 2 Cor 5:20, where, after apparently affirming that conversion comes "from God" (5:18), Paul describes God as "making his appeal (παρακαλοῦντος)" through the Christian preaching. He then personalizes this by addressing the audience directly: "we entreat you (δεόμεθα) on behalf of Christ, be reconciled to God." This again seems to depict God's activity as an invitation to rational response. Since Paul is addressing believers it is unclear whether he regards conversion in the same light, but here he does seem to be recalling the substance of his initial preaching to the Corinthians.

wage war according to human standards; for the weapons of our warfare are not merely human, but they have divine power (δυνατὰ τῷ θεῷ)[40] to destroy strongholds. We destroy arguments (λογισμοὺς) and every proud obstacle raised up against the knowledge of God, and we take every thought (πᾶν νόημα) captive to obey Christ." Here Paul is describing the character of his apostolic ministry, affirming that he does not act "according to human standards." As Malherbe has pointed out, such warfare imagery is a common Hellenistic topos for philosophical debates.[41] Paul depicts himself first as fighting these battles with "divine power," a power which apparently allows him to "take captive" the thoughts of those whom he wants to convince of the Gospel and its true application.[42] Yet notice that these weapons, with their "divine power," accomplish their intellectual conquest by demolishing opposing *arguments*.[43] So it appears that while God (by the Spirit?) is

---

[40] Thrall has objected that the reading of τῷ θεῷ represented by the NRSV translation is grammatically impossible, suggesting instead that the weapons are being exercised by Paul on God's behalf (*2 Corinthians*, 2.609–610; so Furnish, *2 Corinthians*, 457). Martin suggests, however, that a dative of advantage can be construed so as to understand God as the one who acts through the weapons (*2 Corinthians*, 305; so Bultmann, *2 Corinthians*, 185; Malherbe, "Antisthenes," 117; cf. Barrett, *2 Corinthians*, 251). I have here accepted the reading which maximizes the idea of divine involvement. If we follow Thrall and Furnish the focus on rational argument and persuasion is simply intensified.

[41] So Thrall, *2 Corinthians*, 2.611; Furnish, *2 Corinthians*, 458; see, e.g., Philo, *Conf.* 129–31. Martin suggests that the image "is calculated to challenge the opponents' use of reason, exactly as the defensive stance of Attic philosophy sought to ridicule the pretensions of the sophists" (*2 Corinthians*, 306).

Malherbe sees Paul drawing on the debate between Stoics who compared reason to an inner fortress, and Cynics who rejected this fortress of "doctrine" and fought vice armed only with their simple garb and natural life ("Antisthenes," 95–112). Malherbe suggests that Paul here defends his humble, adaptable manner of life using the imagery of the Cynics ("Antisthenes," 114, 116). Yet the connection between Paul's self-description and Cynicism is tenuous (see "Antisthenes," 114–17), and the defensive Stoic fortress seems quite different from the offensive fortifications which Paul attributes to his opponents. As Malherbe admits, martial imagery was extremely common in the ancient world, and it was a standard topos in descriptions of debates.

[42] Barrett suggests that νόημα has a negative connotation here, based on its use in 2:11; 3:14; 4:4; and 11:3 (*2 Corinthians*, 252). Yet the νοήματα of 11:3 are not inherently bad. They must be *protected* from corrupting influences. Likewise, in 3:14 the Jews' problem is not that they have νοήματα but that these thoughts have been "hardened" (cf. 4:4). The νοήματα of Satan in 2:11 are evil simply because of their author's wickedness.

[43] Malherbe suggests that the λογισμοί which Paul destroys are the intellectual faculties

involved in Paul's efforts at persuasion, these efforts must still involve rational argument. Paul launches his own reasoned attempts to show that hostile ways of thinking are wrong.[44] There is, of course, some ambiguity as to whether Paul is including his whole apostolic mission (and so the conversion of new believers) under this metaphor of conflict or whether the image is meant more restrictively to depict his conflict with the Corinthian "false apostles."[45] The tension involved, however, is precisely the one which,

---

themselves, but in this case we would expect a singular noun (so Thrall, *2 Corinthians*, 2.612). Contra Martin and Barrett (*2 Corinthians*, 252), Paul displays no broad opposition to the activity of λογίζεσθαι (see 10:2!). As Thrall suggests, Paul probably means by λογισμοί here primarily "the forms of argument" employed by his Corinthian opponents, and perhaps secondarily "intellectual forms of resistance" to the Gospel in general (*2 Corinthians*, 2.612). The ὕψωμα of 5a may include the "arrogant attitude" which tries to establish humanity's autonomy through reason, and the λογισμοί of 10:4 do seem to share this hubris (so Barrett, *2 Corinthians*, 252). This reading does not require, however, either that all thought be corrupt or that Paul avoid rational argument in responding to intellectual arrogance. Some thought can, Paul believes, be "obedient to Christ" (10:5; cf. 11:3) and may well be used to quell more rebellious minds – as Paul attempts to do throughout the Corinthian correspondence.

[44] Barrett has argued that the νοήματα of v. 5 are captured by supernatural demonstrations which do away with all argument (*2 Corinthians*, 252). Malherbe, on the other hand, has argued that the "weapons" with which Paul subdues πᾶν νόημα in 10:3–5 are nothing more than his humble lifestyle ("Antisthenes," 118; see also Stowers, "Reason," 268–70). Neither of these suggestions, though, makes sense in the context of these verses, where Paul is defending his unimpressive rhetoric (10:1, 10). Since this criticism of his oratory seems to have gone along with the charge that Paul lacked spiritual power (12:1–7), it is unlikely that he tried to replace rhetoric with miraculous spectacle. On the other hand, it is just as unlikely that the Apostle's speaking in Corinth lacked the appeals to reason which made his letters compelling (10:10). Paul was probably criticized instead for his lack of oratorical polish, something which would not be so apparent in a letter. His claim here in 2 Cor 10 seems to be that his rough and ready arguments are still able to convince, that they are *more* effective in fact than the declamations of trained speakers precisely because they embody Christ's "meekness and gentleness" (10:1). Far from stressing the inherent weakness of reason (so Stowers, "Reason," 284), Paul argues in 11:6 that what he lacks in oratorical training (ἰδιώτης τῷ λόγῳ) he more than makes up in "knowledge" (ἀλλ' οὐ τῇ γνώσει). Both of the passages to which Stowers points as examples of Paul's supposed anti-rationalism are aimed not at human reason in general, but at the overblown "pneumatic" or "gnostic" claims of some Corinthians (1 Cor 8:2; 13:8–13), and in both passages Paul himself continues to reason forcefully with his audience.

[45] Thrall (*2 Corinthians*, 2.613–14) is representative of those who take Paul to refer narrowly to his conflict with the false apostles and their Corinthian supporters. Bultmann

as we have seen, seems to be involved in Paul's talk about *both* epistemic situations. The divine involvement in the confrontation can be depicted as definitive, and yet this involvement does not do away with the rational, argumentative process by which people move from one way of thinking to another.[46]

How can this tension between the Spirit's power and the believer's reason be resolved? Bornkamm pointed towards a useful model when he suggested that human reason *makes possible* the existential confrontation in which faith arises. Reason, Bornkamm says, first convicts human beings of their helplessness in the face of sin and then grasps the content of the Gospel

---

(*2 Corinthians*, 186) suggests that the Apostle is offering a general description of his ministry which "naturally applies to his missionary activity as well." Notice that the goal is construed in 10:5 as obedience of thoughts to Christ (εἰς τὴν ὑπακοὴν τοῦ Χριστοῦ), recalling Paul's description of his missionary aim in Rom 1:5; 15:18; 16:19, 26 (so Furnish, *2 Corinthians*, 462–3). Verse 10:6 does suggest, however, that this process of bringing thoughts into obedience is one which continues after conversion, since Paul waits for the time ὅταν πληρωθῇ ὑμῶν ἡ ὑπακοή. If what Paul means in "practical terms" is "submission to Paul's kerygma" (Martin, *2 Corinthians*, 306), then the description would apply equally to his missionary preaching and his struggle with opponents who threaten his congregations' right faith.

[46] See also Rom 15:18–19, where Paul describes how God is "winning obedience from the Gentiles" and goes on to say that this happens in Paul's ministry "by word and deed, by the power of signs and wonders, by the power of the Spirit of God." Notice that the references to "word and deed" and to "signs and wonders" all presume a process of rational persuasion. The Gentiles are being persuaded by verbal arguments and by miraculous events which form the basis of inferences about the truth of the Apostle's message. At the same time, the Gentiles' response is also attributed to "the power of the Spirit of God." It is conceivable that this is another reference to miraculous acts, which are understood to be effected by the Spirit. If, however, Paul means that the Spirit's power is *another* cause of the Gentiles' response, he still gives no indication of how that power relates to the persuasive force of verbal arguments and miraculous signs.

This tension is, of course, closely related to (though not quite identical with) the tension between Paul's predeterministic statements and his statements which seem to attribute real effectiveness to human will. It is not my intent here to sort out the way in which divine sovereignty and human will are balanced (or deliberately left in tension) in Paul's account of coming to faith. Ridderbos is probably right to affirm that for Paul "[t]here is a deep mystery here which, on account of the heterogeneity of divine and human freedom, does not, however, admit of being reduced causally to one of the two" (*Paul*, 236). A more straightforwardly "predestinarian" position is represented by Hofius in "Wort Gottes," 172–4. Perhaps the strongest affirmation of the freedom of the human will in relation to God is offered by Bultmann (*Theology*, 1.329–30).

proclamation which offers a solution.[47] There are weaknesses in this approach. On the one hand, it probably emphasizes too much a personal sense of oppression by sin as the driving force toward Christian faith. On the other hand, Bornkamm says very little about the Spirit's involvement and lays stress instead on a kind of existential decision about which Paul himself says little, if anything. Bornkamm encourages us, however, to treat Paul's "rationalist" and "spiritualist" statements about conversion (or subsequent extension of knowledge) as two legitimate but partial perspectives on one event which encompasses them both. A better specific working out of this general solution might be the one we suggested above: that Paul sees conversion to Christianity as the result of a process of rational inference, but that such an inference is always resisted by human beings because of our moral corruption. The Spirit would thus be responsible for faith in the sense that he restores the human moral constitution, making it possible for human beings to follow the logic which leads to the Gospel. This model would also help to explain the hints we find in Paul's letters of a general relationship between ethical virtue (specifically love) and successful reasoning about the divine/human relationship.[48] These kinds of specifics must, however, remain

---

[47] See Bornkamm, "Faith and Reason," 35, 39–40; *Paul*, 119.

[48] Bultmann rightly insists that for Paul knowledge never becomes "a free-floating speculation" or "a neutrally investigating science," because its success depends on one's moral growth (Bultmann, *Theology*, 1.327). The classic text here is 1 Cor 8:1–2, where Paul introduces his discussion of idol meats: "we know that 'all of us possess knowledge.' Knowledge puffs up, but love builds up. Anyone who claims to know something does not yet have the necessary knowledge; but anyone who loves God is known by him." The implication seems to be that the humility which accompanies love is necessary if one is to obtain true knowledge.

Likewise, in Col 2:2–3 Paul wants the audience to be "encouraged and united in love, so that they may have all the riches of assured understanding (πᾶν πλοῦτος τῆς πληροφορίας τῆς συνέσεως) and have the knowledge of God's mystery (ἐπίγνωσιν τοῦ μυστηρίου τοῦ θεοῦ), that is, Christ himself, in whom are hidden all the treasures of wisdom and knowledge." Love is thus the key to achieving right understanding – not just moral understanding, but understanding of Christ.

See also 1 Cor 4:8–13. Here Paul ironically calls the Corinthians "wise" and claims to have become a "fool" in his work for the Gospel. Yet he calls this evaluation into question and renders it ironic by pointing to the history of his own suffering for Christ and contrasting it with the easy life in Corinth. It is thus the moral life of Paul which lends credibility to his claim to have the true wisdom.

This connection between love and right reasoning does not, however, mean that

tentative extrapolations from Paul's own words. Our confident statements can lead us no further than the recognition that when he imagines the process of conversion Paul holds the activities of reason and of the Spirit in some sort of dynamic tension.

We must also leave room in our reading of Paul's thought for prophecy and other charismatic gifts which allow for more direct communication between the Spirit and a Christian community.[49] It is, however, highly unlikely that such charismatic vehicles of knowledge were regarded by Paul as the norm for Christian knowing, since they play almost no role at all in grounding the arguments which we find in his letters.[50] Moreover, Paul seems

---

knowledge simply grows organically "en même temps que se développe la vie chrétienne" (so Dupont, *Gnosis*, 13; cf. pp. 33, 43, 49–50). There is little indication in the Apostle's letters that this moral requirement for discovery excludes or renders unnecessary the process of rational inquiry.

[49] Paul's discussion of these charismata comes largely in the Corinthian correspondence. In 1 Cor 12:4–11 Paul refers to "the utterance of wisdom (λόγος σοφίας)," "the utterance of knowledge (λόγος γνώσεως)," "prophecy (προφητεία)," "the discernment of spirits (διακρίσεις πνευμάτων)," and "the interpretation of tongues (ἑρμηνεία γλωσσῶν)." Each of these is a "manifestation of the Spirit (ἡ φανέρωσις τοῦ πνεύματος)" (12:7). Likewise, in Rom 12:6–7 Paul includes among the "gifts" given by God "prophecy," "teaching," and "exhortation."

Lührmann argues that in many cases Paul's positive talk about "revelation" from the Spirit does not actually denote an immediate message from the Spirit. In 1 Cor 14:6, 26, Lührmann argues that the charisma of revelation (ἀποκάλυψις) cannot be an "ekstatischen Offenbarungsvision" such as we see in 2 Cor 12:1, 7, for in 14:6 it appears among those charismata which take place ἐν voῖ. In fact, Lührmann points out that the common assumption that this revelation is synonymous with a "vision" remains supported only by 2 Cor 12:1, 7 (*Offenbarungsverständnis*, 40). Instead he argues that such a revelation is "eine in der Gemeinde durch Charismatiker vermittelte konkrete Anweisung" (*Offenbarungsverständnis*, 42). In particular, Lührmann suggests that the "revelation" which led Paul to go up to Jerusalem in Gal 2:2 need not have been a visionary experience. The parallel account in Acts, in which Paul goes up in response to the decision of the Antiochian community, may suggest that Paul is actually thinking of the Spirit's will as expressed in the community (*Offenbarungsverständnis*, 41–2, 73).

[50] I pointed out above Paul's reluctance to parade his own visionary experience as authentication of his authority (p. 54). When he does refer to a visionary experience in 2 Cor 12:1–7 he casts it rhetorically as someone else's experience, emphasizing that such boasting is not proper for an apostle of Christ. This suggests to Lührmann that "für ihn die Ekstase kein Offenbarungserlebnis und daher auch nicht Grundlage seiner Verkündigung ist" (*Offenbarungsverständnis*, 58). Perhaps the opponents in Corinth view their mystical

to expect that prophetic messages will still be subjected to rational consideration. He tells the Thessalonians not to "despise the words of prophets" but still to "test everything (πάντα ... δοκιμάζετε)" (1 Thess 5:20–21).[51] Hence prophetic messages seem to present for Paul simply one more phenomenon which must be evaluated by the rational mind under the influence of the Spirit.

At times Paul is also aware of the fallibility of human reason. Often Paul's comparison of "knowledge" to an enigmatic reflection in 1 Cor 13:8–13 is understood as a deep challenge to any confidence in human reason. It turns out, however, that the knowledge to which Paul refers in this passage is almost certainly charismatic revelation, not the fruit of ordinary rational thought.[52] Still, in 1 Cor 4:3–5 Paul urges that people not judge one another, because their judgement is not sufficiently reliable. "I do not even judge myself," he says. "I am not aware of anything against myself, but I am not thereby acquitted" (4:3–4). Rather, God is the only accurate judge. Here

---

experiences as bringing about a spiritual empowerment and transformation, and they view those without such experiences as "weak." Paul, however, emphasizes that his value to the community lies precisely in his "weakness," in his "alltägliche Existenz" (12:9–10; *Offenbarungsverständnis*, 60). Indeed, in 4:10–11 it is precisely Paul's "body" and "flesh" which is the locus of God's revelation in him, a revelation which does not try to transcend history but takes place within history, a revelation in which Paul's ordinary life mirrors that of Jesus himself (*Offenbarungsverständnis*, 61). Hence the "sight" which would make "faith" unnecessary is reserved for the eschaton, when all are brought before the judgement seat of Christ (5:7; *Offenbarungsverständnis*, 65).

[51] Note too that Paul most likely has charismatic knowledge, in view in 13:2–3, where he insists that (as with other kinds of knowledge) it must be subordinated to love. Then, in 13:8–13, such prophetic knowledge is downplayed as only a partial and enigmatic vision, a vision which will "come to an end (καταργηθήσεται)" in the eschatological fulfilment.

[52] So Barrett, *1 Corinthians*, 305; Conzelmann, *1 Corinthians*, 225–6; Fee, *1 Corinthians*, 643–4; Garland, *1 Corinthians*, 620. Thiselton, on the other hand, seems to recognize Paul's initial focus on the charismata, but also treats Paul's discussion of γνῶσις here as if it broadens to include all human knowing (*1 Corinthians*, 1064; cf. 1067–70; see also Garland, *1 Corinthians*, 625; Robertson and Plummer, *1 Corinthians*, 297–9). Yet this reading does not take seriously enough Paul's insistence in 13:13 that *faith*, along with hope and love, will remain in the eschaton when γνῶσις has passed away. Gooch rightly points out πίστις and γνῶσις usually have much the same content in Paul (*Partial Knowledge*, 142–3). The different fates of "faith" and "knowledge" in these verses thus suggest that Paul is not talking about ordinary knowing at all, but only the pneumatics' insight into eschatological mysteries which will be rendered redundant in the eschaton.

again, however, Paul's concerns about human reason are not as severe as they might at first appear. On closer inspection the issue seems to be less the inherent fallibility of reason than the human being's lack of access to complete information. God is the one "who will bring to light the things now hidden in darkness and will disclose the purposes of the heart" (4:5). It is only in light of that complete picture that accurate judgements can be made, and so human judgements must remain tentative. It is perhaps because the problem lies at this level for Paul, at the level of access to information, that he generally shows little concern about the competence of human reason *per se* to comprehend and acknowledge the truth about our relationship with God, provided that the moral corruption which hampers the mind is removed by the Spirit. Paul may introduce here a certain tentativeness about human knowledge, a recognition that it must be open to revision. This tentativeness does not, however, issue for Paul in a fundamental mistrust of the human intellect.

3. The Nature of the Reasoning Act

Before we move on to ask about the kind of reasoning which Paul treats as a valid path to knowledge, we must take a brief glance at the Apostle's language for the reasoning act. Up to this point I have treated terms such as "reason" and "rationality" as if they are transparent and universal, as if we can assume that Paul understood these concepts in the same way we moderns do. If we look at the way in which Paul uses language to talk about human reasoning, however, we discover that he does not conceive of "human reason" in precisely the same way that many contemporary readers would.

It is important, in the first place, to notice what Paul does *not* talk about. He does not use any term which would correspond with our formal, self-conscious "logic." That is, he never talks about ordered structures or methods of reasoning. Paul never mentions a "premise" or a "conclusion," and still less does he employ the technical language of Aristotelian or Stoic logic or of the Platonic Skeptics. Instead, the Apostle's language for the reasoning act falls into two closely related semantic fields. On the one hand he can talk about an act of "understanding" in which one organizes the disparate phenomena of one's perceptions, of memory, of language, and produces a coherent and true model of some part of the world.[53] So in Rom 1:20 the Apostle writes: "Ever since the creation of the world his [God's] eternal power and divine nature, invisible though they are, have been understood (νοούμενοι) and seen (καθορᾶται) through the things he has made." Here the verb νοέω seems to denote an activity of understanding in which a human being works with a set of perceived phenomena (the created order) and recognizes in those phenomena true patterns, in this case the traces of divine activity. In 2 Cor 10:12, on the other hand, "understanding" is interpretation of one's own ethical status. The Apostle suggests that his opponents, despite their commendation of themselves, "do not understand (οὐ συνιᾶσιν)."[54] It appears that these opponents have a wrong estimation of themselves, and their lack of understanding arises "when they measure themselves (μετροῦντες) by one another, and compare themselves with one another (συγκρίνοντες)." Their evaluative interpretation of their own actions fails because they employ in their comparisons the wrong standards of value. These two passages provide a sense of the variety of interpretive acts to which Paul can refer with language of "understanding" – from the theological to the ethical, from purely synthetic insight to comparative evaluation. In each case, however, the basic act involved is an interpretation in which

---

[53] On this use of νοέω in Rom 1:20, see LSJ, 1177 (I.2); BDAG, 674 (1.a); L-N, 380 (νοέωª). We might read κατανοέω in this sense in Rom 4:19, where Paul describes how Abraham "perceived" or "recognized" (κατανόησεν) that his body was dead. See also συνίημι in 2 Cor 10:12 (L-N, 380 [συνίημιª]; LSJ, 1718 [II.3]; BDAG, 972), the cognate σύνεσις in Col 1:9 (BDAG, 970; L-N, 383; LSJ, 1712 [II.1]), and αἴσθησις in Phil 1:9. Cf. the adjective ἀσύνετος in Rom 1:21, 31 (LSJ, 265 [I.1]; BDAG, 146; L-N, 386). Paul also frequently uses metaphors of vision for this kind of "understanding." See καθοράω in Rom 1:20 (BDAG, 493; LSJ, 856 [II.1]) and βλέπω in Rom 7:23; 11:8; 2 Cor 7:8. LSJ does not clearly recognize such a use of βλέπω, although under the heading of the transitive use, "see, behold," we do find that the expression ἐξ αὐτοῦ βλεπόμενον is used to mean "self-evident" in Sext. Emp., *adv. Math.* 1.184 (LSJ, 318 [III.1]). M-M (112) do, however, find attested the "metaphorical" use of βλέπω for moral self-understanding in P. Oxy. 9.1220.22 (iii CE) (cf. P. Lond. 964.9 [ii/iii CE]). It is in this same sense that Paul can characterize the limitations of human understanding using a metaphor of obscured vision (1 Cor 13:12). Cf. Paul's use of κατοπτρίζομαι in 2 Cor 3:18.

[54] This is my own translation. The NRSV renders the phrase "do not show good sense," but this suggests too much the idea of "common sense."

disparate phenomena are brought together in the mind in such a way that the resulting model of those phenomena is true.

The second category of language which Paul employs to describe the reasoning act is language of "judging."[55] Here the basic mental act seems identical to the act which is involved in "understanding." The difference is simply that his terms for "judging" denote the act itself, without implying anything about whether or not the act is successful. Hence, looking once more at 2 Cor 10:12, we find that the opponents' lack of understanding (συνίημι) arises from an improper exercise of the faculty of judgement (κρίνω). Paul denies that he "classifies" (ἐγκρῖναι) or "compares" (συγκρῖναι) himself with his opponents, implying that they do precisely that. Indeed, he says outright that they "measure (μετροῦντες) themselves by one another, and compare (συγκρίνοντες) themselves with one another." So the activity expressed by these derivatives of κρίνω and by μετρέω is one in which the opponents *are* engaged. These activities should lead to understanding, but in this case they have failed. The opponents "do not understand (οὐ συνιᾶσιν)."[56] It would seem that, for Paul, every act of

---

[55] Paul expresses this idea of "judging" by means of the verb κρίνω in Rom 14:3; 1 Cor 5:3, 12, 13; 10:29; 11:13; Col 2:16 (BDAG, 567–8 [3]; L-N, 363–4 [κρίνω^c]; LSJ, 996 [I, II.5, II.9]), διακρίνομαι in 1 Cor 11:31; 14:29 (BDAG, 231 [3.a]; L-N, 364 [διακρίνω^a]; LSJ, 399), διάκρισις in 1 Cor 12:10 (LSJ, 399 [I.1]; L-N, 364 [διάκρισις^a]; BDAG, 231 [1]), δοκιμάζω in Gal 6:4; 1 Cor 11:28; 2 Cor 13:5; 1 Thess 5:21–22; Phil 1:10 (LSJ, 442 [I]), συγκρίνω 1 Cor 2:13–14; 2 Cor 10:12 (LSJ, 1667 [II–III]; BDAG, 953 [2]); ἐγκρίνω in 2 Cor 10:12 (LSJ, 473 and 1667 [II–III]; BDAG, 274); and ἀνακρίνω in 1 Cor 2:13–15; 4:6 (BDAG, 66 [3; cf. 2]; cf. LSJ, 109 [II]), νομίζω in 1 Cor 7:26 (LSJ, 1179 [2]; BDAG, 675 [2], who also suggest that νομίζω has an added "suggestion of tentativeness or refraining from a definitive statement"), ἡγέομαι in 2 Cor 9:5; Phil 2:6, 25; 3:7–8 (BDAG, 434 [2]; cf. LSJ 763 [III]), διερμηνεύω in 1 Cor 12:30; 14:5, 13, 27–28, and ἑρμηνεία in 1 Cor 12:10; 1 Cor 14:26 (BDAG, 244 [2], 393 [2]; LSJ, 425; 690 [I.3]). Notice that this use of δοκιμάζειν seems to be synonymous with διακρίνω in 1 Cor 11:29, 31.

For Paul, συνείδησις ("conscience") may also denote an activity of inner examination and ethical interpretation, though the sense of these terms has been highly contested. See, e.g., Eckstein, *Syneidesis*; Gooch, "Conscience"; Jewett, *Anthropological Terms*, 402–46, 458–9; Lüdemann, "συνείδησις"; Maurer, "σύνοιδα"; Pierce, *Conscience*; Stacey, *Pauline View*, 206–10; Thrall, "συνείδησις."

[56] The intimate relationship between this kind of ethical judgement and the act of understanding is evident, again, in Phil 1:9–10. There the understanding (σύνεσις) of 1:9

"understanding" involves a "judgement." It is only when a judgement yields a true model of the world, however, that it comes to constitute an act of understanding.[57] We can observe some further specialization in Paul's language, more specific semantic fields for judgements that yield positive[58] or negative[59] evaluations of some object, etc. What is important for our purposes, however, is simply that when Paul talks about the activities of human reason, he does not talk about ordered, methodical steps in thought. Instead he talks about acts of interpretation, hermeneutical acts in which phenomena are brought together, synthetically, to construct a model of the world.

Still, it is also important to emphasize the ways in which Paul's conception of human reasoning is like our own. For Paul, acts of understanding and judgement are quite explicitly acts of "thought."[60] They are also acts which

---

consists precisely in being able to "determine what is best (δοκιμάζειν ... τὰ διαφέροντα)" so that the Philippians may be "pure and blameless."

[57] The fallibility of an act of judgement is evident again in Rom 14:5. There Paul reports that "[s]ome judge (κρίνει) one day to be better than another, while others judge (κρίνει) all days to be alike." That is, people differ over their interpretation of different days and their evaluation of the kinds of activities one might perform on them. Paul does not necessarily see this diversity of opinion as a problem, but he clearly thinks that the judgement of the "strong" is true, while the judgement of the "weak" is ultimately incorrect (14:14). He simply does not want the weak to be forced to act in contravention of their ethical judgements where the issue is non-essential (see 14:13–23).

[58] A positive judgement is denoted by δοκιμάζω in Rom 1:28; 14:18, 22; 16:10; 1 Cor 16:3; 1 Thess 2:4 (BDAG, 255 [2]; L-N, 364 [δοκιμάζω^c]; LSJ, 442 [II.1, II.2a]), εὐδοκέω in Rom 15:26–27; 1 Thess 2:8; 3:1; 2 Cor 5:8 (BDAG, 404 [1]), and ἀξιόω in 2 Thess 1:11.

The verb συνευδοκέω is used in parallel ways (though with the added idea of people agreeing about the judgement in question) in Rom 1:31; 1 Cor 7:12, 13. In the latter case, συνευδοκέω approaches the simple idea of "agreeing."

[59] See κρίνω in Rom 2:1, 12, 27; 14:3, 4, 10, 13, 22; 1 Cor 4:5; 5:3; 11:31; Col 2:16, and perhaps ἀνακρίνω in 1 Cor 14:23–24 (see the parallel with ἐλέγχεται; so BDAG, 66 [3]; cf. LSJ, 109).

[60] Notice how Paul can sometimes employ the same words for "judgement" or "understanding" which elsewhere denote the bare activity of thinking. Not only can βλέπω denote, metaphorically, an interpretive act, it also means "thought" in 1 Cor 1:26; 10:18; 2 Cor 10:7 (BDAG, 179 [4 and 6.b]; M-M (112); see BGU 4.1079.24 [41 CE]). On the other hand, the verb λογίζομαι is used in 2 Cor 3:5 for a non-ethical species of interpretive act. The verb λογίζομαι is used for simple thinking in Phil 4:8 (BDAG, 598 [2]), but also for Paul and Timothy's interpretation of their own ministry (see also Rom 6:11; 8:18, 36 [quoting Ps 44:23]; 14:14; 1 Cor 4:1; 2 Cor 10:2; Phil 3:13; LSJ, 1055 [II.1, 2, 5]; L-N, 351

are performed by the "mind."[61] So it is no anachronism when we refer to human reasoning in Paul as a "mental" activity. It is worth emphasizing that this makes such hermeneutical reasoning an activity of the human person. So, regardless of how much influence Paul gives to the Spirit in enabling believers to reason properly, their interpretive reasoning is still a matter of

[λογίζομαι[a]]; M-M, 378; *OGIS* 665.23 [49 CE]). In other places, the terms for judgement and understanding are close cognates of terms for thought. The noun λογισμός, a close cognate of λογίζομαι, is used in Rom 2:15 for one's ethical self-evaluation (BDAG, 598 [1]; L-N, 351 [λογισμός[a]]). It is then the cognate adjective λογικός which is associated with the believer's moral "discernment" (δοκιμάζειν) in Rom 12:1–2 (BDAG, 598; LSJ, 1056 [II.2.a]), while the cognate noun διαλογισμοί seems to denote the Romans' varying ethical judgements in Rom 1:21; 14:1 (LSJ, 402 [II–III]; L-N, 351 [διαλογισμός[a]]; BDAG, 232 [1]; though BDAG, 232 [2], takes διαλογισμός in Rom 14:1 as the *content* of reasoning, not the *process*). Finally, while the νοήματα are "thoughts" in Paul (2 Cor 10:5; LSJ, 1178 [I.1–3]; M-M, 428; BDAG, 675 [1.a]), the cognate verb νοέω appears in Rom 1:20 in the sense "to understand," i.e., to interpret correctly.

[61] Given that the terms for thought such as νόημα and νοέω generally signify the content or activity of the νοῦς (see 2 Cor 10:5), this relationship between the mind and interpretation was implied already when we saw that such interpretive acts were acts of thought. Likewise, in Rom 1:28 it is humanity's improper exercise of judgement (ἐδοκίμασαν) which prompts God to abandon them to an ἀδόκιμος νοῦς, suggesting that the νοῦς was in fact the organ responsible for that failure of judgement. Then, in 1:31, the fruit of humanity's corrupt νοῦς is seen in turn in their lack of understanding (ἀσυνέτους), implying again that the νοῦς is responsible for proper understanding (συνίημι) as well. Likewise, the whole purpose of God's renewal of the νοῦς in Rom 12:2 is to enable the believer to exercise proper moral judgement (εἰς τὸ δοκιμάζειν ὑμᾶς ...), and this judgement seems in 12:3 to issue in proper thinking (φρονεῖν) about one's status. In 1 Cor 14:14–19 Paul treats the νοῦς as the faculty which generates intelligible speech, suggesting that the "interpretation" (διερμηνεύω) of initially unintelligible speech is probably to be assigned to that same faculty. A similar connection between συνείδησις and νοῦς is implied by the fact that in 1 Cor 8:7–12 and 10:25–29 Paul emphasizes the importance of following the dictates of one's own "conscience" in the matter of food associated with idol cults, while in Rom 14:5 Paul makes the mind responsible for this ethical self-evaluation: "Let all be fully convinced in their own minds (ἐν τῷ ἰδίῳ νοΐ)."

The connection between "mind" and interpretation does not prevent Paul from also associating such acts with the "heart" (καρδία), but in such cases "heart" is being used in the sense of the Hebrew בל as the seat of the whole inner life, including rational thought (see further Jewett, *Anthropological Terms*, 305–33; Therrien, *Discernement*, 276). So when Paul pictures the mind being renewed in Rom 12:2 and the heart undergoing a renewal in 2 Cor 4:6 he is probably thinking not of two separate faculties but of the same rational centre of the person.

their manipulating their own thoughts about the world, an act which still takes place within their own minds. When the Apostle talks in Col 1:9 about "spiritual understanding" (συνέσει πνευματικῇ) he is not talking about ideas implanted within the believer's mind by an outside force, but rather about the believer's own thought processes, which are able to interpret the world properly because of the Spirit's aid.[62] This would seem to confirm once again the general picture of Pauline rationality as one which is an autonomous human activity, but which can only function properly (and so yield reliable "understandings") when it is freed from the corrupting influence of the human tendency to reject God.

---

[62] In Col 1:10 Paul explains that he wants them to gain this insight "so that you may lead lives worthy of the Lord, fully pleasing to him, as you bear fruit in every good work and as you grow in the knowledge of God." This is very much like the purpose of the ἐπίγνωσις and αἴσθησις in Phil 1:9, which in Phil 1:10 is also said to produce ethical guidance. In Phil 1:10, however, such ethical understanding is explicitly the product of the believer's own judgement (δοκιμάζειν).

Chapter Three

The Hermeneutics of the Cross:
A Trajectory in Pauline Scholarship

In a sense, we have now arrived back at our initial problem. If Paul affirmed such a strong and central role for human reason, then why have his actual arguments seemed so *un*reasonable to the Apostle's readers, from Lucian's day to our own? In our search for an answer to this question, we need to ask not just how Paul viewed reason, but what *kind* of reason he seems to have regarded as valid. When we ask this second question we soon discover that several scholars have gone ahead of us, and that they have often arrived at strikingly similar conclusions. In particular, a number of studies have suggested that Paul's thought and argument tend to be hermeneutical, drawing out the implications of a new fact within the context of a prior framework, rather than foundationalist, working up from unquestionable premises by way of syllogistic logic.

1. Dieter Lührmann

In his monograph *Das Offenbarungsverständnis bei Paulus* (1965), Dieter Lührmann argues that for Paul revelation is conveyed not in immediate communication from God, but in the human being's reflective interpretation of encounters with the divine. Many interpreters (Bultmann included) have seen such rational interpretation as a secondary activity which worked only to expand a basic deposit of "revelation." So, for instance, when Paul alludes in Gal 1:12 to the "revelation of Jesus Christ" which he received on the Damascus road, many understand this as a visionary experience which furnished Paul with the core of his message, prior to any rational reflection. Lührmann argues, however, that the moment of revelation for Paul comes not in the pre-reflective experience but in the *interpretation* of that experience, when the meaning of the experience is hermeneutically grasped and appropriated.[1] So the "revelation" of Christ to which the Apostle refers in Gal 1:12 includes, when he refers to it again in 1:16, the *interpretation* of the risen Christ as "God's Son."[2] Hence, "Offenbarung ist nicht das Christusgeschehen als solches, sondern eine auf den Menschen bezogene Interpretation dieses Geschehens als den Menschen angehend durch ein neu einsetzendes Handeln Gottes."[3] Lührmann then points out that the Scriptures and early Christian traditional formulae become vehicles of revelation for Paul only when he interprets them, in turn, in light of this interpreted Christ event.[4]

Paul's hermeneutical understanding of revelation helps to explain, for Lührmann, why the Apostle does not claim for himself some special inspiration from the Spirit which authorizes his teaching. Paul places little emphasis, Lührmann argues, on the Gospel as something hidden, to which only a few might be given privileged access. Rather, knowledge of this Gospel simply requires proper interpretation of events and statements which

---

[1] Lührmann, *Offenbarungsverständnis*, 161. Lührmann writes that "Offenbarung ist also für Paulus nicht vergangenes Geschehen, das eine Tradition begründen könnte, sondern als den Menschen angehende Auslegung des Heilsgeschehens in der Verkündigung ein neu einsetzendes gegenwärtiges Handeln Gottes" (ibid., 92).

[2] Lührmann, *Offenbarungsverständnis*, 77, 160. What is revealed, Lührmann argues, is the understanding (evident in Gal 3:23 and Rom 8:18f.) that Jesus was "die eschatologische Zeitenwende" (*Offenbarungsverständnis*, 75).

[3] Lührmann, *Offenbarungsverständnis*, 79. Lührmann also observes that in Phil 3:4ff. (esp. vv. 7–8) "das visionäre Element völlig fehlt" (*Offenbarungsverständnis*, 74).

[4] On Scripture, see Lührmann, *Offenbarungsverständnis*, 82–4. On Paul's use of traditional formulae see *Offenbarungsverständnis*, 88–90. Paul includes clearly traditional formulae in, e.g., Rom 1:3–4, 1 Thess 1:9–10. In Rom 1:3–4, however, Lührmann thinks it is clear that the Apostle uses the tradition in a new context which lends it new meaning. Moreover, with the exception of 1 Cor 15:1ff. and 1 Cor 11:23b–25, Paul does not identify these passages as traditional, so that he does not seem to depend on their traditional nature as grounding for the authority of his teaching. Even in 1 Cor 15, Lührmann argues, Paul adds significant material (15:6–8) without differentiating between the tradition and his own modifications. This is how Lührmann resolves the tension between such traditional passages and Paul's claim that his Gospel does not depend on Jerusalem tradition (Gal 1:11f.). Paul does not use traditional formulae as independent authorities, but rather they become vehicles of revelation once he has properly interpreted them. Along similar lines, see Yu, "Pneumatic Epistemology," 133–6, 140–41, 168–89, 174–5.

are open and public.[5] Lührmann points out, moreover, how others seem to be recipients (through their interpretive activity) of the same kind of revelation which Paul claims. In Gal 3:23, for example, the revelation of faith (πίστιν ἀποκαλυφθῆναι) seems to come equally to Paul and to all believers in general. If we understand "faith" as a new mode of existence made possible by Christ, then the revelation of this faith must involve interpretation of the Christ event as (among other things) the pivotal event in God's salvation of humanity.[6] So, Lührmann suggests, all believers receive revelation from God as they come properly to interpret Jesus' death and resurrection. This makes sense of the fact that Paul does not seem to think in terms of a narrowly or clearly defined group of formal apostles so much as he thinks in terms of individuals who are gifted to serve an apostolic function.[7]

2. Leander E. Keck

Whether or not Lührmann is right about Paul's use of revelation language, the interpretive activity which he identifies as a part of Paul's appropriation

---

[5] So Lührmann, *Offenbarungsverständnis*, 158–9. Lührmann points out that although Paul follows apocalyptic literature in looking for an eschatological "revelation" (emergence in history) of God's plans for the end (e.g., 1 Cor 1:7; Rom 2:5; 8:18–19), he does not emphasize the anticipatory announcement of these plans to seers in dreams and visions. Even Paul's visionary experience on the Damascus road is not interpreted in this sense, since its content is not the eschatological future but the acts of God in the recent past (*Offenbarungsverständnis*, 98–108). Lührmann recognizes, of course, that the motif of "hiddenness" occurs in Paul's letters, but he argues that such examples either do not concern esoteric revelations to the few (Rom 2:16, 28–29; 1 Cor 14:25; 2 Cor 3:13–16; 4:2) or are citations of the Apostle's opponents (1 Cor 2:6ff.; 2 Cor 4:3) or apocryphal texts (1 Cor 4:5; *Offenbarungsverständnis*, 156–7). Nor does Paul emphasize metaphors of light and vision (see *Offenbarungsverständnis*, 159–60).

[6] Lührmann, *Offenbarungsverständnis*, 80.

[7] Lührmann (*Offenbarungsverständnis*, 94–7) points to, e.g., Andronicus and Junia(s) in Rom 16:7 and Paul's inclusion of "apostles" among the groups of those endowed with different charismata in 1 Cor 12:28–29. He also observes that when Paul confronts the challenge to his apostleship in 2 Corinthians he seems not to have a clearly defined concept of apostleship to which he can appeal, but rather focusses more broadly on the legitimacy of his work. In particular, Lührmann here points out that Paul does not use his visionary experience on the Damascus road as evidence of his apostleship, even where one would expect it in 2 Corinthians.

of revelation has been observed by others as well.[8] Some have gone further than Lührmann and have tried to describe the logic by which this interpretation proceeds. Leander E. Keck argues, in his article on "Paul as Thinker" (1993), that the Apostle's interpretation followed an *ex post facto* logic. Such thinking, he writes, "occurs not only after an event but because of it, and with continual reference, explicit or implicit, to it. The event's very "happenedness" requires thinking."[9] In other words, a single event, "the resurrection of the crucified Jesus," becomes for Paul the hermeneutical key and point of reference for all of life.[10] Since his prior understanding of the world took no account of this event, his acknowledgement of the resurrection forces a reinterpretation of everything within these new terms of reference. Such *ex post facto* thinking, Keck observes, is different from thinking which is oriented towards internal problems detected in previous systems of thought. It also differs from "telic or utopian thinking" which projects the necessary future based on an established system of thought.[11] This is not to say that the central event was self-interpreting. Perhaps the most insightful aspect of Keck's article is his observation that Paul's understanding of the resurrection depended on at least three prior beliefs: 1) that resurrection is

---

[8] Robin Scroggs, for example, has argued, in his article "New Being: Renewed Mind: New Perception" that Paul's gospel of justification by faith amounted to a shift to a new reality which brought with it a new noetic situation of the kind described by Berger and Luckmann in their sociology of knowledge. It was this new situation which was the wellspring for new ethical norms. Scroggs does not elaborate, however, on how exactly this new noetic situation produced a new interpretation of the world. This question is particularly pressing, since Scroggs sees Paul's new ethical norms as arising from an inner reorientation which is *not* substantially influenced by interpretation of the Scriptures or other traditional authorities. Moreover, Scroggs suggests that the rootedness of Paul's ethic in such a fundamental shift of perspective explains why Paul ascribes the new knowledge to the Spirit ("New Being," 5). Scroggs does agree, however, with several emphases we have seen: that Paul locates the epistemic problem chiefly in one's struggle to respond to revelation, not in a struggle to attain knowledge in the first place ("New Being," 7); that Paul believes faith in Christ brings the restoration of the corrupted human noetic state ("New Being," 8–9); that is somehow fundamental to proper thought; and that the believer's new situation does not bring a spontaneous perception of the good, but rather initiates a struggle to appropriate and use one's new powers in the context of the community.

[9] Keck, "Paul as Thinker," 29.

[10] Keck, "Paul as Thinker," 30.

[11] Keck, "Paul as Thinker," 29.

plausible; 2) that resurrection happens during the eschatological fulfilment; 3) that resurrection is a part of the "new age" within a two-age apocalyptic schema.[12] Keck's observations thus prompt us to ask exactly how Paul's prior beliefs interacted with his conviction that Christ had been raised. Can we be more specific about how such *ex post facto* logic worked in his case?

3. Jürgen Becker

Jürgen Becker provides us with further hints as to the nature of this interpretive process in his magisterial work *Paul: Apostle to the Gentiles* (1989; trans. 1993). Becker sees "the gospel" as forcing the same kind of radical reevaluation which Keck describes. Becker insists that

> for Paul the gospel does not bring partial knowledge within an otherwise untouched, persistent scheme of reality: it does not sing a variation of an already known song. Conversion to the gospel of Jesus Christ is not only a change of position within the same coordinate system. It is not simply the creation of new and different value judgments about the same things within a fixed whole. No, the gospel has within it the possibility of understanding absolutely everything in a new way. With the gospel nothing remains as it was, for the gospel brings a new content that guides knowledge and necessarily leads to a new view of everything.[13]

For Becker, as for Keck, this gospel, this hermeneutical key, includes primarily the conviction that God has raised Christ. Becker suggests that in fact Christianity in general was born out of the effort to "redescribe" the God of Israel's exodus as "the God who raised Jesus from the dead." Paul simply continues and extends this process of Christocentric interpretation, convinced that "in the destiny of Christ, God interprets himself to humankind."[14] As does Lührmann, Becker insists that Paul's understanding of God's self-revelation is one in which human beings are not called to transcend "world and history" in an attempt to comprehend God directly, whether in Platonic contemplation or in ecstatic mysticism. It is, rather, in the historical life,

---

[12] Keck, "Paul as Thinker," 30.

[13] Becker, *Paul*, 377. As examples of this radical reorientation of perspective, Becker points to Phil 3:7–8; 2 Cor 10:5; Gal 1:11–12, 15–16.

[14] Becker, *Paul*, 378.

death, and resurrection of Christ that we are given the means to properly interpret both the world and the actions of its Creator.[15]

Becker is more specific than either Lührmann or Keck, however, about the effect of this reinterpretation on Paul's world view. In light of Christ, Becker argues, Paul "infers not only the depth of human lost-ness (in sheer classical form in Gal. 2:17, 21) but also the depth of divine grace and love, which alone are efficacious in achieving the deliverance of humanity."[16] Becker also suggests that Paul's ethics, with their emphasis on "faith, love, and hope," arise from the interpretation of the believer's life as one which should follow Christ's pattern of living. These principles of action "are the living expressions of one who is "crucified with Christ" (Gal. 2:19; Rom. 6:4–5), who has put on Christ like a piece of clothing (Gal. 3:27)."[17] Love, Becker argues, "has its norm in the model of Christ (Phil. 2:1ff.; Rom. 15:1ff.)." Indeed, the sphere of salvation is "in Christ," the Church is Christ's body, and the believer's hope is to be made like Christ.[18] All of human identity has been reimagined by Paul in reference to Jesus. Becker even suggests that when Paul calls faith a kind of "obedience," he is talking in large part about the willingness to allow the Christ event to reinterpret one's own identity and obligations.[19]

Becker also goes further than previous authors in pointing out that, beyond the historical occurrence of the resurrection, the believer's own experience of God's activity plays an important hermeneutical role for Paul. Becker describes Paul as speaking "out of the experience of his call," out of his experience on the Damascus road.[20] More broadly, though, Becker points to the influence of the broader experience of the Spirit in the Apostle's communities. Paul often points, Becker observes, to the church's original experience of the Gospel as the ground for his argument that the believers need to understand themselves and their actions with reference to that Gospel (1 Thess 1–2; Gal 3:1–5). Hence Becker calls Paul's theology "the theology of experience under the influence of the gospel and of the Spirit connected

---

[15] Becker, *Paul*, 378.

[16] Becker, *Paul*, 378–9.

[17] Becker, *Paul*, 379.

[18] Becker, *Paul*, 379.

[19] Becker, *Paul*, 413. For this theme in Paul, see Rom 1:5; 16:19; 2 Cor 10:5; cf. Rom 10:3, 16; 15:18; 2 Cor 9:13.

[20] Becker, *Paul*, 374.

with it."[21] As with both Lührmann and Keck, however, Becker is simply sketching the outlines of Paul's interpretive logic. The very suggestiveness of his observations prompts us to ask how exactly the Christ event and the experience of believers work in the Apostle's mind to reinterpret the world.

4. John D. Moores

More than anyone else, John D. Moores has taken up the challenge of unpacking this Pauline logic in its details. In his book *Wrestling with Rationality in Paul* (1995), Moores reads Romans 1–8 through the lens of Umberto Eco's theory of semiotics. Paul "recognized" the crucifixion, Moores argues, as a sign that particular eschatological events were taking place, much as one might recognize a footprint on the beach as a sign that some particular human being had walked there recently.[22] Paul's preaching is, Moores suggests, primarily a matter of pointing out that one event and trying to help others recognize it as a sign which carries a certain significance, an indicator of these other eschatological events.[23] Yet the significance of a sign is not always immediately apparent, and this is where Moores sees reasoned argument coming into play for Paul. For the meaning of any sign is constituted largely by the relationship in which it stands to other signs and sign systems. In order to "spell out" the meaning of a sign, one must point out the impact which that sign has on these other signs. Hence, in order to spell out the meaning of the sign of the cross (or, Moores suggests, even to understand the event himself), Paul must produce a series of "texts" which describe the relationship of the crucifixion to other ideas and entities, statements such as "A man is crucified"; "That man is the son of God"; "God gave him up to be crucified"; "It was for us that God gave him up to be crucified"; etc.[24] Reason must be employed in order to work out exactly how this new sign will affect Paul's whole world of sign entities and their

---

[21] Becker, *Paul*, 374. Becker writes that Paul speaks out of "the experience gained by him and the churches through the effect of the gospel on the worldwide mission field. Thus the apostle expresses himself on the basis of the new being effected by the Spirit, the common experience of all Christians with the gospel that changes people" (*Paul*, 373).

[22] Moores, *Wrestling*, 5–6.

[23] See Moores, *Wrestling*, 6–7.

[24] Moores, *Wrestling*, 9–10.

relationships to one another. For it is only by describing these relationships verbally that he can help his hearers "recognize" the significance of the cross for themselves.[25]

There are some problems in Moores' treatment of Paul's thought. Moores spends much of the book dealing not with this logic itself, but with the convoluted "enthymematic" arguments which it spawns in Romans 1–8. "Premises are constantly being taken for granted," Moores observes, "where it is far from easy to identify precisely what they are."[26] This part of Moores' analysis is less useful for our purposes, since in most cases the confusion seems to lie more in his reading than in Paul's argumentation.[27] Moores' attempt to justify the Apostle's complexities by an appeal to theories of "fuzzy" logic also seem unable, in the end, to clarify much of Paul's thought.[28] It is not clear, in any case, that the semiotic setting of Paul's

---

[25] Moores follows several of the other authors we have surveyed in suggesting that traditional materials are not understood by Paul as independent authorities (see *Wrestling*, 30). The primary authority for Paul is the interpreted sign of the cross.

[26] Moores, *Wrestling*, 28.

[27] Moores objects, for example, to the enthymeme which supports the assertion of Rom 5:5. The argument is, he says, actually an inductive argument from signs to a probable conclusion, not a deductive argument from premises to a necessary conclusion (*Wrestling*, 77–81). Yet Paul did not claim to be employing deductive argument. Nor is the certainty of which the Apostle speaks meant to be logical certainty. The whole problem here seems to arise from Moores' overly narrow definition of logic as deductively certain reasoning, while inductive, probabilistic reasoning is dismissed as mere "rhetoric" (*Wrestling*, 79–80).

Likewise, when Paul argues for the peace of the justified in 5:1, Moores takes this peace to be one which "has yet to mature" but which is deduced by Paul from the justification by God which is "an accomplished fact." Moores finds it illogical to deduce "what-is-not-yet-accomplished from what-is," and so finds problems in Paul's attempt "to draw a conclusion whose ambit is experiential ('peace') from a premise whose ambit is forensic ('acquittal')" (*Wrestling*, 100; cf. 68–76). Yet the logical problem here eludes me. Even if Moores is correct that the syllogism which lies beneath the verse (as reconstructed in version "a" on p. 74) would be invalidated by the introduction of a third premise, it seems that an alternative solution is ready to hand: recognize that one of the premises is complex and is itself based on a prior syllogism. This is, in fact, an analytical strategy which Moores himself employs liberally elsewhere.

[28] "Fuzzy" concepts, such as "tallness" or "security," are concepts which for some reason defy precise abstract definition but which nonetheless prove extremely useful, even in logical deductions. In fact, their clarity in practice depends on their remaining fuzzy (see Moores, *Wrestling*, 145–9). In a few instances this notion seems to be useful. Moores argues, for example, that in Rom 1:16–17 the enthymematic nature of the argument allows

communication about the cross really prevents logical coherence or requires such "fuzziness" in his thinking.[29] Moores' own analysis of Paul's use of logic thus seems, in many ways, to be a false start.

The most useful part of Moores' study is, for our purposes, his basic semiotic description of Paul's interpretive situation. He is able to clarify an idea towards which Lührmann, Keck, and Becker were all groping when he suggests that it is the primary "recognition" of the crucifixion as a sign which drives all of Paul's thought and provides its ultimate justification.[30] The specific role of reason in interpreting such a sign also helps us to understand why Paul could both emphasize the role of rational thought and at the same time depict God's wisdom as unjustifiable in terms of "worldly wisdom," ordinary human experience, or ordinary human standards for plausibility. For in this semiotic situation Paul is not using reason to build a world view from the ground up based on unquestionable premises. Rather, he is beginning with phenomena such as the crucifixion and his Damascus road experience, applying reason to work out the implications of such phenomena when they are taken as a sign. In this process reason can work not to build on ordinary

---

at least four different syllogisms to be reconstructed from the explicit statements (*Wrestling*, 37–40). Yet the ambiguities entailed are "attributable, not to indifference to logical rigour or abuse of logic, but to profundities of meaning which human reason and language have extreme difficulty in encompassing" (*Wrestling*, 45).

In several cases, however, it is unclear in what sense Paul's ideas are fuzzy (e.g., *Wrestling*, 76, on 5:1). It is often no more clear how the notion of fuzzy concepts contributes to our understanding of Paul's logic. Moores argues (*Wrestling*, 150–53) that by identifying Paul's concepts as fuzzy he can save Paul from the charge that he capitalizes on the polysemy of his terms in order to surreptitiously shift the ground of his argument. Moores never explains, though, how the fuzziness of a concept legitimizes such semantic shifts in the midst of an argument.

[29] Moores argues that the use of reason to explicate the significance of a sign, where the recognition of that sign is based on an immediate experience such as Paul's Damascus road epiphany, will necessarily lead to "inescapable" and "baffling" problems over "the jurisdiction of reason" (*Wrestling*, 31). It remains unclear, however, just why such a logical impasse is inevitable. On the other hand, it is no more clear why Paul's use of fuzzy concepts would necessarily lead the Apostle into such confusing, enthymematic argument. In other spheres, the whole point of fuzzy set theory is that fuzzy concepts *add* clarity to a discussion or analysis.

[30] Moores, *Wrestling*, 130–31.

terms of reference, but to subvert and undermine them in light of the new sign.[31]

What is more, Moores' analysis of Paul's semiotic situation points to a fascinating interplay between sign and interpretive reason which will bear significant fruit in later chapters of this study. On the one hand, Moores suggests that "[r]ecognition occurs only insofar as what has been recognised can be spelt out," and this spelling out necessarily involves reason.[32] On the other hand, "spelling-out is only spelling-out if it remains within the boundaries of what has been recognized." Hence, Moores writes,

> although the spelling-out of the content of what has been recognised relies on reason, once the content recognised is spelt out, only such further reasoning as is compatible with the established content of the Recognition can be tolerated. The very object of recognition which it has been instrumental in explicating deprives it of its autonomy.[33]

Moores is suggesting that in this kind of interpretation neither sign nor code has the upper hand. Each constrains the other, but in asymmetrical ways. Moores does not make this kind of use of the idea that a "code" is necessary in order to understand (or "decode") any sign, but that semiotic model allows us to clarify his insights here. It is not simply that Paul must employ reason in interpreting the sign of the cross. That phenomenon must be interpreted by Paul *in terms of a prior code*. Yet once the sign has been decoded, it exerts a reflexive interpretive force on the code itself. Moores simply mistakes the location of the constraint which the interpreted sign imposes. It constrains not reason, but rather *the code which gave it its meaning*.[34] For that code can now

---

[31] Imagine, for example, that an astronaut on a lone mission in space leaves his dinner for a few minutes and comes back to find it half-eaten, presumably by someone else, yet he knows there has been no other spaceship within thousands of miles. Such a phenomenon, taken as a sign, would imply a reality which would subvert the astronaut's deep-seated assumptions about his situation – e.g., that he is alone in the spaceship, that other beings would have to come to him in another spacecraft, etc. Such subversive signs are, in fact, the stock and trade of many contemporary films.

[32] Moores, *Wrestling*, 29.

[33] Moores, *Wrestling*, 29.

[34] It may be due to this analytical mistake that Moores introduces this dynamic as a problem rather than as the opportunity which I think it represents. Moores is, of course, very much aware of the role of codes in sign functions. His mistake in missing the role of the code here may arise from his mistaken suggestion that Paul's reinterpretation of the crucifixion in the wake of his Damascus road encounter involved the *replacement* of one code with another one (*Wrestling*, 8–9). Yet this idea of an entirely new code being

be applied in other situations only in a way which is in keeping with the significance of this new sign. In a real sense the code has not only given the sign its meaning, it has also been reshaped in turn through the process of interpreting the sign. This is the sense in which Paul's interpretive activity can be both eminently rational *and* deeply subversive of ordinary frameworks of thought.

Space has allowed me to survey only one thread of scholarship on the nature of Paul's reasoning.[35] I would suggest, however, that the trajectory which we have followed here is one which we will find sets us on the proper footing for our analysis of Galatians in Part Three. There we will take up again the interpretive dynamic to which Moores (almost) introduced us. In the meantime, however, we must look to the objects or content of Paul's knowing and ask what logical structure we find there. This task will not only confirm the basic insights of the "hermeneutical" trajectory in the study of Paul's thought, but will also suggest a set of terms within which to frame Paul's argumentation which will prove more useful, for our purposes, than the often arcane terminology of semiotics.

---

introduced raises the problem of explaining where the new code came from. Moores suggests that this new code might have been "provided by experience alone" (*Wrestling*, 8). How, though, could a code sophisticated enough to interpret the cross be produced instantaneously, "by experience alone"? When we actually look at Paul's understanding of Christ we see that his terms of reference tend to be derived from Jewish apocalyptic and sapiential thinking. Hence it is more likely that the Damascus road event prompted Paul to re-evaluate the significance of the cross in the context of his traditional Jewish code.

[35] For another approach see, e.g., T. E. Boomershine, "Epistemology." There are also countless places in which various other scholars have in passing observed elements of the models which we have examined here. Soards, for example, suggests in his commentary on 1 Corinthians that, while Paul employs reason throughout his letters, this reason is always operating "in reflection on the significance of God's revelation in and through the cross" (*1 Corinthians*, 40).

Part Two

The Structure of Paul's Knowledge

Chapter Four

Paul's Mundane Knowledge

1. Tracing the Structure of Paul's Knowledge

In order to elaborate further the kind of interpretive logic which Paul assumes will lead to knowledge, it is helpful to begin by looking at the knowledge which he thinks that logic can produce. When we gather together Paul's claims to knowledge, can we detect any logical structure implicit in that knowledge itself? To answer this question I will begin by surveying every instance[1] in the main Pauline letters of the standard terms of knowing (γινώσκω, γνῶσις, γνωστός, ἀγνοέω, ἀγνωσία, ἐπιγινώσκω, ἐπίγνωσις, γνωρίζω, οἶδα, and σύνοιδα)[2] and asking what common patterns we can

---

[1] Here at the outset I set aside those instances in which it is denied that one may actually know the object of the verb. See γινώσκω in Rom 11:34; 1 Cor 2:11, 16 (cf. LXX Isa 40:13); οἶδα in Rom 8:26; 1 Cor 7:16 (twice); 2 Cor 12:2b, 3b. It is also sometimes impossible to be certain about the content of Paul's γνῶσις (see 1 Cor 1:5; 12:8; 13:2, 8, 9, 12; 14:6; 2 Cor 1:13a; 6:6; 8:7; 11:6; Col 2:3). Zimmerman thinks that several of these instances should be understood as the experiential and volitional "knowledge of God" which characterizes the OT, but he offers nothing by way of justification for this and his reading is far from self-evident ("Knowledge of God," 476). Finally, I will leave out of consideration those passages in which God is the one who knows (Rom 8:27; 11:33; 1 Cor 3:20; 8:3; 2 Cor 11:11, 31; 12:2b, 3b). For a listing of the passages which do fall within our purview, see pp. 91, 95, 119, 123, and 143.

[2] Bultmann represents the consensus when he says that "ἐπιγινώσκειν is often used instead of γινώσκειν with no difference in meaning" ("γινώσκω," 703; cf. Robinson, *Ephesians*, 248–54). See, e.g., the parallel between ἀγνοούμενοι and ἐπιγινωσκόμενοι in 2 Cor 6:9. For the discussion, see also BDAG, 369; M-M, 236; Lightfoot, *Colossians and Philemon*, 136; Picirelli, "Epignosis"; Trench, *Synonyms*, 285–86.

In classical Attic use, οἶδα denoted "knowledge of facts absolutely," while γινώσκω was "relative," highlighting either "the *attainment* or the *manifestation* of knowledge" (Lightfoot, *Galatians*, 171; cf. LSJ, 350, 483). In the first century CE, however, the meanings of γινώσκω and οἶδα have likewise become similar enough to be generally

discern in the kinds of things which Paul claims to know.[3] In the interest of space I will not be able to pursue a full exegetical treatment of each passage, but will instead highlight the patterns in Paul's use of knowledge language and deal in more depth with those passages which prove difficult or seem to resist schematization. What we will find is that Paul talks about knowing in four distinct but interrelated senses. Three of these classes of Pauline knowledge are a matter of having three different kinds of belief: beliefs about mundane realities; beliefs about realities which reach beyond the mundane sphere and can only be called "theological"; and "ethical" beliefs, which bring the mundane into contact with the theological and suggest how one ought to live. The fourth class of Paul's knowledge is quite distinct from these three in that it is not primarily a matter of holding beliefs. The fourth category includes the contexts in which Paul's "knowledge" is a matter of direct experience of or familiarity with something or someone. This fourth category of Pauline knowledge is, as we will see, the point and goal of his belief-oriented knowing. Indeed, we might say that Paul seeks knowledge only so that he may know God and Christ. We are, however, running ahead of ourselves here and must come back to focus in the first place on Paul's knowledge of mundane realities.

---

indistinguishable. Note, e.g., the parallels in 1 Cor 14:9, 11, 16, and see Burdick, "οἶδα," 354; Porter, *Verbal Aspect*, 281–7; Seesemann, "οἶδα," 118; Silva, "Pauline Style."

[3] These are most of the words used by Paul which Louw and Nida include in the semantic domains "know" (the process of knowing), "known" (the content or object of knowing) and "able to be known." See L-N, 334–8. The only words which they include in these domains but which are omitted from consideration here are σοφία/σοφός, ὀνομάζομαι, συνείδησις, and ἀφικνέομαι. As we have already seen, the σοφία language plays a specific role in the Corinthian correspondence. The use of ὀνομάζομαι in Rom 15:20 can, as L-N admit, be read in a "more literal sense" in which it means simply "to be named" (L-N, 337). While the noun συνείδησις can mean a kind of "knowledge" or "consciousness" (BDAG, 967), it is used by Paul in the more specific sense of "conscience" (assuming that συνηθείᾳ should be read in place of συνειδήσει in 1 Cor 8:7a), a concept whose meaning continues to be a subject of debate (for bibliography see above, p. 70, n. 55). Finally, ἀφικνέομαι usually means "to arrive at" or "to reach" (BDAG, 157). The verb is used in Rom 16:19 to say that the (report of) the Romans' obedience has reached everyone, but this does not mean that the verb itself should be considered to carry the idea of knowing.

2. Paul's Mundane Knowledge

A significant amount of Paul's knowledge has as its object ordinary, mundane realities. In calling this knowledge "mundane" I mean that it has as its object those ordinary realities which belong to the world of immediate and public observation.[4] These are realities about which people can often agree, even when they are approaching them from widely different world views.[5] By definition, then, this mundane knowledge does not involve any distinctively Christian assumptions. A great deal of this knowledge concerns the public actions of Paul or his associates. The Apostle does not want his Corinthian converts to be unaware (ἀγνοεῖν), for example, of what he and his co-workers have suffered in Asia (2 Cor 1:8; see also Gal 4:13–14; Phil 2:19; 4:15; Col 4:7–9; 1 Thess 1:5b; 2:1–2; 4:2).[6] While the people involved in these events and interactions are all Paul's fellow Christians, there is nothing here which would prevent Paul and his pagan neighbours from agreeing that he does indeed know that they took place. Even when, in Phil 1:12, Paul wants the Christians in that city to know (γινώσκειν) that his imprisonment has led to the advancement of the Gospel, he is speaking in terms which are not peculiarly Christian. For, when he goes on in verses 13–14 to elaborate on his experiences in Rome, he describes this "advancement" in terms of the plainly observable reactions to his preaching.[7]

---

[4] See γινώσκω, 1 Cor 14:7, 9; 2 Cor 2:4; Phil 1:12; 2:19; 4:5; Col 4:8; 1 Thess 3:5; γνωρίζω, Phil 1:22; 4:6; Col 4:7, 9; ἀγνοέω, Rom 1:13; 2 Cor 1:8; οἶδα, Rom 11:2; 1 Cor 1:16; 2:11; 5:6; 9:13, 24; 14:11, 16; 16:15; 2 Cor 9:2; 12:3a; Gal 4:13; Phil 1:16; 4:15; Col 2:1; 1 Thess 1:5b; 2:1, 2, 5, 11; 3:4; 4:2; Phlm 21.

[5] To be more precise, we might say that mundane knowledge claims are those for which a great variety of hearers would understand both what the speaker was claiming to know and how the truth or falsehood of that claim might be tested.

[6] See also the Thessalonians' knowledge of their own suffering in 1 Thess 3:4. In 1 Cor 1:16 Paul admits that he does not know (οἶδα) whether he baptized anyone at Corinth other than Crispus, Gaius, and the household of Stephanas. He seems, however, to treat this as something which could easily be known if one could remember. We should likely also include Rom 11:2 in this category, where Paul asks (rhetorically) whether the Romans do not know (οἴδατε) "what Scripture says of Elijah, how he pleads with God against Israel."

[7] Cf. Phil 1:16. Something similar goes on in 1 Cor 16:15, where Paul reminds the Corinthians that they know (οἴδατε) that the household of Stephanas were the first Achaians to come to faith. If we understand him to be referring to their public shift from pagan practices to membership in the local Christian community and participation in its

At times Paul's mundane knowledge moves beyond the simple fact that certain observable events happened, to claim knowledge about patterns which can be observed in those events. Paul wonders whether the Corinthians do not know (οὐκ οἴδατε) that a little leaven will make the whole lump rise (1 Cor 5:6), and that of the runners in a race only one wins the prize (1 Cor 9:24).[8] Here it is not an isolated event that he knows but a pattern of similar events which take place under certain circumstances. Yet the events are still mundane, and his claims here would not meet with any resistance from the average Greek or Roman. Anyone who can observe that a small amount of yeast is enough to leaven a whole batch of dough can also learn by experience to expect that the same thing will happen whenever bread is made. In the same way, Paul can talk about people hearing sounds and knowing what is being said, or hearing the strains of a flute and knowing the tune (1 Cor 14:7, 9). This knowledge is simply a question of performing an act of "judgement" to recognize a pattern in mundane events.

From this recognition of patterns in mundane events it is a short distance to Paul's knowledge about the habits and temperament of the people around him. When he knows (οἶδα), for example, the Corinthians' willingness to take part in the Jerusalem collection (2 Cor 9:2), he is not talking about some mysterious inner quality but rather observing the fact that, just as leaven acts in a certain way, so too the Corinthians show a tendency to act generously towards the Jerusalem community. When Paul sends Timothy to find out about (εἰς τὸ γνῶναι) the Thessalonians' faith, this is a matter of Timothy

---

practices, then this too is a mundane event about which Paul could expect widespread agreement. Again, in 1 Thess 2:1 Paul appeals to the Thessalonians' own knowledge that his arrival there was not κενή, in vain. This is, however, simply a question of the observable reality that they have continued to maintain their new Christian community with its distinct practices.

[8] Cf. 1 Cor 9:13 on the priests' eating from the temple offerings. One might object that the knowledge to which Paul appeals in these instances is not mundane, but rather a kind of traditional, proverbial knowledge. Yet, while it is true that the knowledge in these cases is contained in proverbs or maxims, we are not at this point concerned with the surface form of Paul's knowledge or with its mode of acquisition. Rather, our focus here is on the *content* of Paul's knowledge claims. The knowledge to which Paul appeals in 1 Cor 5:6 and 1 Cor 9:24 does have as its content easily observable patterns in everyday events. Moreover, in both cases this content has not been eclipsed by the proverbial nature of the saying, for Paul makes analogical use in these verses of the yeast's behaviour and the runner's victory.

observing their actions to see the pattern they betray, that is, whether they live and speak according to Paul's teaching or whether they have "been tempted" and begun to act differently (1 Thess 3:5; see also Phil 4:5). This mundane knowledge of people's habits or character is a matter of observing ordinary, public events and discerning in them patterns which everyone in Corinth or Philippi would agree were significant.[9]

Paul also assumes that one can know about one's own internal states. In 2 Cor 12:3–4, for example, Paul does not know (οἶδα) whether the man who saw the vision (presumably Paul himself) did so in his body or was transported out of it. Yet he does know (οἶδα) that he was carried off to paradise and heard unutterable words. Paul claims to know that he had certain experiences, but explicitly brackets out any claims about how those experiences related to physical reality. Similarly, Paul says in 1 Cor 2:11 that τὰ τοῦ ἀνθρώπου are only knowable by one's own spirit (πνεῦμα). In other words, one's subjective world is not accessible to anyone else. This kind of inner state might not seem like the content of mundane knowledge as I have defined it, since such introspective knowledge is, by definition, not publicly observable. Paul's statement in 1 Cor 2:11, however, plays on the broad agreement that people *do* have privileged access to their own inner world. Hence, Paul's claims to know his own inner states would not meet many objections from outside the Christian community. In this sense, such introspective observations are also mundane knowledge.[10]

Finally, we should notice that much of Paul's mundane knowledge is based on testimony. He does not require that someone observe events for themselves, but allows that a report about those events (presumably from a reliable source) constitutes a basis for claiming knowledge about that event. This is equally true for internal states. Not only does Paul's mundane knowledge include an awareness of his own inner world, but that knowledge can be shared with others if he describes his inner states to them. In

---

[9] Similarly, in Phlm 21 Paul writes that he is "confident of your obedience . . . knowing (εἰδώς) that you will do even more than I say." The basis for this confident prediction about Philemon's future behaviour would seem to be the Apostle's knowledge of his past patterns of behaviour, although we must also take into account here the rhetorical function of Paul's statement as a spur to action. See also 2 Cor 2:4.

[10] See also Phil 1:22 where Paul confesses he does not know (οὐ γνωρίζω) his own preference – to stay in this world with his communities or to die and join Christ. The presumption seems to be that a person usually *can* tell what he or she prefers.

Rom 1:13, for example, Paul wants the Romans to know (οὐ θέλω δὲ ὑμᾶς ἀγνοεῖν) that he wanted to come to visit them, and his words constitute his sharing of that privileged knowledge with the audience.[11]

Do we learn anything of significance from this mundane knowledge? It demonstrates, at the outset, that Paul is not using knowledge language in the same sense as Plato. Paul is evidently willing to grant the status of knowledge, γνῶσις, to the observations about the world which arise from his senses, from introspection, or from reliable testimony about either one. This confidence is a long way from Plato's apparent skepticism about the fruit of the senses.[12] Paul's willingness to talk about "knowing" these mundane matters also suggests that the absolute certainty and timelessness which are often said to play such a key role in Plato's understanding of knowledge are not so important for the Apostle. We must resist the tendency to imagine that all Greeks fit the stereotype of the Platonic idealist. Strong is not unusual when he writes that for the Greek "knowledge did not derive from experience with the object as in the Hebrew understanding."[13] Yet to pose this kind of opposition between "Greek" idealism and "Hebrew" empiricism is to forget the amount of energy that the Stoics and Epicureans of Paul's day spent on defending the reliability of the senses.[14] In his willingness to call these mundane observations "knowledge," Paul is not siding with a putative "Hebrew" mindset over against the "Greeks," but rather siding with the ordinary person's confidence in such mundane knowledge over against the idealism of the Academy. Nevertheless, it is important at the outset to recognize that Paul is willing to be much more pragmatic than some of his contemporaries about what he calls knowledge.

---

[11] See also Col 2:1. In Phil 4:6 the believers in Christ are told they should make their requests known (γνωριζέσθω) to God. While the agent of knowing here is unusual, the kind of knowing is not.

[12] See the famous analogy of the "divided line" (*Resp.* 6.509d–511e), in which sense perception is only able to furnish "opinion," δόξα (6.511d), or mere "belief," πίστις (6.511e), and gives no purchase on reality. See further *Resp.* 6.506c–d, 534a.

[13] Strong, "Knowledge of God," 26.

[14] See Long, *Hellenistic Philosophy*, 21–30 (Epicureans), 123–31 (Stoics).

Chapter Five

Paul's Theological Knowledge

Although Paul's mundane knowledge will come to play an important role in his thought, the knowledge which he sees himself as set aside by God to declare to the Gentiles is something much less obvious and far more controversial. To understand its shape we must turn to those places in his letters where the Apostle claims to know things which lie beyond the sphere of ordinary human observation, which are not available to the senses. Since this kind of "supra-mundane" knowledge consistently deals with the relationship between God and humanity, we can appropriately refer to it as Paul's "theological" knowledge.[1]

1. Paul's Theological Knowledge as Story

When we pull together the individual statements which represent Paul's theological knowledge, we see that together they form an overarching narrative. I am by no means the first person to suggest that such a narrative is central to Paul's thought.[2] The "story" to which I am pointing is the same

---

[1] See γινώσκω, Rom 6:6; 10:19; 1 Cor 2:8 (twice), 14; 2 Cor 8:9; Gal 3:7; γνωρίζω, Rom 9:22, 23; 1 Cor 12:3; 15:1; γνωστός, Rom 1:19; ἐπιγινώσκω, Rom 1:6, 32; 2 Cor 13:5; ἐπίγνωσις, Rom 10:2; ἀγνοέω, Rom 2:4; 6:3; 7:1; 10:3; 11:25; 1 Cor 12:1; 2 Cor 2:11; 1 Thess 4:13; οἶδα, Rom 2:2; 3:19; 6:9, 16; 7:14, 18; 8:22, 28; 13:11; 1 Cor 2:2, 12; 3:16; 6:2, 3, 9, 15, 19; 8:4; 11:3; 15:58; 2 Cor 1:7; 4:14; 5:1, 6; Gal 2:16; Col 3:24; 4:1; 1 Thess 5:2; 2 Thess 2:6. The γνῶσις in 1 Cor 8:1, 7, 10, 11 is theological insofar as its contents are outlined in 8:4–6 (cf. below, p. 123, n. 7). In Rom 16:26 Paul refers to the Gentiles having been given knowledge (γνωρισθέντος) of the "mystery," that is, the "proclamation of Jesus Christ." The knowledge of God (γνόντες τὸν θεὸν) in Rom 1:21 also seems to be primarily the ideas laid out in 1:20.

[2] In 1936 Gyllenberg had already drawn attention to the narrative dynamic in Paul's thought and contrasted this with the approach of Philo: "Bei Philon ist alles statisch

"narrative substructure" which Richard Hays and others have observed at work beneath much of Paul's argument,[3] and the analysis which follows will contribute some methodological rigour to the discussion about the role of narrative in Paul's thought. Where the argument has been made that there is a pervasive narrative structure underlying Paul's theology as a whole, this idea has tended to be imposed as an heuristic category rather than derived inductively from the texts.[4] Ben Witherington, whose book *Paul's Narrative Thought World* represents the most ambitious attempt yet to read Paul in narrative terms, tells us that he has "become convinced that *all* Paul's ideas, all his arguments, all his practical advice, all his social arrangements are ultimately grounded in a story."[5] Yet, as suggestive as his narrative reading of Paul is, he relies on the force of a synthetic reading of Paul's whole "thought world" to convince us as readers that we too should try to

---

aufgebaut, bei Paulus ist alles dramatisches Geschehen" ("Glaube bei Paulus," 624). See also Leisegang, *Der Apostel*, 20, 28.

[3] Hays has pointed to early intimations of the central role of story in Paul's thought in Wilder, *Early Christian Rhetoric*, 58–9, and Crites, "Angels We Have Heard," 26–7. For full-blooded treatments of Paul's thought using narrative as a central structural feature, see Beardslee, "Narrative Form"; Fowl, "Some Uses of Story"; *idem*, *Story of Christ*; R. B. Hays, *The Faith of Jesus Christ*; Keesmaat, *Paul and His Story*; Petersen, *Rediscovering Paul*; J. A. Sanders, "Torah and Christ"; J. T. Sanders, *Christological Hymns*, 24–25; Witherington, *Paul's Narrative Thought World*, 5 et passim; and N. T. Wright, *The New Testament and the People of God*, especially 403–9. Most recently, see B. W. Longenecker (ed.), *Narrative Dynamics in Paul* and Longenecker's brief overview of such narrative studies in his opening chapter, "Narrative Interest."

Of course, as with any valid insight into a text, hints were made in a narrative direction long before these studies. Hays (*Faith of Jesus Christ*, 37–83) points to what amount to narrative structures in Bousset and Schweitzer. Bultmann's demythologization also represents a backhanded recognition that a narrative "myth" was central for Paul (see Hays, *Faith of Jesus Christ*, 51–55). Something closer to an explicit recognition of Paul's dependence on a narrative arises in Oscar Cullmann's emphasis on *Heilsgeschichte* (*Salvation in History*; *Christ and Time*), in Käsemann's stress on the narrative character of Paul's apocalyptic thought ("The Beginnings of Christian Theology" and "On the Subject of Primitive Christian Apocalyptic"), in Dodd's reconstruction of the primitive *kerygma* behind Paul's letters (*Apostolic Preaching*; *Scriptures*, 102), and in Dan Via's exploration of the "comic structure" of the pauline *episteles* (*Kerygma and Comedy*).

[4] Much of the work on narrative underpinnings in Paul has been less ambitious. Fowl, for example, has focussed on the function of isolated narratives about Christ as "exemplars" in communicating Paul's ethical vision ("Uses of Story"; *Story of Christ*).

[5] Witherington, *Narrative*, 2.

understand Paul's thought in terms of a story.[6] This kind of narrative reading has thus been open to the charge that it imposes an artificial structure on the text. In *The Faith of Jesus Christ* Richard Hays grounds his use of narrative categories in more detailed exegesis, but does so only in the isolated case of Galatians 3–4. In order to further strengthen the basis for a narrative reading of Paul's thought, I will sketch out inductively how a narrative structure is apparent in the content of Paul's theological knowledge.

1.1. Knowledge of Events and Actions

To begin with, we must observe how much of what Paul knows is knowledge of *events*. This is, of course, true of straightforward historical reminiscence as in 1 Cor 15:1–11. Yet it is also true in the midst of his most abstract theological discussions. What does Paul know? In Rom 2:2 Paul's hypothetical dialogue partners claim: "We know that God's judgment on those who do such things is in accordance with truth." This includes at least knowledge that God will judge sinners.[7] In 1 Cor 6:9 he asks the Corinthians: "Do you not know that wrongdoers will not inherit the kingdom of God?" This knowledge includes both the future advent of God's reign and an event in which some enter that reign while others are refused. Of course, Paul's theological knowledge includes the events of Jesus' crucifixion (1 Cor 2:2) and resurrection, and that Christ "being raised, will never die" (Rom 6:9). Paul reminds the Corinthians of their knowledge that Christ, despite being "rich," "became poor" (2 Cor 8:9). This most likely refers to Christ's incarnation as a human being, though it may also look back to the event of the cross.[8] Whatever the event, it is coupled with another in which the Corinthians "become rich," that is, gain access to the eschatological blessings (2 Cor 8:9). The Apostle recalls for the Romans their knowledge that "all of us who have been baptized into Christ Jesus were baptized into his death," and points out that this involves being "buried with him by baptism into

---

[6] There is even less exegetical support in Sanders, "Torah and Christ," and Wright, *New Testament*. For some pointers towards positive evidence of such a narrative structure, see Witherington, *Narrative*, 2. Of course, as Witherington emphasizes (ibid., 4), such a narrative is no more artificial a framework than the *ordo salutis* which still frames much of the thinking about Pauline theology (e.g., Ridderbos, *Paul*; Whiteley, *Theology*).

[7] Rom 2:3 makes it clear that Paul envisions the future, eschatological judgement.

[8] The NRSV translators highlight the fact that this "becoming poor" is an event by translating τὴν χάριν τοῦ κυρίου ἡμῶν as "the generous act of our Lord."

death, so that, just as Christ was raised from the dead . . . so we too might walk in newness of life" (Rom 6:3). Their knowledge is thus focussed on the event of their baptism and highlights the fact that this event brought about their identification with Christ's death. It also includes the knowledge not only of Jesus' resurrection, but also of a future event in which the Romans too will be raised from the dead.[9] In the knowledge of Rom 13:11–12, "salvation" appears as a future event and is connected with the image of dawning day. On the other hand, in Rom 11:25 Paul wants the audience to know "this mystery," that "a hardening has come upon part of Israel, until the full number of the Gentiles has come in." This is knowledge of a past event in which part of Israel was "hardened" – became unresponsive to God.[10]

Even where Paul's theological knowledge is not a knowledge of specific events, it tends to be knowledge of personal actions. In Rom 8:23 Paul refers to the knowledge that "we ourselves, who have the first fruits of the Spirit, groan inwardly while we wait for adoption, the redemption of our bodies."[11] Not only does this knowledge include the future event in which the Romans will be "adopted," but it also includes their ongoing activity of "groaning" in anticipation. In 1 Cor 6:2–3 Paul asks, "Do you not know that the saints will judge the world? . . . Do you not know that we are to judge the angels – to say nothing of ordinary matters?" Paul's knowledge thus includes the fact that believers will carry out the activity of judgement. The "kindness" of God

---

[9] This reading assumes that the "newness of life" which the Romans are to enjoy is the life of the resurrection. See also 1 Cor 15:58, where Paul appeals to the Corinthians' knowledge that "your labor is not in vain." Since Paul is referring to their participation in the coming eschatological fulfilment, their knowledge is primarily a knowledge that they will share in that event. These same events constitute the knowledge of 2 Cor 4:14, where Paul writes: "we know that the one who raised the Lord Jesus will raise us also with Jesus, and will bring us with you into his presence."

[10] If the content of this "mystery" extends to v. 26, Paul's knowledge here also includes a future event in which "all Israel will be saved." See also 2 Cor 1:7, where Paul knows that "as you share in our sufferings, so also you share in our consolation." He knows that they are experiencing events much like those he is experiencing, and that they too can look forward to experiencing the events of the eschatological restoration.

[11] Notice too that this knowledge implicitly involves knowledge of an event in which they received the "first fruits of the Spirit," and that this deposit of "first fruits" implies a future event of harvest.

about which Paul knows in Rom 2:4 is a matter of his actions, his patient restraint of his judgement.[12]

In each case these are actions pursued by a personal agent. The strength of this tendency to talk in terms of personal actions is evident in the way in which Paul consistently personifies inanimate objects or abstract principles and describes them as taking action.[13] Sin and obedience both act to *enslave* those who serve them, though with quite different results for the slave (Rom 6:16). Within believers, the "old man" *was crucified* and they were *freed* from the domination of personified sin (Rom 6:6). The law *speaks* to those who are under its control and *seals* their mouths (Rom 3:19), it *rules* a person as long as he lives (Rom 7:1). Good does not *dwell* within the generic "I" of Romans 7:18. Creation *suffers* and *groans* along with the "saints" (Rom 8:22). In the Apostle's theological knowledge these realities are all transformed into actors on the grand stage of cosmic events.

In other passages Paul's theological knowledge is directed towards the relationships among the agents who are involved in those events and actions. Even these relationships, however, turn out to be a matter of patterns in the way the agents act towards one another. In Rom 6:9 the Apostle claims to know that "death no longer has dominion over him [Christ]." Paul's knowledge here involves the nature of the relationship between Christ and the

---

[12] See also 2 Cor 5:1, where Paul knows "that if the earthly tent we live in is destroyed, we have a building from God, a house not made with hands, eternal in the heavens." In context, this "building from God" is the resurrected body of the believer. Hence Paul's knowledge here amounts to knowledge that at death believers will receive a new, better, embodied form. God has acted to make it, and they look forward to the event of its reception.

Likewise, see Col 1:6, where Paul says that the Gospel has been bearing fruit among the Colossians ever since the day when they heard and truly knew (ἐπέγνωτε) the grace of God. The NRSV translates ἐπέγνωτε here as "comprehended," and this is made more plausible by the way in which Paul adds ἐν ἀληθείᾳ (so Lightfoot, *Colossians*, 136; Lohse, *Colossians*, 21). Given that this "grace of God" seems to be equated here with the Gospel message, knowledge of that grace constitutes a knowledge of the gracious actions which God has performed on behalf of human beings. It is also equivalent to the "hope stored up in heaven" which Paul describes in v. 5, the events which the Colossians can expect to experience in the future.

Likewise, see 2 Cor 2:11, where Paul's knowledge includes the thoughts of Satan. If we consider thoughts to be a kind of inner activity, then even this would constitute knowledge of someone's actions.

[13] This was observed several years ago by Stephen Crites ("Angels," 26–7).

personified death. Notice, however, that in defining this relationship Paul is essentially defining the kinds of actions which death can take in relation to Christ. This relationship means that Christ "will never die again" (Rom 6:9). Death cannot carry out certain actions, and Christ will not undergo certain events. Notice too that this relationship between Christ and death has also come about as a result of an event. Death, we are told, "no longer has dominion" over Christ (Rom 6:9). For Paul this relationship is inseparable from an event which brought it about. Similarly, in Rom 11:25, where Paul knows about Israel's "hardening," this amounts to knowledge of the way in which they are responding to God. They are not embracing the divine action in Christ, but resisting it. They are not taking the right kind of actions. Moreover, here too we find that this relationship between God and some of the Jews is the result of an event, for in the preceding verses Paul has made it clear that God *made* them unresponsive.[14] In Rom 1:32, Paul claims that all human beings "know God's decree, that those who practice such things [the vices he has just listed] deserve to die." Once again we find Paul claiming knowledge of a relationship between human beings and God. This time the relationship is defined by the kind of actions which God will take towards human beings who pursue certain patterns of behaviour, and again this relationship is established by a unique event: "God's decree."

Another example of this knowledge of relationships appears in 1 Cor 3:16 and 6:19, where Paul asks whether the Corinthians do not know that they are the Temple of God. What does it mean to call them a "temple"? In 3:16 that rhetorical question is set in parallel with another which explains it: "Do you not know that you are God's temple and that God's Spirit dwells in you?" To know that they are a temple is simply to know that the Spirit is exhibiting a certain pattern of action in relation to them, manifesting his power within them. Moreover, just beneath this claim is the assumption that a remarkable event has taken place: the Holy Spirit has come to dwell in their midst, just as he did in the sanctuary in Jerusalem. Even Paul's knowledge in 1 Cor 8:4 that "no idol in the world really exists" and that "there is no God but one" amounts to the traditional Jewish claim that only Israel's God can do certain

---

[14] See, e.g., Rom 11:7–8, where Paul uses a divine passive to say that some Jews "were hardened" and then elaborates on this by citing what seems to be a variation on Deut 29:3(4) and Isa 29:10: "God gave them a sluggish spirit, eyes that would not see and ears that would not hear."

things.[15] Thus Paul goes on in a traditional vein to affirm that "though there may be so-called gods in heaven or on earth . . . yet for us there is one God, the Father, *from whom are all things* . . . and one Lord, Jesus Christ, *through whom are all things and through whom we exist*" (1 Cor 8:5–6, my italics). To know that there is only one God is to know that there is only one being who has acted in the past to create and who acts in the present to hold this creation in being. In each of these cases, Paul's knowledge is not merely knowledge that a single event or action has taken (or will take) place. Nor is it unrelated to events and actions. It is knowledge of recurrent patterns in action, knowledge of the kind of actions which certain agents pursue, often under specific circumstances.

Paul seems to be thinking of this same kind of knowledge of relationships in Rom 1:19. Here what human beings can know about God (τὸ γνωστὸν τοῦ θεοῦ) amounts to an awareness of the kinds of actions God can take in relation to the world. What can be known appears in verse 20 to be God's eternal power and majesty (ἥ τε ἀΐδιος αὐτοῦ δύναμις καὶ θειότης), terms which sound very much like the abstract "attributes" of God which dominated scholastic and reformed theology. We must notice, though, that humanity comes to know that God is like this through their experience of the created world. In other words, human knowledge of what God is like is actually knowledge that he is *the kind of God who does this kind of thing*, who makes this kind of world. Likewise, when God wants to make his power and glory known (γνωρίσαι) he does it by bearing patiently with objects of wrath which were made for destruction, for example, by acting towards Pharaoh in a certain way (Rom 9:22–23). Such a pattern of actions even seems to lie behind Paul's knowledge (οἴδαμεν) in Rom 7:14 that the

---

[15] Bauckham (*God Crucified*, 6–13) argues that Jewish monotheism was in fact understood primarily in functional and not ontological terms. That is, there was only one God, not primarily in the sense that this being was composed of a different kind of substance than everything else, but rather in the sense that Yahweh could do things which no-one else could. Most specifically, Yahweh alone creates all things and rules all things. On God's creation see Isa 40:26, 28; 42:5; 44:24; 45:12, 18; 48:13; 51:16; Neh 9:6; Hos 13:4 (LXX); 2 Macc 1:24; Sir 43:33; Bel 5; *Jub.* 12:3–5; *Sib. Or.* 3:20–35; 8:375–376; Frag. 1:5–6; Frag. 3; Frag. 5; *2 En.* 47:3–4; 66:4; *Apoc. Ab.* 7:10; *Jos. Asen.* 12:1–12; *T. Job* 2:4. On God's sole rulership see Dan 4:31–32(34–35); Bel 5; Add Esth 13:9–11; 16:18, 21; 3 Macc 2:2–3; 6:2; Wis 12:13; Sir 18:1–3; *Sib. Or.* 3:10, 19; Frag. 1:7, 15, 17, 35; *1 En.* 9:5; 84:3; *2 En.* 33:7; *2 Bar.* 54:13; Jos. *A. J.* 1.155–156.

law is "spiritual." This is not an abstract ontological pronouncement. Paul is certainly not speaking in general terms about the law having a non-physical mode of existence. Dunn rightly observes that the adjective "spiritual" (πνευματικός) is consistently used by Paul in connection with the activity of God's Spirit.[16] Paul's knowledge here is knowledge of the relationship between two active agents: the Spirit and the law. In calling the law "spiritual" Paul is saying that this law is to be associated somehow with the activity of the Spirit of God.[17] Thus, even in claiming theological knowledge which seems at first to be highly abstract, we can see that what the Apostle knows amounts to a pattern of actions pursued among actors in the cosmic drama.[18]

---

[16] Dunn, *Romans*, 387; *Jesus*, 207–9; cf. Rom 1:11; 1 Cor 2:13; 10:3–4; 12:1; 15:44, 46; Col 1:9; 3:16.

[17] Exactly how the law is related to the Spirit's action is unclear. Several commentators see here at least the idea that the law was brought into being by the Spirit (So Barrett, *Romans*, 137; Cranfield, *Romans*, 355; Dunn, *Romans*, 1.387; cf. Matt 22:43; Mark 12:36; Acts 1:16; 4:25; 28:25; 2 Pet 1:21). Cf. *m. Sanh.* 10:1 on the divine origin of the law. Nor is it clear what more the association between the law's action and the Spirit's action implies about the *human* relationship with the law, but commentators usually suggest that Paul is thinking of the aid of the Spirit as necessary for properly understanding the law (Barrett, *Romans*, 137; Cranfield, *Romans*, 356) or for carrying out its commands (Cranfield, *Romans*, 356; and perhaps Dunn, *Romans*, 387). On any of these readings, what Paul is trying to convey is that the Spirit acts in crucial ways through the law. Lest this seem forced, we should notice how Paul goes on to contrast the "spiritual" (πνευματικός) law with the "fleshly" (σάρκινος) way in which one acts when one is "under sin." When the personified power Sin rules a person, that person's actions are motivated by the unchecked desires of his sensual body, whereas the lifestyle of the law is one which must be driven by God's Spirit. Paul's point is thus that where we see the activity of the law we are also seeing the activity of the Spirit, which is its originating and motivating force.

[18] Even 1 Cor 11:3 may involve knowledge of relationships. Here Paul wants the Corinthians to know "that Christ is the head of every man, and the husband is the head of his wife, and God is the head of Christ." The difficulty in this passage is discerning what Paul intended by the image of headship. If, as is probable, he was thinking in terms of authority, then this relationship would be a matter of one partner issuing instructions while the other partner acts in accordance with those instructions – again, we would have a pattern of action. The notion of authority, however, carries added ethical connotations. To know that someone has authority is often to know that it is *right* to act in accordance with that person's instructions. To this extent Paul's knowledge in 1 Cor 11:3 might better be understood as ethical knowledge (see Chapter VI below). If, on the other hand, we understand headship to mean that one partner is the "source" of the other, then we can see Paul as pointing to the

1.2. Knowledge of Causally Related Events and Actions

This collection of events, actions, and patterns of action which constitutes the object of Paul's theological knowledge is not an assemblage of isolated happenings – the events and actions are *causally interrelated*. Such causal connections are already visible within the individual passages in which Paul refers to his theological knowledge. For example, if one obeys Sin, this causes death, while obedience to God brings about righteousness (Rom 6:16). Similarly, the law's speech causes every mouth to be sealed (Rom 3:19). Again, if one participates in Christ's suffering, this means that one will also share in both his consolation (2 Cor 1:7) and his resurrection (4:14). That participation even causes the domination of Sin to be broken for the believer (Rom 6:6). Likewise, since all and only those who have faith like Abrahams are his sons, the believers' faith is clearly the cause of their justification and their inheritance of Abraham's promise (Gal 2:16; 3:7), much as possession of the Spirit is a sufficient cause of one's declaration that Jesus is Lord (1 Cor 12:3).

Perhaps more important than this, however, is the way in which the theological events about which Paul knows in one passage are clearly causally related to events about which he claims knowledge elsewhere. The fact that the law performs this negative function is in turn linked with the reign of Sin in human lives (Rom 6:6) and the fact that no good dwells within them (Rom 7:18). It is also because, in serving Sin, human beings earn death (Rom 6:16) that they need resurrection (1 Thess 4:13) and to be saved from impending judgement (1 Thess 5:2). In fact, the whole crisis in which humanity now stands, whether imagined as a universal "groaning" (Rom 8:22), as a "night" (Rom 13:11–12), or as "poverty" (2 Cor 8:9), is the result of the humans' slavery to Sin and their inability to free themselves. Finally, it is because sin is rebellion against the one who created the world (1 Cor 8:4) that its consequences have this catastrophic scope.[19]

---

specific roles each partner played in a specific event – the emergence of one partner from the other. For an exhaustive summary of the evidence and a third, more complex interpretation, see Thiselton, *1 Corinthians*, 811–23.

[19] Examples touching on the role of the law are difficult to deal with in this kind of survey because the role of Torah in Paul's thought is subject to so much debate. On a traditional reading of Paul's view of the law, it is because the law "seals" the mouths of those under its sway (Rom 3:19) that human beings must depend for deliverance on God's

As solution is called forth by plight, the action of God in Christ is prompted by this sin and deals with it definitively (2 Cor 8:9; cf. 1 Cor 15:1–4), bringing about the dawning of the day (Rom 13:11–12) and delivering the cosmos from its groaning (Rom 8:22).[20] Second Corinthians 1:7 (cf. 4:14) makes it clear that the resurrection (1 Thess 4:13) and blessed life after death (1 Cor 6:2–3; 2 Cor 5:1, 6; Col 3:24) which God now offers human beings depend on their being identified with Christ in his passion. It is likewise because they have died with Christ that members of the Christian communities stand in a new relationship to the law, a relationship like that which follows an ordinary death (Rom 7:1–6).[21] The believers' identification with Christ (cf. 1 Cor 6:15; 2 Cor 13:5) is, in turn, effected by their participation in baptism (Rom 6:3). Likewise, in 1 Cor 12:3 the believers' identification with Christ and their filling with the Spirit (1 Cor 3:16; 6:19) are causally connected, though it is not clear in which direction the causation runs.[22]

This is not the strict causal relation of physics. We are rarely presented with cases of a sufficient cause and its inevitable effect. Rather we find the more ambiguous causality which is more common in narrative, in which one event serves as *part of* the reason for another.[23] Events cause one another in the sense that one contributes to the other, but the relationships are not

---

action in Christ, and not on one's own legal obedience (Rom 10:2–3, 19; Gal 2:16; 3:7). Adherents of the "new perspective" of Sanders, Dunn, and others will construe the causal connections here differently, but these actions and events still remain causally linked.

[20] This central importance is implied too by Paul's use of the crucifixion as a cipher for his whole theological message in 1 Cor 2:2.

[21] Somewhat more speculatively, we might imagine that it is because God (by his Spirit) was the origin of the law that, despite their freedom, those who flout its basic moral vision will lose their place in the kingdom (1 Cor 6:9).

[22] The particular relationship between man and woman in 1 Cor 11:3 is, again, an exception here. It is not easily linked in a causal fashion with the relationships between God and Christ and Christ and the man. It is also difficult to integrate the "man of lawlessness" (2 Thess 2:6) and his restraint into this causal network, but in this case the ambiguity is likely because we have in Paul's letter to the Thessalonians only a dislocated fragment of what must be a much more involved apocalyptic scenario.

[23] See the discussion of different approaches to causality in historical narratives in Dray, "Narrative in History," 28–37. Of particular interest is W. B. Gallie's insistence that there remains in historical events an irreducible contingency which often makes them unpredictable, even in retrospect. See his *Philosophy and the Historical Understanding.*

precise. So the sinful lives of human beings prompt God's judgement (Rom 1:32; 2:2; cf. 1 Cor 6:9). Yet the judgement is avoidable because there are other factors at play. God's patience with sinful humanity is intended to bring about repentance (Rom 2:4), though not everyone is so affected. It is in this sense, as a necessary but not sufficient cause, that Christ's voluntary poverty causes the believers' spiritual wealth (2 Cor 8:9), that baptism is a prerequisite of identification with Christ (Rom 6:3), and that the apostasy of Israel contributes to the Gentiles' entry into God's people (Rom 11:25). Yet the causal relationships here are no less real for their complexity. On the contrary, this very ambiguity reflects the kind of causation which is usually built into narratives, stories which are concerned less about providing universal laws than with giving insight into lived events which are irreducibly complex.

1.3. Knowledge of Causally and Temporally Related Events and Actions

Of course, to have pointed out that Paul's theological knowledge constitutes a chain of causally related events and actions is still not to have demonstrated that this knowledge is a story. One further narrative dimension which we find in Paul's theological knowledge is time. These events are related not only in terms of causation, but also in that they precede or follow one another in a particular order. The sinful actions of humanity occupy the past and present and near future, while the judgement is anticipated in a more distant future (Rom 1:32; 2:2). Humanity has been groaning along with the rest of creation for some time and looks forward to a deliverance which is yet to come (Rom 8:22–3), a future resurrection (1 Cor 15:58; 2 Cor 4:14; 5:1; Col 3:24; 1 Thess 4:13). The night in which humanity wanders is soon to give way to the new day (Rom 13:11–12). The passion, resurrection, and post-resurrection appearances of Christ are all past, and these are all later than the origin of the problem of sin (though not the ongoing commission of sins) since they were a solution to that problem (1 Cor 15:1–11; 2 Cor 4:14; cf. 1 Cor 2:2). The impoverishment of Christ lies in the past, and though the enrichment of the believers is temporally ambiguous, its full fruition likely lies in the future (2 Cor 8:9).

It is already evident that these events are temporally located, not only in relation to one another, but also in relation to Paul's audience. The problem of sin and the frustration of creation began in the audience's past, though their lingering effects are still felt. On the other hand, it is in the audience's future that the day of the Lord will suddenly come (1 Thess 5:2), that the saints will judge both human beings and angels (1 Cor 6:2–3), that all of creation will be made new (Rom 8:22–23). It is between their present and that future consummation that they can expect the advent of the man of lawlessness (2 Thess 2:6). What this means is that Paul not only knows in what relative order the events of the story take place, but also in what stage of the tale humanity stands as he writes. What is happening at that point in the story? This is the time of creation's agony (Rom 8:22–23), in which human beings are powerless to resist Sin (Rom 7:18). Those with faith, however, are already sons of Abraham (Gal 3:7), are already indwelt by Christ (2 Cor 13:5), are already members of Christ's body (1 Cor 6:15), are already the temple of the Holy Spirit (1 Cor 6:19). These believers participate in Christ's sufferings (2 Cor 1:7) and, having been freed from the domination of Sin (Rom 6:6), occupy themselves with "the work of the Lord" while they await their salvation (1 Cor 15:58).

All of this marks the present of Paul's audience as the crucial time in the story. It is the time at which human beings are given the choice which will determine what role they play in the rest of that narrative. For, in that narrative future, Paul knows that some will be judged (Rom 1:32; 2:2) and others raised to blessed life (13:11–12, etc.). There will be nothing to do at that point but bear one's fate. In his present, however, things are different. While baptism and its accompanying identification with Christ are past for believers, those events are presumably still a present opportunity for others (Rom 6:3). Human beings are still actively engaged in the choice whether to serve Sin or obedience (Rom 6:16). Gentiles can still enter God's people, and Jews can still fall away (Rom 10:2–3; 11:25). The repentance of Romans 2:4 is a present possibility, but one which will not last forever. The present of Paul's audience is thus in many ways the fulcrum around which the whole story moves, the pivotal point at which one's future place in the story is determined.

1.4. Dramatic Tension in Paul's Theological Knowledge

If we are looking for further, conclusive evidence that Paul's theological knowledge is a story and not merely a chronicle, we find it here in the dramatic tension with which the present of Paul's story is charged.[24] His

---

[24] So far we have satisfied M. J. Toolan's basic definition of narrative as "a perceived

theological knowledge does not consist merely of a series of events, some causing others, organized in chronological order. These events are also imbued with significance because they involve human agents and a personal God, all of whom have intentions and anticipations, hopes and fears. Not only is God patient towards the sinner, but he takes this attitude with the intention of bringing about repentance (Rom 2:4). He intends to save his creatures. From the perspective of human beings, judgement is obviously something to instill terror, while salvation in Christ fulfils human hopes of escape from the fallen world and of final happiness. Thus Paul can allude to the certainty of the Corinthians' resurrection by simply assuring them that "your labour is not in vain" (1 Cor 15:58), for that resurrection represents their whole hope. Injected with these hopes and fears, what would otherwise be a simple chronology of events becomes a story in the fullest sense of the word. It becomes a cosmic drama in which God acts to save a creation which has gone terribly wrong, with human beings now standing at the climactic point in the plot. This is the moment of decision which will determine whether, for each individual, the story will turn out to be a comedy or a tragedy. For the fatal flaw of sin will indeed bring the final downfall of some, while others will find themselves at the end in the eschatological dawn.

That narrative is never expressed as a whole in Paul's letters. Rather, as Ben Witherington has written, "Paul is always alluding to larger narratives by means of brief phrases or quotations," and it is left to the audience to fill in

---

sequence of non-randomly connected events" (*Narrative*, 7). This definition is employed by Edward Adams ("Paul's Story"). Both Toolan and Adams also look, however, for further elements in a narrative: characters, setting, and trajectory (Adams, "Paul's Story," 21–2; Toolan, *Narrative*, 103–4). We saw above that the events in Paul's theological story are driven by specific characters, whether individual or corporate. The setting of Paul's story is more diffuse, but it seems to be the same cosmic setting which forms the background, e.g., of many mythological narratives, both in the Ancient Near East and in the Greco-Roman world. In any case, Toolan recognizes that a highly specific setting is not as crucial as the other elements in a narrative (*Narrative*, 103). What remains to be shown here, however, is that Paul's theological story is driven by a "trajectory," some development towards conclusion or climax. As Adams observes, this is essentially what Aristotle meant when he wrote that plots must have "a beginning and middle and end" (*Poetics*, 7.4–7, in Adams, "Paul's Story," 23).

the gaps.[25] Indeed, some sections of the narrative may remain comparatively undeveloped in Paul's own mind. Some aspects of the story may even have changed as Paul's thinking developed and his rhetorical needs shifted.[26] I am not primarily interested in establishing a fixed, stable "core" to the Apostle's thought. The point of this analysis is, rather, the observation that Paul's theological knowledge is *structured as* a grand unified story,[27] an epic narrative of the relationship between humanity and its creator which stretches from creation to the final eschatological fulfilment.[28]

2. Narrative Knowledge and Paul's Analytic Discourse

To some it may seem strange to say that Paul's knowledge is fundamentally narrative in shape, when there is so little actual narration in his letters. If what he knows is basically a story, then why do we not find him simply

---

[25] Witherington, *Narrative*, 2. Three attempts to sketch out the shape of the whole narrative can be found in Ben Witherington, *Narrative*, 5 et passim; Hays, *Faith of Jesus Christ*; Wright, *New Testament*, especially 403–9.

[26] So, e.g., Adams, "Paul's Story," 42; B. W. Longenecker, "Sharing in Their Spiritual Blessings," 73–81; Matlock, "The Arrow and the Web," 51–52. Others argue that apparent shifts in Paul's theology reflect different facets of a single larger narrative (e.g., Dunn, "The Narrative Approach," 230; Hooker, "Heirs of Abraham," 88–96; Wright, *New Testament and the People of God*, 405).

[27] It may be analytically useful, at times, to subdivide this grand narrative (so Cuppitt, *What Is a Story?* 114–15; Dunn, *Theology*, 18; B. W. Longenecker, "Narrative Interest," 11–13; Matera, *New Testament Christology*, 86; Witherington, *Narrative*, 5). Structurally, though, the theological story reflected in Paul's letters is a single temporal and causal sequence (so Hooker, "Heirs of Abraham," 86–87; Lincoln, "Stories of Predecessors," 198, 201; cf. Witherington, *Narrative*, 5). B. W. Longenecker also observes how a multi-story scheme often requires vague language about the "interpenetration" or "superimposition" of various stories ("Sharing in Their Spiritual Blessings," 82–3). This fuzziness disappears when we describe these narrative elements as different "episodes" within a single narrative.

[28] It is not at all clear to me that shifts in Paul's theology require us to speak of entirely different narratives in different letters. This thesis requires that we say Paul "just didn't have a Grand Story" (so Matlock, "The Arrow and the Web," 51). Yet we have now seen that many of the narrative elements which Paul employs a) appear in more than one letter and b) are causally and temporally interrelated, even across different letters. Paul may place more emphasis on (say) Adam in Romans and Abraham in Galatians, but are we really to think that Paul did not understand both Adam and Abraham to be part of a single larger narrative? Cf. Lincoln's comments in "Stories of Predecessors," 199–200.

telling the story? It is not, in fact, the case that the Apostle "never actually tells a story."[29] Passages such as Gal 3:19–29, Phil 2:6–11, and even Rom 1:18–32 do seem to meet all the criteria to qualify as narratives, however brief and condensed. It remains true, however, that Paul's usual mode of discourse is not simple narration. He is not primarily a storyteller. One way of accounting for this situation is to point out that in fact Paul is constantly alluding to the large narrative by referring to its individual episodes. We know that the Apostle relates in precisely this way to the text of Genesis when he mentions figures like Abraham (Gal 3; Rom 4) or Adam (Rom 5). Nor can we say (with Watson) that the only story to which Paul alludes is the one written in the texts of Israel's Scriptures. Surely the many mentions of Christ's cross allude to a series of events surrounding Christ's passion.[30] Still, if Paul's knowledge is structured as a story, why does he depend so heavily on allusion and leave its narration in the background? Why not simply tell the story over and over again?

2.1. Narration and Analysis

In order to answer this question we need to make some general observations about the relationship between narrative and analytical prose as genres. We are used to the idea that a story can be used to serve reflective language, to "illustrate" an abstract proposition. So, for example, when we teach children that curiosity can be dangerous, we will often reinforce this idea with a story, perhaps about Pandora and all of the evil that came from her insatiable curiosity. Yet there has been an increasing recognition that the reverse can also be true, that at least sometimes reflective speech serves simply to help in the appreciation of a story. Richard Hays has explained this relationship with the help of Northrop Frye's typology of literature and in particular his notions of *mythos* and *dianoia*.[31] In Aristotelian terms, the *mythos* of a tale is the simple sequence of events as they are narrated, the story as it is told. Frye complements this with the notion of a story's *dianoia*, a term which in Frye's hands encompasses what we often mean by the "theme" of a narrative.[32]

---

[29] Watson, "Is There a Story?" 239.

[30] Paul seems to allude to his presentation a connected passion story in Gal 3:1.

[31] See Hays, *Faith of Jesus Christ*, 21–23.

[32] In Aristotle, *dianoia* means simply those portions of a dialogue in which arguments are explicitly set forth (Aristotle, *Poetics*, 1450b).

Dianoia, for Frye, is "the *mythos* or plot examined as a simultaneous unity, when the entire shape of it is clear in our minds."[33] It can be expressed without narrating the story's events, but it is no less integral to the story because of that. Hays points out that Paul Ricoeur makes a similar observation about the relationship between "sequence" and "pattern" in stories when he observes how

> all narratives combine in various proportions two dimensions, one chronological and the other non-chronological. The first may be called the episodic dimension of a narrative . . . . But . . . the activity of telling does not merely consist in piling episodes on top of one another. It also construes significant values out of scattered events. To this aspect of story-telling corresponds on the side of story-following an attempt to "grasp together" successive events. The art of telling and, accordingly its counterpart, the art of following a story requires that we be able to elicit a configuration from a succession. This "configurational" operation . . . constitutes the second dimension of narrative activity.[34]

These two dimensions of a story cannot be separated. Nor does one have priority over the other. Rather, as Frye explains, *mythos* and *dianoia* are "the same in substance," the distinction being merely one of point of view. While *mythos* follows the events as they unfold, *dianoia* approaches the sequence of events "in relation to a unity, not in relation to suspense and linear progression."[35] But both *mythos* and *dianoia*, both sequence and pattern, are inherent in the story itself.

What this distinction helps us to see is how a narrative might generate modes of discourse, speech and writing, other than straightforward narration. For if one is interested in exploring and analysing the *dianoia* of the story, one cannot simply continue to narrate its *mythos*, or tell the tale. Instead one must use other modes of discourse to point out the connections between various elements of the story. Otherwise the relationship between these elements might not be obvious, perhaps because they remain widely separated in the sequence of the told narrative, or because that relationship is

---

[33] Frye, *Fables*, 24. Elsewhere Frye explains: "The word narrative or *mythos* conveys the sense of movement caught by the ear and the word meaning or *dianoia* conveys, or at least preserves, the sense of simultaneity caught by the eye. We *listen* to the poem as it moves from beginning to end, but as soon as the whole is clear in our minds, we 'see' what it means" (*Anatomy*, 77).

[34] Ricoeur, "Narrative Function," 183–4. See Hays, *Faith of Jesus Christ*, 23–4.

[35] Frye, *Fables*, 24.

obscured by being intertwined with other narrated events. This is precisely why literary critics are not simply storytellers. In order to discuss the *dianoia* of a narrative they must employ analytic modes of discourse, including the kind of reasoned argumentation which Paul so often employs in his letters. Paul cannot merely narrate the story again, precisely because his letters are occasional documents, written to address various particular situations in specific communities. In order for Paul to draw out the implications of the theological narrative for these audiences, to "apply" it to their situations, he must help them (among other things) to perceive that aspect of the story's *dianoia* which is most relevant. He must analyse the narrative in a way which makes its implications plain, and so he must speak in analytic language. Still, as Richard Hays observes, that "reflective discourse" can still legitimately be understood as "growing organically out of the process of narration."[36]

2.2. *Paul's Irreducible Story*

In individual cases one's interest in the pattern of a story may be more or less attached to the particular events in view. On the one hand, as with the myth of Pandora's box, we might see the story itself as entirely dispensable. It is only a tool with which we can help someone to see the narrative pattern which it embodies. In such cases we would be justified in saying that analytic discourse is primary. Any other story which embodied that pattern could serve our purpose just as well. It is in cases like these that we might speak of stories as serving reflective speech. In other cases, however, the pattern in which we are interested cannot be separated from a particular story. The pattern is for some reason dependent on these particular events, and without them it cannot be preserved. In such cases the narrative itself would seem to be primary, while the analytical discussion to which it gives rise is always inseparably tied to this story.

John M. G. Barclay seems to come close to arguing that most of what we have called Paul's theological narrative was in fact a dispensable illustration of a universal pattern. Instead of being related as part of an overarching story, Barclay claims, these various episodes are related only through "their

---

[36] Hays, *Faith of Jesus Christ*, 24. Cf. W. B. Gallie's recognition of a similar pattern at work in historiography: "If it is true that in the physical sciences there is always a theory, it is no less true that in historical research there is always a story ("Historical Understanding," 50).

homology, their common 'syntax' or pattern."[37] Matlock is more explicit, suggesting that Paul viewed Israel's Scriptures as "a vast theological and rhetorical repertoire . . . to be performed in endless variation and improvisation on the themes of humanity, death, and transcendence," rather than as a tale to be taken "referentially, as a depiction of a certain grand movement of history."[38] In stark contrast, Hans Frei has argued that until the modern age the Gospel story was understood in Christian tradition to be irreducible. Its meaning and import were treated as "functions of the depiction or narrative rendering of the events constituting them."[39] Thus, even as the Church fathers wrote copious discursive treatments of that story, all of that writing was ultimately in service of the story. The patterns towards which they pointed were patterns which could not survive outside the narrative which included these particular events. This is why, Frei suggests, the mythological reading of Strauss or the existentialist, demythologizing interpretation of Bultmann has so often been seen by traditional Christians as threatening. Each in his own way was attempting to find in the Gospel narrative a pattern which *could* exist without the particular events of the New Testament, eternal truths which could find expression in other particular events.[40]

In the end it is Frei's approach which seems to do justice to what Paul actually says in his letters. Contrary to the claims of Barclay and Matlock, we have seen above that Paul's theological statements do, in fact, form a

---

[37] Barclay, "Paul's Story," 154–5. See the critique of Horrell in his response, "Paul's Narratives," 160–66.

[38] Matlock, "The Arrow and the Web," 54.

[39] Frei, *Eclipse*, 13.

[40] This was in both cases bound up explicitly with the interpreter's conviction that the events of the Gospel story could not have happened as they were narrated there. Both thus tackled the task of finding in the Gospel a pattern which could also be embodied in events which *did* happen, particularly in the events of ordinary life in the interpreter's own world. See Frei, *Eclipse*, 233–44; Strauss, *Life of Jesus*; Bultmann, *Jesus Christ and Mythology*. While Frei is correct (*Eclipse*, 337, n. 10) that Bultmann and Strauss took different self-conscious stances towards "myth," the outcome of their methods was remarkably similar.

Leisegang exhibits similar tendencies, for while he emphasizes the narrative shape of Paul's theology, he places all of his emphasis on the synchronic pattern, the "Gebilde" which Paul sees in this "Geschichte" (*Der Apostel*, 18). Leisegang believed that Paul envisioned the individual as reliving the cosmic story, moving from the role of Adam to the role of Christ (ibid., 28).

coherent story, one whose episodes are related as part of a single temporal and causal complex. It is simply not the case that Paul resists tracing "linear lines through historical processes or human continuities."[41] In fact, both Bultmann and Strauss recognized that Paul was concerned to construct such a "myth," and even as they tried to relativize this mythology they recognized that in distilling a universal pattern from the Gospel story they were moving beyond Paul himself. The widespread critique of both Strauss and Bultmann has revolved around the recognition that in attempting to peel away the narrative "myth" from Paul's message, they were in fact removing what the Apostle regarded as its essence. Paul clearly did not think that the Gospel story was of any value apart from the particular events which it narrated.[42] He told the Corinthian believers, "If Christ has not been raised, your faith is futile" (1 Cor 15:17). Why? Because then "[Y]ou are still in your sins. Then those also who have died in Christ have perished. If for this life only we have hoped in Christ, we are of all people most to be pitied" (15:17–19). Nor can we say (as Barclay seems to imply) that it was the Christ event alone which constituted the narrative core of Paul's thought. For the Apostle, the death and resurrection receive their meaning only in the context of the larger interconnected story which I traced out above. It is only if the God of Israel actually created the world that the death of Israel's Messiah represents the dawning of a new creation. It is only if Abraham actually received a promise from God that the Christ event can open the door for the Gentiles to receive its fulfilment. It is only if the law was actually given to Moses at Sinai that the advent of Christ could mean the liberation of Israel from the law's enslavement.

The importance of the story lay, for Paul, in the hope that he and his churches would *actually experience the events which it narrated.* If the episodes in the story were reduced to mere ciphers for a universal pattern of life, it would be of little religious use in Paul's eyes. For as one who had been

---

[41] Barclay, "Paul's Story," 154–5.

[42] Michael Root distinguishes between an "illustrative" interpretation of the story, in which "the story illustrates certain redemptive truths about self, world, and God", and a "storied" relationship between narrative and reader in which "the reader is included in the Christian story. The relation of story to reader becomes internal to the story. . . . The story is good news because redemption follows from the primary form of inclusion in the story" ("Narrative Structure," 147). He also notes that "rightly or wrongly, few theologians have sought to interpret the redemptive relation along strictly illustrative lines" (ibid., 147).

beaten and hunted for his belief in Christ, he had in the present received little more than pain from that belief. It is only if Jesus was actually raised, only if that event is actually the climactic moment in the story of Israel's Scriptures, that he can hope for the new life which makes such a gruelling existence worthwhile. As Paul declares to the Corinthians, "This slight momentary affliction is preparing us for an eternal weight of glory beyond all measure. . . . For we know that if the earthly tent we live in is destroyed, we have a building from God, a house not made with hands, eternal in the heavens" (2 Cor 4:17). If, however, the episodes in Paul's theological story are only illustrations of some universal ethical or existential paradigm, then this hope which drives his apostolic mission simply evaporates.

2.3. A Continuous Narrative or a Radical Irruption?

For Barclay at least, this resistance to the idea of a continuous narrative underlying Paul's thought seems to arise from a particular understanding of the Christ event in the Apostle's letters. There is a school of Pauline interpretation which insists that the Apostle conceived of the Christ event as a radical novelty, an irruption into human life and history which had no precedent or precursor, which stood in no relation to other ideas or events. This approach, in its present form, arose out of Ernst Käsemann's objection to Oscar Cullmann's notion of *Heilsgeschichte*, but it has gained a staunch recent advocate in J. Louis Martyn.[43] For those who take such an approach to Paul's thought, it will seem obviously impossible that the Apostle would include the sending and exaltation of God's Son in a continuous narrative along with the creation of the world, the call of Abraham, Israel's desert wanderings, etc.

There is considerable theological promise in this kind of approach to the Christ event in Paul, but we must be careful not to allow the power of such a theological vision to blind us to what Paul actually says. When we look

---

[43] See, e.g., Martyn, *Galatians*, 347–8; *idem*, "Events in Galatia." See also Watson, "Is There a Story in These Texts?" As Horrell points out ("Paul's Narratives," 163), Martyn makes his perspective more appealing by describing the alternative as a process of "gradual maturation" through history, reminiscent of the older *Heilsgeschichte* approach (Martyn, *Galatians*, 389). Surely, though, one can find some middle ground between a model of radical, punctiliar novelty and one of gradual evolution. See, e.g., D. J. Lull, "Salvation History." For an account of the older debate between Bultmann, Cullmann, and Käsemann, see Hays, *The Faith of Jesus Christ*, 51–63.

carefully at the Apostle's extant writings, what we find is that Paul *does* in fact construct just the kind of continuous story which Barclay and Martyn suggest he would find unthinkable. We have already seen above that Paul places the "sending," death, and resurrection of Christ firmly within a temporal and causal sequence which stretches from creation to cosmic renewal. Likewise, David G. Horrell has pointed out that even as Paul makes claims in Gal 1–2 about the radical novelty of his message and its independence from human tradition, he articulates that new experience and message *in terms of Israel's tradition*. Thus the relationship of Paul to Israel's tradition seems to be one of dialectic rather than a radical break.[44] Christ's advent is *"the* definitive, climactic moment" in Paul's theological story, and it does come as a radically transformative and surprisingly novel act of God, but Paul's very willingness in Galatians 3 to make the Galatian believers in Christ heirs of God's promise to Abraham suggests that the Christ event, however sudden, is the pivotal moment in a much larger story.[45]

Barclay may claim that Paul resists locating Christ within a linear history and Watson may claim that God's saving act in Christ *"cannot* be located on the same horizontal plane as the events of (for example) exodus, conquest, and exile – or even the creation and the fall."[46] Yet this seems to be precisely what Paul *does* do when he makes Christ the "seed" who inherits Abraham's promise, or when he makes the advent of Christ the turning point from the "imprisonment" of Israel under the Mosaic code to a new state of liberation (Gal 3:1–4:7). Indeed, Paul's declaration that Christ was sent "when the fullness of time had come" (Gal 4:4) seems to locate this event within the same historical sequence as the previous events of Israelite and Gentile history.[47] Far from being "essentially nonnarratable,"[48] Paul's message

---

[44] Horrell, "Paul's Narratives," 160–62. See also the comments of I. H. Marshall, "Response to A. T. Lincoln," 212–13.

[45] So Horrell, "Paul's Narratives," 163.

[46] Watson, "Is There a Story?" 234.

[47] Watson's argument is based largely on the ambiguities of the relationship between Christ and Adam in Romans 5 ("Is There a Story?" 235–8). Precisely because this passage is so ambiguous, however, we should not allow it to obscure these clear ways in which the Apostle locates the Christ event within a larger cosmic and historical story.

Watson focusses heavily on the "story of Jesus," drawing a sharp opposition between the "vertical plane" of Jesus' "descent and ascent" and the "horizontal plane" of the "unfolding of the life of Jesus." He suggests that the vertical plane was so dominant in Paul's thinking

centres around a chain of events which, as I have shown above, bear all the marks of a coherent story. We may recognize that for Paul the Gospel brings about an existential confrontation between the individual who hears the message and the God who is its source. We can even acknowledge that this existential dynamic draws each individual, in that moment, into God's eternal present and does away with the ordinary distinctions of temporal distance. Such a picture of individual confrontation with the Gospel would fit well with my own suggestion above that, in Paul's view, a deep moral struggle emerges when human beings try to think certain truths about God. We should not, however, confuse that experience of encountering the Gospel with the message itself. The *message* is one which *can* be narrated, which is in fact structured as a story about God's relationship with his creation.

2.4. The "Location" of Paul's Story

One more knotty problem plagues narrative treatments of Paul's thought. Where precisely is the story of which we speak to be located? Does it exist *in* the text of Paul's letters, as textual signals with an inherently narrative relationship? Does it exist *behind* or *beneath* the text, in the mind of Paul? Or does it exist *in front of* or *above* the text, in the mind of the interpreter who perceives and reconstructs it? We should probably acknowledge that Paul's theological story exists in part at each of these levels. Indeed, while it may be analytically fruitful at times to distinguish these moments in the life of the narrative, they are no more separable in this case than when we talk about

---

that the linear life story of Jesus was never told by Paul as such (ibid., 233). Yet, even if we grant to Watson that Paul never told a linear story of Jesus' earthly life, this still does not mean that Paul's *Gospel* did not possess a narrative form. The "descent and ascent" of Christ – the "vertical plane" of Paul's message – is itself described as a series of temporal events within a larger outline of cosmic events. Watson is right (ibid., 233) that, if Jesus' earthly life is left out of view by Paul, the descent and ascent of Christ do not provide enough of a sequence to seem like much of a story. The problem here, however, is that Watson has artificially bracketed out the "story of Jesus" from the other cosmic and historical events to which it is related in Paul's letters. This isolation of the "story of Jesus" was an artificial heuristic exercise in the article by Douglas A. Campbell upon which Watson is commenting, but Watson takes this isolation as though it reflects Paul's own practice. The presentation of Paul's theological story above should suffice to show that, when these other events are taken into account, a much more robust narrative is evident.

[48] Watson, "Is There a Story?" 239.

meaning in any text, particularly an ancient one in which the historical question of the author's thought is often of interest to the interpreter.[49]

The more interesting question may be to ask in precisely what sense the Apostle's theological story existed in his own mind. Any historical interpretation operates in the hope that, when Paul wrote (or dictated) his letters, his thoughts resembled the ideas we reconstruct when we interpret those texts. So to the extent that our interpretation is accurate we can assume that Paul entertained in his own mind something like what we imagine when we examine his individual claims to knowledge. To what extent, however, did the events about which he claims to know exist in Paul's mind as a connected story? The obvious causal interrelationships between the various elements of the story mentioned in his letters strongly suggest that Paul thought of these various events as interconnected in something like the way we have outlined above. Since the structure of these connections qualifies as a narrative structure, we can thus be optimistic that something very much like the story which we reconstruct from Paul's letters existed in the author's own mind. At least we can posit that such an entity existed and make it the ideal (if unattainable) goal of our interpretation when what concerns us is the thought of the historical Paul.

Did Paul's theological narrative exist behind his letters in the sense that he ever told that story in a single continuous performance? Likely not. The Apostle does not betray any self-consciousness about the narrative structure in his theology, and there would be no particular reason for him to attempt an exhaustive presentation of his beliefs on any one occasion. He may well have told elements of his theological story in fuller form, as he seems to have done

---

[49] So, essentially, Adams, "Paul's Story," 41–2. The one point at which Adams may disagree with me is in our construal of what it would mean for the story to exist behind the text. Where for me this means that it existed in Paul's own mind, for Adams this means that it is involved in intertextual interactions with prior narratives. Watson wants to make this intertextual level the *only* level on which Paul's theological story exists, arguing that the "narrative substructure" of the Apostle's thought is nothing more than the texts of Israel's Scriptures ("Is There a Story?" 232). It is strange, however, to suggest that Paul's theology is grounded in the scriptural narratives and yet to deny that these stories also existed in his mind. Moreover, Watson himself admits that Paul is offering a "reinterpretation of these narratives" ("Is There a Story?" 232). To the extent that the Apostle viewed the scriptural narratives as part of a continuous story, he would thus have to hold some model of this reinterpreted narrative in his own mind.

with the story of Christ's crucifixion (Gal 3:1). He is not likely, however, to have given a full "recitation" of his theological narrative, any more than other Jews gave full recitations of Israel's Scriptures. At the same time, the continuous narrative structure of Paul's theology need not be denied simply because that story was never performed by Paul as a continuous whole. A story is not identical to any of its tellings, and it can exist without ever being told all at once. Many historians, for example, construct a story about the past without ever narrating that story as if they were novelists or bards. It would be strange to deny that the historical narrative exists in the historian's own understanding. Hence, when I suggest that Paul's theological narrative existed behind his texts, I am suggesting that when Paul thought about theological matters his thoughts in fact had a narrative structure. He thought of actions and events which were both causally and temporally related, and which were all governed by the overarching plot of God's rescue of his creation.

Chapter Six

Paul's Ethical Knowledge

In the previous chapter I defined Paul's theological knowledge as the opposite of his mundane knowledge, as that knowledge which extended beyond the mundane sphere and which was entirely independent of any information about the specific events and experiences of his present Christian communities. There is, however, another sphere of knowledge which stands between these poles, which links the supra-mundane realm of Paul's theological story with the contingent realities of life in Paul's churches. This is the Apostle's ethical knowledge.

1. Knowledge as Ethical Discernment

Paul often refers in his letters to a knowledge of how one ought to live.[1] In Rom 2:20, for example, Paul's hypothetical Jewish interlocutor believes that he possesses the form of knowledge and truth (τὴν μόρφωσιν τῆς γνώσεως καὶ τῆς ἀληθείας) in the law. What is this "knowledge" of which the law is (as the NRSV translates μόρφωσιν) an "embodiment"? Paul goes on:

> You, then, that teach others, will you not teach yourself? While you preach against stealing, do you steal? You that forbid adultery, do you commit adultery? You that abhor idols, do you rob temples? You that boast in the law, do you dishonor God by breaking the law? (Rom 2:21–23)

Paul does not intend to say merely that his imaginary opponent has knowledge of these few specific ethical rules. The knowledge which (as Paul

---

[1] See γινώσκω, Rom 2:18; 7:15; 2 Cor 2:9; 13:6; Phil 2:22; and perhaps also Rom 3:17 (quoting LXX Isa 59:8); γνῶσις, Rom 2:20; 15:14; ἐπιγινώσκω, 2 Cor 1:13b–14; ἐπίγνωσις, Phil 1:9; Col 1:9; 3:10; Phlm 6; οἶδα, Rom 14:14; Col 4:6; 1 Thess 4:4; 2 Thess 3:7; σύνοιδα, 1 Cor 4:4. The γνῶσις in 1 Cor 8:1, 7, 10, 11, which is also the object of

seems to grant) is embodied in the Torah is a comprehensive understanding of how one should live. This is what the Jew knows (γινώσκει) in 2:18, namely God's will (τὸ θέλημα).[2]

Paul seems to be thinking of this same ethical understanding in Rom 15:14 when he says that the Roman believers are "full of goodness, filled with all knowledge (γνώσεως), and able to instruct one another (ἀλλήλους νουθετεῖν)." Likewise, the Apostle prays that the Colossians will be "filled with the knowledge (τὴν ἐπίγνωσιν) of God's will" (Col 1:9), knowledge of how to "lead lives worthy of the Lord (περιπατῆσαι ἀξίως τοῦ κυρίου)" (1:10). He writes that they "have clothed" themselves "with the new self, which is being renewed in knowledge (εἰς ἐπίγνωσιν) according to the image of its creator" (Col 3:10). What is this knowledge "towards" which (εἰς) they are being renewed? It is that which characterizes the "new self," that self which is defined in opposition to sin (3:1–10). The Colossians are moving towards an understanding of how to live in harmony with the will of God.[3]

Paul generally seems to emphasize the function of this ethical knowledge, not its content. This knowledge allows people to make proper ethical

---

γινώσκω in 8:2, probably includes not only the theological ideas summarized in 8:4–6 but also some insight into their implications for dealing with idol meats.

[2] Zimmerman ("Knowledge of God," 475) thinks that this knowledge of God's will includes an acknowledgement of it, a submission to it. He also reads Rom 15:14 in the same sense (ibid., 476). Yet the emphasis in each case is clearly on being able to discern what God wants, not on a commitment to doing it. For a discussion of the kind of personal, volitional knowledge with which Zimmerman is concerned, see Chapter VII below.

More ambiguous is Rom 3:17, where Paul quotes Isa 59:8: "the way of peace they have not known (οὐκ ἔγνωσαν)." This could mean either that they do not practice that "way" (in which case this would be an example of knowledge as direct familiarity) or that they lack the kind of ethical judgement we are discussing here.

[3] Cf. Phlm 6, where Paul prays that Philemon's faith will become effective in knowledge (ἐπιγνώσει) of "all the good that we may do for Christ." This is hardly, as Piper contends, "the realization of [Christ's] saving significance" ("Knowledge," 45).

See also Rom 7:15, where Paul writes: ὃ γὰρ κατεργάζομαι οὐ γινώσκω. Barrett is almost surely correct that this is not a matter of the subject's literally not knowing what he does, but rather that his actions are "incomprehensible" to him (*Romans*, 138; so Lagrange, *Romains*, 175). Dunn wants to read the verb here as the same "experiential knowledge" which he thinks we find in 7:7, so that here "Paul existentially disowns his action" (*Romans*, 1.389; cf. Cranfield, *Romans*, 1.358–9). Yet the emphasis in what follows falls on the subject's sense of confused helplessness at his inability to reform his actions. So Paul is likely highlighting the fact that the sinner cannot figure out how to stop sinning.

judgements, to accurately interpret the moral quality of human actions. Hence, both in Rom 2:18 and in Phil 1:9–10, this knowledge allows people to "determine what is best (δοκιμάζειν . . . τὰ διαφέροντα)." Only in Rom 14:14 does Paul talk about knowing (οἶδα) a specific ethical rule, and this is merely the negative judgement that "nothing is unclean in itself." Elsewhere Paul simply talks about people having (unspecified) knowledge which allows them to make such judgements properly. The Colossians are enjoined to know (εἰδέναι) "how you ought to answer everyone" (Col 4:6). Paul wants the Thessalonians to "know how (εἰδέναι) to control your own body in holiness and honor, not with lustful passion, like the Gentiles who do not know God" (1 Thess 4:4–5).[4] Nowhere, though, does he mention knowing specific moral injunctions which would guide these ethical judgements.

At times Paul can use language of "knowing" to denote the interpretive act itself. So, in 1 Cor 4:4 he declares that does not know (σύνοιδα) anything for which he would condemn himself. He does not interpret any of his actions as violating the will of God. Similarly, in 2 Cor 1:13b–14 the Apostle expresses his hope that the Corinthians will come to know (ἐπιγινώσεσθε) him and his companions perfectly. Here he hopes not simply that the Corinthian believers will produce an accurate record of Paul's mission but rather that he and his company will become their boast, just as the Corinthians are his. He hopes that they will come to understand how well Paul and the others have acted, so that they may once more become proud to claim an association with him.[5] Here again Paul and his companions stand as the direct object of the verb of knowing. To "know" them is to interpret their moral character properly.

We catch a glimpse of this ethical judgement in action when Paul recalls for the Philippians their knowledge (γινώσκετε) of Timothy's character. In order to prompt a correct evaluation of Timothy, the Apostle reminds his

---

[4] See also 2 Thess 3:7, where they "know (οἴδατε) how you ought to imitate us," that is, not by being slack, but working for their own food.

[5] The sense of ἐπιγινώσκω here verges on the idea of "recognition" of someone's authority, and so it is taken by Thrall (*2 Corinthians*, 1.134–5). Yet the emphasis on "partial" versus "complete" knowledge fits better with the idea of proper moral evaluation than with recognition of authority. Moreover, Paul begins this paragraph in 1:12 talking about the purity of his actions towards the Corinthians. Hence Paul is most likely talking about their interpreting his actions properly, i.e., as pure (so Barrett, *2 Corinthians*, 73). Along similar lines, Martin understands Paul to be calling for the Corinthians' "acceptance of his honesty" (*2 Corinthians*, 21; cf. Furnish, *2 Corinthians*, 131).

audience of the man's faithful work in Paul's mission (Phil 2:22). The Philippians' ethical "knowing" thus seems to be a matter of properly interpreting someone's pattern of behaviour. Paul looks to a person's actions in order to see trends and patterns which reveal something of that person's quality as a moral agent. This is why, when the Apostle wants to know (γνῶ) the character of the believers in Corinth, he pens his "tearful letter" (2 Cor 2:9). It is in their response to a crisis like this that their character, their inclination to act well or badly, is laid open to view and can be interpreted by others as pure or corrupt. In fact, the hermeneutical character of this knowledge is implied by the very word which Paul uses for such "character," for the noun δοκιμή generally denotes what is left over from an act of "testing" (δοκιμάζω).[6]

So the general nature and the purpose of Paul's ethical knowledge is plain. This is an interpretive skill, an ability to make judgements about the moral quality of human actions. What is not clear, however, is where Paul derives the standards against which to test these actions. How does the Apostle recognize God's will in the first place so that he can evaluate whether or not a person is following it? Why is Paul so reticent about saying that he knows specific ethical rules? Before we can answer these questions we must take a step back to explore the ways in which Paul brings his theological knowledge into contact with the everyday events around him.

2. The Intersection of Paul's Mundane and Theological Knowledge

2.1. Locating the Audience in the Story

In some instances what Paul knows seems to be the location of specific, living people within his theological narrative. Paul does not leave his story self-contained, detached from lived experience. Its events are not restricted to a mythic time, disconnected from the time of everyday life. Rather, he seems to understand mundane time to take place within the central moments of the narrative. Likewise, his narrative not only includes generic roles for human

---

[6] See LSJ, 442; BDAG, 256 (2). Cf. 2 Cor 13:6, where Paul hopes that the Corinthians will know (γνώσεσθε) that his company are not ἀδόκιμοι.

beings ("the elect," "the perishing," "Israel," etc.), but it also allows him to identify the narrative role which individual human beings are playing.[7]

Beardslee points out how Paul's own self-understanding is shaped in this way by his theological narrative, how "the 'little story' of Paul's life finds meaning by being related to the 'big story' of which the organizing center is Christ."[8] Hence in Rom 15:29, for instance, Paul says he knows (οἶδα) that when he comes to Rome it will be "in the fullness of the blessing of Christ." In other words, when he disembarks at the wharf in Ostia, makes his way up to Rome, and is greeted on the Romans' own thresholds, he will be doing so (in terms of the story) as one who is endorsed by God, one in whom God's benevolent power is at work, one who is experiencing the dawning of the eschatological fulfilment. Similarly, in 1 Cor 14:37 Paul specifies that anyone who claims to be a prophet or to be spiritual should "recognize (ἐπιγινωσκέτω) that what I am writing to you is a command of the Lord."[9] Paul is claiming that anyone who can interpret his life properly will understand his very ordinary acts of thinking and writing to be the actions of God's representative.[10] In Gal 2:9 it is Peter, James, and John who know (γνόντες) "the grace that had been given" to Paul, that is, his role as God's agent sent to invite the Gentiles to accept salvation in Christ. In each case, this knowledge is a matter of discerning that Paul occupies a certain role in

---

[7] See γινώσκω, 1 Cor 4:19; 2 Cor 3:2, 5:16; Gal 2:9; γνωρίζω, 2 Cor 8:1; Gal 1:11; ἐπιγινώσκω, 1 Cor 14:37; ἀγνοέω, 1 Cor 10:1; 14:38a; οἶδα, Rom 5:3; 8:28; 15:29; 1 Cor 6:16; 12:2; 15:58; 2 Cor 1:7; 5:6, 16; Phil 1:19, 25; 1 Thess 1:4; 3:3. Note that this kind of knowledge statement can sometimes also be drawn into discussions of Paul's theological knowledge, since in these passages the Apostle often provides us with glimpses of the narrative within which he locates a given individual or group. Hence, Rom 8:28; 1 Cor 15:58; 2 Cor 1:7 and 5:6 are also discussed in Chapter V above.

[8] Beardslee, "Narrative Form," 306–7.

[9] Here I have altered the NRSV translation, in which ἐπιγινωσκέτω is rendered as "acknowledge." The translators seem to follow Bultmann's suggestion that Paul is calling on the "pneumatics" to "acknowledge" his apostolic authority in the sense of submitting to it. Yet the idea of authority here is merely implied. What Paul wants them to do is primarily to recognize *that* Paul's speech is an expression of God's will (so Collins, *1 Corinthians*, 522; Fee, *1 Corinthians* 712 n. 15). If they do not interpret his words in this way, he implies, this error in their judgement demonstrates that they do not possess the spiritual inspiration which they claim. See further p. 54, n. 16 above.

[10] See also Gal 1:11, where the Apostle claims to know that his Gospel is from God.

the theological narrative, a matter of "emplotting" him correctly within that story.

In the same way, Paul encourages his audience too not only to discern the outlines and patterns of the theological story, but also to recognize *where they are located* in that cosmic drama. So, for example, when Paul writes to the Thessalonians he tells them that he knows (εἰδότες) not merely that God chooses some people, but, more important, that God has chosen *them* (1 Thess 1:4). That is the role which they occupy in the narrative: the role of the elect.[11] In 1 Thess 3:3 Paul then reminds his audience of their knowledge (οἴδατε) that this role they are playing requires them to suffer persecution. They are appointed to it (εἰς τοῦτο κείμεθα). That is to say, they occupy the role in the cosmic story which is characterized by innocent suffering.

2.2. Correlating Mundane Events with the Story

Often, however, there can be different, competing interpretations of a person's life, interpretations which locate that individual in widely divergent narrative roles. Paul recognizes as much in 2 Cor 5:16, when he writes: "We do not regard anyone (οὐδένα οἴδαμεν) from a human point of view (κατὰ σάρκα); even though we once knew (ἐγνώκαμεν) Christ from a human point of view, we know him no longer in that way." Paul is alluding here to the initial ambiguity of Jesus' role within Israel's narrative. If one adopts a "fleshly" interpretive stance, as Paul himself once did, the man from Nazareth appears to play the part of a cursed enemy of God. Paul's shift from persecutor to evangelist involved his adopting a new hermeneutical perspective in which Jesus could be seen to occupy the role of God's own Messiah. Moreover, Paul seems to be saying here in 5:16 that the same kind of interpretive mistake can be made when attempting to locate anyone in the theological story. Now that his perspective on Christ has shifted he realizes that no one (οὐδένα) should be understood from such a "fleshly" interpretive angle. The sheer volume of argument in Paul's letters makes it plain that the location of living people and current events in the theological story was often far from obvious. As Hays writes, "Paul's letters may be read as running arguments with opponents who draw different inferences from the same story."[12] All the same, the Apostle does not retreat into an interpretive

---

[11] See also Beardslee, "Narrative Form," 305.
[12] Hays, *Faith of Jesus Christ*, 6.

relativism. In 2 Cor 5:16 he clearly believes that his own "emplotment" of individuals is correct, and that competing attempts to locate these figures within the story are flawed, distorted by ordinary human interpretive habits (κατὰ σάρκα).

So how does Paul help his audiences to avoid misinterpretations and locate people accurately within the story? How does he convince them that his own interpretive emplotment of some person is correct? By making what Fowl calls a "critical correlation" between the story and "the specific situation faced by each audience."[13] Paul claims to be able to discern in someone's life an action or event which is characteristic of a particular role in the theological story. This is, in effect, what Paul is doing in 1 Thess 1:4–5a: "We know (εἰδότες) . . . that he has chosen you, *because our message of the gospel came to you not in word only, but also in power and in the Holy Spirit and with full conviction.*" Here he reminds the Thessalonians of their first acceptance of his Gospel and interprets that event, in the context of the theological narrative, as God's choice of them.[14] The "characters" in the story who accept the Gospel in this way and experience this "power" are those whom God has chosen.[15] A similar dynamic is at work in 1 Cor 4:19. Here

---

[13] Fowl, *Story of Christ*, 201.

[14] Paul's reference to the Thessalonians' experience of and reaction to Paul's preaching is introduced in 1:5a with ὅτι. I have taken this ὅτι clause as describing the reason or basis for the knowledge of their election to which Paul refers in 1:4 (so Morris, *Thessalonians*, 56; Richard, *Thessalonians*, 64). Lightfoot suggests alternatively that the phrase εἰδέναι τι ὅτι is idiomatic and that in this context the ὅτι clause should be taken epexegetically (as an expansion or elaboration on the content of the knowledge) rather than causally (*Notes*, 12; so Best, *Thessalonians*, 73). Lightfoot points to parallels in Acts 16:3; Rom 13:11; 1 Cor 16:15; 2 Cor 12:3–4; 1 Thess 2:1 (so Best, *Thessalonians*, 73; cf. 2 Cor 9:2). Yet we have the same construction in Rom 8:27 and 2 Thess 3:7, where most commentators take the ὅτι to be causal. Even if we take 1:5 as a further elaboration of what Paul means by the Thessalonians' "election," however, his logic remains much the same. These experiences in the Thessalonians' initial confrontation with the Gospel message are interpreted by Paul as typical of divine election. The observable events are linked to certain stereotyped events in Israel's narrative and then used to locate the congregation within that story.

[15] It is unclear precisely what kind of "power" Paul is thinking of in 1:5. Is it the effective force of the message itself to produce belief, perhaps as an expression of the Spirit's activity (so Bruce, *Thessalonians*, 14; Morris, *Thessalonians*, 57; Richard, *Thessalonians*, 65)? Is it the salvific impact of the message for those who believe, or the spiritual empowerment of the preachers (so Best, *Thessalonians*, 75)? Or is the Apostle referring to miraculous or ecstatic experiences which accompanied that reception (so

Paul looks forward to being in Corinth and knowing (γνώσομαι) "not the talk of these arrogant people but their power (τὴν δύναμιν)."[16] In effect he offers a (thinly) veiled threat that, when he arrives, the events in the community will immediately make it clear whether these would-be leaders actually occupy the role in the story which they claim for themselves.

When Paul discusses the use and abuse of prophecy in the Church he writes: "I want you to understand (γνωρίζω) that no one speaking by the Spirit of God ever says 'Let Jesus be cursed!' and no one can say 'Jesus is Lord' except by the Holy Spirit" (1 Cor 12:3). Here he identifies two kinds of prophetic action and tells the audience that these correspond with two different roles in the story. A person who speaks in the latter way is thereby identified as being aligned with and empowered by the Spirit, while someone speaking in the former manner is by definition excluded from that role. More broadly, Paul can interpret the former paganism of the Corinthian believers as

---

Donfried, *Thessalonica*, 91–2, 239–40; Holtz, *1. Thessalonicher*, 46–7; Jewett, *Thessalonian Correspondence*, 100)? The singular δύναμις may tell against the latter, miraculous interpretation (so Lightfoot, *Notes*, 13; Best, *Thessalonians*, 75; see the plural in 1 Cor 12:10, 28, 29). True, in Rom 15:19 the singular denotes miraculous power, but there it is explicitly qualified as the power of "signs and wonders" (δυνάμει σημείων καὶ τεράτων). On the other hand, in Rom 1:16; 1 Cor 1:18; 2 Cor 6:7 the Gospel itself is said to be God's δύναμις in that it is the site of human encounter with God's salvation. Hence it is probably best to understand this "power" as the salvific impact of Paul's preaching on the Thessalonians, an impact which may have been visible in changed lives as well as charismatic manifestations in the community.

[16] Fee (*1 Corinthians*, 191) argues that the "power" which marks a true apostle here is miraculous or charismatic power, pointing to miraculous demonstrations (cf. Hays, *1 Corinthians*, 75). I argued above, however, that the powerful "demonstration" in 1 Cor 2:4–5 probably consists of the Spirit's internal persuasion of Paul's audience (see above, pp. 30–34). We should also remember that Paul consistently downplays the importance of charismatic displays in 1 Cor, and that in 2 Cor 12:1–7 he seems to have been criticized for his lack of such powers. In 1 Cor 4:19, it is thus more likely that the "power" which is present in his work is the power of God to bring salvation through the Gospel message. As Thiselton points out (*1 Corinthians*, 376), the contrast here between "power" and mere "words" suggests that Paul is thinking of the "valid effects" of someone's preaching and lifestyle, effects which can only be produced by God's Spirit (cf. 1 Cor 2:4–5; Barrett, *1 Corinthians*, 118; Collins, *1 Corinthians*, 201–2). The following statement in 4:20 that "the kingdom of God depends not on talk but on power" certainly suggests that Paul is thinking of this "power" primarily as God's power to save. See further n. 15 above on 1 Thess 1:4–5.

having marked them as those in the story who were deceived, living against God. They know, he claims, that when they were pagans they were "enticed and led astray to idols which could not speak" (1 Cor 12:2). This is certainly not how they would have understood their sacrifices at the time, but, in light of the new narrative with which they interpret their own actions, they realize that those religious rites were the kind of thing that the "deceived" would do. Then, in 2 Cor 8:1, the Apostle wants them to know (γνωρίζομεν) "the grace of God that has been granted to the churches of Macedonia." What is this "grace"? It appears to be the joy and resultant generosity which flowed from them despite their severe hardships. The very fact that they can act in this way marks the Macedonian believers as those in whom God is at work. Likewise, in Rom 5:3–5 Paul claims to know that "suffering produces endurance, and endurance produces character, and character produces hope, and hope does not disappoint us." Those who endure suffering without abandoning their faith in Christ, who maintain their hope in God's eschatological blessing, are the ones who will see that blessing dawn. This is no abstract generalization. It is "we" in Rome and in Paul's company who can be located among the heirs of God's kingdom because of "our" perseverance. In each of these passages the knowledge to which Paul refers is a matter of locating a person accurately within the theological story, and in each case the interpretive key which allows this identification is a point of contact between mundane (i.e., observable) events and the theological narrative.[17]

2.3. Knowing the Future of the Role

Why is it so important to Paul that his communities know how to locate themselves in the theological story? Because whatever role one plays, that role carries with it very concrete implications for the future. The story within which the members of the Apostle's churches understand their existence extends beyond their present towards the eschatological consummation of God's creation. So if Paul's hearers can identify both where their present lies in the timeline of the story and their own narrative role, they need only look

---

[17] This is likely how we should read 2 Cor 3:2 as well, where the Corinthians are said to be Paul's letter of recommendation, known (γινωσκομένη) and read by everyone. The very existence of this community founded by Paul marks his mission as the mission of one approved by God.

at how that role fares further on in the story in order to know the kind of end they can expect to meet.

The stakes are high. Depending on what role they play in the story they will either be sheltered from wrath or left to bear its brunt in the coming judgement. Paul knows (εἰδότες) that because of the Corinthians' faithfulness their "labor is not in vain" (1 Cor 15:58), knows (εἰδότες) that the one who raised Jesus will raise them as well (2 Cor 4:14), and knows (οἴδαμεν) that if their earthly home is destroyed they have an eternal home in the heavens (2 Cor 5:1).[18] It is because the story provides such insights about the future of its various characters that Paul can rejoice in Phil 1:19 and claim to know (οἶδα) that his present sufferings will eventually result in "salvation" (σωτηρίαν). Because he knows (οἴδαμεν) that "all things work together for good for those who love God," those who are "called," the Apostle can assure the Romans who play this role that their future is secure (Rom 8:28).[19] On the other hand, those who act out the role of the "wicked," who stand outside God's saving action in Christ, will be excluded from the eschatological kingdom and face judgement instead (see, e.g., Rom 2:2; 1 Cor 6:9). The end which awaits human beings is entirely determined by the role which they play in the theological narrative.[20]

---

[18] Cf. 2 Cor 5:6, where Paul knows (εἰδότες) that being at home in the body means being away from the Lord. Similarly, in 2 Cor 1:7 Paul knows (εἰδότες) that since the Corinthians share in the sufferings of Christ (cf. 1:5), so the members of that church must also share in the comfort which Christ brings, i.e., eschatological comfort.

[19] It is clear that Paul wants the Romans to understand themselves as being among those who are called. This statement in 8:28 stands as the culmination of Paul's talk in verses 26–27 about the way in which the Spirit helps us in our weakness and intercedes for us when we do not know what to pray. The assumption seems to be that the Romans are included in Paul's "we" in these verses, and it may well be that Paul understands the co-operation of the cosmos for their good as the direct consequence of the Spirit's intercession.

[20] See also Phil 1:25, where Paul claims to know that he will not die in prison, but will "remain and continue" with the Philippians for the sake of their "progress and joy in faith." This knowledge seems to be based on Paul's awareness of his apostolic commission (i.e., his role in the narrative) and the perception that his communities still have need of his guidance (see 1:24).

3. Knowing How to Navigate the Story

3.1. Knowing How to Live a Good Role

This knowledge of the role one is playing in the story and of what the future holds for that role is not yet truly ethical knowledge. We can, however, call such knowledge "pre-ethical," because it is this understanding of one's narrative location (and hence one's narrative future) which seems to provide the basis for Paul's moral discernment, his fully ethical knowledge.

In the first place, Paul's emplotment of individuals within the story often seems to provide the motivation for his ethics. For the Apostle does not regard a person's role in the story as set and unchangeable. His passionate aim is to help his audiences to see how their narrative location is intimately connected with what they do in the present. If they can come to recognize their role in the story by looking (in part) at the way they behave, they can also *change* that role by adopting a new course of action. This is a possibility for Paul and his audience because, as we have already observed, their present marks the pivotal moment in the theological story. They stand in the moment of decision, when human beings are able to shift their allegiances before the consummation begins and the fate of human beings is sealed. It is thus crucially important that the members of his communities not only learn the story, but also learn what must be done in order to play a good role.

This is why Paul's specific ethical instructions are often accompanied by reminders about what his hearers know is in store for those who play the part of the wicked and faithless. Paul asks the Corinthians "Do you not know that wrongdoers will not inherit the kingdom of God?" (1 Cor 6:9). When he accuses those who stand in judgement over sinners of being guilty themselves, he reminds them of their knowledge that "God's judgment on those who do such things is in accordance with truth" (Rom 2:2). The clear implication in both of these passages is that the addressees must change their actions (and hence their part in the story) if they want to reach a good end. Similarly, Paul wants the Philippians to grow into a deeper ethical "knowledge (ἐπιγνώσει)," to develop the skill of ethical discernment (δοκιμάζειν), so that they will be "pure" when the eschatological "Day of Christ" dawns (Phil 1:9–11). The impetus for seeking ethical knowledge seems again to spring from the need to position oneself well in the religious story before it is too late. Hence it is vital to know which actions place one in a role which receives blessing and which lead to destruction.

The importance of this ethical knowledge also explains why in Rom 10:2–3 Paul regards it as so tragic that Israel's zeal for God is not κατ' ἐπίγνωσιν, is not guided by an accurate understanding of the theological story. Paul says that they are unaware (ἀγνοοῦντες) of the righteousness of God – that is, the kind of relationship with God by which the "redeemed" are distinguished – and seek to establish their own righteousness on a different basis.[21] The implication is that despite all her zeal Israel is left (at least for the time being) excluded from God's act of gracious salvation. Without a proper knowledge of the theological story, they cannot hope to make accurate judgements about how to play a role which leads to salvation.[22]

3.2. Knowing What Behaviour Fits a Good Role

So the skill of moral discernment which constitutes, in general terms, Paul's ethical knowledge seems to be the ability to distinguish actions which align one with a good role in the theological story from those actions which identify a human being as headed towards destruction. But how does the Apostle think we can know which kinds of action are associated with which role? To what extent does Paul's theological narrative give rise to his specific ethical standards? Does the story provide the *content* of the Apostle's ethics, or merely their context and motive?

This is a question which cannot be adequately answered within the confines of this chapter, in which we are looking specifically at the content of Paul's knowledge claims. Yet some of these claims do suggest ways in which

---

[21] See also Gal 2:16, where Paul and Peter came to faith in Christ, "knowing (εἰδότες) that a person is justified not by the works of the law but through faith in Jesus Christ."

[22] In fact, this seems to be the context of Paul's ethics generally. See, e.g., Gal 5:21, where Paul sums up his survey of the works of the flesh by warning (again) that "those who do such things will not inherit the kingdom of God."

Note too how Paul is convinced that if the powers of this age had known (ἔγνωσαν) the proclamation of Christ, if they had known the story, their actions would have been radically different. They would not have crucified the lord of glory (1 Cor 2:8).

One case in which Paul's ethical knowledge appears to be unmotivated by his religious narrative is Phil 4:11–12, where he claims to know how to be αὐτάκρης. This characteristic appears to be valuable not because it helps one to salvation, but simply for its own sake. Yet notice that this claim does not actually ground any ethical injunctions. It seems that Paul is simply appealing to what he knew was a primary value of his Greco-Roman hearers in order to bolster his own authority and the attractiveness of his example.

the Apostle's theological story contains within itself an understanding of the kind of behaviour to be expected of one who lives out the role of the "redeemed." In Rom 6:6 Paul helps his Christ-believing audience to recognize the kind of lifestyle which their role requires, not by appealing to set laws or ethical codes, but by exploring with them the nature of that narrative role itself. In 6:1 the Apostle's fictive conversation partner wonders why those who enjoy redemption in Christ should not "continue in sin in order that grace may abound." Paul responds in 6:2–5 by reminding his opponent of the mechanism by which believers participate in this grace – their identification with Christ in death and (in the future) resurrection. The Apostle then points out the key aspect of this narrative situation which provides believers with a continuing ethical imperative. "We know (γινώσκοντες)," Paul says, "that our old self was crucified with him *so that the body of sin might be destroyed, and we might no longer be enslaved to sin.*" Within the Apostle's theological narrative, the purpose of the Christ event seems to have been (in part) to free human beings from the sin which makes their relationship with God impossible and places them under the threat of divine wrath. Hence one's identification with Christ's death, his salvific act, naturally also commits one to avoid sin and to live as God intends. Such a commitment is built into the believer's identification with Christ, precisely because of the purpose Christ's death serves within the story.[23] Since his death was a death "to sin," so too the believer who is identified with Christ must live as if "dead to sin" (6:10–11).[24]

Still, a general injunction to avoid "sin" does not provide much basis for making ethical judgements. What, after all, does "sin" look like? In 2 Cor 1:5–7, however, we see an indication that Paul can derive a much more specific standard for behaviour from the audience's narrative role. In 1:5 Paul describes the suffering and opposition which Paul and Timothy endure as "the sufferings of Christ," and he describes these trials in verse 6 as

---

[23] Paul continues to explicate the Roman believers' place in this story through to 6:12, where he concludes with the exhortation "Therefore, do not let sin exercise dominion in your mortal bodies . . ."

[24] See also Rom 6:16, where Paul asks whether the Romans know (οὐκ οἴδατε ὅτι) that whatever one obeys, one becomes a slave to that entity. Notice here the dramatization of what would otherwise be abstractions. Paul envisions the Romans in a cosmic drama, dwarfed on all sides by much greater powers which will either help them to salvation or drag them off to be numbered among the doomed.

benefiting the Corinthian community. Their "affliction" is "for your consolation and salvation." The Apostle seems to be assuming, once again, that the believer's role involves an identification with Christ in his death, and his own sufferings on behalf of the Corinthian community are an example of what that union can mean in day-to-day life. In 1:7 Paul then seems to go further and to make such suffering on behalf of others a necessary sign that one is "in Christ." The Apostle claims to know (εἰδότες) that "as you share in the sufferings, so also you share in the consolation."[25] Their future share in the resurrection depends on their union with Christ, and that participation includes a share in the cross as well. The very nature of the Corinthians' role in the cosmic narrative gives rise to a concrete ethical commitment to imitate Christ's own self-giving sufferings.

Nor should we overlook Paul's habit of asking the Corinthians, perhaps with a note of rhetorical exasperation, whether they do not know some aspect of the theological story. His point is not that they are uneducated, that they actually lack knowledge of the narrative, but rather that they are living in a way that would cast them in a bad role in that story.[26] Do they not know that the saints will judge the world? If so, then why are they submitting their complaints to public courts (1 Cor 6:2)? The Apostle seems to be saying that it is foolish for those who are supposed to be competent judges to submit their disputes to the incompetent. If they are so incapable of running their own affairs, this might even mean that they need to question their status as

---

[25] The NRSV reads "our sufferings" and "our consolation," but the possessive pronouns are not present in the Greek. By supplying them, the NRSV rendering obscures the way in which Paul characterizes these sufferings (in v. 5) as a participation in Christ's own passion.

[26] These passages also show that such knowledge in Paul often carries no idea of obedience. Paul has to remind the Corinthians of their knowledge precisely because they often act in defiance of its implications. This highlights the difficulty with Bultmann's suggestion that knowledge language in the NT was used primarily in the sense of "acknowledgment, and obedient or grateful submission to what is known" ("γινώσκω," 704–6). In fact, some of his examples are read more easily in the sense of simple intellectual understanding ("γινώσκω," 706; see Rom 2:20; 3:17; 1 Cor 8:4–6; Gal 2:9). Another of his examples which does talk about obedience does not mention knowledge ("γινώσκω," 705; 1 Thess 1:9), while some clearly indicate that one can have knowledge *without* any acknowledgement of God or obedience (Rom 2:18, 21; 10:19). This is not to say, however, that the usage to which Bultmann points is entirely absent from Paul. In 1 Cor 16:18 knowledge probably does include submission (see also, e.g., 2 Cor 10:5). See also Chapter VII below.

members in God's people. Similarly, Paul asks whether they do not know (οὐκ οἴδατε) that their community constitutes the temple of God in which God's spirit dwells (1 Cor 3:16)? This implies that they are, as a community, holy. The destruction of such a holy "site" through factionalism and power struggles will bring God's wrath on the ones responsible, just as God visits punishment on anyone who violates his holy place in Jerusalem (3:17). On the other hand, Paul reminds the Corinthians in 6:19 that as individuals their physical bodies also house the Holy Spirit. Thus the "fornication," which pollutes a holy space, is inappropriate. Instead the believer's body should be used as a site of worship, to "glorify God" (6:20). Just above this passage, in 1 Cor 6:15–16, Paul objects to the fact that some Corinthians are having relations with prostitutes. In order to explain why this is wrong, he reminds them that "your bodies are members of Christ" and then points out that (according to Gen 2:24) sexual unions involve the fusion of the partners into "one flesh." The implication is that a prostitute thus united with a believer is an inappropriate (perhaps impure?) intrusion into the union between a human being and Christ.[27]

In several of these cases Paul leaves some steps unspoken in his reasoning. How does he know, for example, that intercourse with a prostitute involves impurity in a way that intercourse with one's spouse does not? We need not insist that all of these missing premises are to be supplied directly from the Apostle's theological story. The idea of prostitution as impure seems to derive, rather, from Israel's customs of cultic purity, particularly as they were developed metaphorically by the prophets. In this case, a key idea in Paul's ethical judgement would seem to be derived from Israel's tradition of non-narrative teaching, not simply from narrative events. All the same, it is

---

[27] See also 1 Cor 8:1–13. Here some Corinthians are convinced that it is perfectly acceptable to join in the religious banquets of pagan temples. This ethical insight seems to be based on the knowledge (γνῶσις) summarized in 8:4–6, that idols are unreal and only one God has the power to create and sustain life. The Corinthians seem to have reasoned that if the gods of the idol-cults were unreal, powerless, no negative spiritual "power" could reside in the food. So here again their ethical judgement was based on the implications of the theological narrative for one who seeks to play a good role. Paul takes issue with the Corinthians' application of this knowledge in community life (8:7–12), and seems ultimately to say that their basic moral judgement is mistaken (10:1–22), but his own arguments are equally based in the shape of the theological story. See further Hays, *1 Corinthians*, 136–43, 159–71.

important to notice that in none of these cases does Paul's ethical knowledge seem to constitute a direct appeal to Israel's written moral codes. When, as here, his ethical knowledge does seem to rely on non-narrative formulations, he consistently interprets them in light of the key events in his theological narrative. It is not simply that prostitution renders one impure. Such impurity is illegitimate for one who has become a temple for God's Spirit through identification with Christ. It is illegitimate because the story of Eve's creation implies a profound physical union between sexual partners. Moreover, it would seem from our examples here that Paul's appeals to non-narrative elements of Israel's tradition are very selective, and that he tends to appeal only to very general principles such as moral impurity, principles which so pervade the narratives of Israel's Scriptures that they are hardly separable from those stories themselves.[28] We can thus say that the activity of moral discernment which constitutes Paul's ethical knowledge seems in large part to be a matter of a) deciding whether or not a given action is appropriate for the narrative role of the "saved" b) by asking whether the action is consistent with the identity of the saved as it is defined in the theological story.

3.3. Ethical Analogies within the Story

We should also notice that in some cases Paul's ethical knowledge does not seem to be derived directly from the narrative role of Christ-believers, but rather by analogy with the obligations which accompany other roles in that story. I argued above that for Paul the theological story is what Hans Frei would call a "realistic narrative."[29] It is not simply a story which illustrates a pattern of life but rather a story within which Paul wants to locate the experiences of the Christian communities. In keeping with this, we have seen now that Paul's ethical knowledge – even of specific standards for behaviour – is often grounded in the believer's unique role in that "realistic" story. This is not to say, however, that individual episodes within that narrative cannot also, at the same time, illustrate patterns which recur elsewhere in the larger story. Paul's assumption seems to be that if one group is playing a role that is somehow similar to that of another group, there will likely be similarities in their ethical responsibilities as well. This is the essence of Paul's

---

[28] In fact, it is in the sphere of sexual ethics and gender relations that we find most of Paul's appeals to such non-narrative principles.

[29] See above, p. 112.

"typological" interpretation of Scripture. His hermeneutical task involves identifying the similarities between the narrative role of the "types" and that of the "antitypes," so that he can identify any pattern of obligation which might arise from that common aspect of their different roles in the story. As Fowl puts it, this analogical ethical knowledge involves identifying the relevant "similarity-in-difference" between the life of his audience and the lives of others who occupy a similar place in the narrative.[30]

In 1 Cor 9:13–14 this kind of ethical analogy involves a comparison between two contemporary groups. Paul asks whether the members of the Corinthian community do not know (οὐκ οἴδατε) that "those who are employed in the temple service get their food from the temple, and those who serve at the altar share in what is sacrificed on the altar." Just as those servants of God gain their living from their work, those who serve God by preaching the Gospel have a right to do the same, even though the form of their divine service is different.

In 1 Cor 10:1, on the other hand, Paul's ethical analogy is drawn between his audience and those who played a similar role at an earlier stage in the theological narrative. Here Paul warns the Corinthians not to be unaware (ἀγνοεῖν) of the Israelites' experience during the exodus and the desert wanderings which followed. Since Paul clearly assumes that his audience already knows the biblical account,[31] it seems that what Paul wants them to do is recognize the significance of that incident for their own situation. The biblical events are "types" (τύποι; 10:6), providing a template for understanding the similar events in Corinth, and as Paul recounts the incident in vv. 1–5 his focus lands on the fate of that first generation which left Egypt. "God was not pleased with most of them," Paul says, "and they were struck down in the wilderness" (10:5). The point of the episode for Paul is that the Corinthians are in danger of falling into the same "evil" practices which the Israelites "desired" (10:6) and for which they were destroyed: idolatry (10:7;

---

[30] Fowl, *Story of Christ*, 202. Fowl compares the function of these narratives to the function of the "exemplar" in Thomas Kuhn's philosophy of science (*Story of Christ*, 203).

[31] G. Wenham (*Story*, 132) points out that Paul's only mention of the golden calf incident is the allusive reference in 10:7: "Do not become idolaters as some of them did; as it is written, 'The people sat down to eat and drink, and they rose up to play.'" As Wenham observes, such an oblique allusion assumes that "the Corinthian church was well versed in the Old Testament, knew its stories intimately" (*Story*, 132).

cf. 14:1), sexual immorality (10:8), and complaining against God (10:10). Paul urges the Corinthians that, as God's people, they will face the same judgement if they repeat the same mistakes (10:6; cf. 10:11).[32] It is simply assumed here that one can predict God's actions in the present phase of the story, and thus flesh out the ethical implications of the Corinthians' role in that narrative, by looking at the experience of those who played an analogous role in the past.[33]

What is perhaps most striking, however, is that this kind of analogical reasoning is comparatively rare as the basis of Paul's ethical knowledge. In the majority of cases Paul's ethical discernment seems to involve a more direct attempt to understand the obligations which arise from the particular role which believers in Christ seek to occupy in the theological narrative. What is more, it is only in the context of this overarching story that Paul's analogical knowledge makes sense. For it is only because he knows that, for example, the Corinthians and the Israelites under Moses are playing similar roles in that narrative that he can assume so confidently that God will deal in the same way with both groups. In fact, the distinction between these two uses of narrative in Paul's ethical reasoning is blurred when we think again of his appeal to Christ as an ethical paradigm. For Jesus provides a pattern to be imitated, but this imitation is itself required by the plot of the overarching story.[34] This ambiguity simply serves to reinforce the fact that all of Paul's

---

[32] As G. Wenham observes, Paul "identifies the experiences of the exodus generation of the Israelites with those of the Corinthian church" (*Story*, 132). See too Witherington, *Narrative*, 38.

[33] Such ethical analogies, which seem to have real heuristic value for Paul, should probably be distinguished from simple illustrations from daily life. The latter remain disconnected from Paul's grand narrative and do not provide any new ethical insight. They simply serve to make his injunctions more vivid and memorable. See, e.g., Paul's appeal to athletic metaphors in 1 Cor 9:24.

[34] Indeed, the imitative aspect of Paul's ethical appeals to the Christ event are often dominant enough that Fowl could devote a very fruitful study to the Apostle's analogical ethical use of discrete "hymnic" narratives about Jesus (Phil 2:6–11; Col 1:15–20; 1 Tim 3:16b). See Fowl, *Story of Christ*. Fowl himself recognizes, however, that his "exemplar" model is not the only way in which story functions to shape Paul's ethics (*Story of Christ*, 207). As an example of a different approach Fowl points to Rom 6:1–11, where, he says, "Paul uses a series of metaphors to narrate how Christians have been transferred from the realm of sin into Christ, and to identify what this new identity entails for their relationship to the realm of sin" (*Story of Christ*, 207; cf. *idem*, "Uses of Story," 296–8).

ethical knowing appears to depend, not just on isolated paradigms to be imitated, but on the cosmic narrative as a whole. This may well be why we do not find Paul claiming to know specific ethical rules. His ethical knowledge does not consist first and foremost of such rules. Its content is, rather, the theological story itself and an understanding of how one must live in order to be raised with Christ in the final chapter.

4. Paul as a Narrative Ethicist

4.1. Paul's Ethical Knowledge and the (Re)discovery of Narrative Ethics

As we come to the end of our treatment of Paul's ethical knowledge, it would be good to pause and address what might be a suspicion in the reader's mind: Is this emphasis on a narrative structure in Paul's ethical thought not just another scholarly fad? The question is justified. Although their insights have been fruitful, some scholars have tended to write as if contemporary theories about narrative and ethics should simply be assumed as the basis for our reading of Paul. Fowl is well aware of the dangers of anachronism and of forcing a text into foreign analytical categories. One can understand, though, the skepticism of some readers when he writes that "Paul's ethics *necessarily* draw their force and coherence from a common narrative tradition which he shares with his audience," adding in a footnote that "any particular formulation of a tradition need not be cast as a narrative, but *it must be sustained by a narrative* as the ground of the tradition."[35] We have now seen that in fact Paul's theological knowledge *is* a story and his ethical knowledge is a matter of interpreting the immediate events of life in terms of that story,

---

[35] Fowl, *Story of Christ*, 208, 208 n. 3 (emphasis mine). Concerning his use of Thomas Kuhn's theory of exemplars, Fowl writes: "It may seem that linking Paul and T. Kuhn is a gross anachronism. We would answer this charge on two levels, historical and methodological. As a matter of historical fact the type of practical reasoning outlined above goes back to Aristotle and his concept of *phronesis*. . . . Even if this were not the case, we would argue there is no a priori reason why Kuhn's notion of exemplars should not be seen as heuristically useful for understanding a particular aspect of the Pauline corpus, as long as certain qualifications are recognized. We are not claiming that language about exemplars and analogy would have been intelligible to Paul and his audience. Rather, this is a description we have imposed from our own contemporary perspective on our exegetical findings" (ibid., 205–6).

learning to manoeuvre skilfully to a good end. Simply because so many writers have not given their narrative approach this kind of inductive, exegetical foundation, however, we should take a moment to ask just how applicable recent theories of narrative ethics are to Paul's thought.

By far the most influential theorist in this area is Alisdair MacIntyre, whose book *After Virtue* almost single-handedly set in motion the current wave of studies on "narrative ethics."[36] What many outside this field do not realize is that MacIntyre's book was primarily an historical and sociological study. While many of his disciples have simply taken his models and applied them wholesale to contemporary issues, MacIntyre himself began with an attempt to find the roots of our ethical vocabulary in pre-Homeric Greek civilization and to trace the shifts in their use over the centuries. In response to the contention that moral language is meaningless, MacIntyre sets out in *After Virtue* to rediscover the social and intellectual context in which that language once made sense. He argues that in pre-Homeric Greece language of "good" and "bad" was intimately tied to common stories, stories about what it meant to live and die well. Virtue, ἀρετή, was not some free-floating moral quality which was simply intuited. Rather, the Greeks had a very concrete sense of their obligations and duties within the πόλις and of what the ideal life looked like. This basic story of a life lived well was embodied over and over again in concrete tales which were not only entertainment but also the chief form of moral education. To have virtue, then, meant quite simply to have the qualities of the hero who succeeded in living that ideal life, to do what contributed to one's εὐδαιμονία. MacIntyre writes:

> If a human life is understood as a progress though harms and dangers, moral and physical, which someone may encounter and overcome in better and worse ways and with a greater or lesser measure of success, the virtues will find their place as those qualities the possession and exercise of which generally tend to success in this enterprise and the vices likewise as qualities which likewise tend to failure. Each human life will then embody a story whose shape and form will depend upon what is counted as a harm and danger and upon how success and failure, progress and its opposite, are understood and evaluated. To answer these questions will also explicitly and implicitly be to answer the question as to what the virtues and vices are.[37]

---

[36] See, e.g., Hauerwas, "Reforming"; *idem, The Peaceable Kingdom*; Goldberg, *Theology and Narrative*.

[37] MacIntyre writes that "the difference between the heroic account of the virtues and the Sophoclean amounts precisely to a difference over what narrative form captures best

MacIntyre goes on to argue that in fact there must be a narrative structure to any coherent ethical discourse,[38] and that the apparent bankruptcy of ethical categories in the modern West is a symptom of our peculiar modern loss of the narrative understanding of life and identity in which the notions of good and evil developed.[39]

Whether or not that further step in his argument works is, for our purposes, neither here nor there. For it is in the midst of that Greek culture, with its virtues and vices grounded as they were in stories about a good life, that Paul wrote his letters. Of course, MacIntyre does not say very much about the Jewish society which nurtured Paul even in a centre of Hellenistic culture such as Tarsus. One might argue that these concepts of virtue and vice are essentially foreign to that Jewish tradition, and thus that Paul's ethics need not be tied to a particular narrative. Still, the Jews were also a storytelling people, and it is not by accident that the Hebrew Bible is full of stories, stories which (as Gordon Wenham has recently reminded us) were considered Torah, instruction.[40] Surely, then, if MacIntyre's analysis of Greek ethical thinking is even broadly accurate, we should not be surprised to find a similar dependence on narrative in Israelite ethics as well.[41]

4.2. The Necessity of the Narrative Category in Paul's Ethical Knowing

Yet is it true that Paul's ethical discernment is fundamentally narrative in structure, that (as MacIntyre claims for the Greeks) it cannot properly be understood without reference to his theological story? After all, we seem in some cases to be able to talk about Paul's approach to an ethical issue without recourse to any narrative events. We can say that the Corinthian community constitutes a living temple without involving ourselves in obvious appeals to a story. Likewise, in 1 Corinthians 8:4 Paul seems to acknowledge that the Corinthian "gnostics" are right to deny that idols have any real

---

the central characteristics of human life and agency. And this suggests an hypothesis that generally to adopt a stance on the virtues will be to adopt a stance on the narrative character of human life" (*After Virtue*, 143–4).

[38] For a similar approach see Hauerwas, "Vision"; "Character, Narrative, and Growth."

[39] See *After Virtue*, 204ff.

[40] See Wenham, *Story*.

[41] MacIntyre himself suggested at least that the centrality of storytelling in moral education was common to ancient Mediterranean and Middle Eastern cultures generally (*After Virtue*, 121).

existence, and he does not immediately reject their resultant ethical conclusion that one may eat food which has been offered in pagan sacrifice. Can we not describe their ethical reasoning here as an inference drawn from their strong monotheism, without mentioning a theological story at all?

In one sense we must answer yes to these questions. In cases like these we may discuss the Apostle's approach to ethical knowing in purely non-narrative categories. Yet there remain clear advantages to speaking in narrative terms, even in passages where the narrative element is not immediately evident. On the one hand, a narrative description of Paul's ethical knowing allows us to perceive the common pattern in his ethical reasoning across a wide range of passages. The reason we question the necessity of narrative categories in some passages is that the theological substance from which Paul extrapolates an ethical imperative is in these cases not clearly an event. We have seen, however, that in other cases the theological substratum for the Apostle's ethics is transparently narrative in character, as when Paul appeals to the events of Christ's death and resurrection, the believer's identification with him, and the resurrection for which the believer hopes in the future. Moreover, theological ideas like the status of a community as a temple and the non-existence of pagan gods can also be understood as first-level analytic statements about Paul's grand narrative. The Corinthians are a temple because God chose them and sent the Holy Spirit to dwell in their midst in anticipation of the final eschatological restoration. The idols in Corinth have no power because it is only Israel's God who creates and only Israel's God who acts to save. By bringing out the dependence of these analytic statements on Paul's underlying theological story, we can see that in all these cases the Apostle follows a common approach to ethical reasoning, seeking to understand how the place of the "saved" in the events of that narrative constrains the activity of those who wish to play that role.

Still, this suggests only that there are certain heuristic advantages to viewing Paul's ethical reasoning through a consistently narrative lens. Can we say that there is an *irreducible* narrative pattern in the Apostle's ethical knowing? We saw above that Paul's theological narrative cannot be reduced to the pattern it represents, but can his ethical reasoning be reduced to a series of timeless principles, if we want to describe it in those terms? Paul does seem to be able to detach paradigmatic patterns of behaviour from their specific setting in the story. Israel's desert wandering, the support of the temple functionaries, even the self-sacrifice of Christ on the cross can all be employed by Paul to highlight a pattern of behaviour which believers in Christ are obligated to imitate or to avoid. As I suggested above, however, we should not pit this kind of paradigmatic, imitative use of narrative in Paul against the approach which locates human beings within the grand narrative, as if the Apostle could employ only one strategy or the other. In fact, the paradigmatic use of stories in Paul depends for its validity on the idea that the audience is acting within the same overarching narrative as Abraham and the Israelites and Christ. It is the connections in the grand narrative between the believer and each of those figures which make these episodes valid paradigms for Christian ethics. Since believers in Christ want to inherit the promise to Abraham by gaining a status as his sons, they must imitate his pattern of faith (Gal 2:6–9). Since they too are God's chosen people, the believers must beware of the "grumbling" and factionalism which derailed God's people in the past. Since they are "in Christ," they must follow the pattern of Jesus' death.

In the end it is precisely because Paul's theological story cannot be reduced to a non-narrative paradigm that his ethics also involve an irreducible narrative element. The key aspects of the narrative which constrain the behaviour of the "saved" are precisely the events which gain their primary theological significance for Paul as singular events, not as mere instances of a pattern. God's creation of the world, his promise to Abraham, the events of Christ's passion and resurrection, the Church's reception of the Spirit, the future restoration of God's world – these events are significant for Paul either because human beings are experiencing their lasting effects in the present or because they hope to experience them in the future. Thus, to the extent that Paul's ethics arise from the implications of these same events, his ethical reasoning involves a narrative element which cannot be eliminated.

This narrative element in Paul's ethical knowing is not identical to the pattern of ethics which McIntyre traced out in Greek culture. The narrative of an ideal life, which for McIntyre formed the kernel of Greek ethical thought, is comparable only to the paradigmatic, imitative dimension of Paul's ethical reasoning. With its thorough grounding in a larger narrative, however, the Apostle's ethical knowledge turns out to be even more profoundly determined by a story. For Paul, ethical reasoning is not simply a matter of trying to relive an ideal story. It is a matter of understanding oneself within a narrative which encompasses all of history, and trying to discern how one must live if one hopes to be among the blessed when the final chapter is played out.

Chapter Seven

Beyond Conceptual Knowledge

1. Non-cognitive Modes of Knowledge in Paul

1.1. Knowledge as Experience

In all of the varieties of knowledge which we have examined so far, Paul's knowing has been a matter of his having a certain kind of *conception* of some object. In traditional philosophical language, Paul's knowledge has been a matter of his claiming to have various true *beliefs*. But in some of the passages where Paul talks about knowing things his focus does not fall primarily on the beliefs of the knower.[1] In many of these passages Paul talks

---

[1] See γινώσκω, Rom 7:7; Phil 3:10; and possibly Rom 3:17 (which is complicated by its being a quotation from the LXX of Isa 59:8); 1 Cor 1:21; 2 Cor 5:21; Gal 4:9a; γνῶσις, 2 Cor 2:14; 4:6; 10:5; Phil 3:8; γνωρίζω, Col 1:27; ἐπιγινώσκω, 1 Cor 16:18; 2 Cor 6:9; and perhaps Col 1:6; ἐπίγνωσις, Rom 3:20; Col 1:10; 2:2; ἀγνοέω, 1 Cor 14:38b; 2 Cor 6:9; Gal 1:22; ἀγνωσία, 1 Cor 15:34; οἶδα, Rom 7:7; 2 Cor 5:11; 12:2a; Gal 4:8; Phil 4:12 (twice); 1 Thess 4:5; 5:12; 2 Thess 1:8.

We might also include ἐπίγνωσις in Rom 1:28, where retaining such knowledge of God is a matter of worshipping him (see Cranfield, *Romans* 1.128). In Rom 1:21, on the other hand, humanity's knowledge of God (γνόντες τὸν θεόν) seems to consist primarily of the theological ideas outlined in 1:20. It cannot include acknowledgement of God, since in 1:21 humanity holds this knowledge and yet fails to give God worship. On the other hand, when Paul speaks in Rom 7:1 to those who know the law (γινώσκουσιν . . . νόμον) he may well mean those who have an experiential familiarity with legal institutions.

Bultmann thinks that ἐπίγνωσις in Rom 10:2 implies the "obedient recognition" of God's will and not simply awareness or understanding of it (Bultmann, "γινώσκω," 1.707). True, Paul does say in 10:3 not only that Israel lacks knowledge of the righteousness of God but also that their crucial failure is a failure to *submit themselves* to that righteousness. Yet is their failure to submit themselves to God's righteousness a sign of their ignorance – because knowledge here includes such submission to God – or is it simply that they could not submit themselves because they did not come to the intellectual recognition that this message about God's righteousness was true? Likewise, Bultmann's reading of Rom 2:18

about knowing an object in the sense of having an *experience* of it.

Take, for example, Phil 4:12, where Paul reminds the Philippians, "I know what it is (οἶδα) to have little, and I know what it is (οἶδα) to have plenty." He is not claiming to have the right kind of beliefs here, but rather reminding them that he has had both of these kinds of experience. Similarly, in 2 Cor 5:21 the Apostle declares that "he [God] made him to be sin who knew no sin (τὸν μὴ γνόντα ἁμαρτίαν)." Surely this is supposed to mean not that Jesus had no conception of sin, but rather that he had no first-hand experience of sinning.[2] In 2 Cor 5:11 Paul describes himself as "knowing (εἰδότες) the fear of the Lord" and therefore trying to persuade others. This again means not simply that the Apostle has an idea of what such fear is like, but that he actually lives in the fear of the Lord. This fear of God which he is persuading others to adopt is not merely an idea but an attitude of submission to and reverence for God, and his point is that his persuasion of others grows out of his own experience of this way of living.

1.2. Knowledge as Personal Relationship

A specialized case of Paul's use of knowledge language to denote personal experience of something is his talk about knowing someone in the sense of having a relationship with that individual. When in 2 Cor 12:2 Paul says, "I know (οἶδα) a person in Christ who fourteen years ago was caught up to the third heaven," he is not primarily concerned with claiming to have certain beliefs about this person. He is saying that this is a person with whom he has had a relationship, with whom he has some direct familiarity. This is all the

---

and 2 Cor 5:16 in terms of "acquaintance" is unconvincing (Bultmann, "γινώσκω," 1.703–4).

[2] This is better than Bultmann's suggestion ("γινώσκω," 1.703) that we understand it in the sense of "mastery." The point is not about whether Jesus had mastered sin (whatever that would mean), but whether he had experienced it first-hand.

Likewise, in Romans 7:7 Paul says that he would not have known sin (τὴν ἁμαρτίαν οὐκ ἔγνων) apart from the law's influence (cf. the ἐπίγνωσις ἁμαρτίας in Rom 3:20). One could suggest that this is simply a matter of the law's framing certain actions in terms of a story, in the context of which those acts come to be understood as sin. Yet Paul seems to envision the law as actually provoking sin: ἀφορμὴν δὲ λαβοῦσα ἡ ἁμαρτία διὰ τῆς ἐντολῆς κατειργάσατο ἐν ἐμοὶ πᾶσαν ἐπιθυμίαν . . . (7:8). Indeed, it brought death to Paul (7:10). Thus, while the knowledge of sin here seems sometimes to be a matter of having an interpretive story which makes it visible (see 7:13), Paul can also understand knowledge of such a power in terms of experiential familiarity (so Bultmann, "γινώσκω," 1.703).

more plain when we realize that in this case the person about whom Paul is so delicately talking seems to be himself. He is not saying "I have good beliefs about this person" but "You can trust me on this because I have intimate familiarity with this person." Likewise, in Gal 1:22 Paul assures the Galatians that after his conversion he remained "unknown by sight" (ἀγνοούμενος τῷ προσώπῳ) to the churches in Judea. There is no question of the Judean believers not knowing about him, for Paul tells us that they were amazed at his conversion: "The one who formerly was persecuting us is now proclaiming the faith he once tried to destroy" (Gal 1:23). What Paul wants to convey is, rather, that they were not personally familiar with him.

1.3. Knowledge as Personal Recognition of Authority or Merit

This sort of direct familiarity is not the only non-cognitive mode in which Paul "knows." We also find in Paul what Bultmann somewhat misleadingly called the "Old Testament" view of knowing, in which "knowledge is also a movement of the will."[3] We have already glanced at the passage in 1 Cor 14:38 in which Paul insists that if a would-be prophet does not recognize Paul's writing as a command of the Lord, then that person "is not to be recognized (ἀγνοεῖται)." Plainly what Paul means here is that the person's claim to a prophetic role in the community should not be accepted. This does involve some cognitive content. The community members are not to interpret the pretender's actions in terms of the role of a legitimate prophet in the theological story. Yet, as Bultmann pointed out, a movement of the will is also involved here which was not involved with Paul's mundane and theological and ethical knowledge. To "know" people in this sense would be to recognize their legitimate role in the story and then act appropriately towards them.

In the case of the would-be prophets, this element of appropriate response would be a matter of, among other things, granting them a measure of authority. Yet this mode of knowledge need not be a matter of submission. In 1 Cor 16:18 Paul has been talking about people such as Stephanas and Fortunatus and Achaicus, apparently members of a delegation to Paul from the Corinthian church. Paul is thankful for the way in which "they refreshed my spirit as well as yours," and so he urges the Corinthians to "give recognition to (ἐπιγινώσκετε) such persons." This is not so much a matter of

---

[3] Bultmann, "γινώσκω," 704.

submitting to their authority as it is one of granting them honour in the community.[4] What is common to both of these passages, however, is that this knowledge involves not only a recognition of someone's role in the theological narrative, but also one's willingness to treat them accordingly.[5]

2. Paul's Knowledge of God/Christ

2.1. *"Knowledge of God" in the Old Testament*

By far the most frequent object of Paul's experiential and volitional knowledge is God himself, and here we cannot do justice to Paul's conception without at least a glance back at the way the writers of the Old Testament would speak of the "knowledge of God." As we do so, however, we must avoid the common tendency to say that this idea of knowledge as experience is characteristic of the "Hebrew mind," while the "Greek mind" occupies the more arid realm of objective, conceptual thought. C. H. Dodd, for example, wrote of the Greek knower, "it is the thing in itself, as static, that he seeks to grasp, eliminating in so far as may be its movements and changes, as being derogatory to its real, permanent essence."[6] This might be true enough if one were talking about Plato (and even there the issue is controversial), but such static idealism certainly does not represent all of

---

[4] See also 1 Thess 5:12, where Paul wants the Thessalonians "to respect (εἰδέναι) those who labor among you, and have charge of you in the Lord and admonish you." Clearly Paul expects that this "knowledge" will go along with a submission to their authority, but this is not his primary focus when he pens these words. He goes on in 5:13 to urge the people to "esteem them very highly in love because of their work."

[5] See also 2 Cor 1:13a, where Paul claims to write only about ἃ ἀναγινώσκετε ἢ καὶ ἐπιγινώσκετε. Thrall suggests that what Paul means by their "knowing" what he writes is actually their "acknowledgment" or active "recognition" of its truth or validity (*2 Corinthians*, 1.133; so Furnish, *2 Corinthians*, 128, and perhaps Martin, *2 Corinthians*, 19). Other commentators, however, tend to understand ἐπιγινώσκετε in 1:13a as "understand," so that Paul is emphasizing their ability (or the ability which they *ought to* possess) to understand his message (so Barrett, *2 Corinthians*, 73; Bultmann, *2 Corinthians*, 36, and perhaps Martin, *2 Corinthians*, 19).

[6] Dodd, *Interpretation*, 152. Bultmann ("γινώσκω," 1.689) writes that "γινώσκειν . . . denotes in ordinary Greek the intelligent comprehension of an object or matter, whether this comes for the first time, or comes afresh, into the consideration of the one who grasps it . . ."

Hellenistic philosophy, let alone popular Greek thought.[7] So it is important to recognize that the Greeks too can talk of knowledge in terms of immediate familiarity. Homer himself, in the *Odyssey* (21.35), said of Odysseus and his old friend Iphitus that they never shared a meal: οὐδὲ τραπέζῃ γνώτην ἀλλήλων.[8] A first-century decree boasts that a certain citizen of Olbia "had advanced to personal acquaintance with the Augusti (τῆς τῶν Σεβαστῶν γνώσεως)," that is, with Augustus and Tiberius.[9] This gives us cause to wonder whether when the tendency of the LXX translators to render ידע with γινώσκω, even where the "knowledge" is experiential, can really be explained in terms of their wooden adherence to one Greek equivalent for the Hebrew word.[10] On the other hand, while it is true that דעת does typically express this kind of knowledge by familiarity more often than, say, the Greek γνῶσις, we must not forget that Hebrew does have a verbal construction (the hiphil of נכר) which comes closer to the more "objective" use of γινώσκω.[11]

With this major caveat in mind, we may ask what the "knowledge of God" means in the Old Testament. More than anything else, this knowledge means, in the words of Johannes Botterweck, "*a practical and active recognition of God.*"[12] It is most often a passionate devotion to Yahweh. Mays describes the "knowledge of God" (דעת אלהים) which is so prominent in Hosea as

---

[7] E. R. Dodds' classic study *The Greeks and the Irrational*, while now somewhat dated, is still a very useful antidote to this tendency to view all of Greek civilization through the Platonic dialogues.

[8] Cf. Xenoph., *Cyr.* 1.4.27, where γινώσκω connotes the idea of friendship. So Strong, "Knowledge of God," 27.

[9] See M-M, 130. Deissmann suggests that this use of γνῶσις directly illuminates Paul's use of the noun for "familiarity" with Christ in Phil 3:8 (*Light*, 383, n. 8). Moulton and Milligan also point to an old and not unusual use of γινώσκω as a euphemism for sexual relations from the time of Menander, just as דעת is used in the Hebrew Bible (M-M, 127; see the references in Durham, *Vocabulary of Menander*, 51). The verb γνωρίζω is commonly used in the papyri in the sense "to recognize" another person (M-M, 129; P. Oxy. 7.1024.18; 6.976; P. Hib. 1.28.6), so the noun γνωστήρ can mean a "witness" of someone's identity (see P. Oxy. 3.496.16). The verb can also be used in a mystical sense, as in *Poimandres* 10.15. Note too how the phrase ἕως γνώσεως περὶ τῆς δίκης in P. Hib. 1.92.13 is translated by the editors "until the *decision* of the suit" (M-M, 129; cf. P. Hal. I. 1.25; P. Lond. 234.18).

[10] Lev 4:14, 23, 28; 5:3, 4, 17.

[11] See *HALOT*, 1.700.

[12] Botterweck, "Knowledge of God," 473. Italics original.

"Israel's personal response to the salvation-history of election and obedience to the requirements of the covenant."[13] God's desire, according to the prophet, is for "steadfast love and not sacrifice, the knowledge of God rather than burnt offerings" (Hos 6:6). Indeed, throughout the Old Testament those who "know" God are those who "seek" him (Ps 9:11[10]),[14] who "serve" him wholeheartedly (1 Chr 28:9), who "return" to him (Hos 6:3 [cf. 6:1]), who show "steadfast love" (Hos 2:19–20 [MT 2:21–22]; 6:6).[15] To have the "knowledge of God" is to live in the "fear of the LORD" (Prov 2:5; cf. 9:10). Hence, when the people forget God and worship idols they show that they do not "know YHWH." As Hosea writes, "Their deeds do not permit them to return to their God. For the spirit of whoredom is within them, and they do not know the LORD" (Hos 5:4).[16]

Along with this devotion, the knowledge of God entails an ethical way of life. To know God is to live in harmony with the divine will, and only the righteous can enjoy that knowledge. Thus Jeremiah warns Jehoiakim in no uncertain terms:

> Are you a king because you compete in cedar? Did not your father eat and drink and do justice and righteousness? Then it was well with him. He judged the cause of the poor

---

[13] Mays, *Hosea*, 63–4.

[14] Although in Ps 9:12(11) it is actually God's name which is known (יוֹדְעֵי שְׁמֶךָ), this is clearly a circumlocution for YHWH himself. Isa 58:2 is less clear: it is God's "ways" which are known by those who seek him. In Hos 10:12, however, the declaration that it is time to seek YHWH (וְעֵת לִדְרוֹשׁ אֶת־יְהוָה) is a call to the same repentant obedience which is described as "knowledge of God" in 6:3, 6. The equivalence of the two expressions is underlined by the fact that in both 6:6 and 10:12 this knowledge is set in parallel with חֶסֶד.

[15] Note how in Isa 19:21, where it is predicted that Egyptians will "know YHWH," this means that they will perform acts of cultic worship to him.

[16] Cf. Jer 2:8; 4:22; Hos 4:6, 10. In 1 Sam 2:12 the sons of Eli are described as not "knowing YHWH" (לֹא יָדְעוּ אֶת־יְהוָה), and this manifests itself in their desecration of the cult. In Isa 1:3 Israel's apostasy is described as a lack of knowledge, though here there is no explicit object of the knowing.

1 Sam 3:7 is unusual in that here the knowledge of God seems to be less a matter of proper devotion than of intimate relationship. We are told that "Samuel did not yet know the LORD, and the word of the LORD had not yet been revealed to him." This does not mean that Samuel lacked devotion to YHWH, but simply that he was not yet on speaking terms with the deity. This passage should likely not be understood, however, as exhibiting a completely different idea of "knowing God." Rather, here the idea of relationship (which is always present in talk about knowledge of God) is emphasized, while the element of proper devotion recedes into the background.

and needy; then it was well. Is not this to know me? says the LORD. (Jer 22:15–16; cf. Hos 2:19–20)[17]

Likewise, it is when his Torah is inscribed on the hearts of the people that God says they will all "know" him (Jer 31:33f.). Indeed, Isaiah foresees a time when "they will not hurt or destroy on all my holy mountain" because "the earth will be full of the knowledge of the LORD" (Isa 11:9). On the other hand, when the knowledge of God is missing in Israel, this manifests itself in corrupt dealings between human beings (Jer 9:2[3]; Hos 4:1f.) and in Israel's refusal to turn from wickedness (Hos 5:4). When Israel abandons the knowledge of God, the result is, as Walter Harrelson writes, "an age of violence, of breaking all boundaries."[18] Moreover, those who do not know God, whether Israelite or not, face not only chaos but also divine judgement. So the Psalmist prays, "Pour out your anger on the nations that do not know you, and on the kingdoms that do not call on your name, for they have devoured Jacob and laid waste his habitation" (79:6–7; cf. Jer 10:25).[19]

---

[17] See also Deut 4:39–40, where knowing "that the LORD is God in heaven above and on the earth below" is closely tied to keeping "his statutes and his commandments." Cf. Jer 9:23(24).

[18] Harrelson, "Knowledge of God," 12.

[19] See also Job 18:5–21, where we read of horrific punishments and are then told: "Surely such are the dwellings of the ungodly, such is the place of those who do not know God."

We should also acknowledge here the similar talk in the OT about knowing that God is YHWH. The refrain "know that I am the LORD" draws many of Ezekiel's oracles of judgement and blessing to a close (e.g., Ezek 6:7, 13; 12:20; 15:7; 25:7, 11, 17; 26:6; 28:22, 23). Zimmerli argues that the formula "know that I am the LORD" originates in "the sphere of legal examination in which a sign of truth was demanded" (*Ezekiel*, 1.37). Thus, to know that God is YHWH is to receive a demonstration proving, and at the same time revealing, God's unique identity. Zimmerli also observes, however, that this knowledge formula always follows a description of the great acts of God which the people will experience. Thus this knowledge that God is YHWH is not detached assent to some theoretical affirmations. It is a *recognition* of God's identity which flows from the experience of YHWH as he destroys the high places, desolates the altars, and lays waste Judah's towns (*Ezekiel*, 1.38). It is the acknowledgement of YHWH as the one who ends the mourning of Jerusalem, who brings the people back into their land and establishes an eternal covenant with them (Ezek 16:59–63; 20:42, 44; 24:19–27; 28:24, 26; 29:21; 34:27; 36:11, 38; 37:6, 13–14; 39:22, 28). Indeed, in Ezek 20:5, 9, the divine voice says that it was in the exodus, with the establishment of the covenant, that YHWH made himself known to Israel. Hence, in 25:14 the prophet can exchange the formula "then they shall know that I am LORD" with the declaration "they shall know my vengeance" (cf. 17:21).

2.2. Paul's Knowledge of God

When we turn back to Paul it does not take long to realize that when the object of Paul's knowing is God himself it is usually this same kind of relationship of which he is thinking.[20] In these contexts, at least, Bultmann is right that "[k]nowledge of God is a lie if it is not acknowledgement of him."[21] Knowledge of God is, for the Apostle, a matter of shifting from the hostile opposition which is humanity's default state into a harmonious relationship with the Creator. So the Gentiles are, by definition, those who do not know (τὰ μὴ εἰδότα) God (1 Thess 4:5).[22] Likewise, in Gal 4:8–9 the Galatians were ignorant of God (οὐκ εἰδότες θεὸν) prior to their conversion, but now know him (γνόντες θεόν).[23] This passage is particularly instructive when we notice how Paul immediately stops himself and adds, as if by way of an

---

This knowledge is precisely the recognition of God as God which arises from an experience of his deeds. Notice too that in Ezek 20:11, 12, 20 the regular practice of the Sabbath seems intended to embed this recognition of YHWH's identity in Israel.

In Ezekiel the formula "know that I am the LORD" does seem often to lack the idea of intimacy and ongoing relationship which is present in other Israelite talk of "knowing God." In many places God promises to make foreign nations "know that I am YHWH," not only when they see Israel restored by God (36:23; 37:28; 39:7; cf. 36:36) or see Gog destroyed at his hand (38:16, 23), but also when they themselves are destroyed (29:6, 9; 30:8, 19, 25, 26; 32:15; 39:6; and see perhaps 35:15). Yet language about "knowing" that God "is YHWH" also appears elsewhere in the OT (Exod 6:7; 16:12; 29:46; 1 Kgs 20:13, 28; cf. Exod 16:6; Deut 4:35; 2 Kgs 5:15), and in these cases outside Ezekiel the construction seems to include the idea of relational familiarity more prominently. Since this acknowledgement of God as God springs from experience of his involvement in history, it also entails a recognition of God's reliability, a trusting dependence on Israel's God as the one who saves (see, e.g., Deut 7:9; Ps 100:3). In fact, knowledge of God and "knowledge that God is YHWH" are not clearly distinguishable outside Ezekiel (see Jer 9:23–25[24–26]; 24:6–7; Exod 5:2; Judg 2:10).

[20] So Piper, "Knowledge," 44. Zimmerman ("Knowledge of God," 475) understands the element in Paul's knowledge of God which he owes to the OT as "*an expression of genuine religious feeling.*" This formulation does not do justice to the powerfully ethical and soteriological character of Paul's knowledge of God (both of which Zimmerman elsewhere acknowledges), but it does highlight the element of devotion. See, e.g., 2 Cor 4:6, where, in order to give the believers this "knowledge of the glory of God," he "has shone in our hearts."

[21] Bultmann, *Theology*, 1.213.

[22] So Dupont, *Gnosis*, 1–2. See also 2 Thess 1:8.

[23] There is little evidence for the distinction which Bultmann saw between οἶδα and γινώσκω here ("γινώσκω," 1.705). Cf. above, pp. 89–90, n. 2.

afterthought, μᾶλλον δὲ γνωσθέντες ὑπὸ θεοῦ . . . The Galatians' knowledge of God might more accurately be understood as their having been *known by* God. This reluctance to speak simply of the Galatians knowing God suggests that Paul's emphasis in his talk about "knowledge" here is not on the cognitive content of the Galatians' beliefs, but rather on their conversion, the shift in their allegiances, and the salvific relationship with God which resulted.[24] Perhaps in order to guard against the impression that the choice and reconciliation were entirely the Galatians' doing, he shifts the agency to God. It was God who brought them near, God who transferred them from a hostile camp to his own. The emphasis falls not on what narrative one has in mind but rather on the end goal of those narratives, allegiance to God and the relationship with him which that allegiance makes possible. Thus, when Paul reminds the Corinthians that the world, through its wisdom, did not know (οὐκ ἔγνω) God, the positive counterpart to this lack of knowledge is God's salvation of those who believe (1 Cor 1:21).[25] As in Jer 10:25 and Ps 79:6, those who do not share this knowledge of God face "flaming fire" and "vengeance" when God's judgement is realized, though for Paul this event is located at Christ's parousia (2 Thess 1:7–8).

For one to emerge from spiritual ignorance into the knowledge of God is not, for Paul, simply a matter of adopting new beliefs. It involves devotion and worship. Whether or not Paul believed that the sequence of events narrated in Rom 1:18–32 actually took place in a primordial age, it is instructive to observe the relationship there between knowledge of God and proper worship. In Rom 1:21 Paul describes humanity initially as knowing God (γνόντες τὸν θεόν) through the created order, but not worshipping him as God (οὐχ ὡς θεὸν ἐδόξασαν). It seems that their knowledge of God calls for a certain kind of worship, a relational response which fits God's unique character.[26] Indeed, when they refuse to give God proper worship, the knowledge which requires that worship is lost. The result in 1:22–23 is that their knowledge turns to folly (ἐματαιώθησαν ἐν τοῖς διαλογισμοῖς αὐτῶν) and they descend to a ludicrous worship of animals. So, in 1:28, Paul says that they did not see fit to retain their knowledge of God (οὐκ ἐδοκίμασαν τὸν θεὸν ἔχειν ἐν ἐπιγνώσει). To abandon their proper devotion to God was

---

[24] So Strong, "Knowledge of God," 74.

[25] So Fee, *1 Corinthians*, 72.

[26] So Strong, "Knowledge," 47.

at the same time to abandon the knowledge of him, the familiar relationship with him, which that worship sustained.[27]

Even clearer in Paul is the way in which, as in the Old Testament, the knowledge of God involves for Paul a willingness to obey the divine will.[28] In 1 Thess 4:5 Paul defines the righteousness which he wants to encourage in them by contrasting it with the "lustful passion" of "the Gentiles who do not know (μὴ εἰδότα) God" (see vv. 3–5). In 2 Thess 1:8 "those who do not know (μὴ εἰδόσιν) God" are "those who do not obey the gospel of our Lord Jesus." Paul's strategy in 1 Cor 15:34 – to shame the Corinthians into abandoning their sin – involves pointing out that this is the way of life which characterizes an ignorance of God (ἀγνωσίαν . . . θεοῦ). Even in 2 Cor 10:5, where Paul describes his fight against "arguments and every proud obstacle raised up against the knowledge of God," this knowledge involves a particular moral will. The Apostle's description of these "proud obstacles" which are exalted against God evokes images of idolatry and certainly suggests that the knowledge of God which is being attacked involves the opposite – fitting devotion to the Creator.[29] Yet, in order to keep one's hold on this knowledge, Paul says that he must also "take every thought captive to obey Christ." It comes as no surprise, then, when in Col 1:10 we find that Paul can talk about walking in a way which pleases God, bearing fruit, and then restate this way of life in terms of growing in the knowledge of God.

As was evident in the Old Testament, this knowledge is not simply a matter of having experience of something. For Paul, knowledge of God does involve some cognitive content. Paul implies as much in 2 Cor 10:4, where his defence of his knowledge (γνώσεως) of God against "every proud obstacle" involves controlling his *thoughts*. Yet even here, as we have seen, this knowledge cannot be reduced to merely having the right conceptions about the deity. The knowledge of God is for Paul, just as much as for his

---

[27] See also Wis 13:1ff., where those who "were ignorant of God" are described as "foolish in nature," and this foolishness issues in idolatry. In 14:8–11 the sage describes a future judgement on this folly, while in 14:12–14 such idolatry is linked to sexual immorality. Hence a lack of knowledge of God results, as in Rom 1:18–32, in all other sin, and in both passages this lack of knowledge is linked with idolatry, improper worship. The difference is that, for the sage, idolatry is the result of ignorance, while for Paul ignorance springs from idolatry.

[28] So Dupont, *Gnosis*, 2.

[29] So Strong, "Knowledge of God," 68–9, 94, 100.

Hebrew ancestors, a relationship in which one responds with loving obedience to the God who is encountered in history.

2.3. Paul's Knowledge of Christ

The new note sounded in Paul's talk about the "knowledge of God," however, is the remarkable way in which Christ, a human being, becomes involved as a mediator of that knowledge – and even as an object of this devotion in his own right.[30] When God gives the believers "the light of the knowledge of the glory of God," they meet this knowledge "in the face of Jesus Christ" (2 Cor 4:6). Indeed, what God makes known (γνωρίσαι) in Col 1:27 is "the riches of the glory of this mystery, which is Christ in you, the hope of glory," and in Col 2:2 Paul's desire is that the Laodiceans will have "the knowledge (ἐπίγνωσιν) of God's mystery, that is, Christ himself." In 2 Cor 2:14 he praises the God who "in Christ always leads us in triumphal procession, and through us spreads in every place the fragrance of his knowledge (τῆς γνώσεως αὐτοῦ)."[31] Whose knowledge is this? The pronoun "his" (αὐτοῦ) is ambiguous, but in the following verse the ambiguity is resolved when Paul writes that "we are the aroma of Christ . . ." (2 Cor 2:15). It is thus the fragrance of the knowledge of *Christ* which the believers radiate into the world. Christ himself has become an object of the same special knowledge which had before been reserved for God alone.

Lest we imagine that this knowledge of Christ is somehow inferior to the knowledge of God, we must recognize that for Paul this knowledge of the crucified saviour is tantamount to salvation itself. In Phil 3:8, for instance, Paul declares that his knowledge of Christ (γνώσεως Χριστοῦ) is so exceedingly valuable that he considers all else "loss" (ζημίαν) in comparison.[32] Already the implication is that salvation itself must lie in this knowledge of Christ, and in the following sentence Paul rephrases his declaration of profound devotion by saying that he is willing to consider everything else dung (σκύβαλα) in order to "gain Christ" (Χριστὸν κερδήσω).

---

[30] So Zimmerman, "Knowledge of God," 476.

[31] My adaptation of the NRSV translation.

[32] It is commonly assumed that in these verses Paul is thinking of his experience on the Damascus road (e.g., Dupont, *Gnosis*, 35). We should note, however, that this experience is nowhere mentioned explicitly in Phil 3, and that Paul's focus here seems to lie less on the

Surely to gain Christ (and likewise, then, to know Christ) includes for Paul the experience of the salvation which Christ brings. Notice too that the things which Paul gives up for the sake of this knowledge are the marks of Jewish piety which he has just mentioned. He was "circumcised on the eighth day, a member of the people of Israel, of the tribe of Benjamin, a Hebrew born of Hebrews; as to the law, a Pharisee; as to zeal a persecutor of the church; as to righteousness under the law, blameless" (Phil 3:5–6). These are precisely those things which mark a Jew as a faithful member of the covenant. Thus, to know Christ is more important to Paul than to maintain these old marks of his salvation, of his "knowledge of God" in the old sense of that expression. To know Christ is to gain a salvation which cannot be gained anywhere else.

Nor can we overlook the way in which, in Phil 3:9, Paul so closely associates "gaining" Christ (and thus "knowing" him) with being "found in him." Knowledge of Christ is thus inseparable from that very identification of the believer with his lord which looms so large in his theological story. To know Christ is to somehow share in his cross and in his resurrection. So we read in Phil 3:10 how the Apostle desires

> to know Christ (τοῦ γνῶναι αὐτόν) and the power of his resurrection and the sharing of his sufferings by becoming like him in his death, if somehow I may attain the resurrection from the dead.

Here is the root of the "peculiarly personal intensity" which G. B. Caird saw in Paul's knowledge of Christ.[33] To know Christ is not simply to have the right concepts about him, nor is it simply to be devoted to him. It is not simply a matter of changing one's life to conform with Christ's will, though this is present in Paul's thought as well.[34] Knowledge of Christ includes all of these things, but more than that this knowledge is for Paul a matter of somehow living Christ's life along with him, passing through his passion and yearning for the day when he will experience Christ's resurrection.[35]

---

point in time when knowledge of Christ was gained than on the contrast between the old state and the new one in Christ.

[33] Caird, *Letters from Prison*, 137; so Zimmerman, "Knowledge of God," 476. Cf. Piper, "Knowledge," 45: "for Paul [knowledge of Christ] is primarily the experience of the risen Lord's operation in the life of his church. . ."

[34] Notice, e.g., how in Rom 16:26 the knowledge of Christ which goes out to the Gentiles is εἰς ὑπακοὴν πίστεως.

[35] Cf. Pope, "Faith and Knowledge," 424.

5. Summary: Living the Story

Our goal in this section has been to see whether we could discern in the objects of Paul's knowing any consistent logical structure. What we have found is that Paul's knowledge falls into four distinct categories. The first three of these categories are different kinds of conceptual knowledge. Paul knows, in the first place, about many ordinary events and observable patterns in everyday life. This is his *mundane* knowledge, and in this sphere there is little to distinguish Paul from the average inhabitant of the Roman world. More interesting for our purposes is what we have termed Paul's *theological* knowledge. Here we discovered that when Paul's knowledge moved beyond the mundane sphere of ordinary life, it consisted of a story. The Apostle's individual claims to theological knowledge turned out to be allusions to a grand narrative of humanity's relationship with its Creator.

We saw that this theological story is not an end in itself for Paul, but led us naturally into his *ethical* knowledge. This third category of Paul's knowledge consisted of a hermeneutical skill, the skill of setting the mundane events of one's life properly into the context of the theological story. Here again, however, we found that this narrative interpretation of ordinary events served a purpose beyond itself. For the goal of Paul's ethical knowledge is to live out a good role in that theological narrative in the hope that one will live to experience the blessed life which it offers the elect. At this point Paul's conceptual knowledge comes to an end and points beyond itself to a *knowledge of God and of Christ* which is not merely intellectual. This knowledge is a matter of direct familiarity with the divine Person. It involves being related to God in an attitude of humble worship and obedience, and even more comes for Paul to mean that one is identified with the life of Christ himself, lives out his passion, and waits to experience his resurrection.

What conclusions should we draw from this? Among other things, the narrative structure of Paul's theological knowledge helps us to understand why, as exegetes have been realizing for some time now, Paul's "theological" and "ethical" teachings are so intimately intertwined.[36] Paul's ethical

---

[36] So Victor Furnish: "Because the indicative and imperative aspects of Paul's preaching are so vitally interrelated, it is an exceedingly difficult task to single out and summarize the peculiarly 'ethical' aspects of his gospel. In an important sense the exposition of the themes of Paul's preaching has already, and in the most appropriate way, revealed the character of

knowledge grows out of the conjunction of the theological story with the events of life. The hermeneutical element which enters into Paul's approach to knowledge at this point, as he interprets his "small" story in light of the larger story of God's action in Christ, also confirms the insights of Lührmann, Keck, Becker, and Moores which we surveyed at the end of Part One. The logic assumed in Paul's talk about knowledge is an interpretive, hermeneutical logic.

At the same time, I must not claim too much for this section. We have not surveyed all of Paul's theology or ethics, but have remained narrowly focussed on those theological or ethical statements which constitute the content of the Apostle's statements about "knowledge." This knowledge does seem to be identical to what Paul "thinks" and "believes," and it is tempting at this point to suggest that the interpretive logic which we have uncovered structures all of Paul's thought.[37] It remains to be seen, however, whether this same logic is present in Paul's arguments more generally. We must also ask how much exegetical weight can be carried by my narrative description of the Apostle's theological knowledge. Does that narrative category in particular help us to better understand Paul's reasoning as it appears in his letters? With both of these questions in mind, we turn now to examine the letter to the Galatians as an extended sample of Paul's argumentation.

---

the Pauline ethic" (*Theology & Ethics*, 207). Nor is this situation unique to Paul among early Christian writers. In fact, Hauerwas' account of the rise of "Christian ethics" as a discipline suggests that it was not until the rise of medieval ethical casuistry that ethics was perceived as an enterprise distinct from theology (see his "Christian Ethics").

[37] Note how, e.g., Paul can make the same ideas the object of λογίζομαι in Rom 3:28 and οἶδα in Gal 2:16. In Rom 14:4 the ethical "faith" of 14:1–2 is the fruit of ethical "judgement" (κρίνων), and what he knows seems to be identical with what he has confidence in (πείθω; see Rom 14:14; 2 Cor 5:11; Phil 1:25; Phlm 21). Paul's knowledge often has the same content as his belief (πιστεύω; so Binder, *Der Glaube*, 17; Bultmann, *Theology*, 1.318). In 1 Cor 1:23 Paul sums up the substance of the Christian message as "Christ crucified," and this is the proclamation which in 1:21 brings salvation to "those who believe (τοὺς πιστεύοντας)." In 2:2, however, Paul says that he resolved to *know* nothing (οὐ . . . τι εἰδέναι) when he was with the Corinthians except "Jesus Christ and him crucified" (cf. πίστις in 2:4–5). See also the use of γινώσκω and πιστεύω for the same content in Rom 10:17–19; 14:1–2, 14; 1 Cor 15:1–2; 2 Cor 4:13–14; 1 Thess 4:13–14. Compare Rom 6:9 with 10:9; Rom 6:3–4 with 6:8. See also the identical contents of πίστις and ἐλπίς in 2 Cor 1:7 and Phil 1:19–20.

Part Three

Coming to Knowledge in Paul's Letter to the Galatians

Chapter Eight

Reading the World: Paul's Narrative Reasoning

We are only now coming to the point of my interrogation of Paul. Having uncovered the narrative structure in Paul's knowledge, we are now ready to take a closer look at the kind of interpretive reasoning the Apostle encourages when he leads his audiences to knowledge. In this part of the study we will focus on Paul's letter to the Galatians and examine the logical structure of the Apostle's arguments as he tries to offer his audience convincing reasons for placing their confidence in his version of the Gospel.[1] As we uncover the logic of Paul's reasoned arguments we will be able to infer from this logic something about how the Apostle assumes human beings can come to religious knowledge.

1. Emplotting Paul and His Audience (Galatians 1:1–2:14)

1.1. The Galatians' Hazardous Role (1:1–9)

Although Paul's epistolary opening in 1:1–5 is not explicitly argumentative, we find that already the Apostle is preparing for the argument to follow by carefully locating himself and his audience within his theological story. In an unusually long and elaborate self-identification[2] Paul introduces himself as "an apostle" (one commissioned and sent on a mission[3]) who was "sent

---

[1] On my reasons for selecting Galatians, see above, pp. 6–7.

[2] So Dunn, *Galatians*, 25; R. N. Longenecker, *Galatians*, 4. Romans furnishes the only Pauline introduction which is more elaborate (Rom 1:1–6).

[3] Sandnes is right that the unusual expression here – where the title ἀπόστολος is followed by prepositional phrases supplying the agents who sent (or did not send) him – emphasizes the verbal meaning underlying the term: "one being sent" (*One of the Prophets*, 66; so Martyn, *Galatians*, 83). As Dunn observes, Christians put an increasing amount of theological weight on this common word, and we should understand its sense in Paul here on the basis of the specification which follows (*Galatians*, 25; so Martyn, *Galatians*, 82).

neither by human commission nor from human authorities" (1:1). The one who sent him, who authorized his message, is no mere human being, but "Jesus Christ and God the Father, who raised him from the dead" (1:1).[4] Paul is claiming at the outset that he is an authorized messenger of the God who, in Christ, is rescuing humanity. The implicit thrust of this self-identification is that the Galatians cannot play off other authorities against him or decide that someone else knows better.[5] If they want to occupy a good role in the story, to play the role of "the saved," they must heed the Apostle's word, for his message is the message of the God who saves. Paul's terse identification of the addressees as "the churches of Galatia," while undoubtedly signalling his unhappiness with their conduct, still locates his audience within his theological narrative as members of "churches," communities of those being saved, communities of people aligned with God's act of restoration (1:2b).[6]

The customary wish for "grace and peace" which follows the address (1:3–5) is again greatly expanded and provides a dense reminder of the narrative within which this identity makes sense.[7] Jesus "gave himself for our sins to set us free from the present evil age," and this happened "according to the

---

On the origins and development of the Christian use of ἀπόστολος see Betz, *Galatians*, 74–5; R. N. Longenecker, *Galatians*, 2–4; Rengstorf, "ἀπόστολος"; and P. Barnett, "Apostle" and the literature cited there.

[4] Martyn (*Galatians*, 85) notes that God and Jesus are both identified here primarily by their *action* in the passion and resurrection (so R. N. Longenecker, *Galatians*, 5), reinforcing the impression that Paul's theology has a narrative shape. Bryant observes that only here and in Romans does Paul refer to the crucifixion or resurrection in the opening of a letter, suggesting that Paul is concerned here to bring this basic element of the narrative back to the Galatians' minds and establish an "apocalyptic framework" for what follows (*Crucified Christ*, 114–115).

[5] Here Paul clearly wants to emphasize his independence from other authorities. It is less clear whether Paul faced a prior charge that he *was* dependent on others, though the emphatic position of this reference to his apostleship, combined with its antithetical form as a denial and refutation, suggests that he is rebutting such a charge (so Betz, *Galatians*, 39; Bryant, *Crucified Christ*, 113; Burton, *Galatians*, 2–3; Dunn, *Galatians*, 25; R. N. Longenecker, *Galatians*, 4).

[6] So Bryant, *Crucified Christ*, 116–17. Betz notes the terseness of this identification, which lacks the usual "epithets and polite compliments" (*Galatians*, 40; cf. Rom 1:7; 1 Cor 1:2; 2 Cor 1:1; Phil 1:1; 1 Thess 1:1).

[7] Bryant (*Crucified Christ*, 120–3) suggests that the unusual or stereotyped vocabulary in vv. 4–5 may indicate that Paul is drawing on confessional material with which the Galatians are familiar.

will of our God and Father" (1:4). Paul reminds the Galatians right at the outset of the letter that they are claiming to stand among those who benefit from God's act of salvation in Christ. Indeed, he accepts that as "churches" they are at present heading towards a good end. At the same time, however, he reminds them that not everyone is so fortunate. The present age is "evil" and it is out of this whole order that the Galatians have been rescued by God's mercy. As Paul ends his epistolary prescript in verse 5 with a short doxology, one cannot help but detect a threat lying just below the threshold of speech: that if the Galatian believers continue to reject Paul's message, they will be rejecting the God who sent him, and this must threaten their identity as "churches," as those who are being rescued from this evil age.

Leaving aside the usual thanksgiving and prayer for the addressees' wellbeing,[8] in 1:6–9 Paul leaps directly into a confrontation with the audience: "I am astonished that you are so quickly deserting the one who called you in the grace of Christ . . ." (1:6).[9] Here too the Apostle does not actually argue, but asserts his own position by elaborating in more detail the "emplotment" of the Galatians which he began in the letter's opening. Paul makes explicit the claim which was only hinted at by the silences in his extended address: that their current practice threatens to undermine their identity as "the saved." Their actions are those of apostates, those who have abandoned God.[10] Describing this apostasy in terms of his theological narrative, Paul says that they are abandoning "the one who called you in the

---

[8] So Dunn, *Galatians*, 38–9; R. N. Longenecker, *Galatians*, 13; Jegher-Bucher, *Galaterbrief*, 24. See Rom 1:8ff.; 1 Cor 1:4ff.; Col 1:3ff.; 1 Thess 1:2ff.; 2 Thess 1:3ff.; Phlm 4ff.

[9] There is general agreement that this section presents the reason for writing the letter (Jegher-Bucher, *Galaterbrief*, 39; R. N. Longenecker, *Galatians*, 13; Martyn, *Galatians*, 109), and my division here follows that of Martyn (*Galatians*, 106–7). Betz (*Galatians*, 16) sees 1:6–11 as an "exordium," but his analysis still recognizes a shift from v. 9 to v. 10, since he identifies vv. 1:10–11 as a "transitus" or "transgression." Several commentators extend this section to 1:10 (so Burton, *Galatians*, 18; R. N. Longenecker, *Galatians*, 12–13), but this construal of Paul's argument blurs the shift in verse 10 from his outrage at the Galatian situation to his defence of his own independence.

[10] So Dunn, *Galatians*, 40; R. N. Longenecker, *Galatians*, 14; Martyn, *Galatians*, 108. BDAG (642 [3]) points out that ὁ μεταθήμενος is sometimes used as an epithet for a certain Dionysius, "who left the Stoics and adopted Epicureanism" (see Diog. L. 7.166; Athen., *Deipnos*. 7.281d). This language was also used to describe the apostasy of Jews in 2 Maccabees (so Dunn, *Galatians*, 39–40; 2 Macc 4.46; 7.24; 11.24).

grace of Christ" (1:6). They are "turning to a different Gospel," which is in fact not a gospel at all (1:6c–7a) but a false narrative which does not lead them to salvation. The visiting teachers in Galatia, far from being a positive influence, are "disturbing" the believers there (ταράσσοντες), as one stirs up insurrection in a city.[11] They "want to pervert (μεταστρέψαι) the gospel of

---

[11] This is the first mention of the Galatian "opponents," a group which most regard as a band of Jewish-Christian missionaries who have entered Galatian communities and who are identified as the source of the problematic teaching. Mark Nanos has recently challenged this consensus view, suggesting that they were members of the established Jewish communities in Galatia responsible for the supervision of proselytes. Yet Paul's description in 1:7 of the "influencers" as θέλοντες μεταστρέψαι τὸ εὐαγγέλιον τοῦ Χριστοῦ (while not an objective description of their work) strongly suggests that these people understood themselves as teachers of the Christ-message. This same impression is reinforced by Paul's curse on any who *preach a Gospel* other than Paul's own (εἴ τις ὑμᾶς εὐαγγελίζεται παρ' ὃ παρελάβετε . . .). Given that Paul's whole reason for this curse seems to be to impugn the activity of those who are "disturbing" the Galatians, it is significant that the curse covers only self-consciously Christian teachers. For Paul never uses εὐαγγελίζομαι except in the technical sense, "to proclaim the Christian Gospel." This curse certainly calls into question Nanos' claim that the Apostle does not challenge the status of the "influencers" as righteous members of God's people (*Irony*, 84). The opponents' belief in Christ also seems to be presupposed by Paul's charge in 6:12 that they are motivated by a desire to escape "being persecuted for the cross of Christ" (τῷ σταυρῷ τοῦ Χριστοῦ μὴ διώκωνται). Nanos suggests (*Irony*, 223) that these "influencers" worry about reprisals from civil authorities if some who claim Jewish identity (and the accompanying exclusion from civic cults) are not fully identifiable as Jewish (i.e., are uncircumcised), but in this case it would be strange for Paul to isolate Christ's cross (as opposed to, say, uncircumcision) as the source of pressure.

Nanos also challenges the usual view that these opponents were outsiders, pointing out that Paul's use of the third person to refer to them may be a rhetorical attempt to isolate opponents who would otherwise be seen as a part of the Galatian communities (*Irony*, 159–71; cf. Thurén, *Derhetorizing*, 66–7, and Munck, *Paul and Salvation*). At the same time, if the opponents were Christian teachers inculcating a message at variance with Paul's own, it is unlikely that they would have arisen from the Galatians' own ranks at this early stage. Moreover, we must notice that the Galatian letter is written to all the communities of a region and yet seems to assume that the same problem exists in all of these places: teachers encouraging circumcision. Nanos suggests that Paul is simply assimilating different local issues to the same pattern, rhetorically claiming that various local phenomena all amount to the same thing (*Irony*, 183–4). Yet his view would still require that all the Galatian churches began to desire circumcision at the same time. This is most easily explicable if they were all visited by members of the same group of travelling teachers (so Lightfoot, *Galatians*, 29).

Nanos also criticizes the label "opponents" for those seeking to "influence" the Galatian

Christ" (1:7). This is hardly the role in which Paul's opponents in Galatia would cast themselves, but that is precisely Paul's point. Their preaching relies, he argues, on a faulty version of the Christian narrative and so leads to a dangerous misconstrual of the kind of behaviour which leads to a good end. Thus, right at the outset, we find Paul situating his Galatian audience within his telling of the theological story in an attempt to convince them that their present actions place them in a perilous role. He has not yet provided any *reasons* for accepting his own construal of the theological story over that of the opponents. What he has done, however, is to emplot the audience within his version of that narrative, and so to highlight just how much is at stake for the audience.

1.2. A Methodological Interlude: Focussing on Paul's Reasoned Argument

This polemical emplotment of his audience is not, of course, the only instrument of persuasion which Paul brings to bear in these opening verses. The Apostle is also engaging in a rhetoric of authority designed to win a favourable hearing for his message. So the Galatians are being addressed by God's own apostle, the one chosen directly by divine powers and not through any intermediary (1:1). Wrapped up with this rhetoric of authority is a rhetoric of shaming which appears not only in Paul's refusal in his opening to

---

believers (*Irony*, 119–27). Yet, whether or not these individuals understood themselves as Paul's opponents, Nanos himself admits that this is certainly how Paul understands them (*Irony*, 120–21). Since the Apostle is opposing them, they are his opponents, and the label need mean no more than that. Thurén has suggested that much of the personal polemic against these "opponents" may actually be standard rhetorical vilification, the terms of which were often "so well-known to both parties in communication, that no-one took them at their face value" (*Derhetorizing*, 66–7; cf. DuToit, "Vilification"). He argues that the Galatians' beliefs have been deliberately caricatured in an effort to "exaggerate and redefine them, to reveal their 'true nature'" (*Derhetorizing*, 69). The difficulty with this approach is that it is difficult to corroborate. Moreover, elements such as Paul's curse in 1:8–9 and his wish that the opponents castrate themselves in 5:12 are difficult to read simply as rhetorical flourish. On the other hand, Paul's description of the Jerusalem council seems to confirm that at least some *did* try to compel (ἠναγκάσθη) Titus' circumcision (2:3), suggesting that for some of Paul's contemporaries compliance with this rite *did* represent a pressing concern, and not just a "slightly different nuance" (contra Thurén, *Derhetorizing*, 71). Paul also seems to be responding in 1:10–2:14 to direct challenges to his apostolic authority emanating from within the Galatian community. If such challenges were being made, they increase the likelihood that those teaching circumcision in Galatia also understood themselves to be Paul's opponents.

offer the Galatians the usual polite commendations, but also in his expression of amazement at the course of action they are considering (θαυμάζω, 1:6). These non-rational elements of the letter's persuasive strategy remind us that, as speech-act theorists have long observed, communication is always a complex act of which the cognitive, rational component is only one element.[12] The non-rational, affective elements of Paul's speech-act deserve to be taken with full seriousness, and we will note as we go some of the other points in the letter at which they come to dominate Paul's speech to the Galatians.

At the same time, we must not fall into the reductionist trap of treating these non-rational elements of Paul's strategy as the "real" content of the letter, as if his use of reasoned argument were mere window dressing or a rationalization after the fact of convictions established on other grounds.[13] As important as the non-rational level of his rhetoric may have been, a brief glance at the whole of Galatians will show that the Apostle did not feel this level sufficient to lead his audience back to knowledge. After all, in the bulk of the letter the predominant element of Paul's speech act is neither a call to accept his authority nor a direct appeal to the Galatians' emotions, but an attempt to persuade by means of reasoned arguments. What is more, when these rational and non-rational elements in the Apostle's rhetoric converge in the apostolic curse of 1:8–9, Paul deliberately subordinates the non-rational to the rational. He declares: "But even if we or an angel from heaven should proclaim to you a gospel contrary to what we proclaimed to you, let that one be accursed!" (1:8). Although Paul, as God's commissioned agent, is able to announce the judgement which lies ahead for those who reject the path of faith in Christ, he does not want his audience to accept that message *simply* because an authoritative figure is speaking it.[14] The message is here prioritized over the messenger, so that neither Paul nor any other representative of God should be heeded if their message is inconsistent with

---

[12] See Austin, *How to Do Things with Words*.

[13] Austin, the founder of speech-act theory, did not take such a reductionist view. Rather he emphasized that "constative" speech-acts, conveying "ideas" by making "statements," are themselves a kind of "performative" speech-act, an act in which the speaker uses words to affect the hearer in some way – in this case affecting the way in which he or she thinks (see Austin, *How to Do Things with Words*, 132–46).

[14] Martyn is right (contra the implication of Betz, *Galatians*, 52–3) that both Greek and Jewish readers would understand this as *God's* curse (*Galatians*, 114).

the authentic Gospel.[15] Betz has pointed out that a parallel blessing is pronounced in 6:16 on those who follow Paul's "rule" (τῷ κανόνι τούτῳ), so that the whole body of the letter becomes not just an act of communication but an act of *confrontation* in which the Galatians are forced to decide between reverting to Paul's gospel to receive blessing or following the opponents to receive the curse.[16] The Galatians' response to Paul's words here does become a matter of life or death.[17] Yet the Apostle apparently does not expect their response to hinge primarily on their recognition of his own authority. It is, rather, on the reasoned argument which constitutes most of the letter that Paul places most of his hopes to convince the Galatians that they should trust his message, his version of the story, and thus his account of who will reach a good end. It is on this basis that the analysis of Galatians which follows will focus primarily on the rational level of argument, bracketing out the non-rational rhetoric of authority and of shaming – again, not because these levels of Paul's rhetoric are unimportant for understanding the letter as a total speech-act, but because the Apostle himself subordinates them (in theory and practice) to his reasoned argument.

---

[15] So Dunn, *Galatians*, 44–5; R. N. Longenecker, *Galatians*, 17. If, as most commentators now agree, the προειρήκαμεν of 1:9 indicates that Paul had announced a similar curse (or teaching to the same effect) in his earlier teaching to the community (so Betz, *Galatians*, 53–4; Burton, *Galatians*, 29; R. N. Longenecker, *Galatians*, 17; Martyn, *Galatians*, 115; contra Bruce, *Galatians*, 84; Schlier, *Galater*, 40), this would suggest that the priority of the Gospel message over the authority of the messenger was a stable feature of Paul's thought and not simply an ad hoc ploy to undermine the opponents in Galatia. Dunn (*Galatians*, 47–8) observes that the expression "what you received" (ὃ παρελάβετε) in 1:9 appeals to the fact that his message "was not theirs alone but already traditional" (so R. N. Longenecker, *Galatians*, 18; cf. 1 Cor 11:23; 15:3; Gal 1:12; 1 Thess 2:13; 2 Thess 3:6). Given his insistence in 1:12ff. on his independence from human traditions, Paul likely thought of his own teaching as the start of a new tradition in his communities, rather than the handing on of earlier tradition (contra Martyn, *Galatians*, 149–51).

[16] So Betz, *Galatians*, 25.

[17] Dunn suggests that instead of God's active judgement Paul may have been thinking more about a heretical teacher's being "set apart to God," that is, isolated from the community so that no more harm could be done (*Galatians*, 46–7). Paul is more likely thinking of the term ἀνάθεμα as it was used in the LXX to translate חֵרֶם – "ban" – where it denotes something devoted to God for destruction (so R. N. Longenecker, *Galatians*, 17; see Lev 27:28–29; Deut 7:26; 13:17; Josh 6:17–18; 7:11–13, 15; and cf. Rom 9:3; 1 Cor 12:3; 16:22). Betz finds a close parallel to Paul's curse in *1QS* II 5–17 (*Galatians*, 51).

1.3. Paul's Extraordinary Role (1:10–2:14)

Against this focus on the reasoned argument in Galatians, one might object that all of 1:10–2:14 is geared simply to establish Paul's authority, and hence the audience's obligation to accept his version of the Gospel. Here already, however, we must notice that the Apostle does not simply assert his authority. Instead he takes the time to make a rational argument, to present evidence on the basis of which he believes the Galatians should rationally be led to accept his claim to be God's apostle. In 1:10–12 Paul answers what seem to be challenges to his credibility which were circulating in Galatia[18]: "Am I now seeking human approval or God's approval?" he asks, apparently countering a charge that he panders to his Gentile audience (1:10).[19] It is at this stage that Paul first begins not only to assert his polemical position but also to give some reasons for it. Paul's initial response is simply to ask

---

[18] Most recognize that these verses contain the "thesis" of the first, defensive section of the letter (so Burton, *Galatians*, 35; Dunn, *Galatians*, 52; Jegher-Bucher, *Galaterbrief*, 39–40; R. N. Longenecker, *Galatians*, 20; Martyn, *Galatians*, 136). I have followed the division of Martyn here (*Galatians*, 136–7). Some commentators include v. 10 with the previous section and begin a new section with v. 11 (so Bryant, *Crucified Christ*, 134–5; Burton, *Galatians*, 18; Dunn, *Galatians*, 51; R. N. Longenecker, *Galatians*, 18, 20). As Betz recognizes, however, these verses belong together, since together they introduce Paul's denial of the opponents' charge (v. 10) and his counter-assertion (v. 11, beginning with γνωρίζω . . . ὑμῖν), the point which he will try to establish in the *narratio* which follows (*Galatians*, 46; cf. Jegher-Bucher, *Galaterbrief*, 40–42). Separated from v. 11, v. 10 becomes a disconnected "emotional outburst" (so R. N. Longenecker, *Galatians*, 18).

The relationship of vv. 11–12 to the surrounding verses is likewise disputed. Hester argues that vv. 11–12 constitute the *stasis* of apologetic rhetoric in which the speaker rebuts the basic charge against him (so Sandnes, *Among the Prophets*, 52; Jegher-Bucher, *Galaterbrief*, 39–40). Betz assigns v. 11 to the end of the *exordium* and v. 12 to the beginning of the *narratio*, but the Apostle does not actually begin narrating his defence until v. 13. Note how in his positive "thesis statement" of v. 12 he alludes to the Damascus road incident but then does not return to that incident in the (strictly chronological) narrative until vv. 15–16. Formally, this division at the end of v. 12 is also suggested by the two γνωρίζω ὑμῖν formulae which occur in v. 11 (introducing his defensive thesis) and v. 13 (introducing the evidence for it).

[19] So Burton, *Galatians*, 35; Dunn, *Galatians*, 49; R. N. Longenecker, *Galatians*, 18; Martyn, *Galatians*, 142; Sandnes, *One of the Prophets*, 56–7. Some have argued that the Galatian opponents presented their teaching simply as the completion of Paul's own (so P. Borgen, "Paulus"). Open hostility seems to be implied, however, by Paul's reference in Gal 4:13–20 to having become their "enemy" (ἐχθρός), and by the sheer length of Paul's explanation of his authority in 1:10–2:14 (so Sandnes, *Among the Prophets*, 51).

whether such a charge is really credible: "If I were still pleasing people, I would not be a servant of Christ" (1:10b). It is tempting to hear in these words an allusion to the hostility and violence which Paul's Gospel so often prompted. He then turns to make his own counterclaim to be a messenger sent directly from God. "For I want you to know," Paul says, "that the gospel that was proclaimed by me is not of human origin (κατὰ ἄνθρωπον)" (1:11).[20] Here Paul makes explicitly the same claim which was implicit in 1:1. His message is authoritative not because of some inherent quality of his own, but because the message itself comes directly from God. In verse 12 the Apostle then summarizes the evidence for this claim that his message is God's message: "for I did not receive it from a human source, nor was I taught it, but I received it through a revelation of Jesus Christ" (1:12).[21] His claim to have a message from God is credible because it was taught to him directly by God in "a revelation of Jesus Christ." Paul is probably alluding to his Damascus road experience here,[22] and we need not decide how explicitly the content of Paul's Gospel was communicated in this vision. What is important to note is that Paul's authority derives not from institutional sanction but from a unique religious experience. It is what Max Weber called "charismatic" authority. Yet this is not simply a matter of basing knowledge on heavenly disclosures. For, as Dunn points out, Paul clearly placed (in 1:8) the Gospel revealed to him on the Damascus road in a different category from the products of the "ordinary" heavenly visions which seem to have been common in Second-Temple Judaism and in early Christianity.[23] He situates Christ in a unique relationship to God, different from the position enjoyed by

---

[20] Martyn (*Galatians*, 142) understands κατὰ ἄνθρωπον here to mean something like "according to human expectations" or "according to human standards of judgement," so that Paul is denying any point of contact between ordinary human reason and the Gospel message. Yet, as Burton points out, the phrase (common in Greek literature) can mean simply "human," in which case Paul would be making a global denial that his is a "human" message (*Galatians*, 37). In what sense is it not human? Verse 12 suggests that Paul's concern is primarily with its origin in divine revelation.

[21] We need not decide here whether the genitive Ἰησοῦ Χριστοῦ, which modifies δι' ἀποκαλύψεως, designates Christ as the source of the revelation or as its content.

[22] So Dunn, *Galatians*, 53; Sandnes, *Among the Prophets*, 53.

[23] So Dunn, *Galatians*, 54.

the angels.[24] Hence, to be addressed directly by the risen Christ was for Paul something very much like being addressed face to face by the Creator. This is why he can claim that to reject his message is tantamount to rejecting God, why he can warn that a divine curse will fall on those who depart from his Gospel.

At this point we should observe that, again, Paul's reasoned argument is decisively shaped by his theological narrative. We have seen above how Paul's opening offers a version of the story and then "emplots" the Galatians within it, based on their current behaviour. In much the same way, the Apostle makes his own claim to authority by pointing to his own actions and experiences and arguing that these events locate him in a very specific narrative role – the role of God's messenger. His primary mode of argumentation is a kind of narration in which he alludes to certain aspects of his life story and suggests, in light of those events, how that individual story should be integrated into the larger universal narrative. Hence it is no surprise that from 1:13 to 2:14, where Paul offers the evidence for his claims to an authoritative role, he proceeds by way of a chronological narration of several key aspects of his life story. Negatively, Paul reasserts the narrative of his own life as one who was not taught or authorized by Jerusalem. He lays out an account of his contacts with Jerusalem authorities (the most likely human basis for any delegated or more indirect authority) to show that, in fact, he had no opportunity either to be catechized by Peter, James, and the others or to be sent out under their aegis.[25] Positively, Paul's reference to his Damascus road experience reminds the audience that this event is difficult to construe as anything other than a commission to carry out a specific role in

---

[24] See, e.g., Mehrdad Fatehi's study of the relationship between Christ and the Spirit in Paul (*The Spirit's Relation to the Risen Lord*).

[25] There is general agreement that 1:13–2:14 function as a large unit to substantiate the claims made in 1:11–12 (see Burton, *Galatians*, 43–4; R. N. Longenecker, *Galatians*, 26; Martyn, *Galatians*, 152–3), though there is less agreement about whether (and how far) this unit extends past 2:14 (see Martyn, *Galatians*, 152–3).

This is the section identified by Betz as the *narratio* in which the facts relevant to Paul's defence are recited. Dunn agrees that this new section begins in 1:13 (*Galatians*, 55). Betz begins the *narratio* in v. 12 (*Galatians*, 58), while Hester argues that vv. 13–14 are transitional and should not be regarded as part of the *narratio* proper ("Rhetorical Structure," 228–9; so Sandnes, *Among the Prophets*, 52). This disagreement highlights how smoothly Paul shifts into the *narratio*, lending an element of arbitrariness to any sharp line of division between the two.

the theological story – that of an apostle of God. Of course, the force of this argument depends on his audience's already accepting that the broad Christian narrative is true. But given the context of that story, Paul suggests that the events of his life clearly indicate what role in the narrative he occupies. Thus, even as Paul tries to bolster his own apostolic authority in Galatia, he supports that authority with a reasoned argument whose logic resembles the interpretive activity by which Paul's narrative knowledge gives rise to ethical insight. This is a logic in which the events of Paul's life are taken as clues by means of which one can recognize which role he is playing in the theological narrative, and hence how he should interact with other human beings.

2. Paul's Narrative Logic of Reconfiguration

2.1. Narrative and Experience in Damascus and Jerusalem

In 1:13–2:14 this narrative mode of argument remains fairly straightforward, describing the role which Paul is playing in the theological narrative and pointing to the specific actions and events which demonstrate that he does indeed play this role. Starting in 2:15, Paul's argumentative logic is marked by a more complex interpretive relationship between human experiences and the narrative which constitutes their hermeneutical framework. It is important, however, to note the hints in this direction which appear already in Paul's allusions to his experience on the Damascus road in 1:13–16. As the Apostle describes the event, it was clearly Israel's theological narrative which provided the interpretive context within which this experience found its meaning. Paul's own theological story, as I outlined it in Part Two of this study, was based on the elements of Israel's scriptural narrative, along with common Second Temple elaborations. It described the relationship between Israel's God and his creation, a creation which is rebellious and suffering, but which God is rescuing. God's restoration is expected to come in a great eschatological transformation, an event which will include the resurrection of the dead, and it will be inaugurated by God's Messiah, emerging from Israel. As the Apostle describes his Damascus road experience in 1:12 and 1:15–16, it occurred at a point in his life when these common Jewish narrative elements would have constituted his entire theological story. It is thus important to observe that when he refers here to that experience, Paul does not offer a neutral phenomenological description. He describes the experience *as it would be interpreted in the context of his Jewish narrative*. He did not simply encounter a mysterious apparition of an executed man. He met the crucified messianic pretender from Nazareth after this man had been raised from the dead. He met the Messiah ("Christ" in 1:12) whose claims had been vindicated by God and who would now bring the eschatological restoration. It is only in the context of Israel's story that Paul could interpret his encounter in this way. It is, moreover, only in that narrative context that the experience could have the implications for Paul's life that he believes it did: he is to preach the message that God is offering salvation in Christ.[26] So not only does Paul's theological narrative identify the agent of the vision, but it is also the context within which Paul understands the specific message which the vision conveyed. The narrative of Israel serves as the "code" in light of which the "sign" which he encountered on the Damascus road becomes intelligible.

At the same time, this event itself, once it is interpreted in the context of Israel's story, seems to effect for Paul an irrevocable change in the significance of that narrative. The Apostle understands that revelation as a commission to preach salvation in Christ "among the Gentiles" (1:16). Whether or not Paul immediately understood his experience in this sense is not, for the moment, our primary concern.[27] My interest lies not in the process by which Paul actually came to his convictions, but rather in his own later account of that shift. As Paul goes on to describes the Jerusalem meeting in 2:1–10 and his confrontation with Cephas in 2:11–14, the encounter on the Damascus road, once interpreted within Israel's narrative, seems to have

---

[26] Notice that in 1:15 the experience is interpreted, using motifs from Israel's prophetic tradition, as the call of Israel's God to one who has been chosen to carry his message. The act of proclaiming that message is denoted with the verb εὐαγγελίζομαι in 1:16, a term which is likely derived in Christian use from Isaiah and which often denotes the announcement of God's eschatological blessing for Israel (see Isa 42:9; 52:7; 60:6; 61:1 and cf. Joel 4:5 [3:5]; Nah 2:1[1:15]; Ps 39:10[9]; 68:12[LXX 67:12]; *Pss. Sol.* 11:1). The identification of the addressees of this message as "Gentiles" (ἐν τοῖς ἔθνεσιν) in 1:16 also presupposes the Jewish distinction between God's chosen people, Israel, and the rest of the nations. Hence the term presupposes the narrative of Israel's election.

[27] For various models of the relationship of this event to Paul's later thought, see Dunn, "Light to the Gentiles"; Kim, *Origin of Paul's Gospel*; Lüdemann, *Paul*, 188–91; Munck, *Paul and the Salvation of Mankind*; Segal, *Paul the Convert*; Stendahl, *Paul among Jews and Gentiles*; Theissen, *Psychological Aspects*, 177–265.

given rise to a new understanding of that very story. His commission seems to have issued in a new "Gospel" (2:2, 5, 14) in which Jesus is the Christ, the one through whom salvation comes. This is already an expansion or extension of Israel's story. What is more, when Paul lays out this new Gospel to the Jerusalem leaders, it appears to be one in which God's eschatological salvation is offered to non-observant Gentiles such as Titus (2:1–3). Paul's experience, once interpreted as a commission to preach salvation to the Gentiles, seems to have required a rereading of Israel's story in which Gentiles are fully included in God's people if they place their faith in the Christ.[28] Indeed, the intense resistance of the "false brothers" in Jerusalem (2:4), the evident caution of the Jerusalem "pillars" (2:6–10), and the concern of James and Peter over Paul's practice of common meals (2:11–14) all demonstrate just how radical was the re-imagining of Israel's story which Paul says was prompted by his commission.

The Apostle's experience, as he depicts it, thus seems to have stood in a dialectical relationship to Paul's earlier understanding of Israel's theological story. The story provided the framework within which his experience outside Damascus took on meaning, but that "emplotted" experience in turn exercised an interpretive counterpressure of its own and brought new meaning to the original narrative.[29] This interpretive logic is here only implicit. It must be inferred from Paul's description of his "call" and its interpreted significance, all of which the Apostle relates in order to make a more straightforward argumentative point. Yet Paul's description of later events in 2:1–10 also

---

[28] This inclusion of non-observant Gentiles may not have been unknown in Second-Temple Judaism. Both *Joseph and Aseneth* and *Aristeas* seem to assume that the adoption of ethical monotheism, without any observance of the distinctly Jewish aspects of Torah, is sufficient to qualify Gentiles as righteous. For many Jews, however, it seems to have been assumed that Gentiles would be saved only through a mass conversion in the eschaton (see, e.g., Tob 14:6; *Sib. Or.* 3:616–17; 3:710–23; and probably *Pss. Sol.* 17:31–2). Some texts envision large-scale destruction of Gentiles in the eschaton (see, e.g., Sir 36:1–12; *T. Mos.* 10:7; *Pss. Sol.* 17:24; cf. Judith 16:17 and Tob 13:12, where those nations hostile to Israel will be punished in the eschaton). In some cases this destruction seems to include all who will not convert (*Sib. Or.* 3:670–701), while in other cases all Gentiles are destroyed (*1QM*; *1 En.* 90:19). For an excellent summary of the variety of opinions about the fate of the Gentiles, see Donaldson, *Paul*, 51–80. Note that Paul himself, in 2:15, seems to assume that Gentiles are sinners: ἡμεῖς φύσει Ἰουδαῖοι καὶ οὐκ ἐξ ἐθνῶν ἁμαρτωλοί.

[29] Bryant sees this "interpretive importance" of Christ's resurrection to be signalled already in 1:1 by the Apostle's opening focus on that event (*Crucified Christ*, 143).

allows us to infer a similar kind of hermeneutic at work in the minds of Peter and the others at the Jerusalem meeting. In 2:7 the Apostle reported that those leaders "saw (ἰδόντες) that I had been entrusted with the gospel for the uncircumcised" and that this mission was comparable to Peter's. The Jerusalem group came to a new understanding which Paul sums up in the following verse: "he who worked (ὁ . . . ἐνεργήσας) through Peter making him an apostle to the circumcised also worked through me (ἐνήργησεν καὶ ἐμοί) in sending me to the Gentiles" (2:8). Dunn is probably right that we should hear in the verb ἐνεργέω some "experiential overtones": "What was evidently decisive in the consideration of the Jerusalem leadership was the recognition, or perhaps inability to deny, that Paul's missionary work was having precisely the same results among the Gentiles as Peter's among their fellow Jews."[30] What would be the evidence of such divine activity? Dunn suggests that Paul could probably point to "observable signs of the Spirit's presence among Paul's converts,"[31] charismatic experiences and apparently miraculous events which both Paul and the Jerusalem leaders would interpret (in the context of the theological story) as the activity of God's Spirit.

If Dunn is right in this reading of 2:8, then Paul would here be alluding to an interpretive logic very much like that which we see at work in the account of this same meeting in Acts 15. There Peter refers to what appears to be concrete evidence that the Gentiles had received the Spirit through his own preaching (15:8), while Paul and Barnabas are said to have "told of all the signs and wonders that God had done through them among the Gentiles" (15:12). It is this experiential evidence, interpreted in light of the traditional Jewish eschatological narrative, and especially with reference to the prediction of Amos 9:11 (see 15:13–19), which convinces Peter, James, and the others to accept Paul's law-free mission. The account of Acts 15 cannot, of course, be taken without further discussion as a reliable description of the events in Jerusalem, but neither for that matter can Paul's own account in Gal 2:1–10. What is important is that in Galatians 2 the Apostle seems to assume an interpretive process very much like the one depicted in Acts 15.

Yet notice that in the Acts account these reports of religious experiences among Paul's Gentile converts, though interpreted in the context of the traditional Jewish–Christian narrative, still come as a surprise. Although the

---

[30] Dunn, *Galatians*, 106.

[31] Dunn, *Galatians*, 105. See, e.g., 3:2, 5.

events gain their meaning in terms of the traditional story, that story did not on its own allow the Jerusalem leaders to predict them. The experiences of Paul and his converts thus introduce something genuinely novel to the narrative. More than that, once these events have been understood as signs of the Spirit, the undeniable reality of uncircumcised Gentiles having received that Spirit forces a re-evaluation of the whole prior story. Just as the story gave meaning to the events, so the events (once interpreted) recast the meaning of the pre-existing story.

2.2. A Theoretical Interlude: The Experience of Narrative

This dialectical interplay of story and experience, evident both in Paul's description of his "call" and in his account of subsequent events in Jerusalem, recalls Moores' description of the Damascus road event as a "sign" which produced a new "code" for interpretation. I suggested in Chapter III that this sign must not have produced the new interpretive code *ex nihilo*. Somehow the interplay between the sign and Paul's *prior* interpretive code must have led not only to the interpretation of the sign itself, but also to the *re*interpretation of the very code which gave it meaning. This is precisely the kind of interpretive situation which we can infer from Paul's account of these two events in Gal 1:10–2:14. Since our discussion of Moores' semiotic approach, however, we have seen that the signs and codes which the Apostle employs have a narrative shape. Moores' semiotic model did not furnish us with the theoretical tools to account for the transformation of Paul's interpretive code. How exactly does a sign, in being interpreted, alter the code which gave it meaning? Could it be that the narrative dimension of Paul's knowing is crucial to any successful account of the logic which governs the interplay of sign and code, of story and experience?

In order to follow up this possibility we must stop for a moment to examine the experience of following any narrative, whether read or heard. For this purpose we will look to Wolfgang Iser's phenomenology of reading, which has become in many ways the point of departure for other studies of narrative experience. Iser begins by observing that the individual sentences of which a story is composed do not by themselves constitute a coherent narrative. That coherence is, rather, given to the story by the reader or auditor. As one reads a text or hears a story told one is called on to take the sentences as "component parts" and bring them together in an act of interpretive synthesis to form a comprehensive "world."[32] This is not a completely free process.[33] The author of a story places subtle indications in the sentences themselves as to how they are to be joined together.[34] Likewise, the sentences themselves or their particular collocation usually provide cues as to the "genre" in terms of which the story should be understood, furnishing the audience with a rough structural sketch of the shape which the completed story will take. Still, in order to be brought to fruition as a story, "the literary text needs the reader's imagination, which gives shape to the interaction of correlatives foreshadowed in structure by the sequence of the sentences."[35] Neither completely free nor completely constrained,[36] the activity of reading is an imaginative process in which the audience strives to arrange the ideas conveyed by the sentences in a way which allows them to yield a consistent pattern of meaning.[37]

To the extent that stories require this active synthetic participation on the part of the audience, they are very much like paintings, road signs, or other visual signs which require decoding. The chief difference between stories (which can be reduced to visual signs but can also be communicated through sound) and these visual signs, however, is that the experience of stories is temporal and directional in a way that other signs are not. Whereas in a painting all of the elements are simultaneously available to the eye, in the

---

[32] Iser, *Implied Reader*, 277.

[33] Iser writes: "The author of the text may, of course, exert plenty of influence on the reader's imagination – he has a whole panoply of narrative techniques at his disposal . . ." (*Implied Reader*, 282).

[34] Iser, *Implied Reader*, 277.

[35] Iser, *Implied Reader*, 277. Iser continues: "These connections [between sentences] are the product of the reader's mind working on the raw material of the text, though they are not the text itself – for this consists just of sentences, statements, information, etc." (ibid., 278). "The product of this creative activity," he writes, "is what we might call the virtual dimension of the text . . . This virtual dimension is not the text itself, nor is it the imagination of the reader: it is the coming together of text and imagination" (ibid., 279).

[36] Iser writes: "This whole process represents the fulfilment of the potential, unexpressed reality of the text, but it is to be seen only as a framework for a great variety of means by which the virtual dimension may be brought into being" (*Implied Reader*, 279).

[37] Iser, *Implied Reader*, 283. Iser notes how "even in texts that appear to resist the formation of illusion [i.e., a consistent pattern], thus drawing our attention to the cause of this resistance, we still need the abiding illusion that the resistance itself is the consistent pattern underlying the text" (ibid., 284).

experience of a story (whether read or heard) the sentences emerge into consciousness gradually and in a prescribed sequence. Yet, as with a painting, the meaning of each element depends on its place in the whole work, in the overall pattern which in Chapter V we called (following Hays' use of Aristotle and Frye) the *dianoia* of the story, in contrast to the *mythos* or sequence of events. This means that in experiencing a story, as one moves through the *mythos*, the one-after-the-other of its actions, one must constantly project the shape of the sentences which have not yet been encountered so as to imagine the completed *dianoia*, or pattern in which each event in the sequence becomes meaningful. The sentences which make up the work are, for Iser, "always indications of something that is to come, the structure of which is foreshadowed by their specific content."[38] Each sentence, as it is encountered, shapes the audience's expectations about the whole which is emerging,[39] and it is within the context of that whole that the sentences which have been read thus far are understood.

As we move forward through a story, however, these expectations about what lies ahead are often frustrated and so must constantly be revised.[40] Iser explains that "each intentional sentence correlative opens up a particular horizon, which is modified, if not completely changed, by succeeding sentences."[41] A character whom we thought to be reliable may turn out to be a villain in disguise. As new sentences change our expectations about the shape of the whole story, all that we have already encountered in the narrative may take on a new meaning. Each sentence in the story must now be understood within this newly imagined whole, this new *dianoia*. "While these expectations arouse interest in what is to come," Iser writes, "the subsequent modification of them will also have a retrospective effect on what has already been read. This may now take on a different significance from that which it had at the moment of reading."[42] So, for example, the hero of what we took to be a serious detective novel may in the third chapter fail to escape the plotting of his murderous opponent and come to a painful end. Suddenly we are forced to abandon our expectation that the hero will solve

---

[38] Iser, *Implied Reader*, 277.

[39] Iser, *Implied Reader*, 277–8.

[40] Iser, *Implied Reader*, 278.

[41] Iser, *Implied Reader*, 278.

[42] Iser, *Implied Reader*, 278.

his case. Even more than this, we are forced to ask whether in fact this is really a detective story or whether it is a specimen of a different genre. Perhaps, we think, it may actually be a tragedy focussed on the futile attempts of society to curb overpowering primary human instincts through law and order. All that we remember in those first three chapters now takes on a new significance. This new context allows us "to develop hitherto unforseeable connections" between the elements of the story; it "brings to light new aspects of what we had committed to memory."[43] Finally, having elicited this new configuration of what we have already read, the new sentence, scene, or event is itself recast in light of this newly enriched "past," "thus arousing more complex anticipations."[44]

This process of anticipation, frustration, and reconfiguration does not unfold uniformly or smoothly as we proceed through the narrative. When we come to a sentence with no clear connection to what has gone before we experience some surprise, or even shock.[45] At the death of our detective-hero we may experience a momentary interpretive vertigo in which we are no longer sure how to make sense of the story as a whole. Such points of apparent incongruity represent "gaps" in the matrix of the text which the reader must "fill in" by positing a specific connection and thus restoring the unity of the "virtual" world being presented.[46] As we encounter such gaps the indeterminacy of the text is heightened, for different members of the audience may make different decisions about how to fill them.[47] Still, consistency of pattern is the mark of "better" readings. That interpretation which can best include every element of the story is the one which should be preferred.

The last aspect of this description of the experience of a story which we must borrow from Iser is his observation that progress through the story as it is told is not necessarily correlated with progress through the time of the story world. This movement of interpretation and reinterpretation, although it constantly shifts back and forth between the audience's past (the sentences we have already heard) and the audience's future (the sentences we expect to

---

[43] Iser, *Implied Reader*, 278. "Every sentence," Iser adds, "contains a preview of the next and forms a kind of viewfinder for what is to come; and this in turn changes the 'preview' and so becomes a 'viewfinder' for what has been read" (ibid., 279).

[44] Iser, *Implied Reader*, 278.

[45] Iser, *Implied Reader*, 279.

[46] Iser, *Implied Reader*, 280.

[47] Iser, *Implied Reader*, 280.

hear), need not be matched by a smooth chronological arrangement of the events in the story. A surprising event met halfway through the story as it is told could take the form of a flashback to an event which actually occurred (in the world of the story) *prior* to the events which had been narrated up to this point. Yet that flashback can, in the audience's experience of the story, have the same effect on the audience's experience as a surprising event which is chronologically subsequent. What is important is that it follows next in the *audience's experience* of reading and thus has the power to force a re-understanding of all that has come before.

2.3. Reconfigurational Logic in Damascus and Jerusalem

With this model of experiencing a story in hand, we can see how both Paul's new understanding following his experience on the Damascus road and Peter's insight at the Jerusalem meeting seem, in Paul's portrayal, to arise when they treat their experience of life in the world as new episodes in a traditional narrative. As he set out for Damascus, Paul seems to have understood himself within the traditional story of Jewish apocalyptic. This is a story which in its early "chapters" (those contained in Israel's Scriptures and other oral and written traditions which Paul learned early on in life) already described both the beginning and the end. Since Paul himself lives within this story, however, his subsequent experiences constitute further chapters in that same narrative, the focus of which is not really the eschatological end but the struggle of individual Jews in the present and the question of how or whether they will reach that end. When he encounters the risen Christ, it is that story which gives meaning to the experience. Paul meets Christ not as a mysterious manifestation of the "numinous," but as another chapter in this same story and hence as Israel's Messiah, as one who has experienced the resurrection which traditional apocalyptic predicted, etc. At the same time, however, this event is not like anything which Paul had anticipated in his construal of the story as a whole. Here Paul has an experience which – if he is to integrate it into his traditional narrative – will demand that many of the events of that prior story take on a new meaning. Similarly, when Peter learned about remarkable events among Paul's Gentile converts, he seems to have interpreted those experiences as further events within the Christian story. It was this narrative which provided him with the framework within which to understand them as manifestations of God's Spirit. Yet once again these events represented an unexpected "chapter" in the story which forced Peter to rethink the meaning of the previous "chapters" as he had learned and experienced them. The key in both cases is that the scriptural and traditional story does not stand removed from the present time and space of Peter and Paul, as in most understandings of myth. On the contrary, all distinctions between the timeline of the traditional story and the timeline of the experienced "now" are removed so that the present becomes another episode in the same narrative, a narrative which has God as its author and so must be coherent.[48] As we move from Paul's preliminary defence of his apostolic status to his main argument against the Galatians' being circumcised, we will find that it is this narrative, "reconfigurational" logic which becomes dominant.

---

[48] Note that Iser himself observed how the reading process, driven by anticipation and retrospection, "is closely akin to the way in which we gather experience in life" (*Implied Reader*, 281).

Chapter Nine

The Interpretive "Gaps" at the Heart of Paul's Argument

Although we find hints of this reconfigurational logic in the *narratio* of Paul's letter to the Galatians, it is at the end of chapter 2 that it first appears explicitly in the Apostle's argument. In 2:11–14 Paul ended his narrative argument for his apostleship with an account of his confrontation with the "pillar" Peter at Antioch. The speech rebuking Peter begins in 2:14 as a way of demonstrating Paul's independence and integrity in carrying out his commission. With 2:15, however, the topic clearly shifts from Peter's inconsistency to a more generalized argument for Paul's own position. This marks the point at which the Apostle turns from his focus on re-establishing his credibility with the audience towards the substantive argument with which, as the "parent" of the Galatian congregations, he wants to convince them to return to his authentic understanding of the Gospel.[1] Yet there is no

---

[1] Cosgrove (*Cross*, 5–38) has argued on the contrary that 2:15–21 should be understood as part of Paul's defensive narrative and that the section does not establish the argumentative theme of Galatians. Cosgrove finds the real argumentative theme declared instead in 3:1–5. Yet in 2:15 the argument clearly shifts from establishing Paul's independent apostolic status to justifying Paul's law-free message. On the other hand, the themes of justification, faith, and "works of the law" which appear in 2:15–21 reappear in 5:4–5, where Paul makes his final argumentative appeal to the Galatians before launching into the explicitly hortatory section of the letter.

Cosgrove is right that the language of justification does not dominate the intervening argument in 3:1–5:1 (*Cross*, 32), but his attempt to portray justification as a merely subsidiary matter here does not work. Cosgrove misses the fact that in 3:6, where Paul introduces the figure of Abraham, his focus is on how Abraham achieved "righteousness" (δικαιοσύνη). Moreover, in 3:8–9 Paul interprets the Gentiles' sharing in Abraham's blessing as their being justified on the same basis as the patriarch, "justified by faith" (ἐκ πίστεως δικαιοῖ τὰ ἔθνη ὁ θεός). In 3:11 justification once again appears to be understood as equivalent to participation in blessing (and as the opposite of suffering the curse), while in 3:24 Paul can say that Christ came ἵνα ἐκ πίστεως δικαιωθῶμεν. In the latter passage the end of the law's jurisdiction (a matter which is clearly in focus throughout this argument) is

clear end to Paul's quotation of his words to Peter until 3:1, where the Galatians are explicitly addressed. Why, given the importance of Paul's point here, does he leave it ambiguous to whom he is speaking? Because by maintaining this ambiguity he encourages the audience to lay the situation in Antioch alongside the situation in Galatia, to see the crises as parallel and the true solution as the same in both cases. Since in the one case the demand for legal observance was clearly (in Paul's telling) evidence of the Jerusalem leaders' inconsistency, this suggests at the outset that here too the opponents' law-observant position will turn out to be wrong. This indirect way of introducing Paul's main theological point also allows him to provide the Galatians with an outline or sketch of his position before they are put on their guard by the direct confrontation which comes in 3:1. The end goal of these rhetorical devices, however, is to gain a favourable hearing for the discursive argument which begins in 2:15-21 and will dominate chapters 3 and 4. Our primary interest here is thus to uncover the logic by which that discursive argument moves forward. Before we can face this central task, however, we must sort out the meaning of the controversial verse 16.

1. Clearing Ground: Issues in the Interpretation of Gal 2:16

Paul opens with a concise statement which has become a lightning rod for debates about the Apostle's thought. He and Peter both "know that a person is justified not by the works of the law but through faith in Jesus Christ" (2:16). Almost every word in this clause is the subject of some scholarly dispute, not only between adherents of the so-called "new perspective" on Paul and their opponents, but also within both of those camps. What is more,

---

understood precisely as a shift in the means of justification (cf. 3:21). Hence justification on the basis of faith not only appears as the theme in the conclusion of Paul's main argument, it is also portrayed in the body of the argument as the substance of the blessing and the salvation which the Galatians have put in jeopardy by their considering circumcision (cf. 1:6–9). When Cosgrove argues that Paul's focus in Galatians is on how to experience the Spirit rather than on how to be justified, he is driving a wedge between two realities which Paul held together. Hence in 5:5, in the conclusion of his main argument, Paul says: ἡμεῖς γὰρ πνεύματι ἐκ πίστεως ἐλπίδα δικαιοσύνη ἀπεκδεχόμεθα. The Spirit's activity, as the Galatians have experienced it, is here understood as a *part of their justification*. Hence the statements of 2:15–21 do appear to sum up the thrust of Paul's main argument in Galatians.

these questions cannot be avoided, since they determine how we will read much of Paul's argument in Galatians. Space does not permit me to give a full treatment of these issues here, but I will flag my own position on each one and offer a brief explanation of my reasoning.

1.1. The Nature of "Works of the Law"

We can sidestep the endless discussion about the meaning for Paul of "being justified" (δικαιοῦται) by taking this language in the general sense of "being accepted" by God. This acceptance carries with it, of course, inclusion in the eschatological restoration which marks the denouement of Paul's theological story.[2] Our second problem, however, cannot be so easily avoided. Paul's assertion here is that "no one will be justified *by works of the law* (ἐξ ἔργων νόμου)" (2:16). But what exactly are the "works of the law"? Dunn has been

---

[2] Some treat δικαιόω in Paul's use as judicial terminology, so that when one is "justified" one is awarded a legal status, is pardoned by God for one's sin (so Bruce, *Galatians*, 138; Dunn, *Galatians*, 134; Oepke, *Galater*, 60). Alternatively, Sanders has argued that the verb is "transfer terminology" (*Paul and Palestinian Judaism*, 470–72, 501, 518 n. 5, 544; *Paul, the Law, and the Jewish People*, 5–10). It denotes simply that an outsider to God's people has been made (by God) an insider, moved "from the state of sin and condemnation to the state which is the pre-condition of end-time salvation" (*Paul, the Law, and the Jewish People*, 45; cf. Sanders, *Paul and Palestinian Judaism*, 544–5). Most agree that the cognate noun (δικαιοσύνη) and adjective (δίκαιος) often carry an ethical meaning and denote the quality of acting as one should. Hence δικαιοσύνη can be contrasted with sin (e.g., Rom 3:9; 5:7–8; see Burton, *Galatians*, 468–73; Westerholm, *Perspectives*, 263–73; so Sanders, *Paul, the Law, and the Jewish People*, 10; though see *Paul and Palestinian Judaism*, 491–5, 501, 544–5). Ziesler denies that the verb carries this ethical idea as well (*The Meaning of Righteousness in Paul*), while Westerholm insists that the verb does denote not only an acceptance or transfer but also a recognition that one's actions are ethically good (see 1 Cor 4:4; Westerholm, *Perspectives*, 264–6). Hence, in ordinary use δικαιόω would mean the recognition that one has fulfilled God's ethical demand on humanity (Westerholm, *Perspectives*, 272–3). In the end, however, Ziesler and Westerholm are not far apart, since Westerholm emphasizes that where Paul talks about the justification of sinners (e.g., Rom 5:8–9) he envisions an unusual situation in which God grants sinful human beings the status usually reserved for the righteous (*Perspectives*, 273–84). Others argue that δικαιόω *always* denotes a recognition that one has met God's expectations, but that the expectations of God shift with the Christ event from legal obedience to faith in Christ (so Burton, *Galatians*, 473–4). Dunn moves in this kind of direction when he takes δικαιόω to denote a recognition of one's faithfulness to the covenant (*Galatians*, 134–5; *Theology*, 341–2; see the critique of this covenant association in Westerholm, *Perspectives*, 286–93, and Seifrid, "Righteousness Language").

hailed as champion of the view that Paul's phrase refers primarily to the ethnic "boundary markers" which in practice often defined Jewish identity: circumcision, food laws, and Sabbath observance.[3] The "works of the law" of which Paul speaks are, he argues, a matter not merely of Torah obedience, but rather of the distortion of Torah which arises when it is used as an ethnic boundary marker to maintain Israel's distinctiveness as an end in itself.[4] Yet the Qumran sect (which furnishes our only contemporary parallel to the phrase) seems to have meant by "works of the law" any act of Torah observance.[5] What is more, Paul seems in Galatians 2 to treat "works of the law" as interchangeable with "the law" in a way which would make little sense if he had in mind only some of its commands or its misuse as an ethnic marker.[6] Paul is thus saying that no one will be accepted by God (justified)

---

[3] So Bonneau, "Curse of the Law," 66–7; Bryant, *Crucified Christ*, 176. See Dunn, "4QMMT" and *Theology*, 354–9. Dunn himself emphasizes in recent writings that "'works of the law' characterize . . . the conviction that status within the covenant (= righteousness) is maintained by *doing what the law requires* (works of the law)" ("Yet Once More," 100 [emphasis mine]; cf. *Theology*, 357–8). Indeed, Dunn complains of "repeated misunderstanding" of his initial writing on the subject and insists "that I do not (and never did!) claim that 'works of the law' denote only circumcision, food laws, and Sabbath" (*Theology*, 358, n. 97). Some still find, though, that Dunn's affirmations of the expression's broad meaning sometimes seem inconsistent with his actual exegesis (so Westerholm, *Perspectives*, 314; Matlock, "Sins," 78).

[4] See Dunn, *Theology*, 355, 366.

[5] So C. R. de Roo, "Concept"; Mijoga, *Pauline Notion*, 113; contra Dunn, "4QMMT," and Abegg, "Works Righteousness." The author of *4QMMT*, a sectarian document from Qumran, refers to their collection of legal rulings as "some of the works of Torah" (מקצת מעשי התורה) (*4QMMT* C27). In context, the phrase designates a wide variety of legal observances, many of which are quite technical interpretations of purity law. Moreover, these are described as *"some"* of the "works of Torah," *those works of Torah which are at issue in the dispute*, implying that the term "works of Torah" on its own applies to legal observances more broadly. Note too that *4QMMT* associates the expression with the complete fulfilment of Torah which is required in order to experience the Deuteronomic blessings (see *4QMMT* C20–22; cf. the phrase מעשי בתרה in *1QS* V 21). Eckstein (*Verheißung*, 25) also points to a similar expression (ועשו את כול התורה) in *4QFlor* 1 II 1. See also Schlier, *Galater*, 55–6, for partial parallels further afield.

[6] So Westerholm, *Perspectives*, 314–15. Compare Gal 2:16 with 2:21. Barclay (*Obeying*, 78–9) has also pointed out that since Paul's statement here is made in the context of his confrontation with Peter in Antioch, Paul likely means by "works of the law" those acts which are foisted on Gentiles when Peter pressures them to "live like a Jew" (ἰουδαΐζειν, 2:14). Yet this latter verb refers not merely to keeping kosher but also, more broadly, to the

because they have observed Torah.[7] If, however, Paul means by "works of the law" any acts of Torah observance, then neither is the Apostle here opposing "legalism." He is not opposing supposedly Jewish attempts to earn salvation, and he betrays here no conviction that human efforts to be righteous are in and of themselves sinful.[8] His point is, rather, to emphasize that one's acceptance before God simply cannot be gained through Torah obedience, try as one might.

1.2. The Meaning of Πίστις Ἰησοῦ Χριστοῦ

Instead (ἐὰν μή), Paul says that "justification" will come through πίστεως Ἰησοῦ Χριστοῦ (2:16). Here we meet our third dispute about this knotty verse. Until the last couple of decades it was commonly agreed that this phrase was an objective genitive and should be translated "faith in Jesus Christ." More recently, Richard Hays has led the way in a renewal of the reading which takes the phrase as a *subjective* genitive, "the faith/faithfulness *of* Jesus Christ."[9] Despite the attractiveness of this reading, however, it does

---

adoption of Jewish practices in general. On the meaning of ἰουδαΐζω see BDAG, 478. Note especially the broad sense of the term in Jos., *B.J.* 2.454, 463; LXX Esth 8:17; Plut., *Cic.* 864 (7.5).

[7] So Betz, *Galatians*, 116; Burton, *Galatians*, 124; R. N. Longenecker, *Galatians*, 86; Lührmann, *Galatians*, 46; Martyn, *Galatians*, 250, 261–3; Oepke, *Galater*, 59; Sanders, *Paul, the Law, and the Jewish People*, 46; Schlier, *Galater*, 55–6; Stanton, "Law of Moses," 103; Westerholm, *Perspectives*, 313–15. Lloyd Gaston has argued for taking the phrase as a *subjective* genitive, the "works which the law does" (*Paul*, 100–106). Yet Gaston's reading does not account for either the similar expressions at Qumran or Paul's contrast in Gal 3:2, 5 between ἔργων νόμου and ἀκοῆς πίστεως, two possible courses of action *for the Galatians*.

[8] See Beker, *Paul*, 235–54 (esp. 246); R. N. Longenecker, *Galatians*, 85–6; Moule, "Fulfilment-Words"; Räisänen, *Paul and the Law*, 162–77 (esp. 176–7); Westerholm, *Perspectives*, 319–20; contra Burton, *Galatians*, 120; Bruce, *Galatians*, 137; Cranfield, "St. Paul and the Law"; Oepke, *Galater*, 58–60; Schlier, *Galater*, 56.

[9] See Hays, *Faith of Jesus Christ*, 139–91. Representatives of this position since Hays' influential monograph include Byrne, *Reckoning*, 79–80; Gaston, *Paul*, 117, 172; Hooker, "ΠΙΣΤΙΣ ΧΡΙΣΤΟΥ"; Howard, "On the 'Faith of Christ'"; *idem*, "Romans 3:21–31"; *idem*, "The 'Faith of Christ'"; *idem*, *Crisis*, 46–65; Johnson, "Rom 3:21–26"; B. W. Longenecker, *Triumph*; *idem*, "ΠΙΣΤΙΣ"; *idem*, "Defining," 79–81; R. N. Longenecker, *Galatians*, 86–8; Martyn, *Galatians*, 251–2; 270–71; Matera, *Galatians*, 94; and, somewhat differently, Williams, "Again." Earlier proponents of the subjective genitive reading included Karl Barth, *Romans* (though he reversed his position in *Shorter*); M. Barth, "Faith," 368;

not succeed in making sense of Paul's use of the expression here.[10] For in 3:6–9 Paul sets up Abraham as the paradigm example of justification on the basis of (the human being's) faith. Just as Abraham was justified on the basis of his faith in God, so "blessing" comes to Gentiles such as the Galatians who believe (i.e., believe in Christ). In this context the focus is clearly not on Christ's obedient faithfulness but on the believers' faith in their saviour.[11]

Goodenough, "Paul," 45–7; Haussleiter, "Der Glaube," 109–45, 205–230; Hebert, "Faithfulness"; Kittel, "πίστις Ἰησοῦ"; R. N. Longenecker, *Paul*, 149–50; *idem*, "Obedience of Christ"; Robinson, "Faith of Jesus Christ"; Taylor, "ΠΙΣΤΙΣ ΧΡΙΣΤΟΥ"; Torrance, "One Aspect."

[10] For arguments in support of the objective genitive reading, see Barclay, *Obeying*, 78, n. 8; Barr, *Semantics*, 161–205; Betz, *Galatians*, 117–18; Bruce, *Galatians*, 138–9; Burton, *Galatians*, 121; Cosgrove, *Cross*, 55–6; Cranfield, *Romans*, 203, n. 2; Dodd, *Bible and Greeks*, 65–70; Dunn, "ΠΙΣΤΙΣ ΧΡΙΣΤΟΥ"; Grundmann, "Christ Statements"; Hansen, *Abraham*; Hultgren, "*Pistis Christou*"; W. Johnson, "Paradigm"; Moo, *Romans*, 224–5; Moule, "Biblical Conception"; Murray, *Romans*, 1.363–74; Sanday and Headlam, *Romans*, 83–4; Westerholm, *Perspectives*, 305–6, n. 18.

Traditionally the verbal clause εἰς Χριστὸν Ἰησοῦν ἐπιστεύσαμεν in 2:16 was understood to control the sense of the accompanying genitive phrase (see also Gal 3:22; Rom 3:22). More recently the juxtaposition of the genitive phrase with the verbal expression has been taken to be redundant unless the two formulations mean different things (so, e.g., Hebert, "Faithfulness," 373). Yet one can easily imagine plausible rhetorical reasons for the apparent redundancy (see Betz, *Galatians*, 117; Burton, *Galatians*, 121–2; Dunn, *Romans*, 1.166; "ΠΙΣΤΙΣ ΧΡΙΣΤΟΥ," 739–41; Moo, *Romans*, 225–6; Murray, *Romans*, 371; Westerholm, *Perspectives*, 305–6, n. 18).

It is sometimes observed that when Paul qualifies πίστις with a genitive referring to something or someone other than Christ, the genitive is usually subjective (see Rom 3:3; 4:12, 16; so Howard, "Faith of Christ," 459–60). Yet πίστις can often take an objective genitive in the NT, and Paul himself uses the construction more than once (so Burton, *Galatians*, 121; Dunn, "ΠΙΣΤΙΣ ΧΡΙΣΤΟΥ", 731–2; Moo, *Romans*, 225, n. 26; Moule, "Biblical Conception," 157; Westerholm, *Perspectives*, 305, n. 18; see Mk 11:22; Acts 3:16; Phil 1:27; Col 2:12; 2 Thess 2:13; cf. Phil 3:8–9; Rom 10:2). Moreover, Paul's use of the verb πιστεύω also demonstrates that he does regard Christ as a proper object of faith (e.g., Gal 2:16; contra Williams, "Again," 434, and despite his objections on pp. 442–5). Hence, as Westerholm suggests, "grammar cannot resolve the debate" (*Perspectives*, 305, n. 18).

[11] So Barclay, *Obeying*, 78, n. 8. It remains unclear what Paul would mean by "Christ's faith," particularly since nowhere else does he speak of Christ believing. Hence most who advocate a subjective reading of πίστις understand the noun to mean "faithfulness" (as in Rom 3:3). Yet in the vast majority of clear cases Paul uses πίστις to denote human faith – believing – in a divine object (so Moo, *Romans*, 225; Murray, *Romans*, 365), and in none of the πίστις Χριστοῦ passages is there an unambiguous reference to Christ's faithfulness (so

Notice too that Abraham is said to be justified ἐκ πίστεως, and that those with faith like his are called in 3:9 οἱ ἐκ πίστεως. Yet these prepositional phrases are almost identical to Paul's statement in 2:16 that justification comes ἐκ πίστεως Χριστοῦ. Since in both cases essentially the same prepositional phrase is presented as the basis for the believer's justification, it is most natural to assume that the meaning of the phrase is also the same each time Paul uses it.[12] Those who are justified ἐκ πίστεως (Χριστοῦ) are those who have faith (like Abraham's) in God's salvific activity, now centred in Christ.

1.3. The Role of 2:16 in Paul's Argument

We can now summarize what Paul means to say at the outset of his argument: human beings cannot gain acceptance with God (and the eschatological blessing which goes along with it) by keeping Torah; they can gain that divine acceptance only by trusting God's action in Christ. It is in the wake of this realization, Paul says in 2:16, that he and Peter alike "placed [our] faith in Christ Jesus".[13] As soon as we begin to ask about the flow of Paul's

---

Dunn, "ΠΙΣΤΙΣ ΧΡΙΣΤΟΥ," 736). Paul prefers other terms for Christ's right actions in Phil 2:8; 5:18, 19 (so Barclay, *Obeying*, 78, n. 8; Cosgrove, *Cross*, 56; Dunn, "ΠΙΣΤΙΣ ΧΡΙΣΤΟΥ," 742–3; Westerholm, *Perspectives*, 305–6, n. 18; contra Hays, "ΠΙΣΤΙΣ," 723). In Gal 3 Christ facilitates salvation not by providing a model of πίστις but by becoming a curse (contra Hooker, "ΠΙΣΤΙΣ ΧΡΙΣΤΟΥ," 236–331). Abraham remains the model of πίστις (contra Hays, "ΠΙΣΤΙΣ," 722–3).

This whole question cannot be sidestepped by reading πίστις as both faith and faithfulness simultaneously (as, e.g., Hays, "ΠΙΣΤΙΣ," 718; Ljungman, *Pistis*, 38–40, 47; Torrance, "One Aspect"; Williams, "Again," 437, 443–6), since "faith" and "faithfulness" are (even in Jewish use) two distinct senses of the noun (so Murray, *Romans*, 373–4).

[12] In 3:7, 8, Abraham is justified ἐκ πίστεως, and in 3:9 those who practice the same faith (now obviously in Christ) are οἱ ἐκ πίστεως (see also 3:11, 12, 24). Paul seems simply to have dropped the Χριστοῦ which specified the object of the believing in 2:16 in order to ease the comparison between OT models of faith and the faith of believers in Christ. Likewise the prepositional phrase διὰ πίστεως Ἰησοῦ Χριστοῦ in 2:16 closely resembles the phrase διὰ τῆς πίστεως in 3:14, 26, where again the πίστις is clearly the believer's faith in Christ (so Hultgren, "*Pistis Christou*," 255–6; Murray, *Romans*, 1.366–7). Moreover, in each of these passages, with and without the genitive (Ἰησοῦ) Χριστοῦ, "faith" is being contrasted with ἔργων νόμου (2:16, 21; 3:10, 21; so Dunn, "ΠΙΣΤΙΣ ΧΡΙΣΤΟΥ," 736). This evidence may be weakened slightly by Paul's ἐκ πίστεως Ἀβραάμ in Rom 4:12, 16 (so R. N. Longenecker, *Galatians*, 87), but in both cases this πίστις is still human faith in God, by which (ἐκ) one receives righteousness (so Hultgren, "*Pistis Christou*," 256).

[13] Here I have departed from the NRSV rendering.

argument, however, we run into one final question about 2:16. Does this verse state a premise of Paul's argument or its conclusion? Is this a point of view which Paul shares with his opponents in Galatia, and so can take as a starting point, or is it a position for which he is now beginning to argue? One's answer to this question depends in part on how one understands the "we" introduced in 2:15. For it is this "we" who share the conviction which Paul outlines in 2:16. We have already seen that 2:15–16 continue the Apostle's speech to Peter in the context of the Antioch crisis. In this context, the "we" includes primarily Paul and Peter.[14] The Apostle expands on the identity of this "we," specifying that they are "Jews by birth and not Gentile sinners" (2:15). If we understand 2:15 as a verbless clause, then we arrive at a translation like that of the NRSV: "We ourselves are Jews by birth and not Gentile sinners."[15] Paul is thus drawing attention to the fact that he and Peter are Jews, likely in order to emphasize the reality that even they (as Jews) have realized that Torah obedience does not justify. Nothing is implied here about the extent of agreement about the content of 2:16. It remains quite possible that, while Paul presents this declaration as a point of agreement between himself and Peter, it is a point which deeply divides him from his Galatian opponents.

There has been a tendency among exegetes, however, to argue that Paul's "we" here includes not just himself and Peter but *all* Jewish believers.[16] Those who read 2:15 this way often seem to take the verse not as a verbless clause but as a pronoun followed by two phrases in apposition to that pronoun which further define it.[17] This yields a translation like that of R. N.

---

[14] So Burton, *Galatians*, 117–18; Dunn, *Galatians*, 132.

[15] The Greek reads ἡμεῖς φύσει Ἰουδαῖοι καὶ οὐκ ἐξ ἐθνῶν ἁμαρτωλοί.

[16] So Betz, *Galatians*, 114, 115, n. 20; Donaldson, *Paul*, 181, 352, n. 65; R. N. Longenecker, *Galatians*, 82, 84; Martyn, *Galatians*, 263–4; Oepke, *Galater*, 58.

[17] Many commentators seem to assume this construal of the grammar but do not justify the reading in grammatical terms. One exception is Schlier, *Galater*, 52. Others seem to treat 2:15 as grammatically independent, but still understand Paul to treat the conviction expressed in 2:16 as the common faith of Jewish Christ-believers (see, e.g., Dunn, *Galatians*, 131–5). The assumption in this case seems to be that Paul would only mention the Jewish ethnicity of the "we" in order to highlight the fact that these convictions are common among Jews. Yet there are other reasons why Paul might stress the Jewishness of his "we." He might want, for example, to bolster his credibility or authority in the eyes of the Galatian audience which has been overawed by the authentic Jewish credentials of their new teachers.

Longenecker: "We who are Jews by birth and not 'sinners of the Gentiles' . . ."[18] The opening participle of 2:16 then simply continues this description of the "we" who, as Jewish Christians, know that justification does not come on the basis of Torah observance, etc. In other words, according to this reading of 2:15 Paul and Peter share the convictions outlined in 2:16 *because they are Jewish Christians*. The implication, then, is that the Galatian opponents too, as Jewish believers, also share these convictions.[19] As the Galatian audience listens in on Paul's speech to Peter, 2:16 functions to remind them of the basic points on which the Apostle agrees with their more recent teachers. This interpretation of the passage is particularly appealing now, when scholars are eager to show that Paul did not misconstrue Judaism as a legalistic religion of "works righteousness." On this reading, 2:16 does not contain a (hopelessly inaccurate) rejection of Jewish attitudes, but rather a restatement of a perspective which all Jewish Christians share, precisely because Jews do not understand their legal works to earn their salvation.

One cannot help but applaud the recent moves towards correcting our understanding of Second-Temple Judaism. In this case, however, the reading of 2:16 which appears to help that cause simply does not work. On closer examination it becomes clear that the statements of 2:16 cannot reflect convictions which Paul shares with his Galatian opponents. When, in 2:21, Paul winds up this section of his argument, his concluding statement seems to be a *restatement* of 2:16: "if justification comes through the law (εἰ γὰρ διὰ νόμου δικαιοσύνη), then Christ died for nothing" (2:21). As a parting shot, this denial of justification through the law presumes that the opponents do in

---

[18] R. N. Longenecker, *Galatians*, 81.

[19] Martyn is explicit (*Galatians*, 248) that Paul's "we" includes the Galatian "Teachers." In describing 2:15–21 as the rhetorical *propositio* of Galatians, Betz says that this rhetorical section was generally used first to sum up the points of agreement between speaker and audience and then to state the points which are contested (*Galatians*, 114; so R. N. Longenecker, *Galatians*, 82). Yet we must be careful not to let our exegesis be governed by the dictates of the rhetorical manuals. Notice that the *propositio* is also supposed to sum up "the *narratio's* material contents," but that 2:15–21 manifestly do not do that (contra Betz, *Galatians*, 114). Rather, these verses mark the shift from Paul's defence of his reliability as an apostle to the substance of the message which, as an apostle, he brings to Galatia. Nor do these verses constitute a simple statement of the contested points in the conflict, since they are dominated by actual argument. Betz is only able to read 2:15–21 as such a summary by taking each statement in 2:19–20 as a shorthand reference to some later part of the letter (*Galatians*, 121–5). Few, however, have found this reading convincing.

fact hold such a view, or at least that their teaching implies it. It would make no sense, however, for Paul to insist in this way that justification is not "through the law" if the opponents agreed from the outset that "a person is justified not by the works of the law but through faith in Jesus Christ" (2:16).[20] Thus it seems that the "we" in 2:15–16 does *not* include Jewish believers generally, but refers only to Paul and Peter. On the level of Paul's account of the Antioch incident, 2:16 constitutes a summary of the basic convictions shared by Peter and Paul, convictions which had likely been crystallized for Peter earlier, at the Jerusalem meeting. On the level of Paul's discourse with his Galatian audience, this same verse constitutes a statement of the thesis which will be defended through the following two chapters.[21]

Does this mean that Paul thinks his opponents in Galatia actually taught that one was justified on the basis of legal obedience and not on the basis of one's faith? Does it mean that the Apostle considered "justification by the works of the law" to reflect the self-understanding of his Jewish contemporaries? The answer is probably "no" on both counts. For in 2:16 Paul does not simply deny that justification can come on the basis of Torah obedience. He also sets up such justification through Torah as an *alternative* to justification by faith in Christ. In doing so, Paul is likely driving a wedge between two realities, legal observance and faith in God's action, which in

---

[20] Nor can we differentiate between Paul's statement in 2:16a, which employs the preposition ἐκ, and the statement in 2:21, which uses διά, for the two prepositions are used interchangeably in 2:16; 3:6, and elsewhere.

Note too how Paul seems to restate the thrust of 2:16 in 5:4–5, at the conclusion of his "theological" argument. Paul emphasizes that οἵτινες ἐν νόμῳ δικαιοῦσθε have cut themselves off from Christ, while "we" are receiving ἐλπίδα δικαιοσύνης, and this ἐκ πίστεως.

This concluding statement in 2:21 also renders implausible the attempt to differentiate between justification (which all agree the law cannot bring) and sonship of Abraham (for which the opponents think Torah obedience *is* required). Some Jews in Paul's day may have imagined righteous Gentiles who remained outside the law (see Donaldson, *Paul*, 60–68). In Paul's argument, however, being a son of Abraham seems to be inseparable from righteousness. Note, for example, that it is in a discussion of Abraham's justification ἐκ πίστεως that other believers are said to be υἱοί Ἀβραάμ (3:7). Cf. in 3:8 the equation of being blessed with Abraham and being justified.

[21] So Burton, *Galatians*, 118; Bruce, *Galatians*, 135; Lührmann, *Galatians*, 47. It is generally understood that the section in 2:15–21 establishes the primary thesis of at least chapters 3–4. See above, pp. 179–80, n. 1.

traditional Judaism (including most Christian Jews) had been considered inseparable.[22] He is framing his position in such a way that, instead of legal obedience being the supreme expression of faith in God, faith in his salvific action can come to full expression without any adherence to the Sinaitic legislation.[23] It is likely because the opponents do not separate these facets of Israel's devotion to God that they encourage the Galatian believers to adopt circumcision and complete their adherence to Torah. As E. P. Sanders argues, Paul is not attacking "works righteousness," but rather the "standard Jewish view that accepting and living by the law is a sign and condition of favored status."[24] Instead Paul is claiming that this status can (and for Gentiles *must*) be attained outside of devotion to Torah. What remains to be seen, however, is just how Paul is going to argue in 2:15–21 in order to support this model of the situation. It is to this analysis of the Apostle's argument that we now turn.

2. Reconfiguring the Story after the Cross (2:15–21)

2.1. Paul's Version of the Story as a Plausible Reconfiguration

Paul's thesis in 2:16 is a statement, in general terms, of some implications which flow from his configuration of Israel's story. He agrees with most Jews that people must be "justified" – accepted by God – in order to play a good role in the narrative, one which ends up in the eschatological restoration of the world. Paul insists, however, that one does not come to play this role by keeping Torah. Rather, human beings can play this role in the story only if they place their faith in Christ. In other words, those who believe in Christ will enjoy the eschatological restoration regardless of whether or not they keep the details of the Sinaitic law. These ethical dynamics are very different

---

[22] So Barclay, *Obeying*, 78; Lührmann, *Galatians*, 47. See *4 Ezra* 9:7; 13:23; 4 Macc 15:24–28; James 2:14–17.

[23] Even those who treat 2:16 as common ground often recognize that Paul's dichotomy would have been foreign to many Jewish believers (see, e.g., Martyn, *Galatians*, 267–9).

[24] Sanders, *Paul, the Law, and the Jewish People*, 46. Dunn (*Galatians*, 132–3) points to the attitude towards Gentiles in Ps 9:18(17); Tob 13:6; *Jub.* 23:23–24; *Pss. Sol.* 2:1–2; Matt 5:47//Luke 6:33. Dunn also notes that Jews of one group would sometimes call Jews of another group "Gentiles" when they wanted to question that group's righteousness (*Galatians*, 133; see, e.g., 1 Macc 1:34; 2:44, 48; *1 En.* 5:4–7; 82:4–5; *1QH* II 8–12; *1QpHab* V 4–8; *Pss. Sol.* 4:8; 13:6–12).

from those which most Jews (including many Jewish believers in Christ) traced out in Israel's story. The ordinary Jewish reading of Israel's history, and especially of Deuteronomy, depicted the observance of Torah as fundamental to maintaining a good relationship with God, and hence reaping the blessings promised in Israel's covenant. It is most likely this kind of reading of Israel's story which prompted the opponents to press circumcision on the Galatians. The radical divergence between Paul's thesis here and the position of the opponents thus suggests again that the theological story which forms Paul's hermeneutical framework is different in important ways from the story which his Galatian opponents assume. Something has prompted Paul to reconfigure Israel's story in such a way that its ethical implications are now the reverse of what they are on his opponents' reading of the narrative. Indeed, we will see that the argumentative thrust of this section is to show that Paul's reconfiguration is both coherent and necessary.

Following his thesis statement in 2:16, Paul turns to meet objections which the Galatian opponents seem to have levelled against this position. Echoing these objections in a rhetorical question, the Apostle asks: "But if, in our effort to be justified in Christ, we ourselves have been found to be sinners, is Christ then a servant of sin?" (2:17). We should understand by the term "sinners" here not simply the charge that the Galatians have been left without resources to curb their transgressions.[25] Rather, just as in 2:15 Paul and Peter agreed that neither of them was a "Gentile sinner" (ἐξ ἐθνῶν ἁμαρτωλοί), so here too the "sinners" are primarily those who live like Gentiles, those who live outside the covenant law.[26] It thus seems that the opponents have charged

---

[25] So R. N. Longenecker, *Galatians*, 89; see also Lambrecht, "Paul's Reasoning," 72–3. Thus far in the letter nothing has been said about the danger of ethical chaos in the wake of Paul's Gospel. Rather, the focus rests squarely on the question of whether Torah observance is necessary.

[26] As Dunn observes, Paul is thinking primarily about the kind of behaviour which the "men from James" condemned at Antioch (*Galatians*, 141; so Burton, *Galatians*, 125; Martyn, *Galatians*, 255). Of course, he is also thinking about the non-observant lifestyle which the opponents condemn in Galatia (so Burton, *Galatians*, 125; Martyn, *Galatians*, 255). On the standard Jewish identification of Gentiles as "sinners," see the LXX of 1 Sam 15:18 and Ps 9:18(17); *Pss. Sol.* 2:1–2; 17:25; *Jub.* 23:23–24; 24:28; *4 Ezra* 3:28–36; Matt 5:47; 26:45 (and parallels).

Alternatively, we could understand Paul to be admitting that he is a sinner in the more radical sense that he is "in need of justification through Christ" (so Lambrecht, "Transgressor", 218; *idem*, "Paul's Reasoning," 72; Eckstein, *Verheißung*, 35–6). Yet if we

Paul with encouraging Gentiles to remain ἁμαρτωλοί – "sinners" – and even with descending to that lawless way of life himself. Yet the hypothetical objection raised here does not simply attack Paul's ethical conduct. It pushes further and attempts to show that Paul's reading of the story issues in intolerable internal conflicts. Does Paul not depict Christ as a "servant of sin"? If seeking justification in Christ were really to involve abandoning Torah and living like a Gentile, then would this not mean that the advent and activity of Christ would be aimed at promoting apostasy in Israel? Would it not mean that the God who had acted in Christ was tearing down the covenant which he himself had established? The charge is, in other words, that Paul's reconfiguration of Israel's narrative cannot produce a coherent reading of its "chapters."

Paul's reply is an emphatic "Certainly not!" (μὴ γένοιτο) (2:17). The Apostle does not refute the charge that he (like Peter before the arrival of the "men from James") does in fact live as a "sinner."[27] What Paul objects to is

---

understand Paul to be responding here to a charge that "Christ is a servant of sin" (2:17b), it is difficult to see how anyone could draw that conclusion from the fact that, prior to their coming to faith, believers were radically in need of redemption. It is no more plausible to suggest, with Bruce, that Christ would be seen as increasing the number of sinners by revealing Torah observance as inadequate (*Galatians*, 141). On the other hand, the charge that Christ is being implicated in sin follows quite naturally if it is a response to Paul's encouragement of a law-free lifestyle.

[27] The form of the conditional in 2:17, beginning with εἰ in the protasis and making use of ordinary indicative verbs, usually indicates that the condition indicated in the protasis is true (so Eckstein, *Verheißung*, 32–33; R. N. Longenecker, *Galatians*, 89; Martyn, *Galatians*, 253; contra Bultmann, "Auslegung," 396). On the other hand, Lambrecht has emphasized that the simple conditional form does not amount to a positive affirmation that the protasis is fulfilled in reality ("Unreal Conditions"). Similarly, Betz argues (*Galatians*, 120) that the second part of the condition – that the believers are found to be "sinners" – must be false because they are identified as being "in Christ," while the status of "sinner" means that one is "living outside of the realm of God's salvation." Betz's point is an important counterbalance to B. W. Longenecker's suggestion that Paul in 2:17 accepts the identification of believers as "sinners" because "all people find themselves to be outsiders to the covenant" as defined by Christ ("Defining," 85). For both Paul and Peter (presumably the "we" in 2:17) stand within that newly defined boundary. At the same time, Betz misses the ambiguity in the Jewish use of the term "sinner" upon which Paul plays here. The word could denote either one who had breached (or lived outside of) Torah, or one who had rebelled against God's will. This ambiguity allows Paul here to affirm for rhetorical effect that the believer *is* a "sinner" in the first sense while denying that this makes him or her a sinner in the second sense (so Burton, *Galatians*, 125, 127–30; Martyn, *Galatians*, 255;

the suggestion that Christ's promotion of this law-free lifestyle must make him a "servant of sin," that is, that God's agent would have to be understood as God's opponent. The Apostle defends his thesis by showing how the reconfiguration of Israel's story upon which it depends is, in fact, coherent. The key factor in maintaining this coherence is of course Paul's particular understanding of Christ's actions. In 2:19–20 Paul lays out in schematic form his construal of the implications of the Christ event in the larger narrative: "For through the law I died to the law, so that I might live to God. I have been crucified with Christ; and it is no longer I who live, but it is Christ who lives in me. And the life I now live in the flesh I live by faith in the Son of God, who loved me and gave himself for me." Paul's telling of the story here is necessarily dense and allusive, but we can make out the broad outlines. The event of Christ's death is understood as some sort of punishment for transgression. By placing his faith in Christ, the Apostle is identified with his Lord in that death, so that he has already suffered the judgement marked out for the covenant violator.[28] Since, however, Christ rose from the grave, Paul too has been enlivened again with Christ. Yet once the believer has suffered (through identification with Christ) God's judgement on lawbreakers, the law no longer carries any threat: "For through the law I died to the law" (2:19).[29] For the believer, coming to a good end no longer depends on keeping Torah, for he or she has already vicariously suffered its curse and (as one infused with Christ's resurrected life) has been reborn outside of the deuteronomic

---

Räisänen, *Paul*, 76, n. 173). This reading fits well with Burton's observation that the emphatic denial μὴ γένοιτο is consistently used (in Paul and elsewhere) following a question in order to deny that "the alleged conclusion follows from the premise", rather than to deny the truth of one of the premises (*Galatians*, 128; so Eckstein, *Verheißung*, 34).

[28] In this sense Paul's death to the law came "through the law," διὰ νόμου (so Eckstein, *Verheißung*, 66; Lambrecht, "Transgressor," 229; Martyn, *Galatians*, 257; contra Burton, *Galatians*, 134). Despite the cautions of B. W. Longenecker ("Defining," 87), Lambrecht is almost certainly right to see here an allusion to the same idea expressed in 3:13 ("Paul's Reasoning," 63). Longenecker ("Defining," 87) understands the "death through the law" simply as the verdict pronounced on "all flesh" as "covenant outsiders." This does not account, however, for the close connection between this "death through the law" and the following reference to being "crucified with Christ" (so Eckstein, *Verheißung*, 58–9).

[29] So Dunn, *Galatians*, 144; R. N. Longenecker, *Galatians*, 91–2; contra Burton, *Galatians*, 134, 136. Betz notes (*Galatians*, 120) that Paul seems to presume the idea which he makes explicit in Rom 4:15, that "where there is no law, neither is there violation."

system.[30] It is this construal of the Christ event as part of Israel's larger story which allows Paul to say that obeying Torah will now not bring any benefit to someone who has been included in Christ. On the contrary, if Paul were to "build up again" that way of relating to God, his own (and his converts') law-free behaviour would again come under judgement.[31] They would again be judged as "transgressors" (2:18).[32] Hence it is not Paul but the opponents who by their actions are putting themselves in a dangerous role in the story. As long as one's role in the story is determined by one's participation in Christ, legal observance is irrelevant. The believer has moved beyond the reach of Torah.[33] Hence to return to a system of legal observance would be to "nullify the grace of God" (2:21).

2.2. The Cross as an Interpretive Gap

Thus far Paul has responded to the opponents' challenge by demonstrating how his ethical position can arise from a coherent telling of the theological narrative. It is not until 2:21, however, that the Apostle tries to show why this reconfiguration of Israel's story was necessary. Here Paul offers his own, positive justification for the way in which he has reconstrued Israel's story: "for (γὰρ) if justification comes through the law, then Christ died for nothing

---

[30] So Lambrecht, "Transgressor," 224–5; "Paul's Reasoning," 61; Eckstein, *Verheißung*, 68.

[31] Paul is not likely distinguishing sharply here among re-erecting Torah itself as a code to be observed (so Betz, *Galatians*, 121), reaffirming the conviction that its observance leads to righteousness (so Eckstein, *Verheißung*, 49), and returning to the observance of certain commands (so Burton, *Galatians*, 130; Räisänen, *Paul*, 47).

[32] So Dunn, *Galatians*, 143. Lambrecht ("Transgressor," 231) rightly emphasizes that the term παραβάτης implies transgression of some law (so Eckstein, *Verheißung*, 52). Hence Lambrecht's own interpretation of this "transgression" as the violation of God's act of salvation in Christ ("Transgressor," 234–5; so B. W. Longenecker, "Defining," 84) is much less plausible than a reading which retains the connection between the παραβάτης and Torah (so Eckstein, *Verheißung*, 55). Παραβάτης is never used by Paul of one who rejects salvation in Christ. Nor can Paul's verb συνιστάνω be forced to mean that Paul would simply recognize his past actions as sin if he returned to Torah observance (so Lambrecht, "Transgressor," 232).

[33] Notice how Paul denies not that his Gospel involves "tearing down" Torah, but only that non-observance makes him a "transgressor." Contra Dunn, Paul is thus not simply opposing the use of the law to exclude Gentiles from God's grace (*Galatians*, 149). As an ethnic Jew, he includes himself among those who need no longer keep Torah (so Burton, *Galatians*, 132).

(Χριστὸς δωρεὰν ἀπέθανεν)."[34] Here is revealed the "gap" in the story which forced the Apostle's reinterpretation.[35] Christ's death was a shameful one, which by its very form suggested divine judgement. On the usual understanding of Israel's story, and the role of legal observance within it, Christ would simply be shown as a transgressor who has suffered God's curse. Yet by his resurrection Christ has been vindicated by God and shown to have been God's agent after all. This is the *aporia* which Paul could not resolve without rethinking the whole of the prior story, and at the end of that process of reinterpretation he was left with a reading which was radically novel but which (he believed) could encompass this new and radically novel event. Of course, the question which both the opponents and the Galatian believers will ask is how Paul can reconcile this construal of the Christ event with the story of Israel in which Torah played so great a part.[36] This demonstration of the coherence of Paul's reconfigured story will have to wait, however, for there is another more immediate "gap" to which Paul wants to draw the Galatians' attention.

3. Reconfiguring the Story after the Galatians' Experience (3:1–5)

When Paul turns back to the Galatians in 3:1 he bursts out: "You foolish Galatians! Who has bewitched you?" Here, as in 1:6, Paul's discursive argument is momentarily suspended in favour of a rhetoric designed to shame

---

[34] Whether we read the conditional clause in v. 21 as a (defective) second-class conditional (Betz, *Galatians*, 126) or simply recognize that first-class conditionals do not necessarily imply the truth of the protasis (Lambrecht, "Transgressor," 229), Paul is certainly denying that the law brings righteousness (so R. N. Longenecker, *Galatians*, 95; Martyn, *Galatians*, 260). Paul has denied this possibility three times in 2:16 (so Lambrecht, "Transgressor," 229).

[35] So Bryant, *Crucified Christ*, 166, 169–70; Burton, *Galatians*, 141; Martyn, *Galatians*, 260.

[36] Paul is already beginning to hint at this coherence with the earlier parts of the narrative in his quotation of Ps 143:2 in 2:16. Notice how in Paul's quotation it is the "flesh" rather than the "living being" (LXX: ζῶν; MT: חי), which cannot be justified ἐξ ἔργων νόμου. Paul is here not only pointing to a hint of his approach to Torah within Israel's scripture, but also using wording which emphasizes his new rereading of the passage (so Dunn, *Galatians*, 140).

the audience and encourage their sympathetic attention.[37] He wants their attention, however, in order to reason with them, to show them *why* the opponents' version of the Gospel is a dangerous perversion of that message. Hence, as suddenly as he broke off, the Apostle rejoins his discursive argument in 3:2, now speaking directly to his Galatian audience and presenting them with reasons why the substance of his own position is true.[38]

It is here that the reconfigurational dynamics in Paul's reasoning become most clear. As Betz observes, Paul begins his main argument[39] by eliciting from his audience themselves the chief point of evidence to which he will appeal:[40] "Did you receive the Spirit by doing the works of the law or by

---

[37] Paul reminds the Galatians that Christ was "publicly exhibited as crucified" right "before your eyes" (3:1), implying that it is this unexpected aspect of the Messiah's work which should have pushed the Galatians to a new understanding of Israel's story (so Dunn, *Galatians*, 152).

[38] Cosgrove argues at length that 3:1–5 should be understood not as Paul's opening argument for the position stated in 2:15–21 but rather as a statement of the main argumentative point which Paul wants to make (*Cross*, 45; cf. 39–52). Yet not only does this reading misconstrue the rhetorical function of 2:15–21 (see above, pp. 179–80, n. 1), it also gives insufficient weight to the way Paul presumes in 3:1–5 that the Galatians will simply acknowledge the conditions under which they received the Spirit. Cosgrove objects that the Apostle cannot be appealing to the experience of the Spirit as evidence of the Galatians' justification without law, because if such law-free justification were the issue in Galatia the opponents would certainly have contested the Galatians' experience of the Spirit (*Cross*, 43–4). This argument does not allow, though, either for the possibility that these experiences were powerful enough to stand as evidence even in the face of the opponents' challenges or for the likelihood that the opponents were not as rigorously consistent in their theology as Cosgrove implies. In fact their insistence on circumcision in Galatia may even have been prompted by their realization that the Spirit was being manifested there and by their resultant concern to bring the Galatian believers in line with traditionally comprehensible categories of righteous people.

[39] Betz (correctly) identifies 3:1–4:31 as Paul's *probatio* (so Dunn, *Galatians*, 159). I will treat 4:12–20 and 21–31 under a separate heading because the mode of argumentation changes in those sections. R. N. Longenecker recognizes this shift by marking the end of the *probatio* at 4:11 (*Galatians*, 97). All the same, Paul's the basic task in 4:12–31 is still that which Betz assigns to the *probatio*: to present the "proofs" of one's argument (so Betz, *Galatians*, 128), and it is this task which the Apostle begins in earnest at 3:1.

[40] Betz, *Galatians*, 30. Barclay (*Obeying*, 83) rightly points out that Paul introduces the fact of their reception of the Spirit as "a knock-down proof for his case": τοῦτο μόνον θέλω μαθεῖν ἀφ᾽ ὑμῶν (3:2) (so Eckstein, *Verheißung*, 84).

believing what you heard (ἐξ ἀκοῆς πίστεως)?" (3:2).[41] It is generally agreed that here Paul is referring to some ecstatic or miraculous experience which the Galatians had at their conversion, and he may also be thinking of the fact that such experiences have continued since then.[42] By referring to this experience as their reception of "the Spirit," Paul makes it clear that he is understanding the event as a part of his theological story. This experience represents the general outpouring of God's Spirit on his people which was predicted in Scripture as a part of the eschatological consummation of history,[43] and to that extent it constitutes a further chapter in the story which many Jews had anticipated.

Thus far the opponents would likely agree. Paul's point in recalling this event, however, is to point out that it also opens up an interpretive "gap" for anyone who is trying to understand it as part of the traditional story. For in that narrative the Spirit is not poured out on just anyone. This eschatological event is to be enjoyed by the members of God's people as part of the final covenant blessing. Yet here the Galatians have received the eschatological Spirit *without taking on any of the observance of Torah which was usually understood to define the boundary between God's people and the rest of humanity.* Here is the "gap" – the totally unexpected event, the aporia which demands resolution if the story is to be understood as a coherent whole.

---

[41] Whether we understand the phrase ἀκοῆς πίστεως to denote "believing what you heard" (so Bryant, *Crucified Christ*, 172, n. 19; R. N. Longenecker, *Galatians*, 103; cf. Martyn, *Galatians*, 287–8) or "hearing with faith" (so Burton, *Galatians*, 147; Dunn, *Galatians*, 154; Lightfoot, *Galatians*, 135; Williams, "Hearing of Faith"), Paul's point is the same. Much less likely is the sense "a message (proclamation) which elicited (only) faith" (so BDAG, 36 [4.b]) or "the proclamation that has the power to elicit faith" (so Eckstein, *Verheißung*, 86–8; Martyn, *Galatians*, 284, 287–9; cf. Betz, *Galatians*, 133; Schlier, *Galater*, 122), since the focus here is on the nature of the response which brought on the Galatians' experience of the Spirit (so Dunn, *Galatians*, 154).

[42] So Betz, *Galatians*, 29, 132; Burton, *Galatians*, 151; Dunn, *Galatians*, 153; Eckert, *Urchristliche Verkündigung*, 74, 108. R. N. Longenecker, *Galatians*, 102. Lull (*Spirit*, 69–71) points to 3:5, where being "outfitted" with the Spirit (ὁ οὖν ἐπιχορηγῶν ὑμῖν τὸ πνεῦμα . . .) is set in parallel with God's "working" of "miracles" among the Galatians (. . . καὶ ἐνεργῶν δυνάμεις ἐν ὑμῖν; cf. Acts 2:4, 33; 8:17–18; 10:45–46). While early Christian writers often spoke of conversion in terms of "receiving the Spirit" (e.g., Acts 2:38; John 20:22), this suggests not that "reception of the Spirit" was merely a metonymic reference to a theological idea or to the baptismal ritual, but that the remarkable experiences which believers often had at conversion were attributed to the Spirit.

The opponents seem to have resolved the incongruity between their prior understanding of the story and this new event by trying to eliminate it. If non-observant Gentiles are not supposed to receive the Spirit, then the solution to the problem is to make these Gentiles observe Torah.[44] The Apostle argues, however, that this solution is no solution at all, for instead of integrating the aporetic event into the story it simply denies it. In contrast, Paul insists that the event must be taken seriously in its novelty and does so by heightening the aporetic character of the event. "Are you so foolish?" he asks, "Having started with the Spirit are you now ending with the flesh? Did you experience so much for nothing? – if it really was for nothing" (3:3–4). The Galatians began their life in Christ "with the Spirit" (having received and been empowered by God's Spirit) but not "with the flesh" (without observing the outward acts of obedience to Torah which the opponents are now urging upon them). This means that they had already reached the goal towards which (on a traditional understanding of Israel's story) "the flesh" – Torah observance – was intended to lead. They had already become part of God's eschatological people and had begun to take part in the blessed restoration of creation. Why would they want to go back to "the flesh," to a system of practices which had no part in bringing them to this point?[45] Why not take seriously the meaning which the story gives to their experience: that they are already part of God's eschatological people and need nothing else?[46]

What is more, Paul seems to imply that by going back to "the flesh" they would put their participation in the Spirit in jeopardy. That experience could

---

[43] So Dunn, *Galatians*, 153. See below, p. 215, n. 44 and p. 255–6, n. 54.

[44] This kind of approach might be suggested by Paul's allusion in 3:3 to attempts to become "perfect" or "complete" (ἐπιτελεῖσθε) by means of Torah obedience (so R. N. Longenecker, *Galatians*, 106).

[45] Paul uses σάρξ in 6:12–13 to denote the medium in which the opponents want to see Torah observed, i.e., the body which must be circumcised, etc. (so Martyn, *Galatians*, 290–91; cf. LXX Gen 17:10–13). On the other hand, in 5:16 σάρξ is used to denote the mode of human existence which is characterized by vulnerability to sin (so Martyn, *Galatians*, 292). Here, in chapter 3, the parallelism between vv. 2 and 3 associates the Spirit with faith and the "flesh" with "works of the law," so that σάρξ here seems to fit most closely with the former use for the locus of Torah observance (so Burton, *Galatians*, 148; Dunn, *Galatians*, 156). Yet it is also possible that the Apostle has the other sense of σάρξ in mind as well, heightening the irony that the Galatians would try to reach eschatological fulfilment from within the mode of existence which dooms them to failure (see Dunn, *Galatians*, 155–6).

[46] So Dunn, *Galatians*, 153–4.

end up being "for nothing" (3:4). To the opponents this would have sounded like nonsense. Torah is precisely the path *towards* eschatological blessing. How could observing it mean that one loses out on that reward? Paul implies, though, that in light of this novel event that whole understanding of the prior story needs to be rethought. If these Galatians were not justified while doing Torah, then perhaps the story has been misunderstood all along. Perhaps doing Torah was not necessary for justification after all, and by continuing to act as if it is one may miss what God is really looking for from human beings.

All of these implications are thick in the air in 3:5 when the Apostle repeats his question: "Well then, does God supply you with the Spirit and work miracles (ἐνεργῶν δυνάμεις) among you by your doing works of the law, or by your believing what you heard?" (3:5).[47] The shift to the present tense here, and thus to the ongoing experience of the Spirit in the community, brings Paul's questions to their implicit conclusion. If it was not by Torah observance that the Galatians initially received the Spirit (i.e., became part of God's eschatological people), then why would their ongoing life with God (which continues to be marked by experiences of that Spirit) depend on such observance?[48] Indeed, if they are to "finish," to reach "completion," it will not be by means of Torah obedience but by means of the faith through which they received the Spirit and continue to experience its power. Paul calls the Galatians "foolish" in 3:1 and 3:3 because they have not exercised the interpretive insight to see what are to Paul the obvious implications of their own experience. The reading of Israel's story which the opponents are presenting cannot make sense of their reception of the Spirit, and so the whole story must be reconfigured in a way which can bridge the interpretive gap opened up by this unexpected chapter.

---

[47] As Dunn notes (*Galatians*, 158) the present participles here (ἐπιχορηγῶν, ἐνεργῶν) suggest that experiences attributable to the Spirit were an ongoing reality among the Galatians and were not limited to a single conversion event (so Betz, *Galatians*, 135; R. N. Longenecker, *Galatians*, 105; Martyn, *Galatians*, 285). Note too that the verb used here for God's "working" of miracles (ἐνεργέω) was used in 2:8 for God's "working" through Paul and Peter in their missions.

[48] Martyn (*Galatians*, 285) correctly observes the implications of this shift in tense.

Chapter Ten

The Coherence of the Reconfigured Story

1. Reconfiguring the Episode of Abraham (3:6–9)

What Paul proceeds to do in 3:6–9 is to trace the outlines of a new "reading" of the prior story.[1] This is, he claims, an interpretation which takes seriously both Christ's death (2:15–21) and the Galatians' experience (3:1–5) and can integrate these novel events into the narrative as a whole. He begins where Israel began, with Abraham: "Just as Abraham 'believed God, and it was reckoned to him as righteousness,' so, you see, those who believe (οἱ ἐκ πίστεως) are the descendants of Abraham" (3:6–7). Paul may well have chosen Abraham as the focus of his reinterpretation of the story precisely because it is Abraham whom the opponents held up as a paradigm of those who will be considered righteous.[2] Yet the patriarch also offers Paul important parallels to the Galatians' experience. Like them, Abraham began as a Gentile and then came out of idolatry in response to God's call. Like them, Abraham was granted "righteousness" before he had obeyed any law, before even the first commandment of Torah was written. Like the Galatians who received the Spirit when they "believed" (οἱ ἐκ πίστεως)[3] that God had

---

[1] Most commentators take 3:6–9 as a unit dealing with Abraham as a precursor of the Galatians (so Burton, *Galatians*, 153; Dunn, *Galatians*, 159). Betz (*Galatians*, 142) divides these arguments differently, construing 3:6–7 as a kind of "thesis" with its proof text and vv. 8–13 as a series of scriptural "proofs" for that thesis and the applicability of the proof text. This reading seems, however, to contribute to his perplexity over Paul's logic.

[2] So Burton, *Galatians*, 153; R. N. Longenecker, *Galatians*, 110; Lührmann, *Galatians*, 56; Martyn, *Galatians*, 297 (though Martyn thinks that Gen 15:6 is Paul's own selection).

[3] The preposition ἐκ here can indicate that the πίστις is the source of or the basis for something. In Abraham's case πίστις brought "righteousness," while in the Galatians' case Paul has so far talked only in terms of πίστις bringing a reception of the Spirit, but given Paul's talk in 2:16 about believers being justified ἐκ πίστεως Χριστοῦ, the Apostle is probably assuming that reception of the Spirit is itself an indication that one is righteous in

acted in Christ, Abraham was granted this righteousness when he "believed" (ἐπίστευσεν) that God would act on his behalf to create a nation and bless the world. Here, Paul claims, Abraham represents the paradigm of exactly the same path taken by those in the Apostle's present who "believe" – a path which calls not for obedience to Torah but for "faith" in God's action. In this sense the Galatians are already "descendants of Abraham," those who live according to his paradigm.[4] At the same time, Paul's use of that expression is pregnant with excess meaning here, for the Apostle is quite aware that the title "descendants of Abraham" was also very often used by Jews to define themselves as members of God's people.[5] It may even have been a key phrase in the opponents' rhetoric encouraging circumcision.[6] By calling those who (like the Galatians) believe "the seed of Abraham," Paul is thus restating his interpretation of the Galatians' experience – that it demonstrates they are already accepted as part of God's people – and at the same time showing how, in the context of Israel's story, this is possible.[7] Abraham too gained righteousness with God simply by believing.

God's sight. Given that God is consistently seen as the source of this justification (see 3:6, 8), this πίστις is not the source of that benefit but the proximate basis on which it is received. Longenecker's suggestion that ἐκ means to "rely on" faith (*Galatians*, 114) stretches the sense of the preposition and obscures the nature of πίστις itself as a "relying on" God's action in Christ. Martyn's paraphrase, "those whose identity is derived from faith," is better (*Galatians*, 299), but still does not convey very well the way in which faith is the *sine qua non* of their salvation.

[4] Dunn (*Galatians*, 163) points out that the Semitic idiom "son of X" to denote a person with the quality X "would make the transition in thought from 'like Abraham' to 'sons of Abraham' all the easier for Paul", and he observes that a similar idiom seems to have been common in Greek (see further BDAG, 1024 [2.c.a]).

[5] See the expression "seed of Abraham" in Ps 105:6; Isa 41:8, and the connection between one's descent from Abraham and covenant status in *Pss. Sol.* 9:17; 3 Macc 6:3. As Dunn (*Galatians*, 160) points out, Philo devotes a whole work to the question of who is the heir of Abraham (*Her.*). Abraham was often portrayed as a model of the pious Jew (e.g., *Jub.* 23:10; *CD* III 2) and the prototype of the genuine convert to Judaism (*Jub.* 12; *Apoc. Ab.* 1–8; Philo, *Abr.* 60–88; Jos., *A.J.* 1.155), so that being a descendant of Abraham would mean precisely to be a faithful Jew.

[6] So Martyn, *Galatians*, 299.

[7] Betz (*Galatians*, 141) misses this when he suggests that the claim "is the result of the following argument here anticipated." Rather, it is the (apparently impossible) implication of the Galatians' experience, which has already been made more intelligible by Paul's highlighting of Gen 15:6.

Moreover, the Apostle claims that the Scriptures read in this light can be seen to have predicted that other Gentiles would follow Abraham's example and find righteousness through faith. For this, Paul suggests, is what God meant when he declared to Abraham: "All the Gentiles shall be blessed in you" (3:8).[8] Certainly this was not the way the Abraham episode had traditionally been read, but Paul's implicit claim is that this reconfiguration of the episode allows the Galatians' experience to be taken seriously and so represents a better reading of the narrative as a whole, the narrative which continues to unfold in the present. Confronted with that experience, Paul can now understand that "the scripture" (here personified) gave Abraham this promise "foreseeing (προϊδοῦσα) that God would justify the Gentiles by faith (ἐκ πίστεως)" (3:8).[9] Once it has been thus recast, however, the story suggests a new way of understanding how the role of a member of God's people is defined. It is not those who obey Torah who will be "rescued" (1:4), but instead "those who believe (οἱ ἐκ πίστεως) are blessed with Abraham who believed (ὁ πιστός)" (3:9).[10]

---

[8] Paul's citation is a mixture of Gen 12:3 and Gen 18:18, but, as Dunn observes, "the promise was repeated several times within the patiarchal narratives (also Gen. xxii.17–18; xxvi.4; xxviii.14), and such variation of detail was inconsequential" (*Galatians*, 164; so also Burton, *Galatians*, 160). At the same time, most Jews in Paul's day (and certainly the opponents) took as their starting point the later formulations of the promise which mention Abraham's faithfulness, interpreting Abraham's faith in Gen 15:6 in terms of the faithfulness which is emphasized in other promise passages (Dunn [*Galatians*, 161] points to Sir 44:19–21; 1 Macc 2:52; *Jub.* 17:15–18; *m. Avot* 5:3; Philo, *Abr.* 262–74; Jas 2.23; so R. N. Longenecker, *Galatians*, 110–11, 113–14). Indeed, as Lührmann observes, Abraham is often presented as the model proselyte (*Galatians*, 58; see below, pp. 222–3, n. 56). Paul, on the other hand, begins from the first two formulations in Genesis where that emphasis is missing (so Dunn, *Galatians*, 164–5).

[9] So Martyn, *Galatians*, 301.

[10] Dunn (*Galatians*, 166–7) suggests that the present tense of "are blessed" (εὐλογοῦνται) points to the reality of the Galatians' experience as the fulfilment of this promised blessing.

The emphasis throughout this section on Abraham's having been justified on the basis of believing, and *not* (as in traditional Judaism) on the basis of his faithful obedience, suggests that the adjective πιστῷ should be taken in the sense "believing," "having faith," rather than the more usual "faithful" (so Burton, *Galatians*, 162; R. N. Longenecker, *Galatians*, 116). If this is correct, then Paul would seem to be reworking a traditional epithet of Abraham, ὁ πιστός, which usually refers to the patriarch's righteous *obedience* (see, e.g., Sir 44:20; 1 Macc 2:52; 2 Macc 1:2; Philo, *Post.* 173). In Paul's new reading of the story Abraham is

Betz is not alone when he complains that Paul's interpretation of the Abraham passage, and indeed his scriptural interpretation throughout chapter 3, "appears arbitrary in the highest degree."[11] As we uncover the hermeneutical logic which drives the Apostle's argument, however, we begin to see that this appearance of arbitrariness stems to a large extent from a misunderstanding of what Paul is trying to do. His references to scripture in chapter 3 are not to be taken as "proof texts,"[12] nor are they meant to be free-standing "arguments from Scripture" which have argumentative weight independent of the "argument from experience" in 2:15–21 and 3:1–5.[13] Rather, Paul is demonstrating a reconfiguration of Israel's story which allows one to take seriously both the surprising new events which the Galatians have experienced and the Messiah's shameful death.[14] Paul does not expect his reading of the Abraham story to seem natural. On the contrary, it is only in light of these new events that the Abraham episode comes to take on this new meaning. What Paul insists, however, is that once one recognizes the significance (in the context of Israel's story) of the Galatians' experiences, one *can* go back and reread the Abraham episode in a way which is very much in keeping with these new events.

πιστός before he receives any commands, simply by virtue of his trust in God's promise to bless him (cf. the treatment in *1QapGen*, which does not seem to emphasize Abraham's virtue so strongly; so Fitzmyer, *Genesis Apocryphon*, 182).

[11] Betz, *Galatians*, 137. Betz quotes Loisy to the effect that Paul's interpretation here is "une fantaisie ingénieuse" (in ibid., 137).

[12] Contra Betz, *Galatians*, 138.

[13] Contra Burton, *Galatians*, 153; Dunn, *Galatians*, 159; R. N. Longenecker, *Galatians*, 109; Martyn, *Galatians*, 294–5. This division is made even more sharply by Schlier, *Galater*, 126; Mussner, *Galaterbrief*, 211.

[14] Note that 3:6 begins with the comparative adverb καθώς. The NRSV (cited above) treats this as if the "just as" of 3:6 sets up a "so . . ." in 3:7, but grammatically this completion of the comparison is not present in 3:7. It is much easier to read the καθώς at the beginning of 3:6 as pointing *back* to the experience of the Galatians in 3:1–5, so that Paul is emphasizing that Abraham's experience flowed "in the same way" as did the Galatians' own (so Burton, *Galatians*, 153; Martyn, *Galatians*, 296). This implies a much closer connection between 3:1–5 and what follows than most commentators have allowed. Even Martyn (*Galatians*, 297), who sees this grammatical link, still treats it as co-ordinating two independent arguments (one experiential and the other exegetical) instead of recognizing that the connection it sets up between the Galatians' experience and Scripture is itself the fulcrum of a single argument.

2. Reconfiguring Israel's Broader Story (3:10–14)

2.1. Paul's Convoluted Appeals to Scripture

The obvious objection to Paul's reconfiguration of the Abraham episode is that his rereading cannot account for Abraham's circumcision and the covenant which it constitutes in Gen 17:4–14. There God declares: "Any uncircumcised male who is not circumcised in the flesh of his foreskin shall be cut off from his people; he has broken my covenant" (Gen 17:14). Instead of addressing this difficult passage head-on, however,[15] Paul chooses to widen his reconfiguration of the traditional story in order to establish a reading of the narrative as a whole which coheres with his reconfiguration of the Abraham episode.

Paul begins this broader reconfiguration of the traditional story with a statement which would have been shocking to most first-century Jews: "For all who rely on the works of the law (ὅσοι γὰρ ἐξ ἔργων νόμου) are under a curse" (3:10).[16] On what basis can Paul make such an outrageous claim? Most interpreters have assumed that what follows in 3:10b–12 is a sort of deductive argument, intended to prove on the basis of Scripture that those who take the opponents' approach to law are cursed by God.[17] On such a

---

[15] Precisely why Paul avoids dealing with Gen 17:14 is not clear (though see Rom 4:9–12). Burton suggests that Paul may have felt that "the argument of his opponents on this point could not be directly answered" and so instead sought to establish on broader grounds that the opponents' understanding could not be correct (*Galatians*, 159). In any case, Burton is right in speculating that Paul "may have reasoned that the oracle [of Gen 17:14] ought to be interpreted in view of the fact, to him well established by his own observation, that God was accepting Gentiles on the basis of faith without works of law in general or circumcision in particular" (*Galatians*, 162).

[16] Davis has presented forceful evidence that the expression ὑπὸ κατάραν does not mean "subject to the power or authority of a curse," but rather "cursed" (*Christ as Devotio*, 51; see Jos. *A.J.* 18.287). Dunn recognizes the shocking nature of Paul's statement (*Galatians*, 170) but tries to soften it by understanding those who are ἐξ ἔργων νόμου to be those who emphasize the status of the Jewish nation, as defined by boundary markers such as circumcision (*Galatians*, 172). Yet the following citation of Deut 27:26 addresses the expectation that Torah observance will bring justification, not the question of whether Israel has a specially favoured status. Those who are ἐξ ἔργων νόμου are, as R. N. Longenecker puts it, simply those who view "observance of Torah as obligatory for God's people" (*Galatians*, 166).

[17] Paul is not (contra Betz, *Galatians*, 144) simply setting up "those of the law" as the

reading the Apostle introduces his quotation of Deut 27:26 as a premise in a syllogism intended to prove his shocking thesis that the law-observant are cursed. The difficulty is, however, that the verse which he cites seems to say the opposite what of Paul claims here. At the renewal of Israel's covenant Moses declares: "Cursed is everyone who does not observe and obey all the things written in the book of the law" (3:10).[18] Yet Paul is trying to argue that it is those who *do* try to keep Torah who are cursed.[19] Although there has been a host of recent suggestions as to Paul's train of thought here, the most popular solution is that Paul has another unspoken premise in mind, for example, that no one is actually able to do what the law requires.[20] The result would then be a syllogism which runs like this:

> *Premise A (stated)*: Those who disobey Torah are cursed (3:10b).
> *Corollary of Premise A (unstated)*: Those who obey Torah are not cursed.
> *Premise B (unstated)*: No one successfully obeys Torah.
>
> *Conclusion*: No one by obeying Torah avoids being cursed (3:10a).

---

opposite of "those of faith" in 3:9 and then inferring that if the latter are blessed then the former must be cursed. As Betz himself recognizes, the γάρ which introduces the following citation from Deut 27:26 introduces it as "the reason for the preceding statement" (*Galatians*, 144, n. 58; so Dunn, *Galatians*, 170; R. N. Longenecker, *Galatians*, 118). This implies that Paul is actually trying to argue for his position, not simply to set up an arbitrary dichotomy.

[18] Actually Paul mixes the substance of Deut 27:26 with elements found in Deut 28:58 and 30:10. He has, however, preserved the intent of these passages (so Burton, *Galatians*, 164; R. N. Longenecker, *Galatians*, 117; cf. Betz, *Galatians*, 145).

[19] Davis is concerned that if those who are cursed in 3:10 are restricted to those who attempt to observe Torah, it becomes inexplicable why Christ's liberation from that curse in 3:13 would have any impact on Gentiles (3:14), since those Gentiles would not have been cursed in the first place (*Christ as Devotio*, 52). As becomes clear in 3:19–29, however, Paul believes that between Sinai and Christ's advent there was no route to justification other than Torah obedience. Hence, although his focus in 3:10–12 is on those who attempt that obedience, he seems to be assuming that non-observant Gentiles are, if anything, in an even worse position. When Christ's action frees Jews from the curse to which nomism doomed them, this entails new possibilities for all who fail to keep the law, Gentiles included.

[20] So Berger, "Abraham," 51; Bruce, *Galatians*, 159; Eckert, *Urchristliche Verkündigung*, 77; Eckstein, *Verheißung*, 130–31, 149–50; Fung, *Galatians*, 142; Hofius, "Gesetz des Mose," 54–63; Lietzmann, *Galater*, 11; R. N. Longenecker, *Galatians*, 118; Luz, *Geschichtsverständnis*, 95; Mussner, *Galaterbrief*, 224–6; Oepke, *Galater*, 72; Räisänen, *Paul*, 94–5; Schoeps, *Paul*, 176–7; Schreiner, "Paul and Perfect Obedience," 247; Thurén, *Derhetorizing*, 87; Westerholm, *Perspectives*, 375; Wilckens, "Aus Werken," 92–4.

This reading allows Paul to present a logically valid argument in 3:10. The difficulty with such an interpretation, however, is that it requires Paul to assume what would have been a highly contentious idea: that the law could not be kept. After all, the very verse which he cites seems to presuppose that it *can* be,[21] and this was the standard view among first-century Jews.[22] Is it realistic to think that Paul would leave such an obvious hole in his argument undefended, an opening for easy refutation by his opponents in Galatia? Thus we seem to be left with Paul making an argument which is either extraordinarily weak or obviously incoherent.[23]

---

[21] So Dunn, *Galatians*, 171.

[22] So Dunn, *Galatians*, 171 (despite the exceptions cited in R. N. Longenecker, *Galatians*, 118; *idem*, *Paul, Apostle of Liberty*, 40–3; Schoeps, *Paul*, 177). *4 Ezra* seems to espouse a pessimism almost as deep as Paul's (see esp. *4 Ezra* 4:20–22), but this document comes from after the fall of Jerusalem in 70 CE. If B. W. Longenecker is correct, it was that event which prompted the author of *4 Ezra* to rethink his Jewish beliefs, much as Paul's Damascus road experience was the catalyst for the Apostle's reconfiguration of Israel's story (*Eschatology*, 268 and *passim*).

[23] For a thorough examination of the various other proposals for interpreting these verses, see Wakefield, *Where to Live*, 66–96. Some have suggested that it is the very attempt to keep Torah, i.e., to establish one's own righteousness, which Paul considers sinful (so Schlier, *Galater*, 132f., 134f.). This idea is, however, nowhere actually stated in Paul (so Dunn, *Galatians*, 171, 176). Paul never gives the impression that his past efforts at law keeping were were wrong in and of themselves (see, e.g., Gal 1:14; Phil 3:4).

Others understand the "works of the law" (ἔργων νόμου) in 3:10a to be nomistic observances which fail to satisfy the law's actual demands, demands such as the exercise of faith or love and which constitute "the law of Christ" in 6:2 (so Cranfield, *Romans*, 2.848; Fuller, "Works of the Law"; Lull, *Spirit*, 124–5). Similarly, Dunn suggests that Paul opposes the misuse of Torah as an ethnic boundary marker and the resultant exclusion of Gentiles from God's people (*Galatians*, 172–3; cf. Bryant, *Crucified Christ*, 176). Yet Paul does not encourage any alternative, proper kind of law-keeping. Rather, he claims that believers are beyond the law's jurisdiction (see, e.g., Gal 2:18–19; 5:2, 18). On "fulfilling" the law, see below, pp. 271–3. On the expression "works of the law," see pp. 181–83.

Some see Paul simply assuming a law/faith dichotomy in which law is associated with curse and faith with blessing and life (so Betz, *Galatians*, 146; Martyn, *Galatians*, 311–12). On such a reading Paul does not actually believe that anyone would be justified, even if they kept Torah perfectly (so Burton, *Galatians*, 164–5). Yet this requires that Paul be reading *against* Deut 27:26 when he cites it here (and against Lev 18:5 in 3:12; cf. Rom 2:6–12). On the law's origin with God, see below p. 222, n. 53 and 226, n. 66. Even less convincing is Martyn's suggestion that Paul simply "removes the distinction" between the observant and non-observant and applies the curse spoken by Deut 27:26 to *both* groups without explanation (*Galatians*, 311). Paul would have known that such exegesis by fiat

The Apostle rephrases his claim in 3:11, shifting from talk about curse and blessing to talk about justification: "It is evident that no one is justified before God by the law."[24] Here Paul seems to offer two explicit premises on

---

would not get him far with the Galatians. On the other hand, if Paul cites Deut 27:26 to illustrate the fact that the law is a force which curses, rather than blesses (so Martyn, *Galatians*, 311–12), it would be odd for him to introduce Lev 18:5 two verses later – a verse which presents law as offering life. Cf. pp. 203–4, n. 17 above.

Other suggestions have been even less successful. Lührmann argues that Paul actually interprets the grammar of the LXX of Deut 27:26 as saying that "No one who adheres to all that is written in the book of the law stands under the blessing" (*Galatians*, 61), but it is difficult to imagine the Apostle so badly misconstruing (even for polemical purposes) the point of such a well-known passage. Sanders understands Paul to use his citations here as "proof-texts" which provide the Apostle with key combinations of words (e.g., "law" and "curse") but whose substance is simply ignored as Paul uses these key terms to make his own declarations in 3:10a and 3:12a (*Paul, the Law, and the Jewish People*, 21–2, 54 n. 30; cf. Betz, *Galatians*, 137–8; R. N. Longenecker, *Galatians*, 118). Such a use of scripture would not, however, be in keeping with his use elsewhere, even within Galatians. Young suggests that Paul is simply discussing the *threat* of cursing which hangs over those who try to keep Torah ("Who's Cursed," 86–8), but Christ's "rescue" of believers in 3:13 seems to save them from more than just the curse's threat. Wright (*Climax*, 146–7) argues that 3:10 should be read as a discussion of Israel's *national* fate, and reflects a common Jewish belief that Judea's subjugation to Rome was a manifestation of the deuteronomic curse. Yet nowhere here does Paul mentions the nation explicitly. Moreover, since 3:13–14 seem to require that Gentiles be subject to this curse, Israel's experience would be irrelevant unless their national experience leads to the broader idea that human beings cannot successfully keep Torah (see Wakefield, *Where to Live*, 70, n. 45). There is also little evidence in first-century Judaism for this sense of languishing under the curse (Dunn, *Galatians*, 171–2). Wakefield proposes that Paul is discussing in 3:10–12 only the kind of life which is appropriate to those who have been made righteous by Christ, not how one *gains* or *maintains* righteousness (*Where to Live*, 177–88). Yet the curse of Deut 27:26 is certainly "soteriological" in its original covenantal context, and Paul ends this section with a reference to Christ's act of deliverance from the curse (3:13), an act which elsewhere is always treated as "soteriological" and which in 3:14 seems to make possible (ἵνα) the Gentiles' inclusion in eschatological salvation (i.e., reception of the Spirit). Moreover, the preceding verses (2:16–3:9) have been concerned with law and faith as competing options in the attempt to become righteous. Hence, when he offers a paraphrase of these verses Wakefield himself lapses back into very "soteriological" talk about *how* one can live "in the new age" instead of in "the old age of sin and death and law" (*Where to Live*, 187–88).

[24] The explanatory ὅτι which follows in 3:11b suggests that 3:11a is again a thesis which Paul then goes on to demonstrate (contra Wright, *Climax*, 137–56; Zahn, *Galater*, 152–7). It is unlikely that Paul is setting up in v. 11a "the actual attitude of God" (Burton, *Galatians*, 165; so R. N. Longenecker, *Galatians*, 118; Martyn, *Galatians*, 326) in order to pit it

the basis of which one may draw this conclusion. The first is another quotation, this time from Hab 2:4: "The one who is righteous will live by faith" (3:11b). The second premise is again stated in Paul's own words: "But the law does not rest on faith" (3:12a).[25] The resulting syllogism runs like this:

Premise A: Faith is the means by which one becomes righteous (3:11b).
Premise B: Keeping Torah is not an expression of faith (3:12a).[26]

Conclusion: Keeping Torah is not the means by which one becomes righteous (3:11a).

This time the syllogism appears to be valid as stated. The problem in this second stage of Paul's argument is again that the Galatian opponents would certainly have disagreed with both of his premises. They could easily have criticized his exegesis of Hab 2:4 as faulty. The full text of Habakkuk's words reads: "Look at the proud! Their spirit is not right (לֹא־יָשְׁרָה) in them, but the righteous (וְצַדִּיק) live by their faith (בֶּאֱמוּנָתוֹ)." The noun אֱמוּנָה, which is here translated "faith," can mean either "trust" or "faithfulness." Paul's Galatian opponents would simply have to argue, as have several modern commentators, that Habakkuk is actually extolling the "righteous," that is, those who live "by their [own] faithfulness" to God, by which they distinguish themselves from the "proud," who are not "right."[27] Hence, the opponents might have argued, the verse can hardly be used to justify a distinction between faith and obedience. In fact, those opponents would probably point out that for Habakkuk the law-keeping of the righteous likely

---

against the (false?) judgement of Deut 27:26. Nowhere else does Paul display this kind of hostile approach to scriptural quotations, and he affirms similar ideas in Rom 2:6–12.

[25] The δέ at the beginning of 3:12a is most likely disjunctive, expressing the contrast between the faith described in 3:11b and the law described in 3:12a (so R. N. Longenecker, *Galatians*, 119; contra Betz, *Galatians*, 147).

[26] The affirmation that νόμος is not ἐκ πίστεως is somewhat ambiguous. The ἐκ might suggest the idea of faith as the origin or source of law, in which case Paul would mean that Torah itself originated from somewhere other than the divine source of the Gospel (so Martyn, *Galatians*, 315). Given Paul's positive use of quotations from those Scriptures, however, this is an unlikely reading. It is more plausible to see Paul using ἐκ πίστεως much like he did in 3:7 and to be claiming that the attempt to achieve righteousness based on legal obedience is incompatible with the path to righteousness which relies on God's action in Christ. On ἐκ πίστεως see above, pp. 199–200, n. 3.

[27] This is not to say that Hab 2:4 was always interpreted in this way. See *1QpHab* VII 14–VIII 3 and the discussion in R. N. Longenecker, *Galatians*, 119.

is an expression of their faith(fulness), so that the very passage which Paul cites demonstrates how the law does "rest on faith."[28] This is not to say that either Paul or his opponents would have been concerned to isolate the "original" sense of Habakkuk's prophecy, but Paul's reading of Hab 2:4 depends on the very distinction between faith and legal obedience which it is supposed to demonstrate. Unless all parties were willing to grant that distinction, his argument in 3:11 would lack any force. If they had been willing to allow the distinction in the first place, then the argument would have been unnecessary.[29]

The Apostle does offer one more scriptural quotation, apparently as justification for his disjunction between law and faith, citing Lev 18:5 to the effect that "Whoever does the works of the law will live by them" (3:12).[30] Evidently Paul is thinking of this verse as illustrating the way in which law is

---

[28] This makes it doubtful that Paul would be picking up Hab 2:4 from his opponents and simply applying it "in ad hominem fashion" (R. N. Longenecker, *Galatians*, 119); if so, his *ad hominem* use would be self-defeating.

[29] Alternatively, 3:11 may be tied more closely to 3:10 so that, having established that legal observance does not justify, the Apostle draws on Hab 2:4 as evidence that God has provided an alternative path to "life." In this case the distinction between faith and law observance would be explicable, but the validity of the argument would again depend on the claim that no one can in fact keep Torah.

[30] As R. N. Longenecker observes (*Galatians*, 120), this citation of Lev 18:5 is introduced with the strong adversative ἀλλά, suggesting that Paul viewed the verse as a strong counter-indication against the compatability of faith and law which he had just entertained (and denied).

Dunn suggests that Paul understands Lev 18:5 to define Torah as only "the means of regulating life within the covenant, not the basis of the covenant itself" (*Galatians*, 175). Hence Paul is drawing a contrast between faith which in Hab 2:4 is the basis for one's whole existence before God and Torah, which in Lev 18:5 is only an administrative code. Yet it is doubtful that Jews would have interpreted Lev 18:5 in such a restrictive sense, and Paul's prior citation of Deut 27:26 suggests he is reading Lev 18:5 in similar deuteronomic terms. Wakefield wants to avoid the issue of justification altogether in 3:11–12 and thinks that Paul is simply emphasizing how the mode of one's justification determines the sphere within which one has to live from then on (*Where to Live*, 174–7). This reading stumbles, though, on 3:11a, where Paul introduces the citation of Hab 2:4 as evidence for the claim that ἐν νόμῳ οὐδεὶς δικαιοῦται. This statement seems to require that the following citations which support it in 3:11b–12 are also concerned with how one gains righteousness. Martyn argues that, for Paul, the content of Lev 18:5 is not ἐκ πίστεως and hence not God's word (*Galatians*, 315, 328–34), but we should favour a reading on which Paul would maintain the truth of the Scripture he cites (cf. pp. 222, n. 53 and 226, n. 66 below).

based on the fundamental requirement to "do" (ὁ ποιήσας αὐτά) certain actions, while "believing" is based on a denial that our actions are the crucial factor in the divine–human relationship.[31] Yet unless one has already accepted that faith does not involve "doing," this quotation need not be read as evidence of that disjunction.[32] Paul's argument in 3:10–12 appears to be a complete failure, a skein of superficial verbal parallels which do nothing more than create a first impression of coherence.

Indeed, this is precisely the verdict which several commentators have passed on Paul's thinking in these verses.[33] Even those sympathetically disposed to the Apostle have often felt the need to apologize for his faulty logic here by explaining that it is "Rabbinic" or "Jewish," but one suspects that the Jewish opponents of Paul would not have found it very convincing as a display of syllogistic reasoning.[34] This raises the question whether by

---

[31] So Berger, "Abraham," 52; R. N. Longenecker, *Galatians*, 120. There has, of course, been strong opposition to the notion of a "believing"/"doing" contrast here, but it seems difficult to avoid. The Apostle introduces this quotation in order to ground his last assertion that law is incompatible with faith as a way of maintaining one's "life" (3:12a). The thrust of the quotation is that life comes through law if one *does* it. The quotation certainly suggests, then, that this demand for *doing* is what the Apostle sees as incompatible with πίστις (so Eckstein, *Verheißung*, 148–9). This is, moreover, what Paul says explicitly in Rom 4:4–5. Although it is often suggested that this idea of life as a reward for activity is an inaccurate portrait of Second-Temple Jewish piety, Gathercole has shown that Second-Temple writers very often predicate entrance into eschatological life (or this-worldly blessing and longevity) on one's obedience to Torah (*Where Is Boasting*, 37–111; see also Bauckham, "Apocalypses"; Falk, "Psalms and Prayers"; Evans, "Scripture-based Stories"; Alexander, "Tannaitic Literature"). What Paul is doing is highlighting (in a way which most Jews did not) the real emphasis of Torah piety on the basic requirement of "doing" God's will, a requirement which only now looks so starkly opposed to faith because of the law-free form in which that faith has manifested itself among the Gentiles.

[32] This problem remains even if, as Lührmann suggests, ζήσεται here means simply "will conduct his/herself." Paul's argument still depends on our assuming that the lifestyle of faith in 3:11b is incompatible with the lifestyle of legal obedience in 3:12 (*Galatians*, 61). Betz (*Galatians*, 147) suggests that Paul does simply presuppose the opposition between faith and doing Torah (cf. Bryant, *Crucified Christ*, 177). Yet it seems this distinction is precisely what Paul introduces the quotation from Lev 18:5 to prove: ὁ δὲ νόμος οὐκ ἔστιν ἐκ πίστεως, ἀλλά . . .

[33] Lührmann, for example, writes that Paul "seems indiscriminately to take Old Testament passages out of their context and apply them just as it suits him" (*Galatians*, 58).

[34] On attempts to see specific rabbinic exegetical methods at work here, see Davis, *Christ as Devotio*, 32–44. It may well be that Paul has drawn some or all of these scriptural texts

reading 3:10–12 as a syllogistic argument we have not misconstrued what Paul is doing.

2.2. Demonstrating the Coherence of the Reconfigured Story

Let us try, then, to read 3:10–12 not as a progressive argument which moves from unimpeachable premises to a logically necessary conclusion, but as a paradigmatic re-imagining of Israel's relationship with God which refutes the opponents' version of that story by being more coherent.[35] It is a crucial element of such a reading that we not, as is usually done, separate out these verses as an isolated unit which is supposed on its own to be logically valid and rhetorically forceful. Rather we must begin with the awareness that Paul has already played his "trump cards" in 2:15–21 and 3:1–5; he has already demonstrated on the basis of the Galatians' religious experience and Christ's death that the opponents' version of Israel's story must be wrong. Dunn is right that in Paul's mind the Galatians' "own experience of receiving the Spirit through faith should have been sufficient to confirm [Paul's] basic position."[36] In order to refute the opponents, then, what remains is to

---

from the arsenal of the opponents (see Martyn, *Galatians*, 309), but this still does not change the fact that his use of them appears muddled.

[35] This is, in essence, what Eckert saw when he described this section of Galatians as a revisionist reading of Israel's "Heilsgeschichte" (*Urchristliche Verkündigung*, 102–6). Such an interpretation can fit with Paul's use of connectives in 3:10–12, though it does require that we read them less rigidly. The γάρ at the opening of 3:10a is certainly not to be taken as introducing the strict logical basis for 3:9, but rather as a "marker of clarification" (BDAG, 189 [2]) which introduces the next step or phase in a narrative or discussion without specifying a tight causal connection. The γάρ which introduces 3:10b can then easily be understood in a similar sense, so that the quotation of Deut 27:26 is not the strict *cause* of the statement in 3:10a but (in combination with 3:11a, to which it is joined by a δέ) a further elaboration of that shocking idea. The ὅτι which introduces v. 11b *should* be understood as causal, introducing the reason not just for 3:11a but for all of 3:10–3:11a, for this whole portrait of the fate of the law observant. This ὅτι introduces not just 3:11b, but all of 3:11b–12 (3:11b is co-ordinated with 3:12a by a δέ and 3:11b–12a and 3:12b are then contrasted sharply by the strong ἀλλά) as the basic paradigm which makes sense of the previous statements. The explanatory ὅτι still does not require, however, that 3:11b–12 be understood as the ultimate justification for this whole paradigm. That comes, as we will see below, in 3:13, which is emphasized by the sudden, asyndetic nature of the transition there.

[36] Dunn, *Galatians*, 174. So Eckert, *Urchristliche Verkündigung*, 152–3. Lührmann has this precisely backward when he suggests that the point of 3:6–14 "is to answer the question in v. 5: the Spirit comes indeed from faith and not from the law (v. 14b)" (*Galatians*, 55).

complete the task which he took up in 3:6–9 of demonstrating a reconfiguration of Israel's story which is internally coherent and at the same time allows the surprising events in Galatia to be taken seriously.

What kind of pattern does Paul find in Israel's story? It is emphatically not the straightforward deuteronomic pattern in which those who faithfully keep Torah are the ones who are rewarded. This is clear from his initial statements in 3:10 and 3:11a: "no one is justified before God by the law." That this kind of deuteronomic idea can be found in Israel's Scriptures Paul does not deny. In fact, when he quotes Deut 27:26 he seems to be deliberately drawing on the central text of that deuteronomic theology (Deut 27–28) in order to bring to mind the whole pattern of blessing and judgement which Israel experienced.[37] This same experience is picked up again in verse 12, where Paul characterizes the operation of the law by appeal to Lev 18:5. Paul thus deliberately heightens the emphasis on the necessity of "doing" the Law (ὁ ποιήσας αὐτά), along with the retribution which follows on failure, which he finds present in the Scriptures.

Against this approach to God through obedience and law, Paul sets "faith," πίστις. Paul has already shown in 3:1–5 that in the Galatians' experience this faith constitutes an approach to God which does not require the observance of Torah. He has already found a similar law-free path illustrated by the experience of Abraham (3:6–9). Here he follows through on this new way of reading Israel's story by looking for evidence elsewhere of that different approach to God, and he finds it in Hab 2:4. Whether or not Paul's reading of Habakkuk is consonant with other Jewish readings in his day, and whether his understanding of אֱמוּנָה in 2:4 is in line with the prophet's original conception, do not matter. He is probably well aware that he is, from a traditional perspective, doing violence to the story. Yet he finds here an affirmation of faith, πίστις in the LXX, as the basis of life in which he now hears an echo of the experience of Abraham and the Galatians.

Still, even if Paul can find in Israel's story the material with which to reread it as a story of two different ways of relating to God (law and faith), why does this require that those who take the path of law always suffer the

---

[37] Dunn suggests that Paul's mixture here of elements from several verses in Deut 27–28 "underlines the extent to which Paul was recalling the whole of that concluding section of Deuteronomy, indeed 'the book of the law' itself and the whole mind-set of nomistic covenantalism which Deuteronomy established for Jewish thought" (*Galatians*, 170).

law's curse? Why could law and faith not remain two parallel ways of approach, one for Jews and the other for Gentiles? Again, Paul cannot expect his audience to follow his argument if it depends on a simple assumption that all fail in their observance of Torah. Such a position is so atypical of Second-Temple Jewish thought that it would need some sort of justification. We must remember, however, that Paul has already established in 2:21 that righteousness cannot come on the basis of legal observance, and the key phenomenon there which ruled out any such construal of Israel's story was the crucifixion of Christ.[38] In 3:10–14, then, Paul need not start from scratch with an argument against justification by Torah. The likelihood that the Messiah's death is still in Paul's mind (and, he hopes, in the audience's awareness) as motivation for this whole reconfiguration is confirmed near the end of this phase in Paul's argument, in 3:13. For there Paul returns to remind the audience of this "gap" which has made his reinterpretation necessary in the first place. "Christ," Paul says, "redeemed us from the curse of the law by becoming a curse for us – for it is written, 'Cursed is everyone who hangs on a tree'" (3:13).[39] It is this shocking event, and not any scriptural passage, which serves as the initial impetus and final justification for Paul's narrative reconfiguration in which faith and legal obedience are decisively separated.

Because the Apostle has already argued that the cross rules out a righteousness coming from Torah obedience, he does not explicitly repeat that argument here. It is nevertheless tempting, despite my insistence that I am examining Paul's argument and not his own process of discovery, to transgress that boundary for a moment and trace beneath Paul's explicit argument in 3:13 a narrative hermeneutic in the Apostle's own thought which is reminiscent of 2:15–21 and 3:1–5. Paul alludes in 3:13 to the way in which

---

[38] So, contra Sanders (*Paul, the Law, and the Jewish People*, 26), Paul does present Christ's death as the grounding for his argument against righteousness' coming by the law.

[39] Longenecker observes (*Galatians*, 121) that the absence of a connecting particle between vv. 12 and 13 breaks the flow of Paul's language slightly, adding rhetorical emphasis to his introduction of Christ as saviour.

The citation in the second half of 3:13 is from Deut 21:22–23. For "cursed" Paul has the adjective ἐπικατάρατος, while our LXX has the passive participle κεκατηραμένος. Dunn suggests, plausibly, that Paul adjusted this word in order to echo more closely his citation of Deut 27:26 (*Galatians*, 177–8; so R. N. Longenecker, *Galatians*, 122; Martyn, *Galatians*, 321). While Paul omits the words ὑπὸ θεοῦ, which designate God as the subject doing the cursing, Paul likely took this as assumed (so R. N. Longenecker, *Galatians*, 122).

Christ's crucifixion constituted an interpretive "gap" for anyone who believed that he had also been raised again. For in the context of Israel's story Jesus' glorious resurrection could only mean that he had been vindicated by God. Yet, as Paul points out with his quotation from Deut 21:23, that same traditional story also forces one to interpret crucifixion as a sign of God's curse, of divine judgement on lawbreakers.[40] How could Jesus have both been God's righteous agent and yet have suffered God's curse on unrighteousness? Paul follows the solution offered in early Christian thought generally and interpreted Christ's shameful death, his suffering of the deuteronomic curse, as being somehow "for us."[41] It was not really a punishment for his own violation of the covenant, but rather a God-ordained event which makes possible the vicarious escape of God's people from the judgement which they actually face. If this is the significance of Christ's passion, then that new and unforeseen chapter again forces a reconsideration of what had gone before.[42] For if God had to resort to such measures in order to deliver his people from the deuteronomic curse, then they must have been falling far short of the covenant obedience which would have brought them life.[43] Indeed, if (as the early Christians agreed) Jesus was God's Messiah, the

---

[40] So Berger, "Abraham," 52; Bruce, *Galatians*, 166; Bryant, *Crucified Christ*, 178. Dunn (*Galatians*, 178) points out that Deut 21:23 was already being applied to those who were crucified in the first century (see *4QpNah* I 7–8; *11QT* 64.6–13; cf. Acts 5:30, 10:39). See further Fitzmyer, "Crucifixion in Ancient Palestine." Evidence of the sense of scandal attaching to Christian acceptance of a crucified Messiah can be seen in 1 Cor 1:23; Gal 5:11. Dunn (*Galatians*, 178) seems to miss the interpretive dilemma which the crucifixion would have caused when he portrays Paul as simply using an early Jewish slander against Christ (based on Deut 21:23) in order to establish a connection between Jesus (the outcast) and Gentiles (also "outside the camp"). It is, moreover, doubtful that Paul regarded the resurrection as an indication of "God's acceptance of the 'outsider,' the cursed law-breaker, the Gentile sinner" in any general way (contra Dunn, *Galatians*, 178). For Jesus was not in Paul's mind actually a lawbreaker or sinner, and the Apostle does not imagine that other "outcasts" can find salvation except through Christ, by sharing in *his* death and resurrection.

[41] See also 2 Cor 5:21. We need not decide here exactly how Paul imagined Christ's death (and resurrection?) to deal with the law's curse. For some suggestions, see Berger, "Abraham," 52; Betz, *Galatians*, 150–51; Burton, *Galatians*, 172; Bryant, *Crucified Christ*, 178; Dunn, *Galatians*, 177; Hooker, "Interchange in Christ"; R. N. Longenecker, *Galatians*, 121; Martyn, *Galatians*, 318.

[42] So Barclay, *Obeying*, 103; Eckstein, *Verheißung*, 133.

[43] So, e.g., Räisänen, *Paul*, 108, and cf. 95–101, 109–113; contra, e.g., Martyn, *Galatians*, 316; Sanders, *Paul, the Law, and the Jewish People*, 54, n. 30. See the explicit

one come to deliver Israel, and if this was the unexpected mode of his deliverance, then that curse must have been a general problem for Israel. It was not simply a few "sinners," but *all* of God's people who needed to be rescued from that judgement.

We do not know with any certainty that Paul's own thought actually traversed these particular lines. Yet the lingering presence of 2:21 behind Paul's argument in chapter 3, a presence which makes itself felt in the allusion to Christ's death in 3:13, must be taken into account in our reconstruction of his argumentative logic here. The Apostle did not want his audience to forget that the death of Christ, as an interpretive gap, justified his reconfiguration of Israel's story. Paul's recasting of the narrative in 3:10–13 thus turns out to be justified by the need to incorporate two unexpected chapters into the overall narrative pattern: the Galatians' reception of the Spirit and the passion and resurrection of Christ. It is the presence of these two gaps in the story which, he argues, requires this rethinking of the whole. The former event requires that one reconstrue the story so that it can now be seen to offer a second way of approach to God, the way of faith, distinct from

---

pessimism in Rom 1:18–3:20; 3:23–24; 5:12; 7:14–25. We need not say here that Paul saw *perfect* obedience as the only sufficient response to Torah, but only that Paul did not think any actual law keeping would be sufficient. If this was a conclusion drawn in retrospect, in light of the redemptive event of the cross, Paul may not have had a very clear idea of why the law could not be kept properly, though his musings in Rom 7 suggest that he gave the question some thought. Cf. pp. 205–6, n. 23 above.

Paul does discuss the possibility that people might attaining righteousness "by the law" in Rom 2:6–13, but he never treats this possibility as anything more than hypothetical (contra Räisänen, *Paul*, 103–6). Those passages in which Paul calls believers to be "blameless" or "guiltless" (1 Thess 3:13; 5:23; 1 Cor 1:8) cannot be adduced as evidence that the law could be fulfilled satisfactorily, since they do not attain that state by observing Torah (contra Sanders, *Paul, the Law, and the Jewish People*, 23). Nor can Paul's talk in Rom 8:4 of believers fulfilling the law's "righteous requirement" (τὸ δικαίωμα τοῦ νόμου) be equated with a claim that they successfully keep Torah (contra Dunn, *Galatians*, 171), since such "fulfilment" is distinguished sharply by Paul from ordinary observance of the written code (see below, pp. 271–3). Paul's apparent affirmation of his own former perfection in Phil 3:6 thus appears at most to be a singular throwback to Paul's old views (cf. Räisänen, *Paul*, 106, 109; contra Cranford, "Perfect Obedience," 256–7; Wakefield, *Where to Live*, 68). Moreover, the Christian Paul would hardly have considered his persecution of the Church to be "blameless." The fact that the Apostle can use this term in such an unqualified way in about his pre-Damascus life thus suggests that he is recalling his former self-perception (so Westerholm, *Perspectives*, 403).

the way of law. The latter event pushes one to reconfigure that story in such a way that the path of law could now be recognized as a dead end, from which Christ had to deliver Israel. The only way in which Paul felt he could still read Israel's story as a coherent narrative, while also taking these new events seriously, was to find at its heart a hidden wedge which separated faith in Christ and legal observance. Paul's thinking does indeed seem to move, in E. P. Sanders' words, "from solution to plight," but not in an arbitrary way. The Apostle is simply following through on the implications of his belief that his present experience, and that of all the people around him, constitutes the further unfolding of Israel's story. His logic is the same logic in which we engage whenever we experience a story for the first time. His task in 3:10–14 is not to prove by means of a series of isolated proof texts that faith in Christ and obedience to Torah are opposed, but to illustrate how the broad themes of the biblical story can be read along lines which are consistent with his reconfiguration of the Abraham narrative, and to remind his audience that the death of Christ itself forces us towards this kind of rereading.

Having thus reconfigured the story, however, Paul can read it in such a way that, as he concludes in 3:14, the passion took place "in order that in Christ Jesus the blessing of Abraham might come to the Gentiles, so that we might receive the promise of the Spirit through faith."[44] This is not so much

---

[44] Notice how this explicit reference to the reception of the Spirit picks up again Paul's initial argument in 3:1–5, forming a kind of inclusio surrounding this core argumentative section from 3:1–14 and suggesting that indeed the Galatians' reception of the Spirit has been a driving force behind his thinking all through these verses.

Several authors have pointed out that in 3:14 Paul for the first time conflates the promised blessing through Abraham with the promise of the Spirit. Betz is likely right that this conflation is based in part on the experience of the Galatians, which combines faith and the Spirit (*Galatians*, 152–3). Yet we should not overplay the novelty involved here. Paul already presumed in 3:6–9 that the reception of the Spirit was an indication that one was an heir of Abraham (so Eckstein, *Verheißung*, 168). Moreover, the outpouring of the Spirit was widely assumed to be a sign of the more general eschatological blessing, and that blessing as a whole was generally understood as the inheritance of righteous Israel, i.e., Abraham's heirs. Berger points to the close association between eschatology and the "promises" to the patriarchs in apocalyptic texts such as *4 Ezra* and *2 Bar.* ("Abraham," 53). On the eschatological hope of the coming of the Spirit see Isa 32:15; 44:3; 59:21; Ezek 11:19; 36:26–27; 37:1–14; 39:29 and of course Joel 3:1–2(2:28–29). Eckstein points out that in Isa 44:1–5 the "promises" which will finally come to the "seed" of Jacob (certainly understood as the same promises given to Jacob's grandfather) include the outpouring of God's Spirit (*Verheißung*, 169–70). See below, pp. 255–6, n. 54.

the conclusion of a linear argument[45] as it is the final tying together of the narrative strands into a new configuration. The Apostle does want to draw a conclusion from this reconstrued story, but that conclusion does not concern the status of law or faith. It concerns the concrete ethical question which the Galatians face: should they submit to circumcision?

The "us" for whom Christ became a curse in 3:13 and who receive the promise of the Spirit in 3:14 are most likely Jews *and* Gentiles (so Bruce, *Galatians*, 166–7; Dunn, *Galatians*, 176–7; R. N. Longenecker, *Galatians*, 121; Martyn, *Galatians*, 317; Oepke, *Galater*, 74; Sanders, *Paul, the Law, and the Jewish People*, 26; Schlier, *Galater*, 93). Betz (*Galatians*, 148), Burton (*Galatians*, 169), and Lightfoot (*Galatians*, 139) take the "us" which is liberated from the curse here as referring strictly to Jews, since only Jews stand under the law's curse in 3:10. Yet the "us" who receive the Spirit in 3:14 is almost certainly meant to include the Gentile Galatians (so Westerholm, *Perspectives*, 302 n. 13). The mention of the promise reaching τὰ ἔθνη in 3:14a is not a strong enough basis on which to argue that the identity of the "us" has changed since the previous verse, particularly since Paul elsewhere resists distinguishing between Jews and Gentiles in discussions of salvation (so Martyn, *Galatians*, 317). Paul's explicit identification of the Gentiles as recipients of the blessing is probably intended simply to highlight his point that the benefits of the Christ event extend to the Gentiles as well (so Eckstein, *Verheißung*, 152; cf. 164). Martyn also observes that this deliverance from the curse is said in 3:13b to have taken place when Christ became a curse "for us" (ὑπὲρ ἡμῶν), a phrase which Paul always uses for actions which benefit all humanity (*Galatians*, 317; e.g., Gal 1:4; Rom 8:32).

This reading is supported by the observation that in 3:22–23 the "imprisoning" effect of Torah is extended to τὰ πάντα and not merely to the Jews. Westerholm is probably right (*Perspectives*, 302 n. 13) that Paul sees the Gentiles as trapped in essentially the same situation as the Jews. Both are faced with judgement if they do not fulfil God's will, although this judgement comes to Gentiles "apart from the law" (Rom 2:12; see also Rom 1:18; 5:9; 1 Thess 1:10; so Bruce, *Galatians*, 166–7; cf. Eckstein, *Verheißung*, 152–3). Hence Paul can speak "somewhat loosely" of Gentiles being delivered from the law's curse, since they too had faced the same condemnation if their lives were not righteous (Westerholm, *Perspectives*, 302 n. 13). Paul's turn of phrase here thus anticipates his argument in 4:3, 8–11, in which the Jewish life under Torah is treated as analogous to the Galatians' life ὑπὸ τὰ στοιχεῖα τοῦ κόσμου (so Martyn, *Galatians*, 317; Schlier, *Galater*, 93).

[45] Contra, e.g., Lührmann, *Galatians*, 61.

3. Paul's Use of Analogy in Reconfigurational Argument (3:15–18)

Before the Apostle can address that ethical problem directly he needs first to reinforce the reconfiguration of Israel's story in the context of which his ethical instructions will make sense.[46] Paul's own efforts to reconfigure Israel's story show that he is aware of the indeterminacy involved in the reading of any narrative, a story's capacity to be construed in various ways by different audiences. As we have already suggested, the Apostle is for that reason very concerned to show that his is a better telling of the story than that of his opponents. Yet he knows that from the opponents' point of view (and perhaps from the point of view of their Galatian pupils) the greatest challenge to that claim is that the traditional story is so overwhelmingly dominated by the Mosaic covenant. How can the Torah, which encoded Israel's obligations under that covenant, possibly be understood as a secondary institution, even as counter-productive in Israel's relationship with God? The hardest part of Paul's task will thus be to assign a meaningful role to that covenant within the context of his reconfigured narrative. For all of these reasons Paul wants to prepare for that interpretive task by establishing a basic narrative framework within which to understand the relationship between promise and law. That framework is given in 3:17, where Paul explains simply that the promise to Abraham came first and so must not have been supplanted by the later legal institution under Moses: "My point is this (τοῦτο δὲ λέγω): the law, which came four hundred thirty years later, does not annul a covenant (διαθήκην) previously ratified by God, so as to nullify the promise" (3:17).[47]

---

[46] Most commentators recognize 3:15–18 as a distinct subsection of Paul's main argument in 3:1–4:31 (so Betz, *Galatians*, 154; Burton, *Galatians*, 177; Dunn, *Galatians*, 159, 180; R. N. Longenecker, *Galatians*, 125–6). Martyn treats it as a subsection of 3:6–18 (so *Galatians*, 295), but, as we have observed, this separates it artificially from 3:1–5, which is the heart of Paul's argument.

[47] Cosgrove ("Arguing," 536–8) suggests that Paul adopts, for the sake of argument, the premise that in fact the Mosaic law is in contradiction to the promise, and that here he highlights the legal contradiction to which this situation would lead. Yet nowhere in 3:15–18 does the Apostle actually say that Torah is in conflict with the promise. He is not for the moment concerned with how exactly the two relate. First he wants to establish that the priority of the Abrahamic promise cannot be compromised.

This reconfigured relationship between law and promise is, however, so radically different from the roles assigned to those institutions in the traditional reading of Israel's story that Paul knows he must somehow fix this new pattern in the audience's mind and demonstrate that such a reading carries at least some a priori credibility. The means upon which Paul seizes for this end is a simple analogy from the Galatians' common experience: "Brothers and sisters, I give an example from daily life (κατὰ ἄνθρωπον λέγω)[48]: once a person's will (διαθήκην) has been ratified, no one adds to it or annuls it" (3:15). Here Paul holds up a common situation for the Galatians' inspection. It is not a complete story, but a familiar narrative pattern with generic actors (the deceased, those who might try to alter the will) and generic kinds of action (ratifying a will, adding to a will, annulling a will) which are causally interrelated (if someone ratifies the will, then the other kinds of action cannot take place). By the time we reach verses 17–18 it is clear that the Apostle wants to see this same narrative pattern reflected in Israel's story. God's promise to Abraham's descendants is a kind of

---

[48] Burton observes (*Galatians*, 178) that the standard sense of κατὰ ἄνθρωπον in Greek literature is "as men [i.e., human beings] do," and though it is often employed to contrast the human with the superhuman or divine (so Gal 1:11; 1 Cor 3:3; 15:32; see Cosgrove, "Arguing," 543), this comparison does not usually denigrate what is human (contra Cosgrove, "Arguing," 544; see Plato, *Phileb.* 12c; Athen., *Deipn.* 10.444b; Diod. Sic. 16.11.2; Xenoph., *Cyr.* 8.7.2; *Mem.* 4.4.24). In Philo, what is κατὰ ἄνθρωπον is inferior (compare *Virt.* 217; *Spec.* 1.116; *Legat.* 76), but elsewhere it can be what is healthy and right (Aesch., *Sept.* 425; Soph., *Ajax* 761, 777; *OC* 598). The phrase "to speak in a human way" (λέγω/λαλῶ κατὰ ἄνθρωπον/ἀνθρώπινον) appears in Rom 3:5; 6:19; and 1 Cor 9:8, but appears to be unattested in earlier literature. In Rom 3:5 this speech κατὰ ἄνθρωπον is speech which arises from a false point of view. Paul could thus be saying in 3:15 that he is employing an *ad hominem* argument which does not carry much real validity (so Cosgrove, "Arguing," 543–5; Dunn, *Galatians*, 181; Siegert, *Argumentation*, 228; cf. R. N. Longenecker, *Galatians*, 125). In Rom 6:19, however, Paul speaks ἀνθρώπινον in the sense that he draws (as in Gal 3:15) on an analogy from common experience – the treatment of slaves. In 1 Cor 9:8, again, Paul's κατὰ ἄνθρωπον speech consists of the preceding series of analogies between daily life and his own situation. In neither case is this "human" speech false, though it is contrasted in 1 Cor 9:8 with what is revealed in Scripture (ὁ νόμος). Since in Gal 3:15 too Paul is drawing on an analogy from common experience, the expression κατὰ ἄνθρωπον λέγω here most likely signals that the Apostle is leaving off his discussions of inspired Scripture and speaking "as men do about their affairs," i.e., drawing on common human experience (Burton, *Galatians*, 178; so Betz, *Galatians*, 154; Lightfoot, *Galatians*, 140–41).

"covenant" or "will" (both ideas can be expressed by διαθήκη[49]) which will be inherited by his "seed," and no additional legal stipulations can exclude his offspring from that inheritance.[50]

By first presenting the analogous situation in everyday life, however, Paul accomplishes two things.[51] First, he ensures that the Galatians will perceive the pattern which he wants them to see by isolating a simple situation which they are accustomed to viewing according to an analogous pattern. With this strong and clear image in mind, the Galatians are much more likely to be able to perceive that same pattern in the more complex story which Paul is reconfiguring. This analogical help is particularly important now because the Galatians' sense of the overall shape of Israel's story will be very shaky. Paul has just challenged the configuration to which they have been accustomed, and an analogy like this can serve as an important guide in helping them to

---

[49] The διαθήκη in 3:15 is almost certainly a personal "will" or "testament" (so R. N. Longenecker, *Galatians*, 128; Martyn, *Galatians*, 338; contra Burton, *Galatians*, 179). Not only is this the ordinary sense of the Greek term (see, e.g., Jos. *B.J.* 1.451, 573, 588, 600, etc.; *A.J.* 13.349; 17.53, 78, 146, etc.), but such a sense is also suggested by the way in which the διαθήκη is characterized as ἀνθρώπου and seems to be put in place unilaterally by an individual. Terms such as ἐπιδιατάσσομαι, ἀθετέω, κυρόω, and ἀκυρόω are frequently used in technical discussions of such testaments (so Bammel, "Gottes ΔΙΑΘΗΚΗ," 313). We might not see a direct parallel between a will which one draws up to deal with one's effects after death and a covenant between two living partners, but the LXX uses the term διαθήκη consistently for the Hebrew בְּרִית (see, e.g., Exod 19:5; 24:7–8; Deut 4:13; 28:69; 29:20). Moreover, Paul's talk about ἡ κληρονομία, "the inheritance," in v. 18 highlights the real similarity between the two διαθῆκαι: in both cases there is a unilateral decision which establishes that some person's descendants will receive certain benefits (cf. Heb 9:15–17).

[50] Paul is clearly thinking of Gen 15:18 and especially 17:2–8, where the blessings which God has spoken over Abraham are called in the LXX a διαθήκη and are directed not only to Abraham himself but also to his σπέρμα. Paul seems to read a great deal into what is primarily a promise of land, but possession of the land was often treated as wrapped up with eschatological blessing (see *Pss. Sol.* 7:2; 9:2; 14:3, 10; 17:26; *1 En.* 40:9; *Sib. Or.* 3:47; *T. Job* 18:6–7; cf. Heb 3–4; 6:12; 11:8–16; Acts 2:32; Eph 5:5; 1 Cor 6:9–10; Col 3:24).

[51] That Paul wants the common situation in v. 15 to serve as analogous to his statement in v. 17 is clear from his use of ὅμως, an adverb with which the Apostle often introduces comparisons (so BDAG, 710; Betz, *Galatians*, 156; R. N. Longenecker, *Galatians*, 127; contra Burton, *Galatians*, 178; Lightfoot, *Galatians*, 141; cf. 1 Cor 14:7). This analogy is then highlighted by Paul's use of the same language (διαθήκη, κυρόω/προκυρόω) or synonymous terms (ἀθετέω and ἀκυρόω) for both members of the comparison.

resolve the elements of the story which have become momentarily disconnected in the audience's mind. Nor is this simply a rhetorical device which can be neatly distinguished from epistemology. For, as Bernard Lonergan has emphasized, knowing the world is in large part a matter of being able to perform acts of "insight" in which we construe a group of particulars according to a certain pattern.[52] That is to say, the world in general is characterized by the kind of interpretive indeterminacy which Iser perceives in stories. One cannot know the truth about something if one cannot perceive there the pattern which is "true." A crucial part of our capacity to know the truth thus consists of our familiarity with the patterns which can prepare us by way of analogy to "understand" or interpret our object in a true way, such that the resulting picture is fitting to the world. To put this in terms of Paul's activity here in Gal 3:15–18, the Galatians must be prepared with the analogical tools to perceive the new pattern in Israel's story if they are ever to come to reconfigure it as Paul has and thus come to know the "truth of the Gospel."

The second epistemic task which this analogy performs, however, is to point to an a priori plausibility in this reconfigured pattern. It is no accident that the analogy which Paul chooses is a common scenario, drawn from the ordinary experience of many of the Galatian believers. For the plausibility of any narrative we tell depends on its being structured to a large extent around the kind of narrative patterns which we are accustomed to seeing in daily life. An occasional startling event which breaks through these usual patterns adds interest to a story, but taken too far such anomalies will stretch the credulity of the listeners to the breaking point. Since a striking novelty is already injected into Paul's narrative with the anomalous events of Christ's death and the Galatians' reception of the Spirit, it is imperative that as he fills out his

---

[52] Lonergan characterizes insight as, among other things, sudden and unexpected because it cannot be produced by a method: "Were there rules for discovery, then discoveries would be mere conclusions." "Indeed," he says, "what is true of discovery also holds for the transmission of discoveries by teaching. For a teacher cannot undertake to make a pupil understand. All he can do is present the sensible elements in the issue in a suggestive order and with a proper distribution of emphasis. It is up to the pupils themselves to reach understanding, and they do so in varying measures of ease and rapidity" (*Insight*, 4–5). Thomas Kuhn perceives the intense struggle which can be involved in abandoning one construal of the world in favour of a new one in his discussion of "paradigm shifts" (see *The Structure of Scientific Revolutions*, 77–91).

reconfiguration of the story he draw on patterns which will carry an inherent plausibility by virtue of their familiarity in common life. Again, this should not be thought of simply as a rhetorical trick aimed at making the Galatians accept Paul's story regardless of its truth. This demand for familiar narrative patterns is, after all, essentially what the historian means by the canon of causal uniformity. Just as physical objects are thought to behave in the same ways whether they exist in the first century or the twenty-first, so too human beings are thought (allowing for a certain degree of cultural and individual variation) to behave and interact according to familiar patterns. If an historical reconstruction involves some action on the part of an individual which does not seem to fit any of these familiar patterns, either we call that individual insane (thus showing that we can subsume the behaviour under a familiar pattern after all) or we look for a better construal of that part of the past. In the case of Israel's story, both Paul and his opponents would accept that this basic uniformity of human action and interaction can be extended, at least tentatively, to God himself. The human–divine relationship is understood to be an *interpersonal* relationship, and one in which God's actions and reactions are at least analogous to those of a human being. Israel's narrative revolves, in fact, around God's making promises and covenants, suggesting that at least in a broad sense the divine activity will be understandable in terms of the normal human conduct of those institutions.[53] Hence the narrative pattern which Paul offers up for the Galatians' view, the

---

[53] There is, of course, a tension here. Paul, along with many of the biblical writers, is probably aware that God's action is only analogically comparable to human action and that at some points (as in, e.g., the book of Job) one must abandon the attempt to understand it in terms of those familiar analogies. Note, however, that there is a comparable tension in historiography, since the presupposition of analogy between human thought and action in the past and our own must always be tempered by the realization that in certain ways the world view and experience of people in the past are radically different from our own, giving rise to some kinds of behaviour and thought which are inexplicable in terms of current comparisons. It is not uncommon to see disagreement among historians over just how close the overlap is between past human awareness and our own, with the result that different scholars will disagree over what constitutes a plausible explanation of some past action. So, for example, it is debated whether we must look for a causally familiar model by which to "explain" Paul's sudden shift towards Christianity (such as psychological pressure prompting a psychic break; see, e.g., Lüdemann, *Paul*, 187–91) or whether we can accept that Paul's experience on the Damascus road was radically different from what we normally experience and the "explanation" of his unusual behaviour lies in that difference.

pattern in which a will is established and attempts to alter it fail, not only helps them to perceive a new configuration in the familiar story but also reinforces the Apostle's contention that this construal is eminently plausible. Paul wants to emphasize that God acts, on such a reading, just the way one would expect any person to act.[54]

Finally, in order for this analogy to convince his audience Paul must show that this common situation is actually analogous to Israel's story in the way he claims. He does this, however, not by adducing proofs but by elaborating on his analogy, showing that the reading of the story which results is coherent. The first and by far the more provocative elaboration is his identification in verse 16 of Abraham's heir, the "seed" who was to inherit the promise, as Christ himself. Not a few commentators have here seen Paul taking extreme liberties with the text of Gen 17:1–11[55] and have suggested that Paul's logic must be put down simply to "Pharisaic" ways of thought which are inaccessible to (and invalid for) the contemporary mind.[56] Note again, however, that the Apostle's point is not that an ordinary Jewish reading of the Abraham story would lead them to take the singular "seed" as a reference to some future individual. Paul knows very well that most of his contemporaries have taken it as a collective entity, referring to Israel.[57] He

---

[54] We are here not concerned with the accuracy of Paul's analogy but rather with the manner of his reasoning. It has, of course, been pointed out on many occasions that in both Greek and Roman law a testator *could* replace a will with a later one or could add codicils with further specifications (so Betz, *Galatians*, 155; Dunn, *Galatians*, 182; R. N. Longenecker, *Galatians*, 128–30; see Jos., *B.J.* 2.20–21, 35; *P. Oxy.* 1.106, 107; 3.601). This would seem to take the force out of Paul's analogical argument, since Torah could be likened to such an added codicil. For suggested solutions to this problem, see Bammel ("Gottes ΔΙΑΘΗΚΗ") on the מתנת בריא and Yaron (*Gifts in Contemplation of Death*) on the *donatio mortis causa*, along with the discussion in R. N. Longenecker, *Galatians*, 130, and Dunn, *Galatians*, 182. In any case, Bammel is right ("Gottes ΔΙΑΘΗΚΗ," 317) that we cannot simply assume that Paul thought the νόμος was instituted by the ἄγγελοι of verse 19 and not by God. In 3:21ff. the discussion concerns precisely how law and promise can coexist harmoniously as two products of the one divine will (so Cosgrove, "Arguing," 537, 539–41; cf. p. 226, n. 66 below).

[55] So, e.g., Martyn, *Galatians*, 340.

[56] So, e.g., Dunn, *Galatians*, 184; Eckert, *Urchristliche Verkündigung*, 80.

[57] The context in Genesis implies that this "seed" is to be identified with the descendants of Abraham, who will be as numerous as the sand on the seashore or the stars in the sky (Gen 13:16; 15:5; 16:10; 22:17), and Betz points to this assumption behind the identification of Jews (and proselytes) as Abraham's heirs in Second-Temple literature (*Galatians*, 157;

has already shown, however, that in light of recent events, that construal of the story in which only faithful Jews are Abraham's heirs cannot be maintained.[58] This opens the door to suggest that the identification of Abraham's heir as a singular "seed" actually coheres very well with his reading of the story, a reading in which an individual (Christ) mediates the promise to everyone else who will enjoy it, whether Jew or Gentile.[59] Moreover, as Dunn writes, Paul's point is not actually "to deny that Abraham's seed is multitudinous in number, but to affirm that Christ's pre-eminence as that 'seed' carries with it the implication that all 'in Christ' are equally Abraham's seed (iii.26–9)."[60] So while Paul's identification of Christ with the "seed" of Abraham may have seemed arbitrary to the opponents in Galatia, it is simply another way of stating the claim which the Apostle has already made in 3:6–9 and will make again in 3:29: that in order to inherit Abraham's promise one must be identified with Christ.[61] He is not doing exegesis in the sense of drawing out the human author's "original intent," but rather fleshing out his reconfiguration of the narrative and showing how that

---

see *Pss. Sol.* 12:6; Wis 12:21), the Hebrew Scriptures (Ps 105:8ff.), and Christian writers (Eph 3:6; Heb 4:1ff.; 11:9, 11; Acts 13:22; 26:6–7).

[58] Burton writes: "He doubtless arrived at his thought, not by exegesis of scripture, but from an interpretation of history, and then availed himself of the singular noun to express his thought briefly" (*Galatians*, 182). This is contra Siegert (*Argumentation*, 161), who suggests that Paul, like an Hellenistic rhetorician, is assuming an absolute relationship between grammatical form and ontology. As Burton points out, Paul himself assumes that collective sense in 3:9, 29, and Rom 4:13–18 (*Galatians*, 182; so Dunn, *Galatians*, 183–4). Lightfoot points out, moreover, that the plural σπέρματα would be as unthinkable in Greek as a designation for descendants as would the Hebrew זְרָעִים, so Paul cannot be unaware of the possibility that the singular noun could denote a plurality of descendants (*Galatians*, 142).

[59] Hence Cosgrove is likely right that Paul's point in emphasizing the singularity of the "seed" is to emphasize that the promise "*was not made to law-keepers* (or anyone else, for that matter), and therefore that the law has absolutely no legal voice in the terms of the inheritance" ("Arguing," 548 [italics original]).

[60] Dunn, *Galatians*, 185; so Brawley, "Contextuality," 102; Lightfoot, *Galatians*, 142; R. N. Longenecker, *Galatians*, 132; cf. Eckstein, *Verheißung*, 183–4. Dunn suggests that the Genesis text already invites such interpretive play on the numerical ambiguity of the seed, for that σπέρμα is identified both with Isaac and with Abraham's larger offspring (*Galatians*, 184). See the play on such ambiguity in *4QFlor* 1 I 10–12 on 2 Sam 7:12–14 and especially *Jub.* 16:17–18; 30–32.

[61] So Berger, "Abraham," 55.

reconfiguration reflects by analogy the situation of a will whose heir cannot be disinherited by some alteration of the original testament.

We see here the same element of circularity in Paul's thought which has surfaced before. The identification of Christ as the "seed" already depends on the overall construal of the story, which Paul seeks to reinforce by means of his analogy. Likewise, when Paul elaborates in 3:18 on exactly how the law would be effectively changing the terms of the διαθήκη established with Abraham's "seed," he emphasizes that the right of inheritance was originally ἐξ ἐπαγγελίας, determined solely by the unilateral promise of God, the testator. If that right now becomes ἐκ νόμου, dependent on one's keeping law, then there has been a radical change in the basis upon which one can claim to be an heir of the Abrahamic promise.[62] Yet Paul *assumes* here the distinction between promise and law, the basic incompatability between the two, which is in large part what he is trying to establish.[63] This simply reminds us, however, that the Apostle's argument is not a linear chain forged of syllogistic reasoning and leading from premise to conclusion. It is an effort to demonstrate that his reading of the story is coherent, that it can account best for all of the features of the "text" which consists of Israel's scriptural story and the subsequent experiences of the believers in Christ. He has already shown that his basic reconfiguration can account for recent events,

---

[62] That Paul is thinking here in terms of νόμος and ἐπαγγελία as generally incompatible forms of relationship is made clear by his use of the anarthrous form of both nouns (so Lightfoot, *Galatians*, 144; cf. Rom 4:13ff. and Dunn, *Galatians*, 185–6). Once again this sharp distinction between law and promise was not familiar in Second-Temple Judaism, where the terms tended to be treated as compatible (e.g., 2 Macc 2:17–18; *Pss. Sol.* 12:6; *Sib. Or.* 3:768–9; *2 Bar.* 14:12–13; 57:2). Jewish thought also tended to see the Mosaic code not as a later addition but as present germinally in Abraham's obedience toward God, or even as revealed already in full-blown form to the first patriarch (see Sir 44:20; Philo, *Abr.* 275–6; *Jub.* 21:10; *Gen. Rab.* 44 [27d]; 61 [38b]; *Mek. Exod.* 20, 18 [78b]). Indeed, the text of Gen 26:5 can easily be understood in these terms. As Betz observes, it is Paul who makes a point of Abraham's not having known Torah (*Galatians*, 159).

[63] Something similar might be said of Paul's emphasis in 3:17 on the length of time which passed between the promise to Abraham (the διαθήκη) and the giving of the law at Sinai. The Apostle wants to say that the law would not represent a simple afterthought, but a change added long, long after the original "will" had been set up (for the figure of 430 years see Exod 12:40 and cf. Gen 15:13). This whole way of portraying the situation, however, assumes that Torah introduces a radical change in the conditions of the διαθήκη, precisely the point which traditional Jewish thinking would deny.

recent "chapters," which other construals find difficult or impossible to encompass. Paul's goal in 3:15–18 is then to set up, by means of a simple analogy, a narrative pattern which will provide the framework for his re-imagining of Torah's place in Israel's story, and to show that this pattern has at least some a priori plausibility as a way of reading that narrative.

4. Facing a Possible Incoherence (3:19–24)

Having set up by way of analogy this basic pattern in which the promise is pre-eminent and the later Torah cannot interfere with its terms, Paul is ready to approach his most difficult task in convincing the Galatians: showing that his reconfiguration of the story can integrate God's giving of Torah to Moses as well as it can integrate the more recent divine actions in Galatia.[64] Paul asks, "Why then the law?" (3:19). Given this reconfiguration of the story, what role would Torah play? His answer is that it was "added because of transgressions (τῶν παραβάσεων χάριν προσετέθη)" and that this institution was temporally limited, only intended to be in force "until (ἄχρις) the offspring would come to whom the promise had been made" (3:19). Exactly what role Paul imagines the law playing in relation to "transgressions" will continue to be debated.[65] What is clear is that in the Apostle's radical re-imagining of Torah that law plays a role which not only does not interfere

---

[64] Most commentators extend this section past 3:24, either to 3:25 (so Betz, *Galatians*, 161; R. N. Longenecker, *Galatians*, 137; Martyn, *Galatians*, 295, 352–3) or to 3:29, often with a minor division between vv. 22 and 23 (so Burton, *Galatians*, 187; Dunn, *Galatians*, 159; Lightfoot, *Galatians*, 151; Lührmann, *Galatians*, 71, 74). It is clear that a transition takes place somewhere between 3:24 and 4:1 from a focus on the role of the law in general to a focus on the implications of that role for the Galatians. The smooth nature of that transition is evidenced by the variety of dividing points suggested by scholars, but, as we will see below, it is in 3:25 that the ethical implications of the story for the Galatians are first explicitly introduced. Thus, for our purposes, 3:25 marks a shift to a new argumentative mode.

[65] Is Paul already thinking here of the law as effectively "multiplying sin" (Rom 5:20) and making sin visible by converting it into explicit transgression (Rom 4:15) (so Barrett, *Freedom*, 33; Betz, *Galatians*, 165; Burton, *Galatians*, 188; Lightfoot, *Galatians*, 144–5; R. N. Longenecker, *Galatians*, 138–9; Martyn, *Galatians*, 354)? Or did the law restrain transgression (cf. Eckstein, *Verheißung*, 193–6)?

with the promise but is *temporary* in a way which the promise is not.[66]

Paul adduces no general principles with which to demonstrate ahistorically that "promise" in general is superior to and outlasts the "law." Rather, his argument moves on three levels, each of which is dependent in a circular fashion on the very theological narrative which he is trying to establish. On the one hand, the Apostle reinforces the impression created in 3:15–18 that the circumstances of the institution of Torah are different in kind from the circumstances under which the promise was given to Abraham. He alludes to the indirectness of the law's advent, coming as it did through angelic messengers and through Moses' mediation.[67] Hence the qualitative distinction

---

[66] This is in stark contrast to much of Jewish thinking, in which Torah was regarded as eternal (see, e.g., Wis 18:4; Jos., *C. Ap.* 2.277; Philo, *Mos.* 2.14; *Jub.* 1:27; 3:31; 6:17).

[67] It is not immediately apparent in 3:19b whether the statement that the law was given δι' ἀγγέλων is meant to suggest that angels administered Torah on God's behalf (so Dunn, *Galatians*, 191; Eckstein, *Verheißung*, 200–202) or that the law actually originated among the angels and not with God (so Drane, *Paul*, 34, 113; Lührmann, *Galatians*, 71; Martyn, *Galatians*, 357). The language of "being ordained through" (διαταγεὶς δι') in 3:19 is, however, most naturally read as a "divine passive," the implied subject being God (so Thurén, *Derhetorizing*, 82). Even Räisänen (*Paul*, 130) agrees that this is initially the natural sense, and his subsequent objections are not persuasive (see the rebuttal in Thurén, *Derhetorizing*, 82–3). Moreover, Torah is clearly depicted in 3:21–22 as co-operating with God's purpose (so Thurén, *Derhetorizing*, 82; Westerholm, *Israel's Law*, 178). Even if one opts for the latter position, however, by ἀγγέλων Paul clearly does not understand *evil* angels, as if the law were attributable to demonic influence (contra Hübner, *Law*, 24–36). In any case, the idea of angelic involvement in the giving of Torah seems to have been relatively common in Second-Temple Judaism (see LXX Deut 33:2; Ps 102:20[MT 103:20]; 103:4[MT 104:4]; *Jub.* 1:27–2:1; *1 En.* 60:1ff.; *A.J.* 15.136 [though cf. Davies, "Note on Josephus"]; Philo, *Somn.* 1.143; Acts 7:38, 53; Heb 2:2). Paul's intent too is probably not to distance God from Torah altogether but to emphasize the indirectness of the Torah's revelation and draw an implicit contrast with the direct giving of the promise (so Burton, *Galatians*, 189; Eckstein, *Verheißung*, 200; R. N. Longenecker, *Galatians*, 140).

The second element of 3:19b is the reminder that Torah was given ἐν χειρὶ μεσίτου. This "mediator" is probably Moses (cf. the phrase ἐν χειρὶ Μωυσῆ in LXX Lev 26:46; Num 4:37; 9:23; Jdg 3:4; 1 Chr 16:40; 2 Chr 33:8; Ps 77:21[LXX 76:21]; Bar 2:28; etc.). So this is probably not another reference to the law's angelic mediation (contra Eckert, *Urchristliche Verkündigung*, 83; Eckstein, *Verheißung*, 204–5; Lambrecht, "Abraham," 533; Lührmann, *Galatians*, 71; Stanton, "Law of Moses," 113). More likely the Apostle is contrasting the mediator's role arbitrating between two parties with God's nature as one (see Burton, *Galatians*, 191). The precise thrust of the contrast remains ambiguous. Paul's general goal, however, is clearly to contrast the indirect mediation of the law with the directness of the

between law and promise which runs through the Apostle's reconfiguration of Israel's story is made to appear even more plausible. At the same time, Paul spells out in more detail the role which is left to the law, and does this in such a way that its role now seems naturally temporary. It was given to deal with a specific problem (trangressions) for a specific period in time (until the advent of the "seed"). Its function is not in conflict with the Abrahamic promise (3:21a). On the contrary, Torah co-operates with the promise by "imprisoning" humanity "under sin" (συνέκλεισεν ἡ γραφὴ τὰ πάντα ὑπὸ ἁμαρτίαν) (3:22), acting as a "custodian" (παιδαγωγός), and hence producing the negative circumstances under which the realization of that promise in Christ is possible (3:22–24).[68] For our purposes what is important is that Paul

---

Abrahamic promise (so Burton, *Galatians*, 190; Callan, "Midrash," 554–64; Dunn, *Galatians*, 191; Lightfoot, *Galatians*, 146–7; R. N. Longenecker, *Galatians*, 141–2).

[68] In 3:22 the "imprisonment" is said to have taken place "so that (ἵνα) what was promised through faith in Jesus Christ might be given to those who believe." Exactly how this "imprisonment" accomplishes this task is less clear, and our answer here will inevitably be tied to our reading of 3:19. The verb φρουρέω can have the sense either of negative subjection (see Polyb., 18.4.6; LSJ, 1957–8 [II.b]) or a protective guarding (2 Cor 11:32; Phil 4:7; 1 Pet 1:5; LSJ, 1957–8 [I, II.a]), though συγκλείω is more consistently used in the sense of confinement (LSJ, 1665 [I]; cf. Wis 17:16). It may well be that both the protective and confining ideas are intended and complement one another (so Lightfoot, *Galatians*, 147; R. N. Longenecker, *Galatians*, 145). The thought, though expressed in a tightly compressed form, seems to be much like that of Rom 3:9; 11:32 (so Dunn, *Galatians*, 194; cf. Barrett, *Freedom*, 34–5; Martyn, *Galatians*, 360–61). On the metaphor of the παιδαγωγός in 3:24, see the next section below.

What is evident is that ἡ γραφή in 3:22 must be equated here with the "law" (νόμος) which it records, under which humanity is "imprisoned and guarded" in 3:23 (so Bruce, *Galatians*, 180; Burton, *Galatians*, 195; Oepke, *Galater*, 119; Martyn, *Galatians*, 360; contra Schlier, *Galater*, Betz, *Galatians*, 175). Not only do γραφή and νόμος play the same imprisoning role (συνέκλεισεν/συγκλειόμενοι), but both have their temporal goal in the advent of the promise through "faith." Betz's suggestion (*Galatians*, 175) that Paul introduces γραφή in 3:22 in order to avoid attributing a positive and active role to νόμος is rendered unlikely by 3:23, where (as the agent of a passive verb) νόμος plays just such an active role.

The "faith" which marks the advent of the new state of affairs, through which the promise is realized, should be understood as the new possibility of relating to God on the basis of believing in Christ (so Betz, *Galatians*, 176; Burton, *Galatians*, 198; Lightfoot, *Galatians*, 148; cf. Eckstein, *Verheißung*, 212–13). As Dunn points out (*Galatians*, 195), the dependence of this whole section on the model of Abraham's belief in God in 3:6 makes it very unlikely that the expression πίστις Ἰησοῦ Χριστοῦ in 3:22 refers to Christ's own

pursues both of these argumentative directions in 3:19–24 simply by *narrating more of the story* as he has re-imagined it. This is not to say that the telling of the story is very detailed, complete, or ordered by strict chronology, but none of these qualities is basic to narration *per se*. The sentences describe causally interrelated events, actions (giving law, mediating, imprisoning) pursued by personal or personified agents (God, angels, Moses, Scripture/Law) and suffered by other personal agents (the human race). What is crucial to notice is thus that the Apostle argues here by simply relating what took place in his configuration of the story. Narration itself constitutes a kind of argument for the coherence of the story being told.

The third line of argument in this section appears in 3:21 as the direct answer to the hypothetical objection that Paul has made the law appear hostile to the promise. Paul replies: "Certainly not! For if a law had been given that could make alive, then righteousness would indeed come through the law" (3:21). Here the Apostle's argument does not consist of simple narration but rather forms a brief (and enthymematic) syllogism. Paul offers a hypothetical event and then suggests the implications of that event. *If* a life-giving law had been given (by God), then those who kept that law would be righteous. The assumed premise is that God would not give a law, intended to give life, which did not accomplish its task.[69] The syllogism is valid, but Paul presumes that its conclusion is false. Righteousness has not actually come by means of law observance (cf. 2:16; 3:10–14). Hence, one of the premises must also be false. Since it is inconceivable for Paul, as for most Jews, that the divine purpose could be frustrated, it must be the second, implied premise which is not correct.[70] God must not have given a law which was intended to

---

faithfulness (contra Bryant, *Crucified Christ*, 180; Hays, *Faith*, 124, 157–67; Hooker, *Adam*, 170–75; Howard, *Crisis*, 58, 65; Martyn, *Galatians*, 361; see the discussion above, pp. 183–5).

[69] This reading assumes that Jews would commonly think of the law as a (proximate) source of life. See, e.g., Lev 18:5; Deut 6:24; 30:15–20; 32:47; Prov 3:1–2; 6:23; Sir 17:11; Bar 3:9; 4:1; *Pss. Sol.* 14:2; *m. Avot* 2:8; 6:1ff.; Mk 10:17–20; Matt 5:17–20; 7:13f. The verb ζωοποιέω is not typically used with Torah as its subject. Rather, God is the one who makes people to live (see 2 Kgs 5:7; Neh 9:6; Job 36:6; Ps 71:20; *Jos. Asen.* 8:3, 9; 12:1; 20:7; *Let. Arist.* 16; John 5:21; Rom 4:17; 1 Cor 15:22). Paul thus plays on the nuances of this word to emphasize that, despite traditional Jewish associations between law and life, it is God and not Torah who gives that life (so Dunn, *Galatians*, 193). As Betz emphasizes, for Paul it is usually the Spirit who gives life (*Galatians*, 174; see 2 Cor 3:6).

[70] Though see Rom 7:10.

bring life. Even here, however, where Paul's logic is syllogistic, there are three ways in which his argument is integrally related to his reconfigured narrative. First, the conclusion towards which Paul's syllogism pushes is still an assertion about Israel's story: that the law was not intended by God to give life and so must have had some other purpose. This is not a general statement about "law" or even a timeless truth about Torah. It is a claim about the intentions of a certain agent (God) in pursuing a certain action in history (giving the law to Israel). Second, while the Apostle's argument here is more than just narration, its premises consist of narrative statements, and it is the causal patterns through which those statements are related in the story which allow them together to establish Paul's point. He points to the absence of a particular event in the narrative, that is, the human achievement of righteousness through law (premise 1). Then, based on the fact that an agent in the story (God) was capable of bringing that event about, had he wanted to (premise 2 [implicit]), the Apostle concludes that the agent in question must not have wanted it to happen. In other words, the actual events of the story are not explicable if the character (God) was acting with the motivation in question (to provide a way of achieving righteousness). Yet this syllogism is only valid because the two premises are describing an event and an agent which are causally related in the story. Thus, while the Apostle's logic here is syllogistic, the move from premises to conclusion is possible only because of the narrative relationship between the premises.

Third, we must point out that Paul's point here hinges on his assumption that the conclusion of the syllogism is in fact false, that Israel had not achieved righteousness by law keeping. Yet this assumption can be made only within the context of the Apostle's overall reconfiguration of the story. His opponents would likely have objected that in fact the events of the story were different than Paul described – Israel (following Abraham) had achieved righteousness by her keeping of Torah. Hence a life-giving law had been established. The Apostle's syllogism thus makes the point which he wants it to only if one already grants his reconfiguration of the story in 3:1–18. This highlights the fact that Paul is not pursuing an argument from first principles or on the basis of common assumptions. Rather, he has offered an entirely different construal of Israel's story as a whole, and here in 3:19–24 he is simply showing that this reordering of the narrative can assign a coherent role to the Torah given at Mount Sinai. Where this argumentative task cannot be accomplished simply by telling the story, the syllogism which Paul employs is entirely dependent for its validity on that story. The Apostle's argument appears as a kind of narrative criticism which highlights the pattern, the *dianoia*, into which the experiences of Israel can be resolved most coherently.

Chapter Eleven

Re-emplotting the Audience

1. Emplotting the Audience (3:25–4:11)

In 3:25, beginning with the image of the παιδαγωγός, Paul sets up a series of analogous[1] metaphors in order to help the Galatians see not only the role of Torah in Israel's story but also the implications of that role for their own place in that narrative.[2] When the παιδαγωγός metaphor is introduced in 3:24 it serves primarily to reinforce and crystallize the narrative pattern which is already established – law as a temporary and preparatory institution.[3] The

---

[1] The παιδαγωγός of 3:24–26 is not quite the same figure as the ἐπίτροπος of 4:2 (contra R. N. Longenecker, *Galatians*, 162), still less the οἰκόνομος in the same verse. The situation imagined in the first case is that of a young child living under a slave's discipline. In the second scenario a child lives under others' supervision until he (the scenario assumes a male heir) reaches the age of majority and can direct his own affairs. As Martyn points out, the motif of adoption which Paul introduces in 4:5 is not really related to either of these other metaphors (*Galatians*, 386). The shift from one metaphor to another, however, simply underlines the fact that these analogies are being used primarily as heuristic guides to help the Galatians grasp the underlying shape of Paul's reconfigured narrative.

[2] I am running against the trend of scholarship in holding together 3:25–29 and 4:1ff. On the rationale for this move, see below, pp. 238–9, n. 18. Martyn (*Galatians*, 295) at least treats 4:1–7 as the conclusion of an argument which began in 3:6, suggesting a close connection between 3:25–29 and 4:1ff. Similarly, Eckstein treats 3:19–4:7 as a unified phase of Paul's argument (*Verheißung*, 190). Yet their common decision to place a division between 4:7 and 4:8 obscures the extent to which 4:8–11 sums up and draws the conclusion to 4:1–7 (see the same problem in Betz, *Galatians*, 213; R. N. Longenecker, *Galatians*, 178–9; Lührmann, *Galatians*, 82–3; Martyn, *Galatians*, 409).

[3] On the παιδαγωγός in antiquity see Betz, *Galatians*, 177; Nilsson, *Die hellenistische Schule*; Marrou, *Education in Antiquity*, 201–2; Plato, *Resp.*, 467d; *Lys.*, 208c; *Leges* 7.808d–e. It is not clear how such "supervisors" were usually regarded and so whether (as Betz assumes, *Galatians*, 177) Paul intends by this analogy any denigration of Torah. Dunn

law, as παιδαγωγός, facilitates salvation in Christ by restricting Israel for a period of time, but just as the παιδαγωγός leaves his charge when the child arrives at the classroom, so too Paul imagines Torah having exhausted its role now that Christ has come. The implicit analogy plays the same epistemic role as did the comparison with the institution of the διαθήκη in 3:15–18: it helps the audience to perceive the pattern which Paul is trying to establish and at the same time reinforces the essential plausibility of that pattern. Already in 3:24, however, Paul is shifting into a new mode of argumentation in which he is not only elaborating the story of Israel as an object "out there," but beginning to show how the players in the Galatian conflict fit into that story, are "emplotted" within it. For the law is now said to have been not just a custodian, but "our" custodian (παιδαγωγὸς ἡμῶν). Paul has already made clear that the jurisdiction of the law would come to an end with the advent of Christ and the new possibility which he brings. In 3:25, however, this turn in the narrative is personalized: "But now that faith has come, we are no longer subject to a disciplinarian (οὐκέτι ὑπὸ παιδαγωγόν ἐσμεν)." Having elaborated the place of law in his reconfigured story, the Apostle is locating "us" in that story and making clear how "we" now stand in relation to law,

---

rightly questions this strongly negative impression of the figure of the παιδαγωγός, stressing the function of the slave in protecting and training youths in good manners (Dunn, *Galatians*, 199; cf. *P. Oxy.* 6.930; Brawley, "Contextuality," 107–8). Nor is it entirely clear whether Paul is thinking primarily of the original function of the παιδαγωγός as a supervisor on the way to and from primary school, or whether he is thinking of the broader role such slaves sometimes took on as a guide in manners and morals. If it is the more restricted role which is in the Apostle's mind, the question still remains whether he is focussed on the slave as protector of the pupil en route, as a disciplinarian who constrains the child's conduct, or as a guide who ensures that the child reaches the classroom. Coming as it does after talk of the law as "imprisoning" humanity, it is tempting to see in the παιδαγωγός analogy too a primary emphasis on constraint (so Eckert, *Urchristliche Verkündigung*, 85–6; Eckstein, *Verheißung*, 216; R. N. Longenecker, *Galatians*, 148; Martyn, *Galatians*, 363). The same thing is implied by Paul's equation of life "under the law" with slavery (so Betz, *Galatians*, 178; Gal 2:4; 3:23; 4:1–10; 5:1). Whether, however, this constraining role excludes any idea of νομός contributing to the realization of the blessing is less clear (so Betz, *Galatians*, 178; R. N. Longenecker, *Galatians*, 148; cf. Epict., *Diss.* 3.19.5; Plut., *Num.* 15). In any case, when Paul says in 3:24 that the law, as παιδαγωγός, leads εἰς Χριστόν, the sense of εἰς is probably temporal (so Dunn, *Galatians*, 199; Lightfoot, *Galatians*, 149; R. N. Longenecker, *Galatians*, 148–9; Martyn, *Galatians*, 363).

given "our" place in the narrative.[4] Who is included with Paul in this "us"? Initially it seems that the pronoun refers to Paul and his Jewish compatriots (including the Galatian opponents). In 3:26, however, it becomes clear that Paul has intentionally left the identity of "us" vague, for though the Gentile Galatians did not live "under the law," they too now share in the liberated state which Christ has made possible: "for in Christ Jesus you are all children of God through faith."

Through to 3:29 two things are happening simultaneously. On the one hand, Paul comes back to the basic reconfiguration of the story which he laid out in 3:1–14 under the dual pressure of the Christ event and the Galatians' experience of the Spirit. It is those who are identified with Christ in baptism, those who are "in Christ," who are "Abraham's seed" and thus "heirs according to the promise (κατ' ἐπαγγελίαν κληρονόμοι)" (3:29). This again is not a conclusion to the Apostle's discussion of law in the sense of a conclusion to a syllogistic argument.[5] Rather, Paul is bringing his reconfiguration of the story full circle.[6] He has shown that this new construal of the narrative can even integrate Torah and give it a meaningful (albeit totally re-imagined) role. Now he can return more confidently to his initial claims about who gets to play the role of "Abraham's seed," about who in the story receives God's eschatological blessing. At the same time, however, by locating the audience in his narrative, Paul is beginning to make an ethical

---

[4] Eckstein (*Verheißung*, 217) recognizes that it is here that Paul begins explicitly to draw "die für die galatische Situation entscheidende Konsequenz aus der Darstellung" which has gone before.

[5] Nor is it, as Betz suggests (*Galatians*, 185; so R. N. Longenecker, *Galatians*, 159) an independent argument based on appeal to a baptismal confession. That some or all of 3:27–28 may be such a confessional formula is clear enough (see Betz's discussion in *Galatians*, 181–4; R. N. Longenecker, *Galatians*, 154–5; MacDonald, *There Is No Male and Female*, 4–9; Martyn, *Galatians*, 378–83; though cf. Dunn, *Galatians*, 201). This does not mean, however, that Paul intended the traditional status of the allusion to carry the primary argumentative weight in 3:26–29. Paul certainly does not lay heavy emphasis on its traditional nature (vs. 1 Cor 15:1ff.). Moreover, if the material is traditional it would not be accepted by the opponents as Paul interprets it, so its usefulness to Paul as a traditional authority has probably already been undermined in the Galatian community by the arguments of the opponents.

[6] Dunn rightly observes that the post-positive γάρ which begins v. 26 "indicates that the following assertion is as much the basis of the argument just completed (iii.23–5) as its conclusion" (*Galatians*, 201; so R. N. Longenecker, *Galatians*, 151).

argument. He is emplotting the Galatians in the story and placing them in the role of the blessed "seed" who have become heirs of God's blessing because of their connection with Christ (3:29). Yet his whole reconfiguration of the role of law in 3:19–24 has portrayed the legal institution as coming to an end once this existence by faith in Christ became a possibility. By means of his ambiguous "us" in 3:24–25 Paul has thus highlighted the ethical implication of the Galatians' location in the story. For if the Galatians stand with Paul in a new chapter, a chapter in which blessing comes simply by one's connection with Christ, they must also stand among those who are "no longer subject to a disciplinarian" (3:25), even though they were not actually part of the group which sought to keep that law in the first place (3:24). Their membership in Paul's liberated "us" implies that a return to the previous mode of life led by that "us" is impossible. That chapter in the story is ended.

Here we see in action the ethical "judgement" which we have already observed in Part Two above, in which ethics arise from the story itself as one is "emplotted" within it and perceives how one must act at this stage in the narrative if one wants to play a good role. From 4:1–11 these implications become explicit as Paul seeks to help the Galatians to perform the act of "judgement" which will bring them to a proper understanding of their lack of obligation to keep Torah.[7] In 4:1–2 Paul sets up another analogy from daily life in order to help the Galatians to grasp the narrative pattern which he is suggesting and to reinforce the plausibility of that pattern.[8] "Heirs," Paul observes, "as long as they are minors, are no better than slaves, though they are the owners of the property; but they remain under guardians and trustees until the date set by the father" (4:1–2). Given Paul's reconstrual of the story, including his reconfiguration of Torah's role, the aptness of this analogy seems clear. Life "under the law" was a kind of enslavement (cf. 3:22–24) but was a temporary state which would come to an end once Christ arrived, once the "heirs" of God's promise were able to inherit their estate.[9] Hence the

---

[7] Hence, although the analogy being used in 4:1–7 is closely parallel to that in 3:24–26 and points to the same underlying narrative pattern, it is not the case that 4:1–7 are meant simply "to illustrate what he said in 3:23–25 about living 'under the law' and in 3:26–29 about new relationships 'in Christ'" (R. N. Longenecker, *Galatians*, 162). This is not simply illustration but ethical argument.

[8] On the background of Paul's analogy see Nicholas and Treggiari, *"patria potestas."*

[9] In Greek and Roman inheritance law the death of the father was assumed before such a scenario could take effect (see, e.g., R. N. Longenecker, *Galatians*, 163). Paul is not,

Galatians should not make themselves "minors" again – place themselves back under slavery – by taking on an obligation to observe Torah.

As we have seen, it is not clear at first exactly where the Galatians should be located within Paul's reconfigured narrative, for they did not keep Torah in the past. They were not under its slavery and did not directly experience Christ as emancipation from it. Hence one might still argue that they need to take on Torah in order to reproduce the Jewish experience of Christ. It is in order to clear up this ambiguity that the Apostle carefully emplots not only the Galatians' Christian present, but also their past outside of Christ. Again this is done by means of analogy – this time an analogy between the Galatians' past existence and an established element of the narrative. Notice how Paul compares the quasi-enslavement of the heir under guardians to "our" experience being "enslaved ὑπὸ τὰ στοιχεῖα τοῦ κόσμου" (4:3). In what follows, the identity of these στοιχεῖα is slippery. On the one hand, Paul continues (4:4–5) to describe the deliverance of Christ as a deliverance from the law, as if these στοιχεῖα were identical to Torah.[10] On the other hand, Paul describes in 4:8–9 the Galatians' former life as pagans in terms of enslavement "to beings that by nature are not gods" and speaks of their *returning* to "the weak and beggarly στοιχεῖα."[11] What is going on here? It seems that the Apostle is drawing a second analogy between the existence of Jews under Torah and the existence of the Galatians in their pagan practices. He capitalizes on the ambiguity of the term στοιχεῖα in order to suggest that in certain ways the pre-Christian life of Jews and that of Gentiles are the same.[12] In coming to Christ, both Jew and pagan experience a deliverance

---

however, drawing a perfect correlation between the situation of the heir and the situation of human beings in the theological story. The metaphor serves a primarily heuristic purpose, and neither Paul nor the Galatians would likely have been too concerned by the fact that, like all analogies, this one cannot be pushed too far (cf. Martyn, *Galatians*, 386; Burton, *Galatians*, 211–12).

[10] Contra Barrett, *Freedom*, 39.

[11] Eckstein (*Verheißung*, 228) recognizes that this requires the Gentiles to be part of the "we" who are set free in some sense from the restrictions of Torah.

[12] The noun στοιχεῖον can denote a "letter" of the alphabet or a "syllable," an "element" or basic constituent of the physical world, an "elementary principle" or basic issue, a "heavenly body," or a "sign of the zodiac" (LSJ, 1647 [II.1–5]; Delling, "στοιχεῖον," 671–83). Blinzer ("Lexicalisches") argued that in in extra-biblical Greek the expression στοιχεῖα τοῦ κόσμου refers to "die vier (oder fünf) Grundstoffe" (441; so Rusam, "Neue Belege,"

from a confining, "enslaving" power.[13] Paul likely did not intend to say that life as a pagan Gentile was no worse than life under Torah, or that pagan religion and traditional Judaism were basically equivalent.[14] In comparison to life in Christ, however, both previous states were oppressive, and both come to an end once one is identified with the crucified and risen one.

With this emplotment of the Galatians' past, the opponents' ethical rhetoric appears clearly wrong. The observance of Torah is neither an advance on Paul's initial, rudimentary Gospel nor the key with which they can unlock the full benefit of their faith in Christ. It is, rather, a return to a pre-Christian state, a state which in crucial ways would be no different from

---

124; see Philo, *Aet.* 109; *Her.* 134, 140; Galen, *Nat. fac.* 1.39; Ps.-Lucian, *Am.* 19; *Orphic Hymns* 5.4; Irenaeus, *Haer.* 1.5.4). Yet most of this evidence postdates Paul's letters, often by a century or more. Moreover, the passages from *Sib. Or.* cited by Blinzer (2:206f.; 3:79–82; 8:337f.) seem to refer not to the four/five elements specifically, but to the basic components of the universe more generally (including stars, earth, sea, sky, night, day, etc.). This would suggest that the modification of στοιχεῖα by τοῦ κόσμου need not necessarily rule out a reference to, e.g., heavenly bodies. On the other hand, Rusam cites Sext. Emp., *Pyr.* 3.152, where the Pythagoreans are said to have regarded numbers as the στοιχεῖα τοῦ κόσμου ("Neue Belege," 122). Hence, even this later evidence testifies to a range of common uses for the expression (so Delling, "στοιχεῖον," 683).

What this evidence does suggest is that Paul is thinking of something associated with the physical world, and not primarily of "basic principles" (contra Burton, *Galatians*, 231; R. N. Longenecker, *Galatians*, 165–6; though see Heb 5:12). Some understand Paul's στοιχεῖα here to be deified natural elements which the Galatians used to worship (so Betz, *Galatians*, 204–5; Burton, *Galatians*, 215–16; Martyn, *Galatians*, 396–7; see Wis 13:1–2; Philo, *Decal.* 52–6), and the στοιχεῖα do seem to be identical with the "beings" of 4:8 (so Sanders, *Paul, the Law, and the Jewish People*, 69). But the στοιχεῖα are also equated with the law in 4:3–5, and in 4:3 Paul seems to include himself in the "we" who served them. More plausible is the suggestion of Delling ("στοιχεῖον," 684–5) and Eckstein (*Verheißung*, 230) that Paul here refers to the physical constituents or structuring principles of the world as a metaphor for the "present evil age." To serve the στοιχεῖα τοῦ κόσμου is to remain within the constraints of ordinary human life after Adam. So, inasmuch as both the Galatians' pagan past and Jewish life before Christ were not directed towards the new possibilities opened up in Christ, both states would be for Paul a subjection to such στοιχεῖα (so Dunn, *Galatians*, 213; R. N. Longenecker, *Galatians*, 180–81).

[13] So Eckstein, *Verheißung*, 231. Dunn points out that the common language of "redeeming" (ἐξαγοράζω) in 3:13–14 and 4:4–6 suggests that he is alluding in both passages to the same scenario of Christ's representative suffering of judgement (*Galatians*, 216–17; so Hays, *Faith*, 118–21; contra Betz, *Galatians*, 207, n. 51).

[14] Contra Burton, *Galatians*, 231; Lightfoot, *Galatians*, 172–3.

their pagan existence prior to meeting Paul. With the Galatians' baptism they experienced the shift from life under the στοιχεῖα to life in the new possibility created by Christ, and this is the same shift experienced by Jews who place their faith in Christ. In baptism the Galatians "clothed themselves with Christ (Χριστὸν ἐνεδύσασθε)" (3:27) and took on a new role in Israel's story, the role of Abraham's heirs, of those who enjoy the eschatological blessing.[15] This baptism, this clothing with Christ, was the crucial moment of entry into the best role one can play in the narrative. There is no further shift to make. On the contrary, any further shift towards existence under Torah will, Paul urges, be a retreat from this blessed existence, which will leave the Galatians in the same kind of dangerous role which they occupied as devotees of the στοιχεῖα. A move towards Jewish practice does not place them in a better role in the story, but rather places their status as heirs of God's promise in jeopardy. This is why when Paul hears that the Galatians are "observing special days, and months, and seasons, and years" – that is, taking on Jewish observances – he is afraid "that my work for you may have been wasted" (4:10–11).[16] Here the audience stands at the crisis point of the theological story, the point at which their choice can have wonderful or disastrous consequences. The key is that they choose to play the role of Abraham's heirs and that they discern the shape of that role, not on the basis of the opponents' version of Israel's story, but on the basis of Paul's reconfigured narrative.

What justifies and grounds Paul's ethical conclusions here? Why would the Galatian audience accept the Apostle's claim that his construal of the story is the true one? Here again, the basic grounding for Paul's claim is simply the coherence of the narrative as he has reconfigured it. His argument

---

[15] Whether or not the "clothing" metaphor alludes to baptismal robes (so, e.g., Martyn, *Galatians*, 375–6; contra Lightfoot, *Galatians*, 150), it is unlikely that the expression simply denotes the taking on of Christ's character (so R. N. Longenecker, *Galatians*, 156), since it is here tied so closely with being "in Christ." Such "clothing" language can denote the assumption of another person's identity (see, e.g., Col 3:10 and cf. Burton, *Galatians*, 204).

[16] Paul could be referring specifically here to Jewish Sabbath and festival observance (so Burton, *Galatians*, 232–3; Dunn, *Galatians*, 227–8) or, as Betz says, "the *typical* behavior of religiously scrupulous people" (*Galatians*, 217 [italics original]). The reference may be kept generic in order to highlight the parallel in practice between the Galatians' pagan past and the Jewish practices which they are now contemplating (so Betz, *Galatians*, 218). There is little reason to see an allusion to astrological ideas in the opponents' teaching (as in Lührmann, *Galatians*, 85; Martyn, *Galatians*, 414–18).

still depends in large part on the observation (in 2:21 and in 3:1–5) that there are new chapters in the story which make no sense on the opponents' construal of its plot. Hence, if Paul can offer a rereading which *can* encompass both those new events and all of the previous chapters of Israel's story, he will have demonstrated that his own telling is more trustworthy than that of the Galatian opponents. His assumption is that, by 3:25, this task has been accomplished. He may continue to allude in places (particularly in 4:6–7) to the Galatians' experiences of the Spirit, further illustrating the ability of his version of the narrative to encompass these new events.[17] The Apostle does not, however, feel the need at this point to offer substantial new arguments in favor of his construal of the story. He has shown that his rereading, if disturbingly novel, is eminently coherent, and it is on this basis that he shifts in 3:25–4:11 to begin pointing out the ethical implications which his reconfigured story carries for the Galatian believers.

2. Ethical Analogies Within the Story (4:21–5:12)

We pass over 4:12–20, where Paul suspends for a moment his narrative argument in order to make an essentially non-rational appeal to the Galatians' loyalty and past affection for him. In 4:21, however, Paul returns to his main argument and offers what commentators usually call an "allegorical" reading of the relationships between Abraham's wives and children.[18] Paul recalls the

---

[17] So Burton, *Galatians*, 221. Paul says that "God has sent the Spirit of his Son into our hearts, crying, 'Abba! Father!' So you are no longer a slave but a child, and if a child then also and heir, through God" (4:6b–7). Several scholars see here a reference to a charismatic experience in the Galatians' worship (e.g., Betz, *Galatians*, 210–11; Dunn, *Galatians*, 220–21; Eckert, *Urchristliche Verkündigung*, 91; Lull, *Spirit*, 66–9; contra Eckstein, *Verheißung*, 243). Alternatively, R. N. Longenecker has suggested that Paul is alluding here to the general experience of "a more intimate and truly filial relationship with God the Father" (*Galatians*, 175). On either reading, it is as a consequence of such experiences of the Spirit (ὥστε) that Paul can affirm the Galatians are "no longer a slave but a child" (4:7; so Lull, *Spirit*, 108–9).

[18] Most commentators see a new section beginning part way through these verses, at 5:1 (so Betz, *Galatians*, 238; Burton, *Galatians*, 267–9; Dunn, *Galatians*, 260; Lührmann, *Galatians*, 94; Mussner, *Galaterbrief*, 334), at 4:31 (so Zahn, Lagrange, Bousset), or at 5:2 (Lightfoot, *Galatians*, 203; Martyn, *Galatians*, 432; Bruce, *Galatians*, 228–9). I hold these verses together, however, to highlight the fact that Paul has begun his focussed ethical

events surrounding Hagar and Sarah in Genesis and says that "these things are read figuratively (ἅτινά ἐστιν ἀλληγορούμενα)."[19] When we render Paul's words in this way and avoid the term "allegory," we are reminded that in Paul's time the verb ἀλληγορέω was not yet a technical term for a clearly defined hermeneutical approach. The verb, along with the cognate noun ἀλληγορία, is actually attested little, if at all, prior to the first century BCE.[20] Both words are usually understood to denote a standardized method of interpretation which finds behind the surface of the text a detailed and coded reference to "deeper" meanings,[21] and so Paul is often accused here of "strange and even arbitrary exegesis."[22] Yet in this period we find both the

---

argument already with his interpretation of Hagar and Sarah in 4:21ff., and that 5:1–12 simply lay out the conclusion of this argument. The impression of a major break at 5:1 arises from the misreading which takes the Hagar/Sarah allegory as a secondary illustration and as non-ethical in its orientation. The lack of a connection particle joining 4:31 with 5:1 has been seen by some as emphasis of a major break (so Dunn, *Galatians*, 261) but, as R. N. Longenecker has pointed out, 4:31 serves just as much to introduce the explicit exhortation in 5:1ff. as to sum up the preceding material (*Galatians*, 199, 218). In favour of taking 5:1–12 with the preceding section, Longenecker observes that the note of explicit ethical exhortation began already with Paul's "become like me!" in 4:12 (*Galatians*, 199, 218). Longenecker also notes (*Galatians*, 221–2) how the tone and thrust of 5:1–12 match very closely that of 1:6–10, suggesting that here Paul is summing up his main argument against the opponents, an argument whose final phase is the allegory of 4:21–31 (so Bryant, *Crudified Christ*, 213, n. 60; Dunn, *Galatians*, 260–61; cf. Merk, "Beginn der Paränese"). Bryant also points out (*Crucified Christ*, 213, n. 60) that language about "slavery" continues from chapter 4 into 5:1–12, and that it is not until 5:13 that Paul shifts to mostly second-person pronouns. It is true that 5:1 seems to recapitulate the whole argument since 3:1, and not just 4:21–31. At the same time, 4:12–20 interrupted the flow of that argument, so that the summing up seems to be performed not just by 5:1 but by the whole allegory of 4:21–31 as well. All of this provides sufficient grounds for treating 4:12–31 together with 5:1–12.

[19] The NRSV renders these words "this is an allegory," but the verb ἐστιν is singular simply because the subject of the sentence is a neuter plural (see BDF, 73 §133).

[20] The word group seems to be attested first in Demetrius, *Formae epistolicae* 15; Tryphon, Περὶ τρόπων 191.15; 193.8–9, 16; 206.5 and Dionysius of Halicarnassus, *Dem.* 5.31; 7.64; *Ant. rom.* 2.20.1; *Pomp.* 2.6.5 (not in Philo and Cicero, as per Büchsel, "ἀλληγορέω," 260).

[21] This is assumed by, e.g., Lührmann, *Galatians*, 89.

[22] Barclay, *Obeying*, 91. Barclay is in good company when he attempts to excuse this exegetical abuse as Paul's rhetorical attempt to reuse his opponents' proof texts in an *ad hominem* rhetorical move (see Barrett, "Allegory," 13; R. N. Longenecker, *Galatians*, 199–200, 210; Martyn, *Galatians*, 434). Yet Barrett, who has produced the most formidable

verb ἀλληγορέω and its nominal counterpart ἀλληγορία used to denote any interpretive strategy which recognizes the use of metaphor or analogy in a text, as well as for an author's own use of figurative expression.[23] Hence, when Dionysius of Halicarnassus bemoans the inappropriateness of Pindar's anthropomorphic imagery in his hymn to the sun, he refers to such imagery as ἡ ἀλληγορία (*Dem.* 7.64). Likewise, Josephus can refer derisively to the Greek artists' fanciful depictions of the gods as ἀλληγορίαι, meaning not "allegories" but something like "imaginative representations" (*C. Ap.* 2.255).[24] Certainly there was a very old tradition among the Greek intelligentsia of interpreting Homeric myth as a kind of symbolic code, in much the same way that Philo handles the scriptures of Israel. Up to the first century BCE, however, this hermeneutical approach was not at all associated with the term ἀλληγορέω. So when writers around the turn of the era such as Dionysius of Halicarnassus and Strabo refer to that familiar way of reading Homer as ἀλληγορία it is not because the word group was a hermeneutical *terminus technicus*. On the contrary, they use this language because such Homeric interpretation was recognized as one species of figurative reading, one kind of ἀλληγορία.[25] This is why these same writers feel free to use ἀλληγορέω language for other kinds of speech and reading which have little

---

argument seeing the story of Sarah and Hagar as one of the opponents' favourite texts, has by no means proven his case ("Allegory," 9–10). Nor need we (with Martyn, *Galatians*, 434) see the ἀλλά in v. 23 as intended to "correct the Teachers' reading of the patriarchal stories." Paul could simply be setting the fact that the two sons had the same father (4:22) against the very different manners in which the two were conceived (4:23). McClane goes further to argue that Paul's exegetical technique is itself borrowed from the opponents ("Hellenistic Background," 132), but this does not account sufficiently for the Apostle's use of a similar approach in, e.g., 1 Cor 10:11.

[23] So Trapp, "Allegory." The verb can refer to figurative interpretation of a text (so LSJ, 69[1]; e.g., Philo, *Contempl.* 28; Plut., *Is. Os.* 362b), while both verb and noun can denote figurative expression (so LSJ, 69[2]; BDAG, 46; e.g., Jos., *A.J.* 1.24; *C. Ap.* 2.255; Plut., *Is. Os.* 363d; *De esu* 996b; *Adol. poet. aud.* 19f; *Pyth. orac.* 409d; Strabo, *Geogr.* 1.2.7.5; Aelius Theon, *Progymnasmata* 81.7; Dion. Hal., *Dem.* 5.31).

[24] Likewise, Plutarch can group together τὰ αἰνίγματα καὶ τὰς ἀλληγορίας καὶ τὰς μεταφορὰς in a general reference to the enigmatic expression of the Pythian oracle (*Pyth. orac.* 409d; cf. Tryphon, Περὶ τρόπων 191.15). In his classification of figures of speech, Tryphon defines ἀλληορία as λόγος ἕτερον μέν τι κυρίως δηλῶν, ἑτέρου δὲ ἔννοιαν παριστάνων καθ' ὁμοίωσιν ἐπὶ τὸ πλεῖστον (Περὶ τρόπων 193.9–11).

[25] See Dion. Hal., *Ant. rom.* 2.20.1; Strabo, *Geogr.* 1.2.7.5.

in common with, say, Philo's reading of Scripture, except that they too employ language metaphorically. It may well be that Philo himself and the Alexandrian tradition of which he was a part were responsible for the development of ἀλληγορέω into a specialized term for a distinct hermeneutical approach.[26] All of this means that when Paul announces his intention to read the story of Hagar and Sarah as ἀλληγορία he most likely means nothing more than that he is taking the events described in Genesis as figurative of some broader ideas.[27]

---

[26] In any case Plutarch (in *Adol. poet. aud.* 19f) bears witness to the fact that the use of the noun ἀλληγορία for such Homeric myths is still a relatively new thing in the late first century. The older term, he says, is ὑπονοία.

[27] So Jobes, "Jerusalem," 317–18; contra Betz, *Galatians*, 243; Büchsel, "ἀλληγορέω," 260; R. N. Longenecker, *Galatians*, 209–10). Hence Theodore of Mopsuestia says that by "allegory" Paul means "the comparison, by juxtaposition, of events which have already occurred with present events" (quoted in Löfstedt, "Allegory," 490; cf. Calvin, *Galatians*, on 4:22). Paul is likely thinking of the same approach to the biblical text which he employs in 1 Cor 10:11, where the account of Israel's complaint at Meribah is said to have happened τυπικῶς, in a way which represents a larger idea (so Lightfoot, *Galatians*, 180; cf. above, pp. 134–7).

Explicating precisely how the Alexandrian brand of "allegorical" interpretation (and its Homeric precursors) is distinct from other kinds of figurative reading has often proven difficult. As Büchsel has observed, the difference does not lie primarily in whether or not the exegete maintains the historical truth of the events related in the text ("ἀλληγορέω," 262). Even Philo can insist that the biblical narratives are historically accurate. In all cases, moreover, such interpretation is a matter of finding in the text some analogy to an idea or entity which that text does not explicitly address. The distinction seems to lie in the degree to which the analogy is based on 1) themes and ideas which are native to the text and 2) on prominent features of the story. Hence, while we may call some readings of Song of Songs allegorical (so Büchsel, "ἀλληγορέω," 262), the comparison being made between the lovers' relationship and that between Israel and God rests on a dynamic which is central to the text. This is very different from the way in which the *Letter of Aristeas* takes the Levitical food laws as symbolic of Greco-Roman ethical standards (*Let. Aris.* 148–171). Josephus' symbolic interpretation of the tabernacle's design and furnishings (*A.J.*, 3.179–187) stays close to the central themes of the Exodus account, which already seems to suggest that the construction was intended to represent the cosmos (see Averbeck, "Tabernacle," 816–18; J. Levenson, *Creation and the Persistence of Evil*, 53–127). Where Josephus' reading begins to resemble "Alexandrian" exegesis is in the significance which he extends even to trivial details of the text. In contrast, Aristobulus' figurative explanation of the Bible's anthropomorphic language about God not only highlights ideas native to the texts involved, but also focusses on prominent and recurrent forms of expression associated with those themes (see Frag. 2 [Euseb., *Praep. ev.* 8.9.38–8.10.17]; Frag. 4.3 [Euseb., ibid.

Essentially the Apostle is using the story of Hagar and Sarah to construct an extended analogy, like the analogies from daily life which he employed earlier in Galatians, and like the ethical analogies we observed in Chapter VI. There is a narrative pattern in the Genesis account which Paul sees also in the Galatians' present situation. Hence, just as before, Paul sets the two situations side by side in order to highlight the similar patterns.[28] In this case the analogy draws a parallel between Isaac's relationship with Ishmael and the relationship between those "of faith" and those "of the works of the law."[29] The Apostle's point is to help the audience see that, just as Isaac inherited the promise while his brother was excluded, so too those "of faith" are inheriting the promise while those "of the works of the law" are excluded.

The Apostle opens the analogy by reminding the Galatians that "Abraham had two sons."[30] He seems to presume that the audience will know

---

13.13.3]; Frag. 5.9–13 [Euseb., ibid. 13.12.9–13]). It is because the analogies drawn in much Jewish "allegory" tended to stay closer to the text's central themes and features that this interpretive tradition seems to Büchsel "less arbitrary" than the variety pursued by Philo and Pseudo-Aristeas (Büchsel, "ἀλληγορέω," 262).

Paul's "allegory" of Hagar and Sarah differs from that of Philo in both of these respects (contra Büchsel, "ἀλληγορέω," 263). The Alexandrian understands Abraham to represent the human soul, Sarah divine Wisdom, and Hagar a merely preparatory education, and the narratives are then read as the saga of the soul's quest for mystical wisdom (see Philo, *Congr.* 1–23, 63–69, 71–88, 118–22, 139–62; *QG* 3.18–38; *Leg.* 3.244; *Cher.* 3–10; *Somn.* 1.240; *Post.* 130–31; *Mut.* 261; *Fug.* 209–13; *Sacr.* 43–44). Yet none of these ideas even fall within the horizon of the text taken on its own terms. Paul, on the other hand, focusses on the question of how one is included in the heritage of Abraham, on slavery and freedom, and on the difference between the trust in God involved in Isaac's birth and the human effort involved in the birth of Ishmael – all central motifs in the Genesis account (so Dunn, *Galatians*, 248; Lightfoot, *Galatians*, 199; R. N. Longenecker, *Galatians*, 209). Hence Paul's analogy maintains the integrity of the interpreted text in a way which Philo's does not.

[28] The verb συστοιχέω in 4:26 may simply mean that Hagar "correponds to" – is to be compared analogically to – the present Jerusalem. We need not imagine Paul to be setting up two formal columns of opposite concepts (so BDAG, 979; contra Dunn, *Galatians*, 252; Martyn, *Galatians*, 438).

[29] That the two groups which Paul has in view are those "of faith" and those "of the law" becomes clear in 5:1–12, where the explicit exhortations based on this analogy revolve around the question of whether one should try to be justified ἐν νόμῳ (5:4) or place faith in Christ without obeying Torah (5:2–6).

[30] Exegetes often treat the passage as if Hagar and Sarah were themselves the focus, but notice that Paul begins by focussing on the Patriarch's δύο υἱούς (4:22). It is the distinction

immediately who these two sons were and will at the same time grasp the unspoken point that only one of the boys became heir to the Abrahamic promises. What was the basis for God's inclusion of one and exclusion of the other? Paul emphasizes that "one, the child of the slave, was born according to the flesh (κατὰ σάρκα)" while "the other, the child of the free woman, was born through the promise (δι' ἐπαγγελίας)" (4:23). Thus far the Apostle is offering a straightforward reading of the Genesis story. Ishmael was not allowed to inherit the promises to Abraham because he represented the patriarch's attempt to secure the fulfilment of those promises through ordinary human means.[31] Isaac, on the other hand, was made Abraham's heir because his conception was a miracle, was itself a fulfilment of the promise which (in turn) the child would grow up to inherit.

The surprise, of course, comes in the way in which Paul lines up these two sons as analogous to contemporary groups. Instead of making Isaac analogous to those who faithfully keep Torah, Paul claims that this first "child of the promise" was in a position analogous to the one enjoyed by those "of faith" – by Paul himself and his Galatian (Gentile) converts. Paul writes, "Now you, my friends, are children of the promise, like Isaac" (4:28), and he emphasizes that "we are children, not of the slave but of the free

---

between these children in which the Apostle is primarily interested. Their mothers are introduced by way of explaining the basis for that distinction.

[31] Ishmael is born κατὰ σάρκα (4:23), i.e., in accordance with ordinary human experience and ways of acting (so Dunn, *Galatians*, 246; Lightfoot, *Galatians*, 180), while Isaac is born δι' ἐπαγγελίας. There is no need here to see the "flesh" as a "power" which produces the one child and the "promise" as another, opposing power (contra Martyn, *Galatians*, 435). We must allow for flexibility in Paul's usage of terms such as σάρξ, and the opposition with ἐπαγγελία (not yet with πνεῦμα) suggests that the Apostle is still thinking of the fact that Ishmael represent's Sarah's own effort to produce a child, while Isaac was conceived as a miraculous fulfilment of God's oath. Such a reading allows us to take the preposition κατά in the common sense of "in accordance with" or "according to" (BDAG, 512 [B.5]), marking the conformity of Ishmael's conception to a particular principle of action. While Martyn is right that κατά can verge on "as a result of," this is usually only in the sense that the norm according to which an action is pursued "is at the same time the reason" for its performance, or the action is pursued "according to" (and so "because of") an agent's intention or purpose (see BDAG, 512 [B.5.a.d]). It does not usually mark a material cause or source of an event. Note too that in 4:28, where the believers are κατὰ Ἰσαὰκ ἐπαγγελίας τέκνα, this means that they are "begotten," become heirs of Abraham, in a manner analogous to (following the same pattern as that of) Isaac.

woman" (4:31). While it is these covenant outsiders who are, like Isaac, in a position to inherit Abraham's promises, Paul claims that those who continue to rely on law-keeping as the basis of their position vis-à-vis God are like Ishmael. They will not inherit the Abrahamic promises. Paul writes: "But what does the scripture say? 'Drive out the slave and her child; for the child of the slave will not share the inheritance with the child of the free woman'" (4:30). Just as Ishmael was forced out of the camp and denied any inheritance, so too those 'of the law' will be denied any share in the final fulfilment of those promises.[32]

How can Paul justify such a radical break with traditional Jewish readings of the Abraham story? The key to understanding the Apostle's argument here is to realize again that he is not doing exegesis, if by that term we mean reading the biblical text without any reference to the events involving Christ and the church.[33] He is not suggesting that the Genesis text alone justifies the

---

[32] It is not at all clear that Paul's citation of the biblical instruction to expel the slave woman is intended as a call to expel the opponents (so Löfstedt, "Allegory," 488–9; Martyn, *Galatians*, 446; contra Eckert, *Urchristliche Verkündigung*, 98). The Apostle is probably just driving home the fate of "Hagar," who, along with her offspring (those who do not accept Christ's salvation in faith), is excluded from the covenant people (so Barrett, "Allegory," 13; Dunn, *Galatians*, 258).

Paul's reference to Ishmael's oppression of Isaac (4:29) may also point to the Galatians' experience of some sort of pressure, either from the opponents themselves or (perhaps vicariously through the reports of the opponents) from non-Christian Jews who regard uncircumcised Christians as highly dangerous (so Betz, *Galatians*, 249; Dunn, *Galatians*, 256–7; R. N. Longenecker, *Galatians*, 216). The analogy helps Paul to emphasize that such pressures in the present must not distract the Galatians from the reward which awaits them if they hold fast to his Gospel. In any case, the idea of Esau having oppressed Isaac arose from a reading of Gen 21:9 which understands "playing" to mean "provoking" or "abusing" (so Betz, *Galatians*, 250; R. N. Longenecker, *Galatians*, 217; Lührmann, *Galatians*, 92; see, e.g., *Tg. Ps.-J.* Gen 21:9–11; *Tg. Onq.* Gen 21:9; *t. Soṭa* 6:6; *Exod. Rab.* 1:1; *Pesiq. R.* 48:2; *Pirqe R. El.* 30; cf. Jos., *A.J.* 1.215). It is, however, unlikely (contra Barrett, "Allegory", 13) that Paul would have placed much argumentative weight on the Jewish persecution of Gentile Christians, as if this demonstrated that they were "Ishmael" and so justified his allegory.

[33] Many commentators try to find justification for this identification in some association (verbal or geographical) between Hagar and Arabia (so Betz, *Galatians*, 244–5; Lührmann, *Galatians*, 90; and, tentatively, Berger, "Abraham," 60; Eckert, *Urchristliche Verkündigung*, 96) or between Ishmael and the Arab people. Dunn is likely right that such connections would be "too remote from the movement of thought here" (*Galatians*, 251). One also wonders whether Gentile Galatians would be familiar enough with Targumic

way in which he has applied it to the present situation. Rather, Paul has on other grounds (see 3:1–14) reconfigured Israel's story, and he finds in the relationships within Abraham's household a pattern which is analogous to the pattern of his reconfigured narrative. It is that prior rereading of the overarching story which justifies the use to which the Apostle puts the Genesis story here. On one level, then, this analogy between the Galatians' situation and the story in Genesis is being used, like Paul's previous analogies, as a heuristic device which helps the audience to grasp the pattern of the story.[34] It is precisely because the Apostle is using this incident from the Abraham story in order to illustrate (by way of analogy) a conclusion reached on other grounds that Paul places such a heavy emphasis on the status of the two mothers (slave or free). The slavery of Hagar offers a convenient point of contact with his earlier argument that life "under the law" constitutes a form of imprisonment, confinement, even slavery. It is also because his analogy is justified on grounds outside the text that Paul can equate the mothers of the two children with two "covenants" (4:24). If he has already established that those "of the law" will, like Ishmael, be excluded from the Abrahamic promises, and if they are excluded precisely because of their adherence to a legal covenant which was never intended to bring "life," then Ishmael's mother offers a convenient metaphor for the Sinaitic covenant which holds those "of the law" in "slavery" (4:24–25).

It is likewise Paul's prior reconfiguration of Israel's story which justifies his peculiar use of Isaiah 54:1 in the context of this analogy. Isaiah's call to

---

traditions or Arabian geography to pick up so subtle an allusion (so Lightfoot, *Galatians*, 197–8; Löfstedt, "Allegory," 480). The reference to Arabia may simply be intended to locate Mount Sinai or (with an adversative δέ in v. 25) to highlight Paul's awareness that his allegorical connection between Hagar/Sinai and Jerusalem does some violence to geography (so Dunn, *Galatians*, 251; Mussner, *Galaterbrief*, 322–4). Löfstedt ("Allegory," 481) suggests instead that the connection between Hagar/Sinai and Arabia is intended to further marginalize Torah, setting it outside the land of promise and associating it with Arabs (cf. Eckert, *Urchristliche Verkündigung*, 96; Martyn, *Galatians*, 438, n. 136). Even if Paul is using a linguistic link to connect Hagar with the Sinaitic covenant, Martyn is right that the opposition between this covenant and the promise must still be supplied by the interpreter (*Galatians*, 436). We must also remember that the text of 4:25a is far from certain (see Burton, *Galatians*, 259–61; Mussner, *Galaterbrief*; Metzger, *Textual Commentary*, 527).

[34] So Lightfoot suggests that Paul employs this allegory "rather as an illustration than an argument, as a means of representing in a lively form the lessons before enforced on other grounds" (*Galatians*, 200; so Dunn, *Galatians*, 243).

the "barren woman" to rejoice aids in the Apostle's creative reuse of the Isaac and Ishmael traditions because it provides a precedent for an analogical equation between the stories involving Sarah and the conception of Isaac, on the one hand, and the later Jewish community, on the other. For the Isaianic author clearly seems to be drawing an analogy between Sarah's barrenness and the devastation suffered by exilic Jerusalem.[35] What is more, Isaiah 54:1 furnishes Paul with a clear precedent for his association between the Abrahamic promises and Israel's eschatological hope. The Isaianic prophet seems to be using his Sarah imagery here to cast the exiles of his day as Abraham's (and Sarah's) children, and the final restoration of Jerusalem as the fulfilment of the Abrahamic promise of many progeny. So, by citing Isaiah 54:1, the Apostle highlights the fact that at least some elements of his own analogy are already conventional. The fate of the later Jewish community has long been associated, by way of analogy, with the story of Sarah's struggles and the eventual birth of Isaac. Yet the pivot of Paul's analogy, his equation of Torah-observant Jews with *Ishmael*, still finds no basis in the Isaianic text.[36] The Isaianic author does envision two cities

----

[35] Given the encouragement in Isa 51:2 to view Abraham and Sarah as typological precursors of second Isaiah's audience, Paul's identification of the "barren woman" (i.e., Jerusalem, see 54:11–12) as Sarah, the mother of Israel, is probably already intended by the author (so Lightfoot, *Galatians*, 182; cf. the development in *4 Ezra* 10). Jobes ("Jerusalem," 302) argues that an identification of Sarah with the barren woman of Isa 54:1 "does not seem completely apt," since the barren woman seems to be without a husband, while Abraham was Sarah's husband. Yet we need not push the details of the connection this far in order to recognize that the Isaianic author intended the barrenness of the city and the hope for miraculous children to recall Sarah's plight. The barren woman's lack of a husband is likely due to the effect of other imagery with which Isaiah is working, imagery which depicts a devastated city as divorced by its "husband," its patron god (cf. Jobes, "Jerusalem," 308). This need not detract from the way in which Isaiah associates Sarah's barrenness and expectation with Jerusalem (cf. Jobes, "Jerusalem," 308–9). It is likely this traditional, metaphoric association between Israel's eschatological glory and Sarah's long-awaited progeny which prompts Paul to associate Isa 54 with Genesis (contra Martyn, *Galatians*, 442).

[36] Jobes ("Jerusalem", 311–12) points to the promise in Isa 59:21 that God's Spirit will be placed upon the "seed" of Jerusalem's deliverer, suggesting that on this basis Paul identifies the law-free Galatians (who have received the Spirit) with the citizens of the eschatological city, the eschatological "children" of Jerusalem in 54:1. While the logic which this would involve fits closely with our reading of Paul's thought in Galatians, there is little evidence to suggest that in citing Isa 54:1 Paul is thinking specifically of 59:21.

(devastated Jerusalem and the eschatological Jerusalem) which are represented by two women (barren Sarah and fruitful Hagar), but for him the two cities are distinguished *chronologically*. They are two stages in the ongoing fate of the one Jewish people. *Both* cities are identified with Sarah, while Hagar is present only as a foil for the vindication of her counterpart. It is Paul's own move which separates these two chronological phases in Jerusalem's experience and constitutes them as ontologically distinct economies or institutions, one which continues indefinitely to languish in "slavery" and the other (the "Jerusalem above" of 4:26) which enjoys the eschatological blessing.[37] It is Paul who distinguishes between law and promise in such a way that the heavenly city is entirely divorced from the Sinaitic institution. It is also Paul's innovation to identify of the languishing city and the Sinaitic institution with Hagar,[38] but only the eschatological city

---

Moreover, notice that it is the seed *of Jerusalem's deliverer* who will receive the Spirit in chapter 59, not the seed of Abraham or Sarah.

[37] So Martyn, *Galatians*, 442. Jobes ("Jerusalem," 310) argues that even this move finds some precedent in Isaiah, since the people of Jerusalem are repeatedly condemned as an "evil seed" (σπέρμα πονηρόν, LXX Isa 1:4), while her faithful populace will only be established in the eschatological restoration (e.g., Isa 1:26). Nor are these two groups identical, for even in Isa 40–55 the exiled populace of Jerusalem is still accused of blindness and stubbornness, while the call to participate in the restoration of Jerusalem in chapter 55 implies that a moral return is also necessary for those who will become part of righteous Zion (this note of choice becomes even stronger in 56–66). At most, however, we can say that this distinction between two "cities" was latent in the logic of Isaiah. There is certainly no indication that both cities would coexist at the same time, as Paul envisions them.

[38] In saying that Hagar corresponds to the "present Jerusalem" (4:26) Paul is probably referring to that city as the centre of Judaism in general, not specifically to the Jerusalem church (contra Martyn, *Galatians*, 439). It is because Martyn takes the present Jerusalem as a narrow reference to the law-observant mission whose "children" are "judaizing" Christian converts that his reading runs into inconsistencies (such as the fact that while the "heavenly" Jerusalem is supposed to be "barren," Paul's mission is comparatively fruitful; see Martyn, *Galatians*, 443). It is true that the language of "begetting" in this passage is reminiscent of Paul's use of τίκτω and γεννάω for the conversion of new believers in his mission (Martyn, *Galatians*, 451–2; see Phlm 10; 1 Cor 4:14–15), but this need not mean that the "woman" who "gives birth" to slaves is specifically the law-observant mission. It may be more broadly that stream of Judaism (whether self-proclaimed followers of Jesus or not) which denies the sufficiency of faith in Christ. Martyn is correct (*Galatians*, 457–8) that the Apostle never uses the term "Jerusalem" as a label for Judaism as such. Rather he uses it in most cases as a simple geographical designation (1 Cor 16:3–4; Rom 15:19, 24–26; Gal 1:17, 18; 2:1–2). Yet few commentators would suggest that Paul here uses

with Sarah.[39] What is the basis for these analogical manoeuvres? Again, it can only be the Apostle's prior rereading of Israel's story, a rereading which is in turn necessitated by the interpretive "gaps" constituted by the Galatians' experience of the Spirit and the Christ event.[40]

Yet if the basic justification for Paul's analogy here lies outside the Genesis story, then in what sense can Paul claim that this is what "the law" – that is, the text of Torah – says to those with ears to hear? We must not forget that Paul introduced this whole analogy with a challenge to his audience: "Tell me, you who desire to be subject to the law, will you not listen to the law?" (4:21). This should remind us that even Paul's previous analogies with daily life were not solely heuristic constructs. They were more than mere illustrations. The familiarity and plausibility of the situation held up in the analogy contributes to the inherent plausibility of the pattern which Paul wants the audience to find in Israel's story. The narrative pattern is shown to be "realistic" and hence believable. If this was true of his mundane analogies, however, in Paul's communities (and for the opponents) it is all the more true of analogies to other episodes in the canonical chapters of the story. For we must remember that Paul understands the present as an extension of the scriptural narrative. Hence, to show that there is an analogical similarity between God's actions in the past and a particular interpretation of his action

---

"Jerusalem" as a simple name for Judaism. Rather he uses it analogically, as representative of a particular way of approaching God (so Dunn, *Galatians*, 250). On the other hand, there is only one passage (Rom 15:30–31) in which Paul appears to use "Jerusalem" to denote the church in that city, so it is far from clear that "when he uses the word 'Jerusalem,' Paul thinks in the first instance of the Jerusalem church, not of the city as such" (Martyn, *Galatians*, 458).

[39] The notion of an ideal heavenly city which provides the pattern for the earthly city in the eschatological restoration goes back at least to Ezek 40–48. In the Second-Temple period such expectations become more and more elaborate (cf. *1 En.* 43:6; 90:28–29; *2 En.* 55:2; *Pss. Sol.* 17:33; *4 Ezra* 7:26; 8:52; 10:25–28; *2 Bar.* 4:2–6; 32:2; 59:4; Heb 11:10, 14–16; 12:22; 13:14; Rev 3:12; 21:2). Since the "present Jerusalem" in Gal 4:25 is an actual earthly city, the church is probably not identified with the heavenly city (contra Martyn, *Galatians*, 440), but rather looks forward to receiving that (largely future) fulfilment of Israel's hopes (so Dunn, *Galatians*, 254).

Contra Jobes ("Jerusalem," 317), Paul does explicitly identify Sarah with a non-Sinaitic covenant (4:24) and connect Sarah's free state with the freedom of the Galatian believers (4:22–23; 4:30–5:1).

[40] So Jobes, "Jerusalem," 314.

in the present is to provide a powerful argument for that interpretation of the present.[41]

The particular analogy which Paul draws here is especially effective in making his reading of Israel's story more plausible, because in Abraham's household he finds analogies to precisely those elements of the Galatians' present situation which had before appeared as "gaps." Paul has already drawn attention to the fact that not all of Abraham's physical descendants constitute the "seed" which will inherit. In Genesis we see God passing over Ishmael, despite his having been born first, because he represents Abraham and Sarah's attempt to bypass faith in God, to make the promise of progeny happen through ordinary means instead of relying on God's miraculous intervention. Isaac, though he was born later, inherits the promises to his father because he is the child who was conceived beyond human expectation, at God's intervention, in the fulfilment of that promise. Here the Apostle finds precedent for the unexpected pattern of inheritance which has emerged after the Christ event: beyond all ordinary expectations God has produced new children for Abraham among the Gentile Galatians. They have become "children of the promise, like Isaac" (4:28).[42] He also finds a precedent for the slavery/freedom opposition which he developed in describing the role of Torah in Israel's narrative. For here Hagar and, by implication, Ishmael are slaves, while Sarah and her son enjoy freedom (4:23). This resonates very strongly with Paul's configuration of the broader story in which those who inherit Abraham's promise (and their eschatological fulfilment in the "Jerusalem above") are set free from slavery to Torah/the στοιχεῖα (4:26), while those who insist on the need to keep Torah (quintessentially those in

---

[41] We see a similar logic at work in second Isaiah's imagining of God's activity in terms of a "new exodus" – it is inherently plausible that God will act towards his people in the same way that he has in the past.

[42] Paul's comment here confirms that he is using the Abraham cycle analogically and not simply treating it as a coded reference to his present. The Galatians are "like Isaac," following in the pattern of Isaac (κατὰ Ἰσαάκ). It is for this reason that they can be identified with that patriarch by analogy. Yet the assertion that they are "like Isaac" depends on the fact that, for Paul, Isaac retains an historical/textual identity independent of and prior to the Galatians. Hence for Paul the analogical comparison in 4:29 is structured around the words ὥσπερ τότε . . . οὕτως καὶ νῦν, "just as was the case then . . . so too now . . ." This comparison assumes the independence and distinctness of two events at two times which nevertheless bear a structural similarity.

Paul's present, earthly Jerusalem) remain in bondage (4:25). Hence there is real force to Paul's claim that this is what one hears if one "listens to the law" (4:21). It is not that one would arrive at Paul's understanding of the Isaac and Ishmael episode on a conventional Jewish reading of the story. Rather, once one has been pushed towards Paul's new reconfiguration of Israel's narrative by the "gaps" which have arisen in his own experience and that of the Galatians themselves, one finds in the story of Isaac and Ishmael unexpected parallels to the kind of divine action which is suggested by the Apostle's rereading of the narrative. In this way an analogy which finds its justification in Paul's re-visioning of the whole story can come, in turn, to reinforce the essential plausibility of that new understanding of the story itself. The logic is one which moves not in a linear chain from certainty to dependent certainty, but in a circular effort to establish a coherent reading of the world.

On the other hand, this analogy between the Galatians and Isaac does not simply recapitulate what has already been said. It also helps Paul to express explicitly something which has until this point remained implicit in his argument. Where previous analogies helped the audience to see the relationship between the promise and Torah (3:15–18) or between themselves and Torah (3:25–4:11), here Paul is using the story of Isaac and Ishmael to suggest the shape of the relationship between the Galatians *and the opponents*. The implication of Paul's reconfigured narrative is, as he has already suggested, that no one will be justified, will inherit the Abrahamic promises, by relying on their legal observances. It is not Torah observance which marks one as occupying the role of an "heir of Abraham," but rather it is faith in Christ, a faith which does not require observance of the law. Hence the opponents (and those who follow them into circumcision) will be excluded from the eschatological fulfilment of the Abrahamic promises, a fulfilment which will be enjoyed only by those who hold to Paul's Gospel. Paul introduces this direct polemic against the opponents by means of this analogy, precisely in order to emphasize that his point is not as foreign to Israel's story as it might seem at first blush. If Ishmael was cast out, despite being Abraham's physical descendant, the same could happen to those who appear to be his heirs in the Galatian situation. The crucial question in Galatia, as in Abraham's first family circle, is whether one's status as heir is based on familiar ways of thinking and acting or on reliance on and responsiveness to God's miraculous intervention.

Hence, even more clearly than before, Paul's emplotment of the audience and the opponents constitutes an ethical argument, an argument which draws implications from Israel's narrative about the specific actions which the Galatians must take. As the audience stands poised to choose between two different ways of living, Paul uses this analogy to highlight the fates which await people who play these two roles. The one leads to blessing while the other (appealing as it may seem) ends in rejection. In 4:31 Paul prepares to leave behind the analogy and make this ethical point (now perhaps more plausible to the audience) in direct terms.[43] The Galatians are, he points out, "children, not of the slave but of the free woman" (4:31). This freedom is, Paul adds, precisely the point of their status as heirs of Abraham, and so he urges them to "stand firm" and not to submit themselves again "to a yoke of slavery" (5:1).[44] Concretely, this means that they must not allow themselves to be circumcised, and that if they do, "Christ will be of no benefit to [them]" (5:2). For in Paul's newly reconfigured story it is those who are identified with Christ by faith who experience eschatological blessing. Legal observances are unimportant ("For in Christ Jesus neither circumcision nor uncircumcision counts for anything" [5:6]), and those who try to supplement Christ with such requirements have placed themselves back under the law-based covenant with its curse. Hence, to those who again take on legal observances Paul says, "You . . . have cut yourselves off from Christ; you have fallen away from grace" (5:4). Christ will thus "be of no benefit" to the one who takes on circumcision and with that act deliberately returns to the

---

[43] Notice the διό which opens 4:31 and which usually introduces the conclusion to an argument. Betz (*Galatians*, 251) understands this διό as introducing just the statement in 4:31 that the Galatians and Paul are the "children of the free woman." It seems more likely, however, that the particle introduces Paul's whole ethical conclusion in 4:31–5:1 which is then elaborated and reinforced in 5:2–12. For the statement "For freedom Christ has set us free" in 5:1 is read most naturally as a restatement (in explicitly Christian terms) of the claim to be children of the free woman in 4:31 (this is essentially admitted by Betz, *Galatians*, 255). The injunction to "stand firm" is then the logical conclusion to be drawn (οὖν) from this state of freedom in which the Galatians exist. This reading has the advantage of doing away with what seems to many commentators like an abrupt and awkward new beginning in 5:1 (so Betz, *Galatians*, 255).

[44] The οὖν which connects the injunction of 5:1b with the previous material indicates that Paul is drawing the natural conclusion of his whole analogical presentation in 4:21–5:1a. It is not enough to say that 5:1b is the conclusion to be drawn from 5:1a, for 4:31–5:1a simply sum up the allegory in 4:21–30. 5:1b then states explicitly the ethical implications which have become clear from Paul's allegorical interpretation. A new, more paraenetic phase in Paul's argument does not begin until 5:13 (contra Betz, *Galatians*, 253–6).

old subjection to Torah (5:2–3).[45] The question here concerns how one must live in order to play a good role in the story, a role which ends in blessing. On the opponents' construal of that narrative, it is only those who remain faithful to Torah who will come to that good end. The thrust of Paul's argument, however, has been to show that such a reading of Israel's story cannot integrate recent events, and that a reconfigured story which can do justice to the whole yields a very different picture of what it means to play a good role. Thus, just as Paul's theological argument consisted of a kind of narrative criticism in which the story was read afresh in light of newly emerging "gaps," his ethical argument is a matter of tracing out who comes to a good end in the narrative and how one must act in order to play that role.

3. The Ethical Implications of the Galatians' Role (5:13–6:10)

In many ways 5:1–6 constitute the climax of Paul's argument. As in 4:12–20, verses 7–12 of chapter 5 consist primarily of emotionally charged exhortations with little substantial, rational argument.[46] In 5:13, however, the

---

[45] Paul's assertion that one who is circumcised must then keep the whole of Torah (5:3) fits with the common biblical emphasis on keeping all of the commandments (see, e.g., Deut 27:1; 28:1, 15, 58; cf. 4 Macc 5:20–21; *1QS* I 16–17; *m. Avot* 2:1; 4:2; Jas 2:10). The only way of avoiding this demand, Paul says, is to place one's faith in Christ as providing an alternative to that whole legal system. It is not clear whether this implies that the opponents were not requiring such complete obedience (so Lagrange, *Galates*, 136; Martyn, *Galatians*, 470; Mussner, *Galaterbrief*, 347–8), that the demand to keep the whole law implied a false dependence on it (so Hübner, *Law*, 18–19, 36–9), or that this demand implied a false requirement that Gentiles become Jews (so Dunn, *Galatians*, 266). It is perhaps most likely that here, as in 3:10, the Apostle is assuming the inability of human beings to satisfy that whole law.

Thurén (*Derhetorizing*, 71–2) finds "enormous inconsistency" between Paul's statements here and his slogan in 6:15: ". . . neither circumcision nor uncircumcision is anything; but a new creation is everything"! He suggests that in chapter 5 Paul is deliberately overdrawing the significance of circumcision for rhetorical effect. Yet if 6:15 represents Paul's admission "that he has overreacted to the question about circumcision," it would have to represent a retraction of the whole letter which preceded. Moreover, Thurén overstates the inconsistency. Paul can affirm that circumcision in and of itself has no significance, but also that it will be disastrous if the Galatians undergo the operation *in an attempt thereby to establish themselves in a better role in the story.*

[46] Betz (*Galatians*, 264) notices a shift from the "highly condensed" expression of 5:1–5

Apostle makes one final argumentative turn.[47] Exactly how one understands the relationship of these verses to the rest of the letter will depend to a large degree on how one reconstructs the situation in Galatia.[48] What is clear, however, is that here Paul is concerned to flesh out an ethic based on his reconfigured narrative. It should be evident from the preceding analysis why it is not satisfactory to say that 5:13 marks a shift to an "ethical" section of the letter, as if what came before had no ethical thrust. It is right, however, to recognize that the ethical focus from 5:13 on is different. It is not enough, for the Apostle's purposes, simply to show what the Galatians need *not* do. He is also concerned to show that his reconfigured narrative has *positive* implications about how they must live as believers in Christ.

3.1. Flesh and Spirit

In 5:6 it became clear that Paul had some such positive ethic in mind, for the faith which thus far had been the sole condition of blessing is now described as "faith *working through love*" (πίστις δι᾽ ἀγάπης ἐνεργουμένη). There is broad scholarly agreement that when the Apostle turns in 5:13 and exhorts his

---

and the "freer," "rambling" style of vv. 7–12. Moreover, Paul's statement in 5:13 (ὑμεῖς γὰρ ἐπ᾽ ἐλευθερίᾳ ἐκλήθητε) echoes 5:1 (τῇ ἐλευθερίᾳ ἡμᾶς Χριστὸς ἠλευθέρωσεν), suggesting that Paul here returns to the main thread of his argument. The post-positive γάρ which introduces v. 13 probably just signals a new phase in Paul's argument (*Galatians*, 272). This is not to say that the narrative ground of Paul's exhortation disappears entirely, but no new elements of the narrative are introduced and no new implications drawn out.

[47] Commentators universally recognize at 5:13 a shift in the focus of Paul's exhortations which extends to the end of the letter proper at 6:10 (so, e.g., Betz, *Galatians*, 271; R. N. Longenecker, *Galatians*, 235–6; Lührmann, *Galatians*, 98).

[48] Many commentators understand Paul as here answering the question "How are we to regulate our common life if we do not have to follow Torah?" (So Lührmann, *Galatians*, 100; cf. Dunn, *Galatians*, 284–5). Some suggest that the Galatians were experiencing ethical confusion in the wake of Paul's first preaching (so Barclay, *Obeying*, 70–72, 218; R. N. Longenecker, *Galatians*, 238). If the opponents offered Torah as an antidote to this confusion, Paul's more complete ethic in chapters 5–6 may be offered as an alternative (so Barclay, *Obeying*, 216–20; Betz, *Galatians*, 273; Thurén, *Derhetorizing*, 90). Alternatively, the Apostle may want to insure against libertine excesses in the wake of the success of his letter and the Galatians' rejection of nomism (so Eckert, *Urchristliche Verkündigung*, 134; Lightfoot, *Galatians*, 208). For an excellent survey of other, less plausible models, see Barclay, *Obeying*, 9–23. On Mark Nanos' recent suggestion (*Irony*) that the opponents come from the mainstream Jewish communities in Galatia and want Paul's converts to conform with recognized markers of Jewish identity, see above, pp. 162–3, n. 11.

audience to follow this new ethic, his offer of a new motivation and empowerment for moral living flows directly from his theology. It is thus no surprise that these aspects of the Apostle's teaching appear to be direct corollaries of his emplotment of the Galatians within his theological narrative. To act in an ethical way is, for Paul, to "live by the Spirit (πνεύματι)" and not "gratify the desires of the flesh (ἐπιθυμίαν σαρκός)" (5:16).[49] The immediate presence of God's Spirit within the believer now furnishes not only the motivation for right living, but also specific direction for ethical decisions.[50] The believer is "led by the Spirit" rather than by the explicit statements of Torah (5:18). The community is no longer subject to the ethical authority of the law precisely because its members are guided directly by the divine Spirit. One need no longer be subject to the unreliable urges and drives which are ours simply as human beings, drives which we must counter with formal ethical declarations.[51] Rather, one who is indwelt by God's Spirit has direct access to a different set of "drives" which are absolutely reliable. To this extent the lists of works of the "flesh" in 5:19–21 and the "fruit" of the Spirit in 5:22–23 are probably intended not as a new set of rules, but as a guide to help the Galatians learn to recognize which of their

---

[49] The sharp opposition between these two sources of ethical motivation is highlighted in 5:16 by Paul's emphatic negative οὐ μὴ τελέσητε. The one who is motivated by the Spirit will emphatically not act on "fleshly" desires. Here I take σαρκός in ἐπιθυμίαν σαρκός as an adjectival genitive ("desire associated with/motivated by the flesh") rather than a subjective genitive ("the desire felt by the flesh"). Martyn treats τὰ ἔργα τῆς σαρκός in 5:19 as a subjective genitive, "the effects of the flesh" (*Galatians*, 496), but this this reading springs from his overly reified understanding of Paul's σάρξ language (see below, pp. 256–260).

[50] If the dative πνεύματι in 5:16 is understood in a purely instrumental sense or as a dative of origin (so Betz, *Galatians*, 278; R. N. Longenecker, *Galatians*, 244), then to "walk" πνεύματι might be construed to mean simply to walk "with the help of the Spirit." If the dative denotes the quality of one's "walking" one might think here of a life which reflects the character of the Spirit (so Betz, *Galatians*, 278), but Paul's talk in 5:18 of "being led by the Spirit" (πνεύματι ἄγεσθε) implies positive guidance. Dunn observes that in the same verse this Spirit-guided life is contrasted with life lived "under the law" (ὑπὸ νόμον), suggesting that the inner direction of the Spirit now takes the place of legal guidelines (*Galatians*, 296). If this is correct, then the dative πνεύματι in 5:16 is probably also a dative "of the rule or direction" (Lightfoot, *Galatians*, 14; cf. Bruce, *Galatians*, 243; Burton, *Galatians*, 298; Martyn, *Galatians*, 492; Schlier, *Galater*, 179–80).

[51] Paul also seems to think primarily in terms of such urges in 5:24, where the believers' σάρξ is said to have been crucified σὺν τοῖς παθήμασιν καὶ ταῖς ἐπιθυμίαις. On the meaning of Paul's σάρξ language in chapters 5 and 6 see below, pp. 256–260.

urges originate in the Spirit's proddings and which are the product of their "flesh." It is likely in the wake of this process of learning to distinguish the internal guidance of the Spirit from that of their own "flesh" that the Apostle believes the acts encouraged by the latter will become "obvious" to the Galatians, as they are to him (5:19).[52] The Sinaitic legal code, however, must now give way to the inner direction of the Spirit, the divine presence whose influence bears "fruit" in the growth of new kinds of behaviour (5:22).[53]

What is crucial to recognize here is that only those who are filled with that divine Spirit can enjoy such inward motivation and guidance. What is more, Paul can offer the Galatians the direct help of the Spirit only because of their peculiar place in his reconfiguration of Israel's story. They have, by their faith in Christ, taken on the role of those who are beginning to receive the eschatological blessing which fulfils the Abrahamic promise, and that blessing involves their being indwelt by the Spirit. Their recent experiences are, Paul says, properly interpreted as the outward manifestations of that Spirit's presence among them. The idea that those who received the eschatological gift of the Spirit would be guided directly by God is itself an old part of Israel's story,[54] and so Paul can assure the Galatians that the

---

[52] After all, some of these moral judgements would *not* be obvious to many of Paul's pagan hearers (see below, pp. 274–5). If they were absolutely transparent then the Apostle would have no need to list these examples.

[53] Lührmann suggests that Paul deliberately avoids using the term "works" to designate these Spirit-motivated acts (*Galatians*, 107; so Barrett, *Freedom*, 77; Betz, *Galatians*, 286), but in 5:6 Paul has no trouble talking about faith "working (ἐνεργουμένη) through love" (so R. N. Longenecker, *Galatians*, 259; cf. 6:4, 10; 2 Cor 9:8; Phil 2:12; 1 Thess 1:3). On the other hand, agricultural metaphors can be used for the activity of the "flesh" as well (Gal 6:7–8; Rom 6:21–22; 7:4–5), and the imperatives in chapter 5 speak against the notion that Paul expected such good actions to emerge spontaneously (so Barclay, *Obeying*, 120; R. N. Longenecker, *Galatians*, 259). Metaphors of fruit for ethical virtue are common, especially among Stoic writers. See, e.g., Epictetus, *Diss.* 1.4.32; 1.15.7–8; 2.1.21; Cicero, *Tusc.* 1.119; Philo, *Plant.* 138; *Somn.* 2.272; *Leg.* 1.22f., 3.93; *Migr.* 140, 202, 205; *Deus* 166; *Mut.* 74, 98, 192; *Post.* 171; *Det.* 111; *Agr.* 9; *Mos.* 2.66; *Cher.* 84. For biblical precedents, see Prov 1:21; 31:31; Isa 5:1–7; Jer 17:10; Amos 6:12; and cf. *Let. Arist.* 233. The metaphor may also echo the prophetic demand that Israel "bear fruit" of righteous behaviour and the promise of ethical fruitfulness in Israel's eschatological restoration (so Barclay, *Obeying*, 121; see Isa 5:1–7; 27:2–6; 37:30–32; Jer 2:21; 8:13; 24:8–10; 31:27–28; 32:41; Ezek 17:22–24; Hos 14:6–9[5–8]; Joel 2:18ff.; Amos 9:13–15; Mic 7:1ff. and cf. *Jub* 16:26; *1QS* VIII 20; *1 En.* 93:2–10; *4 Ezra* 5:23–24; 9:31–32; *2 Bar.* 32:1).

[54] Jeremiah's new covenant involves the inscribing of God's Torah on the people's hearts

Spirit's presence among them brings with it motivation for ethical living. To this extent at least, Paul's ethical teaching here in chapters 5–6 arises naturally from his reconfiguration of Israel's story and his emplotment of the Galatians within that narrative.

Yet Paul's ethical theory does not involve just the motivation of the Spirit. It involves an opposition between the Spirit and the negative source of motivation which he labels "the flesh" (ἡ σάρξ). Where in Israel's story does Paul find this concept of a drive towards wickedness within human beings, and why does he call it "the flesh"? Although all agree that the Apostle is not working with a simple Hellenistic dualism of body (evil) and soul (good), our analysis at this point is frustrated by the protracted debate about exactly what Paul's "flesh" language means.[55] The foundational positions in this discussion were established early in the last century by Bultmann and Käsemann.[56] Käsemann understood σάρξ in apocalyptic terms, as a cosmic power enslaving humanity.[57] The difficulty with this interpretation, however, is that there are several indications in these chapters that the "flesh" is not something external to the individual.[58] Neither is it something which is

---

so that they no longer need to be taught. They will all "know" him spontaneously (Jer 31:31–34). On the other hand, there is a common expectation that God's Spirit will be poured out on his people in the eschaton (see above, p. 215, n. 44). These motifs of the Spirit and ethical renewal are connected in Ezek 36:26–27. There God promises to put a "new spirit" (πνεῦμα καινόν) within them (cf. Ezek 11:9; 37:6) and then explains that he will place *his own* Spirit within them, and so make them "follow my statutes" (cf. Ezek 37:14). A more general connection between God's Spirit and ethical guidance is evident in passages like Isa 63:10, where the people's rebelliousness is described in terms of "grieving" God's Spirit. Of course, none of these writers imagined that the inner guidance of the Spirit would replace the written Torah. That aspect of the story arises for Paul only in light of the Christ event.

[55] Paul's high regard for physicality is evident in, e.g., 1 Corithians 15, where he emphasizes that the physical body is renewed along with the whole person and participates in the final resurrection. Likewise, immorality can defile body and soul together (2 Cor 7:1), suggesting that for moral purposes Paul knows little real anthropological dualism (so Erickson, "Flesh," 305).

[56] See the convenient summary in Barclay, *Obeying*, 192–202.

[57] So Eckert, *Urchristliche Verkündigung*, 157; Lührmann, *Galatians*, 106–7; Martyn, *Galatians*, 485, 528.

[58] Dunn (*Galatians*, 287) points to 2:20 and 4:14. The parallelism in expression between σάρξ and πνεῦμα should not mislead us into assuming that the two terms denote comparable ideas. As Barclay points out, the σάρξ is not personified to anything like the same extent as

decisively subdued or destroyed in the way that one would expect if it were a demonic power.[59] Bultmann's position has also continued to be influential and does more justice to Paul's actual use of "flesh" language. Bultmann viewed the Pauline σάρξ as the "world of created things which is the stage and the life-condition for 'natural' life, the world which is at man's disposal, giving him the possibility to live from it and to be anxious about it."[60] This is the world of ordinary human possibilities and limitations within (ἐν) which one necessarily lives, but *for* (κατά) which, according to the norms of which and for the sake of which, one must not live.[61] Something like Bultmann's

---

is the Spirit (*Obeying*, 213). Moreover, Schweizer observes that while God's πνεῦμα and ἐπαγγελία are often introduced in the instrumental dative or with an instrumental διά, the σάρξ which appears in the same contexts is never introduced with this instrumental sense ("σάρξ," 132; see Gal 4:23; 5:18; cf. Phil 3:3; Rom 8:13f.). Similarly, while πνεῦμα often appears as a verbal subject, σάρξ only does in passages where it is set in contrast with πνεῦμα (so Schweizer, "σάρξ," 132). This difference in usage implies that σάρξ and πνεῦμα are not completely parallel as effective powers, and that any hints of the personification of σάρξ are purely figurative. This "anthropological" understanding of σάρξ in Paul is also to be favoured if (as seems to be the case) the concept is derived in part from the Jewish idea of an "evil inclination" within the human being (see, e.g., *T. Asher* 1:5; *1QS* V 5; *CD* II 14–16; Jas 1:14–15). See further Martyn, *Galatians*, 485; 492–3; 526–9; Barclay, *Obeying*, 110.

The most common evidence presented in favour of interpreting the σάρξ as an external power is 5:17, where we read: ἡ γὰρ σάρξ ἐπιθυμεῖ κατὰ τοῦ πνεύματος, τὸ δὲ πνεῦμα κατὰ τῆς σαρκός, ταῦτα γὰρ ἀλλήλοις ἀντίκειται, ἵνα μὴ ἃ ἐὰν θέλητε ταῦτα ποιῆτε (so Eckert, *Urchristliche Verkündigung*, 137; Lightfoot, *Galatians*, 209; Lührmann, *Galatians*, 109). Yet Dunn has argued plausibly that Paul here portrays the Spirit and *one's own human weakness* in a struggle to dominate the will, each suppressing that will to the extent that it is an expression of the opposite influence (*Galatians*, 299). Alternatively, Barclay points to Paul's confidence that the one who walks in the Spirit will avoid the deeds of the flesh (5:16), and argues that the indwelling Spirit here counteracts the influence of the person's corrupt desires, preventing the believer from simply doing "whatever you want" (ἃ ἐὰν θέλητε) (*Obeying*, 113, 115–16). On either reading the "flesh" need not be a cosmic power.

[59] The present tense of ἀντίκειται in 5:17 suggests the ongoing activity of the σάρξ in the believer. Likewise, Paul's positive description of life as lived "in the flesh" in 2:20, i.e., in the sphere of ordinary human limitations (see below, p. 258, n. 62), is difficult to explain if he is going to go on and use the same term to denote a demonic power. In some passages Paul seems to say that the believer no longer operates "in the flesh" (e.g., Rom 7:5; 8:9), but Bultmann offered the plausible suggestion that here the believer's continued existence within the horizon of ordinary limitations is "proleptically denied" (*Theology*, 1.236).

[60] Bultmann, *Theology*, 1.235.

[61] See Bultmann, *Theology*, 1.232–45. Bultmann observes how Paul tends to use the

approach is made more plausible when one observes the associations in the LXX between the σάρξ and human weakness, mortality, limitation.[62] This is, after all, the same sense in which "the flesh" has been used earlier in Galatians.[63] Yet several, more recent writers have offered important qualifications to Bultmann's view. Barclay has rightly emphasized that the problem with living κατὰ σάρκα need not be understood in terms of a sinful *attitude*, a rejection of one's human need for God. Rather, Paul's narrative locates him at a point in history at which life depends on being rescued out of the merely human state by being identified with Christ and empowered with his Spirit. Hence the σάρξ would be, for Paul, all that "*is merely human*, in contrast to the divine activity displayed on the cross and in the gift of the Spirit."[64] To live a life directed solely towards this σάρξ, acting in terms of

---

phrase ἐν σαρκί neutrally. Nor does the fact that one operates "in the flesh" exclude the possibility of simultaneously operating within the higher horizon of possibilities which Christ has opened up (*Theology*, 1.235–6; see Phlm 16). In contrast, where κατὰ σάρκα modifies a verb the phrase usually takes on a negative sense, marking the act as "sinful" (*Theology*, 237–8; see 2 Cor 1:17; 5:16; 10:2, 3; Rom 8:4, 5; though cf. Gal 4:23, 29).

[62] Schweizer ("σάρξ," 109) observes that the LXX introduces a distinction between the heavenly sphere and the mortal and corruptible earthly sphere, the latter being characterized as "flesh" (see LXX Num 16:22; 27:16; cf. Sir 31:1; *Pss. Sol.* 16:14; Judith 10:13). Hence in the LXX of Ezek 10:12 the cherubim have no σάρξ. Paul seems to adopt this sense for σάρξ at least in 1:16 and 2:16 (so Barclay, *Obeying*, 204; Bultmann, *Theology*, 1.233; Erickson, "Flesh," 304).

[63] R. N. Longenecker observes that σάρξ has, prior to 5:13, been used in the sense of "that which is merely human (cf. 1:16; 2:16) or purely physical (2:20; 4:13–14, 23, 29)," and it shows up again in this sense in 6:12–13 (*Galatians*, 239; so Schweizer, "σάρξ," 126–7). Where the flesh/Spirit dualism is introduced in 3:3, σάρξ denotes that legal observance (esp. circumcision), which Paul seems to understand as an attempt to bring about eschatological blessing using the resources of ordinary human existence (so Barclay, *Obeying*, 179; Bultmann, *Theology*, 237; Erickson, "Flesh," 306; see 4:29).

[64] Barclay, *Obeying*, 206; and cf. W. Barclay, *Flesh and Spirit*, 22. This sense would be similar to the use of בשר at Qumran as a metonym for a chronically sinful humanity (so esp. W. D. Davies, "Paul and the DSS," 160–62; cf. Barclay, *Obeying*, 188–91; 205; Erickson, "Flesh," 305; Licht, "Thanksgiving Scroll," 1–13; Meyer in Schweizer et al., "σάρξ," 112–14; Nötscher, *Zur theologischen Terminologie*, 85–6; see *1QS* XI 7, 9, 12; *1QM* IV 3. Erickson points to further evidence of this kind of association between humanity as "flesh" and sinfulness in other apoclayptic literature ("Flesh," 305; *T. Jud.* 19:4; *T. Zeb.* 9:7). What is not clear on such a reading is how much the bodily associations of the term σάρξ should be carried over into Paul's theological/ethical use. Dunn (*Galatians*, 287) puts much more emphasis on this bodily aspect than does, e.g., Barclay.

merely human limitations, would be thus to forfeit God's offer to transform the terms of human existence. On this reading of Paul, actions which are motivated by "the flesh" are actions which spring from our ordinary desires, inclinations, and powers, which, as the Christ event made clear, were not able to motivate human beings towards a life which satisfied God's pattern in Torah. Indeed, since in Paul's narrative the "present age" is "evil" (1:4), is consistently opposed to God, then the desires and habits of ordinary human existence will tend towards this same evil, will "be opposed to" the Spirit (5:17).[65] If this understanding of "the flesh" in chapters 5–6 is correct, even in its general outlines, then we can see that this concept too arises from elements in Israel's story. "The flesh" is simply thrown into new prominence and given a newly problematic significance because of the particular configuration in which Paul has arranged the elements of that story, and because of the particular narrative moment in which he has emplotted himself and his audience.[66]

Paul's ethics in Galatians are not deterministic. He does not imagine believers to be subject to powers (whether good or evil) which determine their actions against their will.[67] Hence, beginning in 5:13, the Apostle's exhortations are peppered with imperatives. He urges them: "[D]o not use your freedom as an opportunity for self-indulgence (εἰς ἀφορμὴν τῇ σαρκί)" (5:13). He calls them to "live by the Spirit (πνεύματι περιπατεῖτε)" (5:16) and to "be guided by the Spirit (πνεύματι ... στοιχῶμεν)" (5:25), and makes this general appeal specific in concrete exhortations to avoid conceited rivalry (5:26), to bear one another's burdens (6:2), to test their own actions (6:4), and to persevere in this Spirit-led lifestyle (6:9), always doing good (6:10). Paul thus holds out to the Galatians a choice: they may co-operate with the Spirit's inner direction or they may resist that inner prompting and continue to live according to their natural drives and tendencies.[68] Here again, however, when the Apostle offers reasons why the Galatians should follow his advice, he points to Israel's story and observes how that narrative holds two different futures: one for those who respond to the Spirit's prompting and

---

[65] So Barclay, *Obeying*, 205; cf. Bultmann, *Theology*, 1.239.

[66] Erickson ("Flesh," 305) observes that the LXX never seems to use σάρξ to denote a power or object which is inherently evil, only what is mortal and corruptible.

[67] Cf. above, p. 255, n. 53.

[68] So Dunn, *Galatians*, 308.

another for those who resist. In 5:21, after listing specific examples of the kind of behaviour which arises from "the flesh," Paul reminds the audience that "those who do such things will not inherit the kingdom of God." Then again, in 6:7–10, where Paul brings his ethical exhortation (and the letter proper) to a close, he writes: "If you sow to your own flesh, you will reap corruption from the flesh." If, however, his hearers "sow to the Spirit," they "will reap eternal life from the Spirit" (6:8). Here the kind of ethical activity which one carries out determines which of two roles one plays in the story – two roles which lead to very different ends in the eschatological denouement.[69] Since these are the only two roles open to human beings, and since it is clear which of the two is more desirable, Paul can finish the body of his letter by drawing a final conclusion from this story: "So (δέ)[70] let us not grow weary in doing what is right, for (γάρ) we will reap at harvest time, if we do not give up.[71] So then (ἄρα οὖν), whenever we have an opportunity,

---

[69] The opening statement in v. 7 ("God is not mocked . . .") indicates that the context of thought is not simply the common idea of moral retribution, but the specifically Jewish notion of God's eschatological judgement. R. N. Longenecker (*Galatians*, 280) points out that the verb μυκτηρίζω appears nowhere else in the NT, but appears very frequently in the LXX and other Second-Temple Jewish writings (1 Kgs [3Kdms] 18:27; 2 Kgs [4 Kdms] 19:21; 2 Chr 36:16; Job 22:19; Pss 44:14 [LXX 43:14]; 80:7 [LXX 79:7]; Prov 1:30; 11:12; 12:8; 15:5, 20; 23:9; Isa 37:22; Jer 20:7; Ezek 8:15; 1 Esd 1:49; 1 Macc 7:34; *Pss. Sol.* 4:8; *T. Jos.* 2:3; *Sib. Or.* 1:171). The idea that one will "reap" what one "sows" is common in Greco-Roman literature, both Jewish and non-Jewish (see, e.g., Plato, *Phaedr.* 260c; Aristotle, *Rhet.* 3.3.4 [1406b]; Demosthenes, *Cor.* 159; Cicero, *Or.* 2.65; Plautus, *Mer.* 71; LXX Job 4:8; Ps 126:5; Prov 22:8; Hos 8:7; 10:12–13; Sir 7:3; *T. Levi* 13:6; *4 Ezra* 4:28–30; Philo, *Conf.* 21; *Mut.* 268–269; *Somn.* 2.76; cf. 1 Cor 9:11; 2 Cor 9:6; Luke 19:21–22; John 4:35–36). Here, though, Paul is not appealing simply to the idea that actions have natural consequences. He is pointing rather to the prospect of eschatological judgement in the future of his narrative (so Betz, *Galatians*, 307).

Martyn (*Galatians*, 553) understands "sowing to the flesh" as a reference to circumcision, taken as a way of curbing the evil impulse (cf. Dunn, *Galatians*, 330). Since, however, this phrase is surrounded by injunctions to act lovingly and avoid the "works of the flesh," Paul is most likely thinking of the willingness to have one's will be directed by the σάρξ (so Barclay, *Obeying*, 164).

[70] On "so" as a rendering of δέ here, see R. N. Longenecker, *Galatians*, 281.

[71] R. N. Longenecker suggests that Paul here is thinking of divine retribution more generally (*Galatians*, 282). Yet the references in v. 9 to a particular future time for moral "harvest" (καιρῷ γὰρ ἰδίῳ θερίσομεν), a time preceded by extended labour which might exhaust the believers (μὴ ἐγκακῶμεν . . . μὴ ἐκλυόμενοι), clearly suggests an eschatological judgement (so Barclay, *Obeying*, 166; Betz, *Galatians*, 309; Dunn, *Galatians*, 332; Eckert,

let us work for the good of all, and especially for those of the family of faith" (6:9–10).[72]

Barclay has observed how Paul's interpretation of the Galatians' situation reduces what must have seemed to them like a range of possible options for living to a simple choice between two "ways."[73] What allows Paul to do this, however, is not simply his "apocalyptic" mode of thought, but more specifically the particular story within which he locates the Galatians. Their responsiveness to the Spirit is, in Paul's reconfiguration of the theological narrative, implicit already in the mode of their salvation. For the Apostle has argued that what marks the Galatians as "children of Abraham" is their experience of being indwelt by the Spirit (3:1–9). At the same time, this presence of the Spirit within and among them is itself a central aspect of the new eschatological possibility which is now open to these believers in Christ.[74] Yet the Spirit is not an impersonal presence but a personal one, with a specific character and moral will. Indeed, we have already noted that the moral guidance of God's Spirit had long been a prominent part of the Jewish hope. Hence Paul seems to be assuming that to resist the Spirit's inner promptings, to reject the new way of life which the Spirit makes possible, is to reject the eschatological blessing itself. "If we live by the Spirit," the Apostle urges, "let us also be guided by (στοιχῶμεν) the Spirit," for that moral re-formation is precisely the point of the Spirit's presence.[75] The only alternative is to reject one's inheritance, to reject the "blessing of Abraham."

3.2. Identification with Christ

If the dependence of Paul's overall ethical theory on his theological story is

---

Urchristliche Verkündigung, 148; Martyn, *Galatians*, 552). Paul consistently talks about receiving "eternal life" in the eschaton, not in the present age (see, e.g., Rom 2:5–8; 6:4, together with 6:22; 11:15). This does not exclude, however, some partial and proleptic experience of that "harvest" in the Galatians' experience of the Spirit (so Martyn, *Galatians*, 554).

[72] Hence Schrage is right that for the Apostle "ethics does not replace eschatology but flows from it" (*Ethics*, 184).

[73] Barclay, *Obeying*, 104.

[74] Notice how in 3:14 the "blessing of Abraham" is equated with the "promise of the Spirit." On the associations which make this equation sensible, see above, pp. 255–6, n. 54.

[75] So Eckert, *Urchristliche Verkündigung*, 154–5. Furnish (*Theology and Ethics*, 61–2) emphasizes that for Paul "the life in the Spirit which the Galatians themselves claim to experience (cf. 3:2, 5) *in and of itself* lays upon them moral imperatives."

easy to see, scholars often confess more difficulty in recognizing any connection between the content of the Apostle's specific injunctions in chapters 5 and 6 and his theology. Since Bultmann it has been common to read scholarly claims to the effect that Paul's theology offers new motivation for ethics but that it provides no new ethical *content*. As Schrage has emphasized, however, Paul's exhortations "not to live in conformity to this eon" seem to suggest that he does not simply accept the ethical standards of the Greco-Roman world wholesale (e.g., Rom 12:2; 1 Cor 5:12–13; Phil 2:15; 1 Thess 4:5).[76] This is not to say that non-Christians have *no* grasp on God's ethical demand, for in some sense that law is "written on their hearts."[77] It does prompt us, however, to ask whether the specific demands of Paul's positive ethic in Galatians 5–6 might also derive from the audience's emplotment within the theological narrative.

The most natural place to begin is the point at which the Apostle's ethic is most distinctive: his ethic of love. In his discussion of the "fruit of the Spirit" in 5:22–23, Betz argues that the terms which describe this "fruit" are all "common in Hellenistic philosophy," except for love, ἀγάπη.[78] This exception is more important than Betz seems to realize, for love, as the first member of the list of virtues in 5:22–23, seems to be the point of reference for the rest of the list. Although "joy" and "peace" may not be obviously related to love, the terms which follow ("patience," "kindness," "generosity," "faithfulness," "gentleness," "self-control") bear a strong resemblance to Paul's famous description of love in 1 Cor 13:4–8. This impression that love is the dominant principle in the fruit of the Spirit is reinforced when we look back at 5:13, for there Paul summed up the ethical responsibility of the believer with the call to serve one another "through love" (διὰ τῆς ἀγάπης).[79] Indeed, the Apostle claims that the entire Mosaic code is "fulfilled" when the believer lives out the single commandment to "love your neighbor as yourself" (5:14; cf. Lev 19:18).

---

[76] Schrage, *Ethics*, 199.

[77] So Schrage (*Ethics*, 200) points to the emphasis on acting in a way which outsiders will approve of and observes that Paul's use of the term εὐσχημόνως in this sense (1 Thess 4:12; 1 Cor 10:32; Rom 13:13) is borrowed from the pagan world.

[78] Betz, *Galatians*, 281.

[79] See also 5:6, where the one thing which Paul recognizes as significant in determining one's ultimate role in the narrative is "faith working through love" (πίστις δι' ἀγάπης ἐνεργουμένη).

What is more, a strong argument can also be made for the suggestion that 5:25–6:6 are intended to serve not simply as a chain of common ethical maxims[80] but as a concrete description of some of the ways in which this ethic of mutual love (as elaborated in the "fruit of the Spirit") should be lived out among the Galatians. After the transitional sentence in 5:25 calls the Galatians to "be guided by the Spirit,"[81] verse 26 describes the kind of behaviour which the Spirit will always lead the believers to avoid: "Let us not become conceited, competing against one another, envying one another." As Betz observes, the behaviour here "is the opposite of 'love' and of 'serving one another.'"[82] Verses 6:1–5 then provide a concrete example of Spirit-directed behaviour[83] by describing a common situation in which conceit and rivalry could normally run rampant.[84] "If anyone is detected in a transgression," Paul writes, "you who have received the Spirit (ὑμεῖς οἱ πνευματικοί)[85] should restore such a one in a spirit of gentleness."[86] This

---

[80] Betz understands all of 5:25–6:10 as a collection of disparate *sententiae* (*Galatians*, 291; cf. Dibelius, *James*, 6; Schlier, *Galater*, 269). Martyn (*Galatians*, 543–4) agrees that Paul here strings together sayings from popular proverbial collections, but he rightly emphasizes that Paul does so in order to make a specific overall point. Cf. n. 86 below.

[81] There is broad agreement that a new section begins in 5:25 (so Barclay, *Obeying*, 155; Betz, *Galatians*, 291; Dunn, *Galatians*, 316; Lührmann, *Galatians*, 114; Martyn, *Galatians*, 542; Oepke, *Galater*, 145; Schlier, *Galater*, 196–7). Others begin the new section in 5:26 (Mussner, *Galaterbrief*) or in 6:1 (Bruce, *Galatians*, 259–60; Burton, *Galatians*, 325; Lightfoot, *Galatians*, 214–15; R. N. Longenecker, *Galatians*, 268–9). Yet the exhortations of 5:25 and 5:26 seem intended to mirror one another as a pair, the positive and negative depiction of life in the Spirit (so Barclay, *Obeying*, 156). Moreover, 5:26 is no longer dealing in the highly abstract terms of 5:22–24, but presents a summary of the attitude which will be treated at length in 6:1–5.

[82] Betz, *Galatians*, 295.

[83] So Barclay, *Obeying*, 157, 167. Note that in 6:1 the believers are to act "in a spirit of gentleness" (ἐν πνεύματι πραΰτητος), recalling the inclusion of "gentleness" (πραΰτης) in Paul's characterization of the fruit of the Spirit (5:23; so Barclay, *Obeying*, 157; Eckert, *Urchristliche Verkündigung*, 160–61).

[84] Barclay observes that Paul has been very selective in his illustrations here, lending weight to the hypothesis that he is responding to a concrete problem with inner-group conflict in Galatia (*Obeying*, 169; see also Martyn, *Galatians*, 544; contra Betz, *Galatians*, 295).

[85] There is little justification for viewing the appellation οἱ πνευματικοί here as ironic, despite such overtones in 1 Corinthians (so Barclay, *Obeying*, 152, 157; Dunn, *Galatians*, 320; contra Lietzmann, *Galater*, 38; Martyn, *Galatians*, 546; Schlier, *Galater*, 270). Paul often speaks of all believers as possessing the Spirit (so R. N. Longenecker, *Galatians*, 273;

offer of help to those who stumble is not to be turned into an excuse for κενοδοξία (5:26), but is to be conducted in humility, which recognizes that all are vulnerable (σκοπῶν σεαυτόν [6:1]).[87] Why is such mutual help important? Because in "bearing one another's burdens (τὰ βάρη)" the community "will fulfil the law of Christ (ἀναπληρώσετε τὸν νόμον τοῦ Χριστοῦ)" (6:2).[88] By "the Law of Christ" Paul probably means the moral will of God, which was at one time most readily accessible in the text of Torah, but which has now gained its highest expression in the life of Christ.[89] The

---

Betz, *Galatians*, 296–7), and this same indwelling is the basis of his ethical exhortation here (e.g., 5:25).

[86] Betz (*Galatians*, 292) argues that the ethic here and in what follows contains "little that is specifically Christian," and offers several parallels to 6:2 in Greco-Roman literature (ibid., 299). As Hays points out, however, Betz's parallels are not as close as he suggests ("Christology," 287–8). Xenoph., *Mem.* 2.7.1–14 refers simply to giving advice to friends in trouble. Aristotle's injunction (*Eth. nic.* 9.11.1–6) to go uninvited to the aid of one's friends is more relevant. Still, Paul's call to mutual love and slavery is stronger than simple appeals to the bonds of friendship. Moreover, there is little in Greco-Roman ethics to correspond with the emphasis in 6:1–5 on humility and on avoiding rivalry. See also the critique in Barclay, *Obeying*, 170–77.

[87] So Barclay, *Obeying*, 158. Eckert likewise sees the connection between this freedom from "Hochmut," this awareness of one's own "Schwäche und Hilfsbedürftigkeit," and one's willingness "die Lasten des anderen wirklich zu tragen" (*Urchristliche Verkündigung*, 145).

[88] Martyn (*Galatians*, 547) sees in these "burdens" the believers' struggle with "transgression" in 6:1, while Dunn (*Galatians*, 322) understands them more broadly (so Pigeon, "La loi," 430–31).

[89] The only other passage in Paul which echoes this talk of a law of Christ is 1 Cor 9:21, where Paul qualifies his statement that he has become like one outside Torah by emphasizing that he is ἔννομος Χριστοῦ, obedient to Christ's law. Barclay observes (*Obeying*, 126–7) that this phrase cannot mean in context being either ὑπὸ νόμον (9:20) or ἄνομος θεοῦ (9:21). In Gal 6:2 most interpreters agree that the phrase is meant to recall the ethic of love in 5:13–14 (so Barclay, *Obeying*, 131; Barrett, *Freedom*, 83; Burton, *Galatians*, 329; Bultmann, *Theology*, 1.262, 268; Furnish, *Theology and Ethics*, 64; Pigeon, "La loi," 435–6; Schrage, *Die konkreten Einzelgebote*, 99–100, 250; Schweitzer, *Mysticism*, 303; Thurén, *Derhetorizing*, 87). More specifically, it is often suggested that νόμος here is the Sinaitic law now understood in the light of Christ (so Barclay, *Obeying*, 132; B. W. Longenecker, "Defining," 91–93; Martyn, *Galatians*, 555; Stanton, "Law of Moses," 116.), interpreted "according to its true intention" as pointing towards the single demand to love (Schrage, *Ethics*, 207). In this case the law may be "Christ's" in part because Paul knows this was Jesus' way of summing up Torah (so Barclay, *Obeying*, 132–3). Others find it rhetorically unlikely that Paul would introduce such a positive role for Torah here (so

talk here about fulfilling and law is almost certainly intended to recall 5:13, where the Apostle first stated his ethic as an ethic of love.[90] Paul thus presents this concrete example of Spirit-led living as an illustration of love in practice. He goes on to emphasize that "all must carry their own loads (τὸ ... φορτίον)" (6:5),[91] in the sense that members of the community must focus on moral self-examination (τὸ δὲ ἔργον ἑαυτοῦ δοκιμαζέτω ἕκαστος) rather than compare themselves to one another in a way which would lead to "boasting" (τὸ καύχημα) about one's superiority or in a competitive way (6:4), a form of the κενοδοξία referred to in 5:26.[92] Hence, 5:25–6:5 are not merely a

---

Eckert, *Urchristliche Verkündigung*, 144; Thurén, *Derhetorizing*, 86–7), and many suggest that νόμος is used in this passage to mean simply "principle" (so Räisänen, *Paul*, 80; Hays, "Christology and Ethics," 268–90; Thurén, *Derhetorizing*, 79; cf. Rom 3:27; 7:21; 8:2), perhaps in a deliberate play on words (so Hays, "Christology," 275). A mediating position is represented by Burton's suggestion that this "law" is not identical with Torah but represents the same basic moral demand of God (*Galatians*, 329). In any case, Paul likely thinks of this injunction to love as Christ's largely because Jesus supremely embodied it. Barclay points to the association between love and Christ's death in 2:20 and also highlights the parallel between 6:2 and Rom 15:1–3, where Paul appeals directly to Christ's example of self-giving (so Barclay, *Obeying*, 133–5).

It is highly unlikely that this νόμος is intended to *oppose* the Sinaitic Torah (as in Martyn, *Galatians*, 555–8; cf. 510–14), since Paul accepts that Torah was given by God. Nor is there much evidence that Paul is thinking of the teachings of Jesus functioning as a new Torah (see Bruce, *Galatians*, 261; Davies, *Paul and Rabbinic*, 144; *Setting*, 341–66; Dodd, "ΕΝΝΟΜΟΣ ΧΡΙΣΤΟΥ"; Dunn, *Galatians*, 322; R. N. Longenecker, *Paul*, 181–208; *Galatians*, 276; *idem, Social Ethics*, 15; Manson, *Ethics and Gospel*, 69, 78; and, hesitantly, Burton, *Galatians*, 329). Davies' evidence for Jewish expectation of a new Torah brought by the Messiah is both thin and late (see *Torah*, 92; *Setting*, 172–9; 188) and we would expect clearer references to such teaching if it were for Paul a new legal code (so Barclay, *Obeying*, 129; Furnish, *Theology*, 59–66; Sanders, *Paul and Palestinian Judaism*, 511–15). There is, in any case, little evidence that 6:2a is dependent on a particular saying of Jesus.

[90] So Barclay (*Obeying*, 158–9), who also observes that both in 6:2 and in 5:13–14 the Apostle emphasizes mutuality in Spirit-led relationships (ἀλλήλων).

[91] Barclay, along with most commentators, understands φορτίον as a weight of "responsibility before God" (*Obeying*, 162; cf. φορτίον for duty in Epict., *Diss.* 2.9.22).

[92] So Barclay, *Obeying*, 159–61; Eckert, *Urchristliche Verkündigung*, 145; Martyn, *Galatians*, 550. It is in this light that we must understand the call in 6:3 not to have an overblown estimate of oneself. The two verses are not merely juxtaposed on the basis of a catchword (contra Betz, *Galatians*, 302). Rather, as Martyn suggests, verse 4 is presented by way of an adversative particle as "the antidote to one's deceiving oneself" (*Galatians*, 544; so Dunn, *Galatians*, 324). The precise force of the γάρ which connects v. 3 with v. 2 is

sampling of generic "paraenesis" but present a coherent picture of humble mutual service which, Paul makes clear, constitutes the love which is the centre of his understanding of the believer's ethical responsibility.

Barclay has even suggested, quite plausibly, that the instruction in 6:6 to pay teachers for their work continues this illustration of the love which is the fruit of the Spirit. Many commentators have felt that the injunction intrudes awkwardly into the flow of Paul's thought, and some have speculated that the instruction must be connected to events in Galatia to which Paul need make no reference.[93] Barclay has suggested, however, that it should be understood as an instance of the "generosity" (ἀγαθοσύνη) which constitutes part of the fruit of the Spirit (5:22). The financial support of those who serve the community may even be intended as another example of how the Galatians ought to replace competitive rivalry with a willingness to bear one another's burdens (6:2).[94]

If this reading of 5:25–6:6 is broadly correct, then we find that all of Paul's positive ethical teaching, from 5:13 to 6:6, is an extended elaboration of the one principle of mutual love. This love is the one thing which fulfils Torah (5:13); it is the focal element of the fruit of the Spirit (5:22), and the demand to love constitutes the law of Christ, which is fulfilled through

---

ambiguous. Is the statement about self-deception the *basis* for the call to carry one another's burdens, a call which only incidentally fulfils the "law of Christ" (so, apparently, R. N. Longenecker, *Galatians*, 276; Martyn, *Galatians*, 549)? Is the real fact that no one has a right to boast the *reason* why one must carry another's burdens in order to fulfil the law of Christ, so that in v. 3 Paul is making explicit an unspoken premise from v. 2? In the latter case, the injunction to avoid moral competitiveness in vv. 4–5 becomes a further explication of how one can "fulfil the law of Christ."

Betz suggests that the background to 6:3 is the Hellenistic topos of the difference between appearances and reality (*Galatians*, 301; cf. Martyn, *Galatians*, 549; *Diog. L.* 8.22), but Paul's emphasis falls on the problem of pride and competition rather than on a general concern about deceptive phenomena.

Again, the γάρ which links v. 4 with v.5 probably does more than string together otherwise isolated sayings (contra Betz; *Galatians*, 303; see Barclay, *Obeying*, 161; Martyn, *Galatians*, 544, who give the particle its explanatory weight). If the image of bearing a load is separated from its context here it would seem to contradict Paul's exhortation in 6:2. Indeed, coming after that call to bear one another's burdens, it would make little sense for Paul to appeal for αὐτάρκεια – "self-sufficiency" – in a typically Stoic sense (contra Betz, *Galatians*, 304).

[93] For possible scenarios, see Martyn, *Galatians*, 551–2.

[94] So Barclay, *Obeying*, 163; cf. Martyn, *Galatians*, 551.

humble mutual service (6:1–6). What is more, although some of the virtues, vices, and maxims which Paul includes in this section find parallels in the ethics of the broader Greco-Roman world,[95] we search in vain outside of early Christian literature for a parallel to this conception of ethical obligation as a whole. In fact, Hays has pointed out that the way in which Paul introduces this love ethic runs directly counter to what we usually find in Greco-Roman literature. In 5:13 he urges the Galatians, as an expression of mutual love, to "become slaves to one another" (δουλεύετε ἀλλήλοις). Nowhere else in Paul's Mediterranean world do we find slavery held up as a positive ethical metaphor. While freedom was often vaunted as an ethical ideal (particularly in Stoic circles), slavery was (if anything) identified with vice.[96] It is beyond the scope of this study to ask how Paul first developed this radical ethic of self-giving love. What we may ask, however, is what grounding, both explicit and implicit, Paul offers for it as he commends this ethic to the Galatians.

Here we must rely on a frustratingly small number of hints, for, in contrast to his teaching about circumcision and Torah, Paul seems to assume that his audience will need little convincing that this love ethic really describes how a believer should live. The clearest hint we receive comes in 5:24, where Paul reminds the Galatians that "those who belong to Christ Jesus have crucified the flesh with its passions and desires." This is no casual statement. On the one hand, such positive use of crucifixion imagery, even after long familiarity, retains some of its original shock value.[97] More important, this reminder of the believers' moral "crucifixion" is the conclusion of Paul's call for the Galatians to choose between the way of the flesh and the way of the Spirit in 5:16–24. In 5:16–17 the Apostle set up the antagonism between these two ways of living. In 5:19–21a and 5:22–23a Paul then sketched out the kind of behaviour which characterizes these two ethical patterns, emphasizing in 5:21b that the Galatians' eschatological future hangs on their decision between them. This description of tension between flesh and Spirit

---

[95] See, for example, the resemblance between Paul's instruction to pay teachers in 6:6 and the section of the Hippocratic oath mentioned by Oepke, *Galater*, 150, and cited by Betz, *Galatians*, 305; Martyn, *Galatians*, 551.

[96] So Hays, "Christology," 283–6; Carter, *Servant Ethic*, 6–11. See Epict., *Diss.* 2.9.4; 3.22.47–49; 4.1.1, 62, 128; Dio Chrys., *Or.* 14.16–18.

[97] Dunn (*Galatians*, 314) highlights the fact that the metaphoric use of "crucifixion" in a positive sense was also unheard of in the Greco-Roman world apart from Christian writings.

is then bracketed by two statements about the relationship between the law and the way of the Spirit (5:18, 23b). Paul's reminder about the believers' "crucifixion" in 5:24 thus stands at the conclusion of a chiastic structure which began in 5:16. In this position it corresponds with the Apostle's initial call to "live by the Spirit" and his description of the flesh/Spirit antagonism. Here, in 5:24, Paul reminds the audience that in fact they have already made their decision. Their reception of the Spirit marks them as those who "belong to Christ," those who are identified with Christ (cf. 3:1–9), and just as this identification involved their reception of the Spirit, so too it already involved the "crucifixion" of their "flesh." This is almost certainly a reference to the believers' baptism and the participation in Christ's death which Paul described in 2:19–20.[98] In being crucified together with Christ, the Galatians chose the Spirit over the flesh. Paul's ethics simply amount to a consistent willingness to continue in that life.

So far, we see again how Paul's ethical theory arises organically from his emplotment of the Galatians within his theological narrative, but what about the substance of this love ethic? Notice that at this crucial juncture in his exhortations Paul reminds the Galatians of Christ's crucifixion. Throughout the letter Paul has emphasized the cross,[99] and in 2:20 this act of self-giving is associated with Christ's love. There Jesus is "the Son of God, who loved me and gave himself for me."[100] Against this background it may well be that here, in 5:24, Paul recalls the believers' participatory "crucifixion" not just to remind them that they have already chosen their path, but also to remind them

---

[98] The aorist verb ἐσταύρωσαν suggests that Paul is thinking not of ongoing moral decisions but of the believer's initial participation in Christ's death, probably to be connected with baptism (so Dunn, *Galatians*, 315). Bryant (*Crucified Christ*, 188) argues that the active form of the verb, which envisages the believers as the agents of crucifixion, indicates that they have ongoing responsibility for making the decision to participate in Christ. Yet where Paul describes the believers' "crucifixion" with an aorist verb, he consistently refers to an event at the beginning of their Christian existence. Hence the active verb is more likely meant to emphasize the fact that the crucifixion of the Galatians' "flesh" was the result of their own decision. As Barclay writes, "[T]o return to the flesh would be to renounce what they themselves have just done (not just what has been done to them)" (*Obeying*, 117).

[99] See Bryant, *Crucified Christ*, 192–4; Hays, "Christology," 277. In 1:4 we are told that Christ "gave himself for our sins." See also 3:1, 13–14; 4:4–7.

[100] So Betz, *Galatians*, 263. Cf. Martyn, *Galatians*, 474, who observes that the love which Paul envisions is "elicited by Christ's love for us (2:20)."

of the form which that path must take. If their entry into the life of the Spirit was effected by their participation in Christ's act of self-giving love, perhaps the Apostle wants to remind the Galatians that this participation implies a call to live out that same love.[101] This is not just a question of the imitation of Christ as an external ethical model. The believers have been "rescued" precisely by becoming, in some sense, a part of Christ.[102] Hence the life they have chosen involves rejecting the self-involved pattern of living which characterizes "the flesh" – ordinary human tendencies and drives – and taking on the self-giving love which characterizes Christ.

All of this is, of course, extrapolating from hints which Paul's text does not explicitly tie together. If this kind of ethical teaching was familiar to the Galatians, then Paul may not have needed to make these connections explicit in order for them to ground his call to love, but our reading remains a reading between the lines. At the same time, the more allusions to Christ's passion which we find in and around Paul's ethical exhortations here, the more likely it becomes that he was assuming his readers would understand their participation in Christ as the basis of their obligation to love. Hence it is important to return to Paul's claim in 6:2 that by bearing one another's burdens the Galatians would fulfil the law of Christ. Coming so soon after the reference to crucifixion in 5:24, it is striking that Paul associates Christ closely with this kind of loving service.[103] As Hays has suggested, it is difficult not to see here something like the thought behind Rom 15:1–6, where the "strong" are urged to put the needs of the "weak" ahead of their own interests, because this was how Christ acted in his passion.[104]

Finally, Hays has pointed out that while the call to follow Christ's pattern of life is not stated explicitly in 5:13–6:7, it *is* discussed explicitly elsewhere in the letter.[105] In 2:19–20, as we have seen above, the Apostle emphasizes his identification with Christ as the basis for his life "in the body" and claims: "It is no longer I who live, but it is Christ who lives in me." In 6:17 it becomes clear that for Paul this identification meant enduring the sufferings

---

[101] So Bryant, *Crucified Christ*, 187.

[102] Could the genitive τοῦ Χριστοῦ in 5:24 even be construed as a partitive genitive, in the sense "those who are a part of Christ"?

[103] Dunn (*Galatians*, 296) agrees that when Paul calls the Galatians to fulfil the law through love, "the paradigm of Jesus is not far in the background."

[104] So Hays, "Christology," 287.

[105] Hays, "Christology," 280–83.

of Christ, for he boasts: "I carry the marks of Jesus branded on my body."[106] This suggests that Paul is thinking of something more than a mere theological metaphor when he says in 6:14 that "the world has been crucified to me, and I to the world"; as Hays points out, the similarity between 6:14 and 5:24 in turn reinforces the impression that Paul is grounding the pattern of his love ethic in the example of Christ. One might argue that the Apostle sees himself as occupying a different position than the ordinary members of his communities, and that such an active participation in the pattern of Christ's life was not intended as the norm. Such a suggestion, however, would run up against Paul's habit of exhorting his audience to imitate his own way of life.[107] What is more, Paul makes it clear in 4:19 that he understands the ordinary Galatian believers to be undergoing a moral transformation in which they become more and more like Christ. There, in the context of a maternal concern for the wellbeing of his audience, he says that he will continue to feel "labour pains" for them "until Christ is formed in you (μέχρις οὗ μορφωθῇ Χριστὸς ἐν ὑμῖν)."[108]

This last statement, in 4:19, is enough to show that our extrapolation based on the hints in 5:13–6:7 has, in fact, been moving along the same lines as Paul's own thought when he penned the letter. The Apostle can expect his ordinarily shocking call for the Galatians to be enslaved to one another to

---

[106] Similarly, there seems to be more than mere hyperbole at work in 4:14 when Paul says that the Galatians received him "as an angel of God, as Christ Jesus." Hays suggests that the point here is not simply that they gave him a reception fit for Christ himself. Rather, he came to them suffering, and they regarded his suffering not as a sign that he was cursed but as the same kind of affliction which Christ bore in the service of others ("Christology," 280–83; so Lührmann, *Galatians*, 86; Martyn, *Galatians*, 421; cf. Dunn, *Galatians*, 234–5). This interpretation would be made even more plausible if we were to follow Bruce (*Galatians*, 209) and Zahn in rendering ἄγγελον in 4:14 as "messenger" instead of "angel," though this would run against the current of scholarly opinion since elsewhere the Apostle uses the noun consistently for superhuman beings (see Betz, *Galatians*, 226; Burton, *Galatians*, 242; R. N. Longenecker, *Galatians*, 192; Oepke, *Galater*, 106).

[107] Hays points to 1 Cor 11:1, where Paul exhorts his audience: "Be imitators of me, as I am of Christ" ("Christology," 282). The same assumption that the Galatians should imitate Paul's example is evident in Gal 4:12, though there the connection with Paul's own imitation of Christ is less self-evident.

[108] Hays is likely right here that ἐν ὑμῖν does not mean "in you" – in each of the individual believers – but "among you" ("Christology," 283). The community as a whole is to be reshaped into Christ's likeness.

gain a sympathetic hearing because he and his audience both hear this exhortation within a very specific narrative context. The Galatians know (and here are reminded) that they have been identified with Christ and that the eschatological life which they experience is the life of Christ. They also know that this identification with Christ involves living a life which is more and more shaped by Christ's pattern of self-giving love.[109] To reject that pattern of life is to reject Christ and to forfeit the good end which can only be reached by one who shares in Christ's own resurrection.

3.3. Israel's Past and Ethics in the Present

All of this suggests that not only Paul's general ethical theory but also the specific pattern of behaviour which he views as the ideal are presented to the Galatian audience as the implication of their emplotment within his reconfiguration of Israel's story. We must not leave off, however, without acknowledging the indications that the Apostle expects the ethical tradition of Israel to play some role in helping the Galatians to recognize those actions which conform to Christ's pattern, to discern the inner promptings of the Spirit. We must notice, first of all, that there is in these verses a peculiar relationship between a Spirit lifestyle and Torah. When the Apostle first introduces the positive ethic of love in 5:13 he immediately gives justification for this ethic: "For the whole law (ὁ γὰρ πᾶς νόμος) is fulfilled (πεπλήρωται)[110] in a single commandment, 'You shall love your neighbor as

---

[109] So Barrett, *Freedom*, 89–90. Hays also points out that it is, for Paul, Christ's passion which is the distinctive source for this ethical pattern. Hays observes that "nothing is said here about any *teachings of Jesus* on humility and servanthood, nor is there any reference to historical incidents in Jesus' ministry such as healings or table-fellowship with 'sinners' or washing the feet of the disciples. Paul focuses in a single-minded fashion on the decisive significance of Christ's incarnation and death" ("Christology," 278).

[110] I have altered the NRSV text here, which rendered πεπλήρωται as "summed up." Paul's idea is clearly not simply that the love command is a summary of Torah's many requirements (which individually remain in force), but that when one carries out this one command, the whole requirement of Torah has been satisfied (so Betz, *Galatians*, 275; Lightfoot, *Galatians*, 208–9; contra Schrage, *Ethics*, 206–7). Hence, as Betz puts it, Paul carefully distinguishes between "doing" the whole law (ὅλον τὸν νόμον ποιῆσαι [5:3]) and "fulfilling" it, a distinction which (again) was unknown in Judaism (*Galatians*, 275; so Barclay, *Obeying*, 139; B. W. Longenecker, "Defining," 91–2; Stanton, "Law of Moses," 115; Westerholm, "Fulfilling"). Where Jewish authors do talk of "fulfilling" the law through observance of a single command, it was always assumed that one would still try to keep the

yourself'" (5:14; cf. Lev 19:18).[111] His supposedly law-free ethic is grounded on the obligation to fulfil what he perceives as the ideal at the heart of Torah. This seems shocking, coming as it does after an extended argument _against_ the idea that Torah is binding on the believer. After all, Paul has made it clear in 5:18 that "if you are led by the Spirit, you are not subject to the law (οὐκ ἐστὲ ὑπὸ νόμον)." Yet the same idea resurfaces at the end of Paul's list of the

---

rest of Torah as well (_Obeying_, 135–6; see Moore, _Judaism_, 2.83–8; Sanders, _Paul and Palestinian Judaism_, 112–14; _idem_, "Fulfilling," 112–17). Barclay (_Obeying_, 138) further highlights the fact that the Hebrew מלא and its LXX equivalent πληρόω are never used in Jewish literature in relation to the law (though πληρόω does appear with objects like ἐντολή in _T. Naph._ 8:7; 1 Macc 1:55; Philo, _Praem._ 83; _Sib. Or._ 3:246). Even the rabbinic passages which might serve as parallels employ קום, not מלא, and thus do not carry the same implications of fullness and completion (Barclay, _Obeying_, 138).

Martyn thinks that this "fulfillment" in Paul is not a matter of the believers' ethical efforts at all, but refers instead to Christ's actions which restored the law to its proper role (_Galatians_, 487–90; 509–514). Yet it is difficult to see in what sense Christ could be said to have completed the law by means of Lev 19:18. True, πεπλήρωται in 5:14 is a perfect verb, but Martyn admits this may be a gnomic (or proverbial) perfect. There is no explicit mention of Christ in 5:13–14, and (as Martyn recognizes) it is the Galatians who fulfil the law of Christ in 6:2 (see Martyn _Galatians_, 490; cf. Rom 13:8–10).

Nor is it necessary to follow Martyn (_Galatians_, 503–6) in his suggestion that in 5:14 Paul isolates a different "voice" of Torah than the one which the opponents want the Galatians to obey in 5:3. Although Martyn places great emphasis on the "singularity" of the law in 5:14 (ὁ . . . πᾶς νόμος), the expression in 5:3 (ὅλον τὸν νόμον) is no less singular (cf. Hübner's emphasis on the attributive position of πᾶς in 5:14, _Law_, 37). Moreover, the shift from talking about "doing" Torah in 5:3 to "fulfilling" it in 5:14 makes sense only if it is the same law which is in view in both cases (so Dunn, _Galatians_, 290; Stanton, "Law of Moses," 115; see also Barclay, _Obeying_, 137). Nor does Paul's reference to a single "word" or "sentence" (λόγος) by which Torah is fulfilled indicate that this law is devoid of commandments, since λόγος is used in the LXX for the stipulations of Torah (see Exod 19:7, 8; 20:1; 24:3, 8; 34:27–28; 35:1; Lev 8:36; Deut 1:18; 9:10; 10:4; 12:28; 27:3, 26; 28:14, 69; 29:8; 31:12, 24). Indeed, the Roman believers fulfil the law's "commandments" in Rom 13:8–10, now apparently reduced to the love command (so Martyn, _Galatians_, 522). For Paul, such love seems to satisfy the whole requirement of Torah, even though some of its specific requirements have not been "done" (so Barclay, _Obeying_, 141; Westerholm, "Fulfilling," 235).

[111] The post-positive γάρ in 5:14 is most naturally understood as introducing the ground or reason for the preceding statement. In isolating the love command as the core principle of Torah, Paul is in agreement with much Jewish tradition (see Matt 7:12/Luke 6:31; _b. Šabb._ 31a; _Tg. Ps.-J._ Lev 19:18; _Gen. Rab._ 24:7; _T. Iss._ 5:2; _T. Dan_ 5:3), but most Jews never imagined love to be a substitute for the law's other observances (Martyn, _Galatians_, 515).

fruit of the Spirit, where he adds, "There is no law against such things" (5:23).[112] On the one hand, with this negative turn of phrase the Apostle seems to be guarding against the implication that Torah is still binding.[113] At the same time, however, it seems to be important for him to show that the behaviour produced by the impulse of the Spirit is in harmony with that code as a whole. Some might suggest that this is only a rhetorical need, that Paul simply wants to say that Spirit ethics are in no way inferior to a Torah-based ethic.[114] It is doubtful, though, that the Apostle would introduce the positive support of Torah for his own ethics, thus introducing the danger that this law be understood as still carrying binding force, unless he himself felt that this harmony between Spirit ethics and Torah ethics was important. It seems, rather, that Paul still believes that the history of God's dealings with Israel *did* point the people towards the lifestyle which God desires for humanity. In this sense the ethical goal of God's interaction with humanity has not changed with the coming of Christ. The believers still "eagerly wait for the hope of righteousness" (5:5). The internal guidance of the Spirit still leads towards that righteousness which God had been encouraging through Torah.[115] On Paul's reconfiguration of Israel's story, what has changed is

---

[112] In context, νόμος in 5:23 should almost certainly be understood as an injunction of the Torah and not simply as law in general. Verse 14 shows that Paul is thinking in terms of the relation of Spirit ethics to that scriptural code. Although νόμος is here anarthrous, this is not determinative in Paul's usage (contra R. N. Longenecker, *Galatians*, 263). The set phrases ἐξ ἔργων νόμου (Gal 2:16; 3:2, 5, 10), ἐκ νόμου (3:18), and ὑπὸ νόμον (3:23; 4:4, 5, 21; 5:18), which in Galatians clearly denote the Jewish law, are all anarthrous (cf. 2:19, 21; 3:11, 17; 5:4, 14; 6:13).

Dunn takes the point here to be that "no law is required in order to produce such virtue" (*Galatians*, 313; so Betz, *Galatians*, 288–9), but this is a forced reading of Paul's words. What he says is that the law does not *forbid* these acts, i.e., that the lifestyle of the Spirit is in harmony with the essence of Torah (so Barclay, *Obeying*, 123–5).

[113] This demonstrates that Paul does not, as Sanders suggests, maintain the necessity of Torah as a means of "staying in" the Christian covenant (*Paul, the Law, and the Jewish People*, 6). As Westerholm observes, Paul nowhere talks about believers "doing" or "keeping" the law, and he does not present precepts from Torah as the basis of his ethical exhortation (*Israel's Law*, 233–7). The turn of phrase also excludes the idea that these virtues themselves constitute a new νόμος (so Betz, *Galatians*, 288).

[114] So Barrett (*Freedom*, 77) takes it as an "*ad hominem* dig."

[115] The idea that when one is guided by the Spirit the law's demand has been fully met is understood here by Burton, *Galatians*, 318–19; Schlier, *Galater*, 262; Mussner, *Galaterbrief*, 389; R. N. Longenecker, *Galatians*, 263. This δικαιοσύνη is probably not to

a) that it is no longer necessary to become a Jew in order to achieve that righteousness, and b) the scriptural expression of that righteousness in Torah is relativized accordingly, since in that written code the temporary markers of Jewishness and the eternal pattern of righteousness are not distinguished. It requires the guidance of the Spirit to see in the scriptural record the pattern of righteousness towards which God has been leading humanity, the pattern which is re-established in God's "new creation" (6:15).[116]

In this light, even Torah, as a part of Israel's story, can be seen to undergird the substance of some of Paul's specific ethical instructions. For although Paul believes, on the basis of the narrative, that the Spirit will now lead the Galatians, he also seems to recognize that they must learn to discern the voice of that Spirit. Otherwise his specific ethical instructions here would be redundant.[117] He claims that the difference between the deeds of the Spirit and those of the flesh is "obvious" (5:19), but he still must list them in order to train the Galatians' moral sensitivity. What is crucial to notice is that in this process of moral education the history of God's interaction with Israel is presupposed.[118] For in what context is "idolatry" an obvious sin, obviously contrary to the will of God (5:20)? Only in the context of Israel's story, in which those who serve idols are excluded from God's blessing, while those who hold fast to the one God find life.[119] Similarly, "fornication" (πορνεία) does not play the kind of role in Greco-Roman ethics which it commonly

---

be understood merely as God's future judicial declaration of a person as acceptable (contra Barrett, *Freedom*, 66; cf. 64–5).

[116] Hence, as Westerholm observes, Paul does not exhort his audience to "fulfil" the law, but rather describes their behaviour as resulting in the law's fulfilment (*Israel's Law*, 235–7). For one cannot know, from the written code itself, how one is to "fulfil" its intent now that one is "in Christ."

[117] So Schrage, *Ethics*, 191–2.

[118] Some commentators suggest that when Paul calls the works of the flesh φανερά – "obvious" – he is suggesting that one does not need Torah in order to see their sinfulness (so R. N. Longenecker, *Galatians*, 252).

[119] The term εἰδωλολατρία appears first in Paul, though it expresses an idea with deep roots in Judaism, and Büchsel speculates that it was likely coined by pre-Christian Jews (Büchsel, "εἴδωλον," 380; so Dunn, *Galatians*, 304). Hence we cannot agree with Furnish when he writes that the works of the flesh are "obvious" in the sense that the Galatians will have always considered them wicked, and "the vices he then lists are typical of those condemned by secular writers (5:19–21)" (Furnish, *Theology and Ethics*, 71–2; so Betz, *Galatians*, 282).

assumes in Jewish ethical literature dependent on the LXX,[120] and the same may be said for sexual "impurity" and "licentiousness."[121] Thus it seems that as Paul offers the Galatians examples of behaviour to be avoided, helping them to learn to recognize the inner promptings of the Spirit, he assumes that there is continued validity in several of the ethical emphases which characterized God's past demand in Torah. This does not mean that the

---

[120] The word πορνεία is common in Jewish literature (see, e.g., LXX Wis 2:16; Sir. 23:23; *Let. Arist.* 166; *T. Jos.* 3:8; *T. Reu.* 5:5; Philo, *Spec.* 1.282; *Mos.* 1.300). In Greek literature it is very rare (see P. Tebt. 2.276.15f. [i/ii cent. BCE]; Athen., *Deipn.* 13.595a; Demosthenes, *Or.* 19.200; M-M, 529; Hauck and Schulz, "πόρνη," 581). In fact, of the 129 occurrences of πορνεία listed in the *TLG* and dated prior to the 2nd century CE, only 11 are found in pagan literature. 51 come from the LXX, 25 from the *T. 12 Patr.*, 25 from the NT, and 12 from the Clementine and pseudo-Clementine writings. Stoics, among others, did oppose adultery and prostitution, but the term πορνεία does not seem to have played a prominent role in this polemic (see Hauck and Schulz, "πόρνη," 581–4). The term is entirely absent from, e.g., Epictetus and Dio Chrysostom. The adulterer, a common target of Stoic ethicists, is instead a μοιχός (Epict., *Diss.*, 2.4.2, 11; cf. Zeno, *Fr.*, 244).

[121] Following πορνεία here, these two terms likely also refer to sexual immorality (so R. N. Longenecker, *Galatians*, 254; Lührmann, *Galatians*, 109; so BDAG, 34 [2]). The term ἀκαθαρσία is not common in non-Jewish literature. It does occur with a moral sense in Demosthenes (*Or.* 21.119) and Epictetus (*Diss.* 4.11.5ff.), but not to denote sexual vice specifically (cf. ἀκάθαρτος in Demosthenes, *Or.* 25.63; 37.48; Plato, *Leges* 716e; *Tim.* 92b; (Ps-)Plut., *Lib. ed.* 17). In Jewish circles ἀκαθαρσία is much more common, first and foremost for ritual impurity (e.g., LXX Lev 5:3; 7:20–21; 15:3, 24–31; Num 19:13; Jdg 13:7; 2 Kgs 11:4; *Pss. Sol.* 8:12), and then for moral "impurity" or sin (e.g., LXX Prov 6:16; Mic 2:10; Ezek 22:15; cf. ἀκάθαρτος in Isa 6:5; Prov 3:32; 16:5; 20:10; Philo, *Spec.* 1.150; 3.209), especially idolatry and pagan worship (e.g., LXX Hos 2:12[10]; Jer 19:13; 39:34; Ezek 36:25; Ezra [LXX 2 Esdr] 6:21; 9:11; 1 Esdr 1:40, 47; 8:66, 80, 84; 1 Macc 13:48; 14:7; 3 Macc 2:17; Wis 2:16; *Pss. Sol.* 8:22; 17:45). Such moral ἀκαθαρσία is also often connected with sexual immorality (see LXX Nah 3:6; *T. Jos.* 4:6; *T. Jud.* 14:5; in Paul see Rom 1:24; 6:19; 2 Cor 12:21; Col 3:5). The closest one comes to this in extra-Jewish literature is when Plutarch calls certain prostitutes ἀκάθαρτος (*Otho* 2.2).

The word ἀσέλγεια is again not especially frequent in Greek literature and is often used in the sense of "wanton licence," "lawlessness," "brutality" (Plato, *Resp.* 424e; Aeschines, *Or.* 3.170; Demosth. *Or.* 4.9; 21:1, 88; Jos., *A.J.* 4.151; Plut., *Alcibiades* 8.1), or even "insolence" (Aristot., *Pol.* 1304b [22]). The term is, however, used by Greek writers to refer to sexual "licentiousness" (Polyb. 36.15.4; 8.10.3; 25.3.7), and the pattern of use in a Jewish writer such as Josephus closely resembles the pattern in pagan writers (see *B.J.* 4.562; *A.J.* 8.318; 16.184; 20.112). In this case the distinctively Jewish element in Paul's use is simply the fact that he would think to count such "licentiousness" as a primary vice (so Dunn, *Galatians*, 303).

Apostle envisions a "third use" for the law in which portions of it serve as an authoritative ethical code for believers.[122] Rather, Torah remains important for Paul *as part of the scriptural codification of the early chapters in Israel's story*, and as part of that story even legal commandments can help the believer to gain a sense of the ethical ideal towards which God wants human beings to move. Remembering how God taught his people to live in other parts of the narrative can suggest how he might want his people to live in the present chapter. Paul always insists, however, that such past legal pronouncements be understood in terms of their purpose and function in his own reconfiguration of Israel's narrative. The source of the Apostle's ethics remains his own reconstrual of the theological story within which he teaches his communities to locate themselves. It is on the basis of this narrative emplotment that he encourages his audience to discern how they must live if they are to come to a good end when the story draws to its close. To the extent, however, that Torah remains a part of his reconfigured narrative, it too can play a role in helping the believers to learn to "walk in the Spirit."

---

[122] Contra Schrage: ". . . the Old Testament and its law are presupposed and enforced as the criterion of Christian conduct" (*Ethics*, 205).

Conclusions

Living the Story

1. Paul's Narrative Logic

What assumptions did Paul make about how human beings can come to religious knowledge? This is the question which has driven the present study. In Part One we found that Paul's attitude towards human reason is much more positive than one might assume. Rom 1:18–32 may not license a straightforward "natural theology," but neither does the passage teach that human reason is inherently problematic. The root of the epistemic paralysis which Paul describes here is *moral*; it is the idolatrous refusal to acknowledge God. Hence the Apostle leaves room for human reason to become fruitful again when the human moral constitution has been restored by the Spirit. Likewise, although Paul has often been understood to teach in 1 Cor 1:17–2:16 that religious knowledge comes only through the irrational inspiration of the Spirit, we discovered that in fact the Apostle presumes that the reasoning faculties are engaged *during* the Spirit's revelation. Again, what Paul opposes in this passage is not reason *per se*, but that "worldly wisdom" in which reason is hijacked by idolatrous vices of control and self-interest. As we surveyed Paul's statements elsewhere in his letters, we found that he constantly assumed the involvement of the believer's reason in the acquisition of knowledge, not only in the ethical sphere but also in the realm of "theological" knowledge as well. I even suggested that Paul seems at times to treat the believer's basic belief in the Gospel as the fruit of rational deliberation.

This surprising openness to human reason in Paul prompted us then to ask what *kind* of reasoning the Apostle presumes can lead to religious knowledge. So in Part Two we looked at the logical structure which is inherent in the content of Paul's knowledge. We found that this content falls naturally into four categories: mundane knowledge, theological knowledge, ethical knowledge, and the intimate knowledge of personal familiarity and devotion. I argued there that the Apostle's theological knowledge is structured as a narrative, a series of causally and temporally related events and personal actions which is shot through with dramatic tension. It is from this theological story, I suggested, that Paul's ethical knowledge arises. Ethical reasoning is for Paul a matter of "emplotting" himself or other human beings within this overarching narrative by correlating the events of the story with his mundane knowledge about himself and others. Ultimately this theological knowledge (and the ethics which are derived from it) is aimed at bringing human beings into that intimate devotion to God and Christ which constitutes their salvation.

Finally, in Part Three we turned to Paul's letter to the Galatians and asked what kind of logical structure could be discerned in the Apostle's reasoning with his audience. I showed how in Galatians Paul's argument is from the very beginning a matter of emplotting his audience within his theological story and pointing out the implications, in that narrative context, of their ethical behaviour. If they adopt circumcision and other legal observances, they will not be playing a good role in the story. Quite the opposite: they will be abandoning their role as God's elect, as heirs of Abraham, and taking on a role which ends in destruction. Likewise, Paul's positive ethical teaching in chapters 5 and 6 arises directly from his theological narrative. It is as believers in Christ that the Galatians can expect the Spirit to give them new ethical impulses, and it is the model of Christ's life and self-sacrificial death which offers the ethical paradigm of love for those who would live "in" Christ and so find resurrection and life in the story's denouement.

Yet all of this ethical argumentation is valid only to the extent that the theological narrative which drives it is a *true* narrative. Paul's argument with the Galatians cannot be a matter merely of emplotting them within his story; he must also show that his own version of the narrative is true and that his opponents' construal of that story is false. For while both Paul and the teachers in Galatia are guided by Israel's story, the two parties construe its shape in two very different ways. In 2:15–3:5 the Apostle presents the basic justification for his reconfiguration of Israel's narrative, and it is here that we uncovered the most intriguing logical dynamics in the argument of Galatians. In order to demonstrate that his construal of Israel's story is more reliable than his opponents', Paul points to two recent events which all parties will agree took place: the crucifixion of Christ and the Galatians' own reception of the Spirit prior to any Torah observance. These two events, Paul insists, were not foreseen in Israel's story. When one tries to understand them as part of a traditional reading of that narrative, they cause irreconcilable contradictions. How can God's agent for the redemption of Israel die as a covenant traitor? How can those outside the covenant of Israel gain the eschatological blessing promised to those who faithfully keep Torah? These events emerge as interpretive "gaps" which resist integration into the ordered pattern of the story's plot. Yet, if that Israelite story is to be understood as the universal narrative, these events must be comprehended within it. Hence Paul argues that in the wake of these novel experiences a reconfiguration of Israel's narrative is necessary. What is more, he insists that it is his own reconfiguration of that story which can succeed in integrating these events, resolving these interpretive "gaps," where the version told by his Galatian opponents must fail. The balance of Paul's theological argument in 3:6–4:11 is then a matter of laying out the reconfigured narrative in enough detail to show that it can indeed remain coherent while integrating both the chapters which have gone before and these new, unforseen episodes.

The core of Paul's argument in Galatians thus turns out to be an argument from coherence. Paul focusses on a collection of "set pieces" of knowledge upon which he and his opponents agree: the episodes in Israel's story along with the cross and the Galatians' experience of the Spirit. He then tries to show that it is only *his* overall paradigm which can make sense of all these pieces together. Yet Paul does not understand himself to be replacing a traditional paradigm with a new one, and here a grasp of the narrative shape of Paul's knowledge is necessary to understand his logic. For if the set pieces of knowledge which the Apostle is rearranging were an atemporal cluster of "facts" or "phenomena" there would be no organic relationship between the old paradigm and Paul's new paradigm, beyond the fact that some of the same individual items were interpreted by both. It is only when these set pieces are understood as events and actions in a coherent story that we can discern not only their essential unity, but also *their inherent and irrevocable connection with surprising and novel events* like the crucifixion and the Spirit's advent. For just as the later chapters in a novel belong to the earlier chapters by virtue of being bound together as a single book, so in a universal narrative *any* new event belongs inherently to the story. Hence, Paul's reconfiguration of Israel's traditional theology was not simply a rejection of that theology. It was the organic and necessary development in understanding which takes place as one follows an unfolding story, a story whose sentences are not yet all spoken.

2. Filling the Gaps in Paul's Talk about Knowledge

If this narrative logic is the kind of reasoning which Paul assumes can lead one to religious knowledge, then we have in hand a hint towards solutions for some of the aporias which emerged early in this study. We can begin, for instance, to understand how Paul could treat human reason so positively and yet could imply that, in giving up "worldly wisdom," one must also sacrifice ordinary standards of plausibility. For Paul's narrative logic tends to be coherentist rather than foundationalist. In an argument from coherence even one's most fundamental values and assumptions may be challenged if one meets a sufficiently coherent view of the world which is structured in different terms.[1] As he argued against his Galatian opponents, the Apostle did not accept many of their assumptions about the shape which a plausible telling of Israel's story must take. The permanent validity of Torah, for instance, an idea which for the Galatian opponents (as for most Jews) seems to have been axiomatic, was deliberately challenged by Paul. Yet he could still argue rationally for his position by pointing out that it was internally coherent. In the same way, we can imagine how believers could have been impelled by the sheer coherence of the Christian message to abandon their ordinary assumptions about what constitutes a plausible view of the world. Paul's message of Christ crucified may be foolishness to Greeks and a stumbling block to Jews because of its violation of ordinary assumptions and values, but the vision of the world which it presents might still possess an internal coherence which rational minds can recognize and find compelling.

What is the measure of coherence for Paul? At times we see the Apostle emphasizing repeated patterns in the narrative. In 4:21–31, for example, Paul points out that while God's acceptance of uncircumcised Galatian Gentiles may defy ordinary human expectations, so too did the miraculous birth of Isaac. Elsewhere we find Paul pointing out how the patterns of action within the narrative are analogous to patterns of action in the world of everyday life. Hence the Apostle's understanding of God's promise to Abraham appears

---

[1] See W. V. Quine, "Two Dogmas."

more plausible when he points out its affinities with human customs around wills and inheritance (3:15–18). Yet both of these approaches appear in Galatians as secondary modes of argument. They bolster Paul's claim that his reconfiguration of Israel's narrative is coherent, but the Apostle does not depend on them to do much of the work of convincing his audience. Rather, Paul's central argument is a matter of showing that his construal of the story *yields a satisfying plot*. The coherence which he tries to demonstrate (and which he claims his opponents' telling of the story lacks) is the narrative coherence of a plot in which the events can all be seen to have causal connections, and in which the characters involved can be imbued with comprehensible motives for acting. How, for example, can Christ's death be God's condemnation of his own agent as a lawbreaker if God then vindicates him by raising him from the dead? What coherent motives can make sense of these apparently contradictory actions? Paul argues that the story can be read coherently only if the Messiah's death is instead understood as (among other things) a vicarious one in which believers can participate, for in this case God's apparent judgement of the Messiah can be understood as the pivotal moment in a larger divine plan.

At first glance we might assume that this narrative logic could operate only in conversations among those who share a common story. It is possible to imagine, however, how such a narrative logic could also lead Paul's Gentile hearers to the conviction that the Christian narrative is superior to entirely different universal stories. This is because, for Paul's converts, coming to faith involves a shift from one way of configuring the phenomena of the world to another, and such a shift could well follow the kind of coherentist logic which Paul uses in Galatians. Even Paul's Gentile hearers may well have been impressed with the internal consistency of the Christian story and so adopted it as a new framework for understanding the world. Of course, such arguments from coherence still assume some common ground between the rival positions. In Galatians Paul shared with his opponents a conviction that the episodes of Israel's narrative were true. This broad area of agreement gave the Apostle a fund of basic "realities" to configure in a more coherent manner than his opposition. When Paul approached pagan listeners in Lystra or in Corinth he would not be able to work with such a broad base of common convictions. This does not mean, however, that an argument from coherence could not make use of a common basic store of data. For, as we saw above, Paul's theological narrative encompasses "mundane" knowledge, knowledge about ordinary and immediate matters with which any inhabitant of Paul's Mediterranean world could agree. To the extent, then, that Paul's narrative furnished a pagan audience with a more coherent account of their everyday experiences, they would have rational grounds to adopt that Gospel.

Moreover, we also saw above that the Galatians' experience of the Spirit constituted a part of the common fund of phenomena which Paul and his opponents were competing to configure. While pagan listeners might not have had these specific experiences, Paul seems to have presumed at times that miraculous phenomena did play a part in the conversion of new believers. Here we should again call to mind the role which prophetic speech plays in conversion in 1 Cor 14:24–25. The point here is that if an outsider arrives at a Christian meeting and is told his innermost secrets, he will have a hard time integrating that experience into his prior account of the world. He will at least be pushed to acknowledge that "God is really among" the believers. What is more, this initial reconstrual of the world will simply heighten the cognitive tension for the outsider. For if God is among the Christians, then presumably their message is true – a message which proclaims such follies as a crucified redeemer. Moreover, if the tradition of the resurrection appearances which Paul repeats in 1 Cor 15:1–8 was a prominent part of his early preaching, one can imagine that eyewitness testimony to the resurrection of this crucified criminal would serve as powerful support for the plausibility of the Gospel. When integrated into a hearer's world view, not only would such an event tend to lend Paul credibility as the (self-proclaimed) messenger of the Risen One, but his message would make much better sense of the cross and resurrection than would the usual Greco-Roman notions of divinized humans.[2] Even Gentile citizens of the Roman world could thus be pushed quite rationally to adopt the new Christian message if they found that it accounted more coherently for their experience of the world, both mundane and miraculous.

---

[2] Such a shameful death would have been difficult for Greco-Roman audiences to reconcile with the divinity which they would associate with resurrection. While the divine Aesclepius was thought to have been slain by Zeus as punishment for his audacious healings (see Diod. Sic. 4.71.2–3; Ovid, *Metam.* 642–649; Pindar, *Pyth.* 3.55–58), even this judgement (being struck by lightning) would not have approached the horror of crucifixion in the ancient mind.

The point here is not that this is how all early Christians actually came to faith (though it is a plausible scenario), but rather that the kind of logic evident in Paul's argumentation allows us to understand how one *could* move from unbelief to faith through a rational process. In other words, Paul's assumptions about the basic viability of human reason make sense if we assume that the reasoning involved is the kind which Paul himself employs with the Galatians. This insight leads in turn to a suggestion about how Paul might understand the Spirit and human reason to work together in the believer's conversion. The rational process involved in conversion would, assuming Paul's style of reasoning, be very much like the kind of "paradigm shift" which Thomas Kuhn observed in the physical sciences.[3] As Kuhn pointed out, there is an intangible element to such shifts. One can become frustrated by inconsistencies within one's own paradigm and can recognize that there seem to be fewer such inconsistencies within another. There is, however, no precise way of determining when this cognitive pressure has built up to the extent that a change of paradigms is rationally justified.[4] In this moment of decision a plethora of non-rational factors may play a role in nudging one towards the new or back into the familiar embrace of the old. If Paul were right that something in the human moral makeup resists any recognition of the Gospel, is offended by its "folly," then Paul might also be right that all the reasoning in the world would still not bring about a single conversion on its own. While the journey towards faith in Christ would be an essentially rational journey, there would still remain the need for the Spirit to remake the human moral constitution and so make possible the decision to adopt the Gospel paradigm.

---

[3] Kuhn, *Structure*. Note the similarity between Paul's constant reference to his own theological story in his argument and Kuhn's account of the use of paradigms in debates where the choice of paradigm is at issue (see Kuhn, *Structure*, 94).

[4] Kuhn (*Structure*, 94) writes: "Like the choice between competing political institutions, that between competing paradigms proves to be a choice between incompatible modes of community life. Because it has that character, the choice is not and cannot be determined merely by the evaluative procedures characteristic of normal science, for these depend in part upon a particular paradigm, and that paradigm is at issue."

3. Dilemmas Old and New

This study of Paul's epistemological assumptions was begun in the hope that the Apostle might help us in the present to find our way back to more workable ways of approaching religious knowledge. Now, at its end, has the search borne fruit? At the very least we can begin to understand why Lucian would be so dumbfounded by the early Christians' apparently groundless beliefs. Doubtless many ordinary believers did not follow the eminently rational process of conversion which has been extrapolated here from Paul's argumentative logic. Yet even if Lucian had met Paul himself and heard the Apostle's arguments, the satirist might still have remained unimpressed. On the logical plane, Paul does not argue in foundationalist terms, following syllogisms from unquestionable premises to unassailable conclusions, but tends rather to follow a coherentist logic. This means that the Apostle does not try to justify his system in terms of the dominant Greco-Roman intellectual traditions; rather, he proclaims a narrative which comes from outside those traditions and seeks to demonstrate its coherence. Hence, one who judged reasonableness in terms of elite Greco-Roman thought would likely miss the coherence in Paul's story and see only that it lacked the "proper" sort of justification. At the same time, if we asked Paul to explain Lucian's response, he would probably say that without the Spirit's aid the Gospel would always remain a stench in the satirist's nostrils. For this is how fallen humanity will, in Paul's view, always react to God's confrontation of our corrupt illusions. While Lucian would hardly accept this explanation of his sentiment, the Apostle does remind us that one's evaluation of a world view always involves a non-rational element, and that criticism of the Christian Gospel as irrational may sometimes arise from a pre-intellectual rejection of its values and its implications.

Beyond explaining this old conflict between elite philosophy and Christian belief, does Paul's way of knowing offer a viable way forward for contemporary Christian theology? I would suggest that it does. On the one hand, the Apostle's implicit epistemology is one which avoids the pitfalls of foundationalism. There is no search here for a neutral vantage point unsullied by prior beliefs and commitments. The prior story is simply assumed as a way of interpreting the world. On the other hand, Paul's narrative logic does not allow for the kind of gulf between religious dogma and lived experience which sometimes plagues confessional movements. His narrative approach to knowing implies a perennial openness to experience and novelty through which the story remains responsive to the world. What is more, Paul's balancing of confidence in the usefulness of reason with a caution about the moral corruption which can paralyze that reason offers a nuanced solution to the apparent conflict in Christian belief between faith and intellect. Coming to faith can be driven by rational thought from beginning to end. At the same time, paradigm shifts of this magnitude also involve a decision to leave one way of living and embrace a new one, a decision in which non-rational factors always intrude. Since the Christian story in particular may challenge basic human tendencies towards idolatry and control, the rational decision to embrace this narrative may be possible only where the believer exerts a moral effort to overcome these corrupt tendencies. One could thus argue that the moral effort involved in conversion is possible only with the aid of the Spirit, while at the same time insist that such conversion is (or at least can be) a fully rational process.

To say that Paul's epistemological assumptions offer theology a useful way forward, however, is not to deny that they raise new problems of their own. How, for example, would the Spirit's aid and the human will work together in the moral effort which faith requires? If Lucian's derision of the Gospel is due to his human moral corruption, is his failure to embrace the story a failure of his own will? Or does Lucian lack the Spirit's aid, perhaps because God has simply excluded him from the "elect"? We are led inevitably back to the question of predestination in Paul's thought and the place of human choice in salvation, a question upon which this study sheds no new light.

Another problem, and perhaps a more fruitful one, arises from the specifically narrative shape of the Apostle's argumentative logic. Does the Christian narrative need to be reconfigured yet again in light of the experience of the Church? We have no reason to think that Paul held his own convictions tentatively. His experience on the Damascus road and the resulting conviction that Christ was risen may have pushed him to reconfigure Israel's story, but he believed that he stood at the dawn of the new age. No further reconstruals of the narrative would be necessary before human beings could follow that story into eschatological communion with Christ and God. Yet by taking theological knowledge to be an unfolding cosmic story, a story of which we are all a part, Paul modelled a kind of reasoning which demands, in principle, that theology remain an open-ended exercise. After all, more than nineteen centuries after the Apostle's death, new chapters of that story continue to unfold in our own experience. Those who would follow Paul's narrative logic are thus left with the perpetual question of whether some new experience might force believers in Christ to reconfigure the Christian narrative once again. Moreover, since Paul understands all of human life as taking place within this story, any human experience (or cumulative set of experiences) could in principle force a reconfiguration of the narrative. If the Galatians' experience of the Spirit could constitute an interpretive "gap" in the story, so could the experiences of geologists examining rock strata or the experiences of a soldier amidst the horrors of mechanized war. Hence, Paul's theological reasoning tends to undo the usual distinction between theology "from above" and theology "from below." For neither the existing narrative nor the new event is given priority. Both must be respected and integrated into the whole.

Still, if the Apostle's logic tends to open up theology to the constant possibility of change, its distinctly narrative shape also offers a model in which tradition and the past are given great authority. The new event gains its interpretive significance from its status as another sentence in the unfolding narrative, but by the same token that new event in turn *must* be configured together with all of the earlier chapters. Paul's strenuous efforts in Gal 3–4 to show how the scriptural episodes can be read coherently in his reconstrual of the story demonstrate his conviction that, no matter how the significance of an episode might change, none can be left behind. Finally, when we consider Paul's narrative logic in light of Iser's phenomenology of reading, it becomes evident that reconfiguration of the theological narrative is a process which is endemic to its nature as narrative. So, while in Kuhn's model the emergence of a new paradigm involves the "destruction" of the old,[5] new readings of the story do not involve the rejection of the old narrative but rather its natural extension. Reconfiguration of a narrative is part of faithfulness to that story, and while old *readings* may die, this is a death brought about in some sense by the narrative itself. There is, of course, no sure way of knowing, according to this Pauline logic, when the theological story needs to be reconfigured or, when it does, which new reading of the narrative is best. In Paul's case we

---

[5] See Kuhn, *Structure*, 97–8.

can see that the debate over his reconstrual of Israel's story raged long past his death. For those who embrace Paul's kind of theological thinking there will be no rest from this type of debate while creation still groans, awaiting its redemption. In the meantime, however, what remains for "Pauline" theologians is the ongoing process of competitive narration – telling the story over and over again in the attempt to read it well, to read it coherently.

Bibliography

1. Primary Texts

1.1. Biblical Texts

Aland, Barbara, Kurt Aland, Johannes Karavidopoulos, Carlo M. Martini, and Bruce M. Metzger, eds. *Novum Testamentum Graece*. 27th ed. Stuttgart: Deutsche Bibelgesellschaft, 2001.

The Holy Bible. New Revised Standard Version. New York and Oxford: Oxford University Press, 1989.

Rahlfs, Alfred, ed. *Septuaginta*. Stuttgart: Deutsche Bibelgesellschaft, 1979.

Rudolph, W., and K. Elliger, eds. *Biblia Hebraica Stuttgartensia*. 4th ed. Stuttgart: Deutsche Bibelgesellschaft, 1990.

1.2. Other Jewish Documents

Aberbach, Moses, and Bernard Grossfeld, eds. *Targum Onkelos to Genesis: A Critical Analysis Together with an English Translation of the Text*. New York: Ktav, 1982.

Brock, S. ed. "Testamentum Iobi." Pages 19–59 in *Testamentum Iobi, Apocalypsis Baruchi Graece*. PVTG 2. Leiden: Brill, 1967.

Charles, R. H. *The Assumption of Moses*. London, A. & C. Black, 1897.

Charlesworth, James H., ed. *The Old Testament Pseudepigrapha*. 2 vols. Garden City, N.Y.: Doubleday, 1985.

———. *Papyri and Leather Manuscripts of the Odes of Solomon*. Durham: International Center for the Study of Ancient Near Eastern Civilizations and Christian Origins, Duke University, 1981.

Clarke, E. G., ed. *Targum Pseudo-Jonathan of the Pentateuch: Text and Concordance*. Hoboken, N. J.: Ktav, 1984.

Colson, F. H., and G. H. Whitaker, trans. *Philo*. 12 vols. LCL. London/Cambridge, MA: William Heinemann/Harvard University Press, 1929–1953.

Danby, H., trans. *The Mishnah: Translated from the Hebrew*. Oxford: Oxford University Press, 1933.

Denis, A.-M., ed. *Fragmenta pseudepigraphorum quae supersunt graeca*. PVTG 3. Leiden: E. J. Brill, 1970.

Epstein, I., ed. *The Babylonian Talmud*. 35 vols (repr. in 18 vols). London: Soncino, 1935–52 (repr. 1961).

Freedman, H., and Maurice Simon, eds. *Midrash Rabbah*. 10 vols. London: Soncino, 1961.

Geffcken, J. *Die Oracula Sibyllina*. GCS 8; Leipzig: J. C. Hinrich'sche Buchhandlung, 1902.

Jonge, M. de, ed. *The Testaments of the Twelve Patriarchs: A Critical Edition of the Greek Text*. PVTG 1. Leiden: E. J. Brill, 1978.

Kittel, G., and K. H. Rengstorf, eds. *Die Tosefta: Text, Übersetzung, Erklärung*. Translated by P. Freimark and W.-F. Kraemer. Rabbinische Texte. Erste Reihe. Stuttgart: Kohlhammer, 1934.

Lieberman, Saul. *The Tosefta*. 4 vols. New York: Jewish Theological Seminary, 1955–1973.

Martínez, Florentino García, and Eibert J. C. Tigchelaar, eds. *The Dead Sea Scrolls Study Edition*. 2 vols. Leiden: E. J. Brill, 1997, 1998.

Marcel Metzger, ed. *Les constitutions apostoliques: introduction, texte critique, traduction et notes*. 3 vols. Sources chrétiennes 320, 329, 336. Paris: Editions du Cerf, 1985–1987.

Neusner, Jacob, trans. *Mekhilta according to Rabbi Ishmael: An Analytical Translation*. 2 vols. Brown Judaic Studies 148, 149. Atlanta: Scholars Press, 1988.

Philonenko, M. *Joseph et Aséneth: Introduction, texte critique, traduction et notes*. Studia Post Biblica 13. Leiden: E. J. Brill, 1968.

Thackeray, H. St. J., ed. "Appendix: The Letter of Aristeas." Pages 531–606 in *An Introduction to the Old Testament in Greek*. By H. B. Swete. Cambridge, U.K.: Cambridge University Press, 1914.

———, Ralph Marcus, Allen Wikgren, and Louis H. Feldman, trans. *Josephus*. 9 vols. LCL. Cambridge, MA: Harvard University Press, 1926–1965.

Ulmer, Rivka, ed. *Pesiqta Rabbati: A Synoptic Edition of Pesiqta Rabbati Based upon All Extant Manuscripts and the Editio Princeps*. 3 vols. Atlanta: Scholars Press, 1997.

1.3. Non-Jewish Documents

Ägyptische Urkunden aus den königlichen (later *Staatlichen*) *Museen zu Berlin: Griechische Urkunden*. Berlin: Widmannsche Buchhandlung, 1895–.

Aelius Théon. *Progymnasmata*. Edited and translated by Michel Patillon with Giancarlo Bolognesi. Collection des Universités de France. Paris: Les Belles Lettres, 1997.

Aristotle. *The Art of Rhetoric*. Translated by John Henry Freese. LCL. London: Heinemann, 1926.

———. *Politics*. Translated by H. Rackham. LCL. London: Heinemann, 1944.

———. *The Nichomachean Ethics*. Translated by H. Rackham. LCL. London: Heinemann, 1947.

Arnim, Hans Friedrich August von, ed. *Stoicorum veterum fragmenta*. 4 vols. Leipzig: B. G. Tübner, 1903–1924.

Athenaeus. *The Deipnosophists*. 7 vols. Translated by Charles Burton Gulick. LCL. Cambridge, Mass.: Harvard University Press, 1987–1999.

Babbitt, Frank Cole, trans. *Plutarch's Moralia*. 14 vols. LCL. Cambridge, Mass.: Harvard University Press, 1949–1967.

Brownson, Carleton L., trans. *Xenophon*. 3 vols. LCL. Cambridge, Mass.: Harvard University Press, 1918–1922.

Bury, R. G., trans. *Sextus Empiricus*. 3 vols. LCL. London: Heinemann, 1949–1957.

Cary, Earnest, trans. *The Roman Antiquities of Dionysius of Halicarnassus*. 7 vols. LCL. Cambridge, Mass.: Harvard University Press, 1937–1956.

Cicero. *Tusculan Disputations*. Translated by J. E. King. LCL. Cambridge, Mass.: Harvard University Press, 1960.

Cohoon, J. W., trans. *Dio Chrysostom*. 5 vols. LCL. Cambridge, Mass.: Harvard University Press, 1939–1951.

Demosthenes. *Orations*. 3 vols. Translated by J. H. Vince. LCL. London: Heinemann, 1930–1935.

Diels, Hermann. *Die Fragmente der Vorsokratiker: Griechisch und Deutsch*. Edited by Walther Kranz. 5th ed. 3 vols. Berlin: Weidmannsche Buchhandlung, 1934.

Dittenberger, Wilhelm, ed. *Orientis Graeci Inscriptiones Selectae*. 2 vols. Leipzig: S. Herzel, 1903–1905.

Epictetus. *The Discourses as Reported by Arrian, Fragments, Encheiridion*. 2 vols. Translated by W. A. Oldfather. LCL. Cambridge, Mass.: Harvard University Press, 1925, 1928.

Eusebius. *Die Praeparatio Evangelica*. 2nd ed. 2 vols. Translated by Karl Mras. Berlin: Akademie, 1982–1983.

Fowler, H. N., et al., trans. *Plato*. 12 vols. LCL. London: William Heinemann, 1917–1937.

Fyfe, W. H., and W. Rhys Roberts, trans. *Aristotle: The Poetics, Longinus: On the Sublime, Demetrius: On Style*. LCL. Cambridge, Mass.: Harvard University Press, 1953.

Graeca Halensis, ed. *Dikaiomata*. Berlin: Weidmann, 1913.

Grenfell, B. P., A. Hunt, E. Turner, and M. Lenger, eds. *The Hibeh Papyri*. 2 vols. Graeco-Roman Memoirs 7, 32. London: Egypt Exploration Society, 1906, 1955.

Grenfell, B. P., A. Hunt, and H. I. Bell, eds. *The Oxyrhynchus Papyri*. 17 vols. London: Egypt Exploration Society, 1898–1927.

Grenfell, B. P., A. Hunt, and J. Gilbart Smyly, eds. *The Tebtunis Papyri*. 4 vols. London: Frowde, 1902–.

Harmon, A. M., trans. *Lucian*. 8 vols. LCL. Cambridge, Mass.: Harvard University Press, 1913–1967.

Henderson, Jeffrey, trans. *Diogenes Laertius*. 2 vols. LCL. Cambridge, Mass.: Havard University Press, 1972.

Jones, Horace Leonard, trans. *The Geography of Strabo*. 8 vols. LCL. Cambridge, Mass.: Harvard University Press, 1959.

Kenyon, F. G., and H. I. Bell, eds. *Greek Papyri in the British Museum*. 5 vols. London: British Museum, 1893–1917.

Miller, Frank Justice, trans. *Ovid, Metamorphoses*. 2 vols. LCL. London: Heinemann, 1916–1921.

Murray, A. T., trans. *The Odyssey*. 3 vols. LCL. London: Heinemann, 1946–1953.

Nixon, Paul, trans. *Plautus*. 5 vols. LCL. London: Heinemann, 1916–1938

Nock, A. D., and A.-J. Festugière. *Corpus Hermeticum*. 4 vols. 2nd ed. Paris: Société d'Édition Les Belles Lettres, 1960.

Oldfather, C. H., et al., trans. *Diodorus Siculus*. 11 vols. LCL. London: Heinemann, 1933–1957.

Ovid. *Metamorphoses*. 2 vols. Translated by Frank J. Miller. LCL. Cambridge, Mass.: Harvard University Press, 1916–1921.

Pantelia, Maria, director. *Thesaurus Linguae Graecae*. No pages. Online: http://www.tlg.uci.edu.

Perrin, Bernadotte. *Plutarch's Lives*. 11 vols. LCL. London: Heinemann, 1914–1926.

Polybius. *The Histories*. 6 vols. Translated by W. R. Paton. LCL. London: Heinemann, 1922–1927.
Sandys, John, trans. *The Odes of Pindar*. LCL. London: Heinemann, 1937.
Spengel, Leonhard von, ed. *Rhetores Graeci*. 3 vols. Leipzig: Teubner, 1853–1856.
Usher, Stephen, trans. *Dionysius of Halicarnassus: The Critical Essays*. 2 vols. LCL. Cambridge, Mass.: Harvard University Press, 1924, 1925.
Xenophon. *Cyropaedia*. 2 vols. Translated by Walter Miller. LCL. London: Heinemann, 1914.
———. *Memorabilia and Oeconomicus*. Translated by E. C. Marchant. LCL. London: Heinemann, 1923.

2. Secondary Sources

2.1. Biblical Commentaries

Abbott, T. K. *A Critical and Exegetical Commentary on the Epistles to the Ephesians and to the Colossians*. ICC. Edinburgh: T. & T. Clark, 1897.
Achtemeier, Paul J. *Romans*. Interpretation. Atlanta: John Knox Press, 1985.
Barrett, C. K. *A Commentary on the First Epistle to the Corinthians*. 2nd ed. BNTC. London: A. & C. Black, 1971.
———. *A Commentary on the Second Epistle to the Corinthians*. BNTC. London: Adam & Charles Black, 1973.
———. *The Epistle to the Romans*. Rev. ed. BNTC. Peabody, MA: Hendrickson Publishers, 1991.
Barth, Karl. *The Epistle to the Romans*. Translated from the 6th ed. by Edwyn C. Hoskyns. Oxford: Oxford University Press/London: Humphrey Milford, 1933.
———. *A Shorter Commentary on Romans*. London: SCM, 1959.
Beare, F. W. *A Commentary on the Epistle to the Philippians*. BNTC. London: Adam & Charles Black, 1959.
Best, Ernest. *A Commentary on the First and Second Epistles to the Thessalonians*. BNTC. London: Adam and Charles Black, 1972.
Betz, Hans Dieter. *Galatians: A Commentary on Paul's Letter to the Churches in Galatia*. Hermeneia. Philadelphia: Fortress Press, 1979.
Binder, Hermann. *Der Glaube bei Paulus*. Berlin: Evangelische Verlagsanstalt, 1968.
Black, Matthew. *Romans*. 2nd ed. NCBC. Grand Rapids, MI: Eerdmans/London: Marshall, Morgan & Scott, 1989.
Bockmuehl, Markus. *The Epistle to the Philippians*. BNTC. Peabody, MA: Hendrickson, 1998.
Bousset, Wilhelm. *Der Erste Brief an die Korinther*. Die Schriften des Neuen Testaments 2. 3rd ed. Göttingen: Vandenhoeck & Ruprecht, 1917.
Bruce, F. F. *The Epistle to the Galatians*. NIGTC. Grand Rapids, Mich.: William B. Eerdmans, 1982.
———. *1 & 2 Thessalonians*. WBC. Waco, Tex.: Word Books, 1982.

Brunner, Emil. *The Letter to the Romans*. Translated by H. A. Kennedy. Philadelphia: Westminster Press, 1959.

Bultmann, Rudolf. *The Second Letter to the Corinthians*. Translated by Roy A. Harrisville. Minneapolis: Augsburg Publishing House, 1985.

Burton, Ernest de Witt. *A Critical and Exegetical Commentary on the Epistle to the Galatians*. ICC. New York: Scribner's, 1920.

Byrne, Brendan. *Romans*. SP 6. Collegeville, Minn.: Liturgical Press, 1996.

Calvin, John. *Commentaries on the Epistle of Paul the Apostle to the Romans*. Translated by John Owen. Vol. 38 of *Calvin's Commentaries*. Edinburgh: Calvin Translation Society, 1845–1849.

———. *Commentaries on the Epistles of Paul the Apostle to the Corinthians*. Translated by John Pringle. 2 vols. Vols. 39 and 40 of *Calvin's Commentaries*. Edinburgh: Calvin Translation Society, 1845–1849.

———. *Commentaries on the Epistles of Paul to the Galatians and Ephesians*. Translated by John Pringle. Vol. 41 of *Calvin's Commentaries*. Edinburgh: Calvin Translation Society, 1845–1849.

Chrysostom, John. *Homilies of St. John Chrysostom on the Epistle of St. Paul to the Romans*. In vol. 11 of *NPNF*, First Series. Translated by J. B. Morris and W. H. Simcox. Revised by G. B. Stevens. Repr. Grand Rapids, Mich.: Eerdmans, 1989.

———. *Homilies of St. John Chrysostom on the First Epistle of St. Paul the Apostle to the Corinthians*. In vol. 12 of *NPNF*, First Series. Translated by Talbot W. Chambers. Repr. Grand Rapids, Mich.: Eerdmans, 1989.

———. *Homilies of St. John Chrysostom on the Second Epistle of St. Paul the Apostle to the Corinthians*. In vol. 12 of *NPNF*, First Series. Translated by Talbot W. Chambers. Repr. Grand Rapids, Mich.: Eerdmans, 1989.

Collins, Raymond F. *First Corinthians*. SP 7. Collegeville, Minn.: The Liturgical Press (Michael Glazier), 1999.

Conzelmann, Hans. *A Commentary on the First Epistle to the Corinthians*. Hermeneia. Translated by James W. Leitch. Philadelphia: Fortress Press, 1975.

Cranfield, C. E. B. *A Critical and Exegetical Commentary on the Epistle to the Romans*. 2 vols. ICC. Edinburgh: T. & T. Clark, 1975, 1979.

Dibelius, M. *A Commentary on the Epistle of James*. Revised by H. Greeven. Translated by M. A. Williams. Hermeneia. Philadelphia: Fortress Press, 1976.

Dodd, C. H. *The Epistle of Paul to the Romans*. Moffat. London: Hodder and Stoughton, 1932.

Dunn, James D. G. *The Epistle to the Galatians*. BNTC. Peabody, Mass.: Hendrickson, 1993.

———. *Romans*. 2 vols. WBC 38a–b. Dallas: Word, 1988.

Fee, Gordon D. *The First Epistle to the Corinthians*. NICNT. Grand Rapids, Mich.: William B. Eerdmans, 1987.

———. *Paul's Letter to the Philippians*. NICNT. Grand Rapids, Mich.: William B. Eerdmans, 1995.

Fitzmyer, Joseph A. *Romans*. AB 33. New York: Doubleday, 1993.

Frame, James Everett. *A Critical and Exegetical Commentary on the Epistles of St. Paul to the Thessalonians*. ICC. Edinburgh: T. & T. Clark, 1912.

Fung, Ronald Y. K. *The Epistle to the Galatians*. NICNT. Grand Rapids, MI: William B. Eerdmans, 1988.

Furnish, Victor Paul. *II Corinthians: A New Translation with Introduction and Commentary*. AB 32A. Garden City, N.Y.: Doubleday, 1984.

Garland, David E. *1 Corinthians*. BECNT. Grand Rapids, Mich.: Baker Academic, 2003.

Harris, Murray J. *Colossians & Philemon*. Exegetical Guides to the Greek New Testament. Grand Rapids, Mich.: Eerdmans, 1991.

Hays, Richard B. *First Corinthians*. Interpretation. Louisville: Westminster John Knox, 1997.

Holtz, Traugott. *Der Erste Brief an die Thessalonicher*. 2. Auflage. EKK 13. Zürich: Benziger/ Neukirchen-Vluyn: Neukirchener, 1990.

Käsemann, Ernst. *Commentary on Romans*. Translated by Geoffrey W. Bromiley. Grand Rapids, Mich.: Eerdmans, 1980.

Lagrange, M.-J. *Saint Paul: Épître aux Romains*. Études Bibliques. 3rd ed. Paris: Lecoffre, 1922.

———. *Épître aux Galates*. 3rd ed. Paris: Lecoffre, 1926.

Lietzmann, H. *An die Galater*. 4th ed. Tübingen: J. C. B. Mohr (Paul Siebeck), 1971.

Lightfoot, Joseph Barber. *Notes on the Epistles of St. Paul*. Repr. Peabody, Mass.: Hendrickson, 1999.

———. *Saint Paul's Epistle to the Galatians: A Revised Text with Introduction, Notes and Dissertations*. Repr. Peabody, Mass.: Hendrickson, 1999.

———. *Saint Paul's Epistles to the Colossians and to Philemon*. Repr. Peabody, Mass.: Hendrickson, 1999.

Lohse, Eduard. *A Commentary on the Epistles to the Colossians and Philemon*. Translated by William R. Poehlmann and Robert J. Karris. Hermeneia. Philadelphia: Fortress Press, 1971.

Longenecker, Richard N. *Galatians*. WBC 41. Dallas, Tex.: Word, 1990.

Lührmann, Dieter. *Galatians: A Continental Commentary*. Translated by O. C. Dean, Jr. Minneapolis: Fortress Press, 1992.

MacDonald, Margaret Y. *Colossians and Ephesians*. SR 17. Collegeville, Minn.: Liturgical Press, 2000.

Martin, Ralph P. *2 Corinthians*. WBC 40. Waco, Tex.: Word Books, 1986.

Martyn, J. Louis. *Galatians: A New Translation with Introduction and Commentary*. AB 33a. New York and London: Doubleday, 1997.

Matera, Frank J. *Galatians*. Sacra Pagina 9. Collegeville, Minn.: Liturgical Press, 1992.

Mays, James Luther. *Hosea: A Commentary*. OTL. Philadelphia: Westminster Press, 1969.

Metzger, Bruce M. *A Textual Commentary on the Greek New Testament*. 2nd Edition. Stuttgart: Deutsche Bibelgesellschaft, 1994.

Michel, Otto. *Der Brief an die Römer*. 12th ed. Kritisch-exegetischer Kommentar über das Neue Testament. Göttingen: Vandenhock & Ruprecht, 1963.

Moo, Douglas J. *The Epistle to the Romans*. NICNT. Grand Rapids, Mich.: William B. Eerdmans, 1996.

Morris, Leon. *The First and Second Epistles to the Thessalonians*. Rev. ed. NICNT. Grand Rapids, Mich.: William B. Eerdmans, 1991.

Murray, John. *The Epistle to the Romans: The English Text with Introduction, Exposition and Notes*. NICNT. 2 vols. Grand Rapids, Mich.: William B. Eerdmans, 1959, 1965.

Mussner, F. *Der Galaterbrief.* HTK 9. Freiburg: Herder, 1974.

Oepke, A. *Der Brief des Paulus an die Galater.* THKNT 9. Berlin: Evangelische Verlagsanstalt, 1973.

Robertson, Archibald, and Alfred Plummer. *A Critical and Exegetical Commentary on the First Epistle of St. Paul to the Corinthians.* Edinburgh: T. & T. Clark, 1911.

Robinson, J. Armitage. *St. Paul's Epistle to the Ephesians.* London: Macmillan, 1903.

Sanday, William, and Arthur C. Headlam. *A Critical and Exegetical Commentary on the Epistle to the Romans.* ICC. New York: Charles Scribner's Sons, 1895.

Schlier, Heinrich. *Der Brief an die Galater.* KEK 7. Göttingen: Vandenhoeck & Ruprecht, 1962.

————. *Der Römerbrief.* HTK 6. Freiburg/Basel/Wien: Herder, 1977.

Schreiner, Thomas R. *Romans.* BECNT. Grand Rapids, MI: Baker Books, 1998.

Soards, Marion L. *1 Corinthians.* NIBC. Peabody, Mass.: Hendrickson/Carlisle, U.K.: Paternoster Press, 1999.

Thiselton, Anthony C. *The First Epistle to the Corinthians: A Commentary on the Greek Text.* NIGTC. Grand Rapids, Mich.: William B. Eerdmans/Carlisle, U.K.: Paternoster Press, 2000.

Thrall, Margaret E. *A Critical and Exegetical Commentary on the Second Epistle to the Corinthians.* 2 vols. ICC. Edinburgh: T. & T. Clark, 1994, 2000.

Wilckens, Ulrich. *Der Brief an die Römer.* 3 vols. EKK 6.1–3. Zürich: Benziger Verlag/Neukirchen-Vluyn: Neukirchener Verlag, 1978, 1980, 1982.

Zimmerli, W. *A Commentary on the Book of the Prophet Ezekiel, Chapters 1–24.* Translated by R. E. Clements. Hermeneia. Philadelphia: Fortress, 1979.

2.2. Other Secondary Works

Aageson, J. W. *Written Also for Our Sake: Paul and the Art of Biblical Interpretation.* Lousiville, Ky.: Westminster/John Knox Press, 1993.

Abegg, Martin G., Jr. "4QMMT C 27, 31 and 'Works Righteousness.'" *DSD* 6 (1999): 139–147.

Adams, Edward. "Paul's Story of God and Creation: The Story of How God Fulfils His Purposes in Creation." Pages 19–43 in *Narrative Dynamics in Paul: A Critical Assessment.* Edited by B. W. Longenecker. Louisville & London: Westminster John Knox Press, 2002.

Alexander, Philip S. "Torah and Salvation in Tannaitic Literature." Pages 261–301 in *Justification and Variegated Nomism: A Fresh Appraisal of Paul and Second Temple Judaism.* Vol. 1, *The Complexities of Second Temple Judaism.* Edited by D. A. Carson, P. T. O'Brien, and M. A. Seifrid. WUNT 2.140. Tübingen: Mohr Siebeck/Grand Rapids, Mich.: Baker Academic, 2001.

Aquinas, Thomas. *Summa Theologica.* 3 vols. Translated by the Fathers of the English Dominican Province. New York: Benziger Brothers, 1947–1948.

Armstrong, Claude B. "St. Paul's Theory of Knowledge." *Christian Quarterly Review* 154 (1953): 438–452.

Austin, J. L. *How to Do Things With Words.* 1st ed. Cambridge, Mass.: Harvard University Press, 1962.

Averbeck, R. E. "Tabernacle." Pages 807–827 in *Dictionary of the Old Testament: Pentateuch.* Edited by T. Desmond Alexander and David W. Baker. Downers Grove, Ill.: InterVarsity Press, 2003.

Baillie, John. *Our Knowledge of God.* New York: Charles Scribner's Sons, 1959.

Bammel, E. "Gottes ΔΙΑΘΗΚΗ (Gal. III. 15–17) und das jüdische Rechtsdenken." *NTS* 6 (1959–1960): 313–19.

Barclay, John M. G. *Obeying the Truth: A Study of Paul's Ethics in Galatians.* Edinburgh: T. & T. Clark, 1988.

———. "Paul's Story: Theology as Testimony." Pages 133–56 in *Narrative Dynamics in Paul: A Critical Assessment.* Edited by B. W. Longenecker. Louisville & London: Westminster John Knox Press, 2002.

Barclay, William. *Flesh and Spirit: An Examination of Galatians 5:19–23.* Nashville: Abingdon Press, 1962.

Barnett, P. W. "Apostle." Pages 45–51 in *Dictionary of Paul and His Letters.* Edited by G. F. Hawthorne and R. P. Martin. Downers Grove, Ill.: InterVarsity Press, 1993.

Barr, J. *The Semantics of Biblical Language.* London: Oxford University Press, 1961.

Barrett, C. K. "The Allegory of Abraham, Sarah, and Hagar in the Argument of Galatians." Pages 1–16 in *Rechtfertigung.* Edited by J. Friedrich, W. Pohlmann, and P. Stuhlmacher. Tübingen: J. C. B. Mohr (Paul Siebeck), 1976.

———. *Freedom and Obligation: A Study of the Epistle to the Galatians.* London: SPCK, 1985.

Barth, M. "The Faith of the Messiah." *Heythrop Journal* 10 (1969): 363–370.

Bauckham, Richard. *God Crucified: Monotheism & Christology in the New Testament.* Grand Rapids, Ill.: Eerdmans, 1998.

———. "Apocalypses." Pages 135–87 in *The Complexities of Second Temple Judaism.* Vol. 1 of *Justification and Variegated Nomism: A Fresh Appraisal of Paul and Second Temple Judaism.* Edited by D. A. Carson, P. T. O'Brien, and M. A. Seifrid. WUNT 2.140. Tübingen: Mohr Siebeck/Grand Rapids, Mich.: Baker Academic, 2001.

Beardslee, W. A. "Narrative Form in the NT and Process Theology." *Encounter* 36 (1975): 301–315.

Becker, Jürgen. *Paul: Apostle to the Gentiles.* Translated by O. C. Jr. Dean. Louisville, Ky.: Westminster/John Knox, 1993. Translation of *Paulus: Der Apostel der Völker.* J. C. B. Mohr (Paul Siebeck), 1989.

Beker, J. Christiaan. *Paul the Apostle: The Triumph of God in Life and Thought.* Philadelphia: Fortress, 1980.

Bell, Richard H. *No One Seeks for God: An Exegetical and Theological Study of Romans 1:18–320.* WUNT 106. Tübingen: J.C.B. Mohr (Paul Siebeck), 1998.

Berger, K. "Abraham in den paulinischen Hauptbriefen." *Münchener Theologische Zeitschrift* 17 (1966): 47–89.

Betz, H. D. "The Foundations of Christian Ethics according to Romans 12:1–2." Pages 55–72 in *Witness and Existence: Essays in Honor of Schubert M. Ogden.* Edited by P. E. Devenish and G. L. Goodwin. Chicago: University of Chicago, 1989.

Blass, F., and A. Debrunner. *A Greek Grammar of the New Testament and Other Early Christian Literature.* Translated and revised by Robert W. Funk. Chicago and London: University of Chicago Press, 1961.

Blinzler, J. "Lexicalisches zu dem Terminus τὰ στοιχεῖα τοῦ κόσμου bei Paulus." Pages 429–443 in *Studiorum Paulinorum Congressus Internationalis Catholicus 1961.* Vol. 2. *AnBib* 18. Rome: Pontifical Biblical Institute, 1963.

Bockmuehl, Markus. *Revelation and Mystery in Ancient Judaism and Pauline Christianity.* WUNT 2. Reihe 36. Tübingen: J. C. B. Mohr (Paul Siebeck), 1990.

Bonneau, Norman. "The Curse of the Law in Gal. 3:10–14." *NovT* 39 (1997): 60–80.

Boomershine, Thomas E. "Epistemology at the Turn of the Ages in Paul, Jesus, and Mark: Rhetoric and Dialectic in Apocalyptic and the New Testament." Pages 147–67 in *Apocalyptic and the New Testament: Studies in Honor of J. Louis Martyn.* Edited by Joel Marcus and Marion L. Soards. Sheffield: JSOT Press, 1989.

Borgen, P. "Paulus Preaches Circumcision and Pleases Men." Pages 37–46 in *Paul and Paulinism: Essays in Honour of C. K. Barrett.* Edited by M. D. Hooker and S. G. Wilson. London: SPCK, 1982.

Bornkamm, Günther. "Faith and Reason in Paul." Pages 29–46 in *Early Christian Experience.* New York/Evanston: Harper & Row, 1969.

———. *Paul.* Translated by D. M. G. Stalker. New York/Evanston: Harper & Row, 1971.

Botterweck, G. Johannes, and Heinrich Zimmerman. "Knowledge of God in the Old Testament." Pages 472–4 in *Encyclopedia of Biblical Theology.* Edited by J. B. Bauer. London: Sheed & Ward, 1970.

Bousset, W. *Kyrios Christos.* Nashville: Abingdon Press, 1970.

Brawley, R. L. "Contextuality, Intertextuality, and the Hendiadic Relationship of Promise and Law in Galatians." *ZNW* 93:1–2 (2002): 99–119.

Brinsmead, B. H. *Galatians:Dialogical Response to Opponents.* SBLDS 65. Chico, Calif.: Scholars Press, 1982.

Bryant, R. A. *The Risen Crucified Christ in Galatians.* SBLDS 185. Atlanta: Society of Biblical Literature, 2001.

Büchsel, Friedrich. "ἀλληγορέω." Pages 260–63 in *TDNT.* Vol. 1.

———. "εἴδωλον, κτλ." Pages 375–380 in *TDNT.* Vol. 2.

Bultmann, Rudolf. "γινώσκω, κτλ." Pages 689–716 in *TDNT.* Vol. 1.

———. *Jesus Christ and Mythology.* New York: Scribner, 1958.

———. "Karl Barth, *The Resurrection of the Dead.*" Pages 66–94 in *Faith and Understanding.* Vol. 1. Edited by R. W. Funk. Translated by L. P. Smith. New York: Harper & Row, 1969.

———. *Der Stil der paulinischen Predigt und die kynisch-stoische Diatribe.* Göttingen: Vandenhoeck & Ruprecht, 1910.

———. *Theology of the New Testament.* 2 vols. Translated by Kendrick Grobel. New York: Charles Scribners Sons, 1951, 1955.

———. "Zur Auslegung von Galater 2, 15–18." Pages 394–9 in *Exegetica.* Tübingen: J. C. B. Mohr (Paul Siebeck), 1967.

Burdick, Donald W. "Οἶδα and Γινώσκω in the Pauline Epistles." Pages 344–56 in *New Dimensions in New Testament Study.* Edited by R. N. Longenecker and M. C. Tenney. Grand Rapids, Mich.: Zondervan, 1974.

Byrne, B. *Reckoning with Romans.* Wilmington, Del.: Glazier, 1986.

Caird, G. B. *Paul's Letters from Prison.* Oxford: Oxford University Press, 1976.

Callan, T. "Pauline Midrash: The Exegetical Background of Gal. 3:19b." *JBL* 99 (1980): 549–567.

Campbell, Douglas A. "The Story of Jesus in Romans and Galatians." Pages 97–124 in *Narrative Dynamics in Paul: A Critical Assessment*. Edited by Bruce W. Longenecker. Louisville: Westminster John Knox, 2002.

Campbell, R. A. "'Against such things there is no law?' Galatians 5:23b Again." *ExpTim* 107 (1996): 271–272.

Carter, Philippa. *The Servant-Ethic in the New Testament*. American University Studies. Theology and Religion 196. New York: Peter Lang, 1999.

Ciholas, Paul. "Knowledge and Faith: Pauline Platonisms and the Spiritualization of Reality." *Perspectives in Religious Studies* 3 (1976): 188–201.

Coffey, David M. "Natural Knowledge of God: Reflections on Romans 1:18–32." *TS* 31 (1970): 674–691.

Cosgrove, C. H. *The Cross and the Spirit: A Study in the Argument and Theology of Galatians*. Macon, Ga.: Mercer University Press, 1988.

———. "Arguing Like a Mere Human Being: Galatians iii.15–18 in Rhetorical Perspective." *NTS* 34 (1988): 536–549.

Cranfield, C. E. B. "St. Paul and the Law." *SJT* 17 (1964): 43–68.

Cranford, Michael. "The Possibility of Perfect Obedience: Paul and an Implied Premise in Galatians 3:10 and 5:3." *NovT* 36 (1994): 242–258.

Crites, Stephen. "Angels We Have Heard." In *Religion as Story*, edited by J. B. Wiggins, 22–63. New York: Harper & Row, 1975.

Cullmann, Oscar. *Christ and Time*. Revised. Philadelphia: Westminster, 1964.

———. *Salvation in History*. New York: Harper & Row, 1967.

Cuppitt, D. *What Is A Story?* London: SCM, 1991.

Danker, Frederick William, ed. *A Greek–English Lexicon of the New Testament and Other Early Christian Literature*. 3rd ed. Chicago and London: University of Chicago Press, 2000.

Dautzenberg, Gerhard. "Botschaft und Bedeutung der urchristlichen Prophetie nach dem ersten Korintherbrief (2:6–16; 12–14)." Pages 131–61 in *Prophetic Vocation in the New Testament and Today*. Edited by Johannes Panagopoulos. NovTSup 45. Leiden: E. J. Brill, 1977.

Davies, W. D. "A Note on Josephus, Antiquities 14.136." *HTR* 47 (1954): 135–140.

———. "Paul and the Dead Sea Scrolls: Flesh and Spirit." Pages 157–82 in *The Scrolls and the New Testament*. Edited by K. Stendahl. New York: Harper, 1957.

———. *Paul and Rabbinic Judaism: Some Rabbinic Elements in Pauline Theology*. 4th ed. Philadelphia: Fortress Press, 1980.

———. *Torah in the Messianic Age and/or the Age to Come*. JBL Monograph Series 7. Philadelphia: Society of Biblical Literature, 1952.

Davis, Basil S. *Christ as Devotio: The Argument of Galatians 3:1–14*. Lanham, Md./New York/Oxford: University Press of America, 2002.

Davis, James A. *Wisdom and Spirit : An Investigation of 1 Corinthians 1.18–3.20 against the Background of Jewish Sapiential Traditions in the Greco-Roman Period*. Lanham, Md.: University Press of America, 1984.

Deissmann, Adolf. *Light From the Ancient East*. 2nd ed. Translated by Lionel R. M. Strachan. New York: Hodder and Stoughton, 1910.

Delling, Gerhard. "στοιχεῖον." Pages 670–687 in *TDNT*. Vol. 7.

Dodd, C. H. *According to the Scriptures: The Sub-Structure of New Testament Theology*. London: Lowe and Brydone, 1952.

———. *The Apostolic Preaching and Its Developments*. New York: Harper & Bros., 1936.

———. *The Bible and the Greeks*. London: Hodder & Stoughton, 1935.

———. "ΕΝΝΟΜΟΣ ΧΡΙΣΤΟΥ." Pages 134–48 in *More New Testament Studies*. Manchester: Manchester University Press, 1968.

Dodds, E. R. *The Greeks and the Irrational*. Berkeley, Calif.: University of California Press, 1951.

Drane, John W. *Paul: Libertine or Legalist?* London: SPCK, 1975.

Dray, W. H. "On the Nature and Role of Narrative in History." Pages 25–39 in *The History and Narrative Reader*. Edited by Geoffrey Roberts. London and New York: Routledge, 2001.

Dunn, James D. G. "4QMMT and Galatians." *NTS* 43 (1997): 147–153.

———. *Jesus and the Spirit*. London: SCM, 1975.

———. "'A Light to the Gentiles': The Significance of the Damascus Road Christophany for Paul." Pages 89–107 in *Jesus, Paul and the Law: Studies in Mark and Galatians*. Louisville, KY: Westminster/John Knox, 1990.

———. "The Narrative Approach to Paul: Whose Story?" Pages 217–30 in *Narrative Dynamics in Paul: A Critical Assessment*. Louisville & London: Westminster John Knox, 2002.

———. "Once More, ΠΙΣΤΙΣ ΧΡΙΣΤΟΥ." Pages 730–44 in *Society of Biblical Literature 1991 Seminar Papers*. Edited by E. H. Lovering, Jr. Atlanta: Scholars Press, 1991.

———. *The Theology of Paul the Apostle*. Grand Rapids, Mich/Cambridge, U.K.: William B. Eerdmans, 1998.

Du Plessis, Paul Johannes. *Teleios: The Idea of Perfection in the New Testament*. Kampen: J. H. Kos, 1959.

Dupont, Jacques. *Gnosis: La connaissance religieuse dans les Épitres de Saint Paul*. Bruges: Desclée de Brouwer, 1949.

Durham, B. D. *Vocabulary of Menander*. Princeton: University Press, 1913.

Du Toit, Andreas B. "Vilification as a Pragmatic Device in Early Christian Epistolography." *Biblica* 75 (1994): 403–412.

Eckert, Jost. *Die urchristliche Verkündigung im Streit zwischen Paulus und seinen Gegnern nach dem Galaterbrief*. Münchener Universitäts-Schriften. Biblische Untersuchungen 6. Regensburg: Verlag Friedrich Pustet, 1971.

Eckstein, Hans-Joachim. *Verheißung und Gesetz: Eine Exegetische Untersuchung zu Galater 2,15–4,7*. WUNT 86. Tübingen: Mohr Siebeck, 1996.

———. *Der Begriff* Syneidesis *bei Paulus: Eine neutestamentlich-exegetische Untersuchung zum Gewissensbegriff*. WUNT 2.10. J. C. B. Mohr (Paul Siebeck), 1983.

Eco, Umberto. *Foucault's Pendulum*. Translated by William Weaver. New York: Ballantine, 1989.

———. *A Theory of Semiotics*. Advances in Semiotics. Bloomington, Ind.: Indiana University Press, 1976.

Erickson, Richard J. "Flesh." Pages 303–6 in *Dictionary of Paul and His Letters*. Edited by G. F. Hawthorne and R. P. Martin. Downers Grove, Ill.: InterVarsity, 1993.

Evans, Craig A. "Scripture-Based Stories in the Pseudepigrapha." Pages 57–72 in *The Complexities of Second Temple Judaism*. Vol. 1 of *Justification and Variegated Nomism: A Fresh Appraisal of Paul and Second Temple Judaism*. Edited by D. A. Carson, P. T. O'Brien, and M. A. Seifrid. WUNT 2.140. Tübingen: Mohr Siebeck/Grand Rapids, Mich.: Baker Academic, 2001.

Evans, C. F. "Rom 12:1–2: The True Worship." Pages 7–33 in *Dimensions de la vie chrétienne*. Edited by L. de Lorenzi. Rome: Abbaye de S. Paul, 1979.

Falk, Daniel. "Psalms and Prayers." Pages 7–56 in *The Complexities of Second Temple Judaism*. Vol. 1 of *Justification and Variegated Nomism: A Fresh Appraisal of Paul and Second Temple Judaism*. WUNT 2.140. Tübingen: Mohr Siebeck/Grand Rapids, Mich.: Baker Academic, 2001.

Fatehi, Mehrdad. *The Spirit's Relation to the Risen Lord in Paul*. WUNT 2.128. Tübingen: Mohr Siebeck, 2000.

Fischer, James A. "Pauline Literary Forms and Thought Patterns." *CBQ* 39 (1977): 209–223.

Fitzmyer, Joseph A. "Crucifixion in Ancient Palestine, Qumran Literature and the New Testament." *CBQ* 40 (1978): 493–513.

————. *The Genesis Apocryphon of Qumran Cave I: A Commentary*. Biblica et orientalia 18. Rome: Biblical Institute Press, 1971.

Fowl, S. "Some Uses of Story in Moral Discourse: Reflections on Paul's Moral Discourse and Our Own." *Modern Theology* 4 (1988): 293–309.

————. *The Story of Christ in the Ethics of Paul: An Analysis of the Function of the Hymnic Material in the Pauline Corpus*. JSNT Supp. 36. Sheffield: JSOT Press, 1990.

Frei, Hans W. *The Eclipse of Biblical Narrative: A Study in Eighteenth and Nineteenth Century Hermeneutics*. New Haven and London: Yale University Press, 1974.

Frye, Northrop. *Anatomy of Criticism*. Princeton: Princeton University Press, 1957.

————. *Fables of Identity: Studies in Poetic Mythology*. New York: Harcourt, Brace & World, 1963.

Fuller, Daniel P. "Paul and 'Works of the Law.'" *WTJ* 38 (1975): 28–42.

Furnish, Victor Paul. *Theology & Ethics in Paul*. Nashville: Abingdon Press, 1968.

Gallie, W. B. "Narrative and Historical Understanding." Pages 40–51 in *The History and Narrative Reader*, edited by Geoffrey Roberts. London and New York: Routledge, 2001.

————. *Philosophy and the Historical Understanding*. New York: Schocken Books, 1964.

Gärtner, Bertil E. "The Pauline and Johannine Idea of 'To Know God' against the Hellenistic Background: The Greek Philosophical Principle 'Like by Like' in Paul and John." *NTS* 14 (1968): 209–231.

Gaston, L. *Paul and the Torah*. Vancouver: University of British Columbia Press, 1987.

Gathercole, Simon J. *Where Is Boasting? Early Jewish Soteriology and Paul's Response in Romans 1–5*. Grand Rapids, Mich.: William B. Eerdmans, 2002.

Gillespie, Thomas W. "Interpreting the Kerygma: Early Christian Prophecy According to 1 Corinthians 2:6–16." Pages 151–66 in *Gospel Origins and Christian Beginnings: Essays in Honor of James M. Robinson*. Edited by J. Goehring, et al. Sonoma, Calif.: Polebridge Press, 1990.

Given, Mark D. *Paul's True Rhetoric: Ambiguity, Cunning, and Deception in Greece and Rome*. Emory Studies in Early Christianity. Harrisburg, Pa.: Trinity Press International, 2001.

Goldberg, Michael. *Theology and Narrative: A Critical Introduction.* Nashville: Abingdon, 1982.

Gooch, Paul W. "'Conscience' in 1 Corinthians 8 and 10." *NTS* 33 (1987): 244–54.

———. *Partial Knowledge: Philosophical Studies in Paul.* Notre Dame, Ind.: University of Notre Dame Press, 1987.

Goodenough, Erwin R., with A. Thomas Kraabel. "Paul and the Hellenization of Christianity." Pages 23–70 in *Religions in Antiquity: Essays in Memory of E. R. Goodenough.* Edited by J. Neusner. Leiden: E. J. Brill, 1968.

Gyllenberg, Rafael. "Glaube bei Paulus." *ZST* 13 (1936): 613–630.

Grundmann, Walter. "The Christ Statements of the New Testament." Pages 527–80 in *TDNT.* Vol. 9.

Hansen, G. W. *Abraham in Galatians: Epistolary and Rhetorical Contexts.* JSNTSS 29. Sheffield: JSOT Press, 1989.

Hanson, A. T. *Paul's Understanding of Jesus.* Hull, UK: The University, 1963.

Harrelson, Walter. "Knowledge of God in the Church." *Int* 30 (1976): 12–17.

Hauerwas, Stanley. "Character, Narrative, and Growth in the Christian Life." Pages 221–54 in *The Hauerwas Reader.* Edited by J. Burkman and M. Cartwright. Durham, N.C./London: Duke University Press, 2001.

———. "How 'Christian Ethics' Came to Be." Pages 37–50 in *The Hauerwas Reader.* Edited by J. Burkman and M. Cartwright. Durham, N.C./London: Duke University Press, 2001.

———. "Reforming Christian Social Ethics: Ten Theses." Pages 111–15 in *The Hauerwas Reader.* Edited by J. Burkman and M. Cartwright. Durham, N. C./London: Duke University Press, 2001.

———. *The Peaceable Kingdom: A Primer in Christian Ethics.* Notre Dame, Ind./London: University of Notre Dame Press, 1983.

———. "Vision, Stories, and Character." Pages 165–70 in *The Hauerwas Reader.* Edited by J. Burkman and M. Cartwright. Durham, N.C./London: Duke University Press, 2001.

Haussleiter, J. "Der Glaube Jesu Christi und der christliche Glaube: ein Beitrag zur Erklärung des Römerbriefs." *Neue kirchliche Zeitschrift* 2 (1891): 109–145, 205–230.

Hays, Richard B. "Christology and Ethics in Galatians: The Law of Christ." *CBQ* 49 (1987): 268–290.

———. *The Faith of Jesus Christ: An Investigation of the Narrative Substructure of Galatians 3:1–4:11.* SBLDS 56. Chico, Calif.: Scholars Press, 1983.

———. "ΠΙΣΤΙΣ and Pauline Christology: What Is at Stake?" Pages 714–29 in *Society of Biblical Literature 1991 Seminar Papers.* Edited by E. H. Lovering, Jr. Atlanta: Scholars Press, 1991.

Hebert, A. G. "'Faithfulness' and 'Faith.'" *Theology* 58 (1955): 373–379.

Hester, J. D. "The Rhetorical Structure of Galatians 1:11–2:14." *JBL* 103 (1984): 223–233.

Hofius, O. "Das Gesetz des Mose und das Gesetz Christi." Pages 50–74 in *Paulusstudien,* 50–74. WUNT 51. Tübingen: J. C. B. Mohr (Paul Siebeck), 1989.

Hooker, Morna D. "Adam in Romans I." *NTS* 6 (1959–1960): 297–306.

———. "'Heirs of Abraham': The Gentiles' Role in Israel's Story: A Response to Bruce W. Longenecker." Pages 85–96 in *Narrative Dynamics in Paul: A Critical Assessment.* Edited by B. W. Longenecker. Louisville/London: Westminster John Knox, 2002.

————. "Interchange in Christ." Pages 13–25 in *From Adam to Christ: Essays on Paul*. Cambridge: Cambridge University Press, 1990.

————. "ΠΙΣΤΙΣ ΧΡΙΣΤΟΥ." *NTS* 35 (1989): 321–342.

Horrell, David G. "Paul's Narratives or Narrative Substructure? The Significance of 'Paul's Story.'" Pages 157–71 in *Narrative Dynamics in Paul: A Critical Assessment*. Edited by B. W. Longenecker. Louisville/London: Westminster John Knox, 2002.

Howard, George. "The 'Faith of Christ.'" *ExpTim* 85 (1973–1974): 212–214.

————. "On the 'Faith of Christ.'" *HTR* 60 (1967): 459–465.

————. *Paul: Crisis in Galatia: A Study in Early Christian Theology*. SNTSMS 35. Cambridge, U.K.: Cambridge University Press, 1979.

————. "Romans 3:21–31 and the Inclusion of the Gentiles." *HTR* 63 (1970): 223–234.

Hübner, H. *Law in Paul's Thought*. Edinburgh: T&T Clark, 1984.

Hultgren, Arland J. "The *Pistis Christou* Formula in Paul." *NovT* 22:3 (1980): 248–263.

Hunt, Allen Rhea. *The Inspired Body: Paul, the Corinthians, and Divine Inspiration*. Macon, Ga.: Mercer University Press, 1996.

Iser, Wolfgang. *The Implied Reader: Patterns of Communication in Prose Fiction from Bunyan to Beckett*. Baltimore: Johns Hopkins University Press, 1974.

Jegher-Bucher, Verena. *Der Galaterbrief auf dem Hintergrund antiker Epistolographie und Rhetorik: Ein anderes Paulusbild*. AThANT 78. Zürich: Theologischer Verlag Zürich, 1991.

Jewett, Robert. *Paul's Anthropological Terms: A Study of Their Use in Conflict Settings*. AGJU 10. Leiden: E. J. Brill, 1971.

————. *The Thessalonian Correspondence: Pauline Rhetoric and Millenarian Piety*. Foundations and Facets. Philadelphia: Fortress Press, 1986.

Jobes, K. H. "Jerusalem, Our Mother: Metalepsis and Intertextuality in Galatians 4.21–31." *WTJ* 55 (1993): 299–320.

Johnson, Luke Timothy. "Rom. 3:21–26 and the Faith of Jesus." *CBQ* 44 (1982): 77–90.

Johnson, W. "The Paradigm of Abraham in Galatians 3:6–9." *TrinJ* 8 NS (1987): 179–199.

Kamlah, Erhard. *Die Form der katalogischen Paränese im Neuen Testament*. WUNT 7. Tübingen: J. C. B. Mohr (Paul Siebeck), 1964.

Keck, Leander E. "Paul as Thinker." *Int* 47 (1993): 27–38.

Keesmaat, S. C. *Paul and His Story: (Re)interpreting the Exodus Tradition*. JSNT Supp. 181. Sheffield: Sheffield Academic Press, 1999.

Kim, Seyoong. *The Origins of Paul's Gospel*. WUNT 2.4. Tübingen: J. C. B. Mohr (Paul Siebeck), 1981.

Kittel, Gerhard. "Πίστις Ἰησοῦ Χριστοῦ bei Paulus." *TSK* 79 (1906): 419–436.

Klein, Günther. "Individualgeschichte und Weltgeschichte bei Paulus." Pages 180–224 in *Rekonstruktion und Interpretation bei Paulus: Gesammelte Aufsätze zum Neuen Testament*. München: Chr. Kaiser Verlag, 1969.

Koehler, Ludwig, and Walter Baumgartner. *The Hebrew and Aramaic Lexicon of the Old Testament*. Revised by Walter Baumgartner and Johann Jakob Stamm. Translated by M. E. J. Richardson. Study Edition. 2 vols. Leiden/Boston/Köln: E. J. Brill, 1994–2000.

Kovacs, J. L. "The Archons, the Spirit, and the Death of Christ: Do We Need the Hypothesis of Gnostic Opponents to Explain 1 Corinthians 2:6–16?" Pages 217–36 in *Apocalyptic and the New Testament*. Edited by J. Marcus and M. L. Soards. Sheffield: JSOT Press, 1989.

Lambrecht, Jan. "Abraham and His Offspring: A Comparison of Galatians 5,1 with 3,13." *Biblica* 80:4 (1999): 525–536.

———. "Paul's Reasoning in Galatians 2:11–21". Pages 53–75 in *Paul and the Mosaic Law*. Edited by J. D. G. Dunn. Grand Rapids, Mich./Cambridge: William B. Eerdmans, 1996.

———. "Transgressor by Nullifying God's Grace: A Study of Gal 2,18–21." *Biblica* 72 (1991): 217–236.

———. "Unreal Conditions in the Letters of Paul: A Clarification." *ETL* 63 (1987): 153–156.

Leisegang, Hans. *Der Apostel Paulus als Denker*. Leipzig: J. C. Hinrichs'sche Buchhandlung, 1923.

Levenson, J. *Creation and the Persistence of Evil*. 2nd ed. Princeton, N.J.: Princeton University Press, 1994.

Liddell, Henry George, and Robert Scott. *A Greek–English Lexicon*. 9th ed. Revised by Henry Stuart Jones and Roderick McKenzie. Oxford: Clarendon Press, 1940.

Lincoln, Andrew T. "The Stories of Predecessors and Inheritors in Galatians and Romans." Pages 172–203 in *Narrative Dynamics in Paul: A Critical Assessment*. Edited by B. W. Longenecker. Louisville/London: Westminster John Knox, 2002.

Löfstedt, T. "The Allegory of Hagar & Sarah: Gal 4.21–31." *EstBib* 58:4 (2000): 475–494.

Lonergan, Bernard J. F. *Insight: A Study of Human Understanding*. New York: Philosophical Library/London: Longmans, 1958.

Long, A. A. *Hellenistic Philosophy: Stoics, Epicureans, Sceptics*. 2nd ed. London: Duckworth, 1986.

Longenecker, Bruce W. "Defining the Faithful Character of the Covenant Community: Galatians 2.15–21 and Beyond." Pages 75–98 in *Paul and the Mosaic Law*. Edited by J. D. G. Dunn. Grand Rapids, Mich./Cambridge, U.K.: William B. Eerdmans, 1996.

———. *Eschatology and the Covenant: A Comparison of 4 Ezra and Romans 1–11*. JSNT Supp. 57. Sheffield: JSOT Press, 1991.

———. "Narrative Interest in the Study of Paul: Retrospective and Prospective." Pages 3–16 in *Narrative Dynamics in Paul: A Critical Assessment*. Edited by B. W. Longenecker. Louisville/London: Westminster John Knox, 2002.

———. "Sharing in Their Spiritual Blessings? The Stories of Israel in Galatians and Romans." Pages 58–84 in *Narrative Dynamics in Paul: A Critical Assessment*. Edited by B. W. Longenecker. Louisville/London: Westminster John Knox, 2002.

———. *The Triumph of Abraham's God: The Transformation of Identity in Galatians*. Edinburgh: T. & T. Clark, 1998.

Longenecker, Richard N. *Paul, Apostle of Liberty*. New York: Harper & Row, 1964.

Louw, Johannes P., and Eugene A. Nida, eds. *Greek–English Lexicon of the New Testament Based on Semantic Domains*. 2 vols. New York: United Bible Societies, 1988.

Lüdemann, Gerd. *Paul: The Founder of Christianity*. Amherst, N.Y.: Prometheus Books, 2002.

———. "συνείδησις." Pages 271-725 in *Exegetisches Wörterbuch zum Neuen Testament*. Volume 3. Edited by Horst Balz and Gerhard Schneider. Stuttgart: Verlag W. Kohlhammer, 1983.

Lührmann, D. *Das Offenbarungsverständnis bei Paulus und in den paulinischen Gemeinden*. Neukirchen-Vluyn: Neukirchener, 1965.

Lull, D. J. "Salvation History: Theology in 1 Thessalonians, Philemon, Philippians, and Galatians: A Response to N.T. Wright, R.B. Hays, and R. Scroggs." Pages 247–65 in *Thessalonians, Philippians, Galatians, Philemon*, 247–65. Vol. 1 of *Pauline Theology*. Edited by J. M. Bassler. Minneapolis: Fortress Press, 1991.

———. *The Spirit in Galatia: Paul's Interpretation of Pneuma as Divine Power*. SBLDS 49. Chico, Calif.: Scholars Press, 1980.

Lütgert, W. *Gesetz und Geist: Eine Untersuchung zur Vorgeschichte des Galaterbriefes*. Gütersloh: C. Bertelsmann, 1919.

Luz, Ulrich. *Das Geschichtsverständnis des Paulus*. BET 49. München: Chr. Kaiser Verlag, 1968.

MacDonald, D. R. *There Is No Male and Female: The Fate of a Dominical Saying in Paul and Gnosticism*. Philadelphia: Fortress Press, 1987.

MacIntyre, Alasdair. *After Virtue: A Study in Moral Theory*. 2nd ed. Notre Dame, Ind.: University of Notre Dame Press, 1984.

Malherbe, Abraham J. "Antisthenes and Odysseus, and Paul at War." Pages 91–119 in *Paul and the Popular Philosophers*. Minneapolis: Fortress Press, 1989.

———. "*Me genoito* in the Diatribe and Paul." Pages 25–33 in *Paul and the Popular Philosophers*. Minneapolis: Fortress Press, 1989.

———. "Gentle as a Nurse: The Cynic Background to 1 Thess 2." *NovT* 12 (1970): 203–17.

Manson, T. W. *Ethics and the Gospel*. New York: Charles Scribner's Sons, 1960.

Marrou, H.-I. *A History of Education in Antiquity*. New York: Mentor, 1964.

Marshall, I. Howard. "Response to A. T. Lincoln: The Stories of Predecessors and Inheritors in Galatians and Romans." Pages 204–214 in *Narrative Dynamics in Paul: A Critical Assessment*. Edited by B. W. Longenecker. Louisville/London: Westminster John Knox, 2002.

Martyn, J. Louis. "Events in Galatia: Modified Covenantal Nomism versus God's Invasion of the Cosmos in the Singular Gospel: A Response to J. D. G. Dunn and B. R. Gaventa." Pages 160–79 in *Thessalonians, Philippians, Galatians, Philemon*. Vol. 1 of *Pauline Theology*. Edited by J. M. Bassler. Minneapolis: Fortress Press, 1991.

Matera, Frank J. "The Culmination of Paul's Argument to the Galatians: Gal. v.1–vi.17." *JSNT* 32 (1988):79–91.

———. *New Testament Christology*. Louisville, KY: Westminster John Knox, 1999.

Matlock, R. B. "Sins of the Flesh and Suspicious Minds: Dunn's New Theology of Paul." *JSNT* 72 (1998): 67–90.

———. "The Arrow and the Web: Critical Reflection on a Narrative Approach to Paul." Pages 44–57 in *Narrative Dynamics in Paul: A Critical Assessment*. Louisville/London: Westminster John Knox, 2002.

Maurer, C. "σύνοιδα, συνείδησις." Pages 898-919 in *TDNT*. Vol 7.

McClane, Curtis D. "The Hellenistic Background to the Pauline Allegorical Method in Galatians 4:21–31." *Restoration Quarterly* 40:2 (1998): 125–35.

Meeks, W. A. "The Social Context of Pauline Theology." *Interpretation* 36 (1982): 266–277.

Merk, Otto. "Der Beginn der Paränese im Galaterbrief." *ZNW* 60 (1969): 83–104.

Mijoga, Hilary B. P. *The Pauline Notion of Deeds of the Law*. San Francisco: International Scholars Publications, 1999.

Milbank, J. *Theology and Social Theory*. Oxford: Blackwell, 1990.

Mitchell, Margaret M. *Paul and the Rhetoric of Reconciliation: An Exegetical Investigation of the Language and Composition of 1 Corinthians*. Louisville, Ky.: Westminster/John Knox Press, 1991.

Moore, George Foot. *Judaism in the First Centuries of the Christian Era: The Age of the Tannaim*. Cambridge, Mass.: Harvard University Press, 1927–1930.

Moores, John D. *Wrestling with Rationality in Paul: Romans 1–8 in a New Perspective*. SNTSMS 82. Cambridge, U.K.: Cambridge University Press, 1995.

Moule, C. F. D. "The Biblical Conception of 'Faith.'" *ExpTim* 68 (1956–1957): 157.

———. "Fulfilment-Words in the New Testament: Use and Abuse." *NTS* 14 (1968): 293–320.

———. *An Idiom Book of New Testament Greek*. Cambridge, U.K.: Cambridge University Press, 1953.

Moulton, James Hope, and George Milligan. *The Vocabulary of the Greek Testament Illustrated from the Papyri and Other Non-Literary Sources*. Grand Rapids, Mich.: Wm. B. Eerdmans, 1930.

Munck, Johannes. *Paul and the Salvation of Mankind*. London: Hodder and Stoughton, 1959.

Nanos, M. D. *The Irony of Galatians: Paul's Letter in First-Century Context*. Minneapolis: Fortress, 2002.

Nicholas, B., and S. M. Treggiari. "*patria potestas.*" Pages 1122–1123 in *Oxford Classical Dictionary*. 3rd ed. Edited by S. Hornblower and A. Spawforth. Oxford: Oxford University Press, 1996.

Nilsson, Martin P. *Die hellenistische Schule*. Munich: Beck, 1955.

Patte, Daniel. *Paul's Faith and the Power of God*. Philadelphia: Fortress, 1983.

Petersen, N. R. *Rediscovering Paul: Philemon and the Sociology of Paul's Narrative World*. Philadelphia: Fortress, 1985.

Picirelli, Robert E. "The Meaning of '*Epignosis*.'" *EQ* 47 (1975): 85–93.

Pierce, C. A. *Conscience in the New Testament*. Studies in Biblical Theology 15. London: SCM, 1955.

Pigeon, C. "'La loi du christ' en Galates 6,2." *Studies in Religion/Sciences Religieuses* 29 (2000): 425–438.

Piper, O. A. "Knowledge." Pages 42–8 in *Interpreter's Dictionary of the Bible*. Vol. 3. New York: Abingdon Press, 1962.

Polanyi, Michael. *Personal Knowledge: Towards a Post-Critical Philosophy*. Chicago: University of Chicago Press, 1962.

Pope, R. Martin. "Faith and Knowledge in Pauline and Johannine Thought." *ExpTim* 31 (1929–1930): 421–427.

Porter, Stanley. *Verbal Aspect in the Greek of the New Testament*. New York: Peter Lang, 1989.

Quine, W. V. "Two Dogmas of Empiricism." *The Philosophical Review* 60 (1951): 20–43.

Räisänen, Heikki. "Galatians 2.16 and Paul's Break with Judaism." Pages 112–26 in *Jesus, Paul and Torah: Collected Essays*. Translated by D. E. Orton. JSNT Supp. 43. Sheffield: Sheffield Academic Press, 1992.

———. *Paul and the Law*. WUNT 29. Tübingen: J. C. B. Mohr (Paul Siebeck), 1983.

Reitzenstein, Richard. *Hellenistic Mystery Religions*. Translated by J. E. Steely. Pittsburgh Theological Monographs 15. Pittsburgh: Pickwick, 1978.

Rengstorf, Karl Heinrich. "ἀπόστολος." Pages 407–445 in *TDNT*. Vol. 1.

Ricoeur, Paul. *Time and Narrative*. 3 vols. Translated by Kathleen McLaughlin and David Pellauer. Chicago and London: University of Chicago Press, 1984, 1986, 1988.

———. "The Narrative Function." *Semeia* 13 (1978): 177–202.

Ridderbos, Herman. *Paul: An Outline of His Theology*. Translated by John Richard De Witt. Grand Rapids, Mich.: Eerdmans, 1975.

Robinson, D. W. B. "'Faith of Jesus Christ' – A New Testament Debate." *RTR* 29 (1970): 71–81.

Roo, C. R. de. "The Concept of 'Works of the Law' in Jewish and Christian Literature." Pages 116–47 in *Christian–Jewish Relations Through the Centuries*. Edited by S. E. Porter and B. W. R. Pearson. Sheffield: Sheffield Academic Press, 2000.

Root, Michael. "The Narrative Structure of Soteriology." *Modern Theology* 2:2 (1986): 145–158.

Ropes, J. H. *The Singular Problem of the Epistle to the Galatians*. Cambridge, Mass.: Harvard University Press, 1929.

Rusam, Dietrich. "Neue Belege zu den στοιχεῖα τοῦ κόσμου (Gal 4,3.9; Kos 2,8.20)." *ZNW* 83 (1992): 119–125.

Sanders, E. P. "On the Question of Fulfilling the Law in Paul and Rabbinic Judaism." Pages 103–126 in *Donum Gentilicium: New Testament Studies in Honour of David Daube*. Edited by E. Bammel, C. K. Barrett, and W. D. Davies. Oxford: Clarendon Press, 1978.

———. *Paul and Palestinian Judaism: A Comparison of Patterns of Religion*. Minneapolis: Fortress Press, 1977.

———. *Paul, the Law, and the Jewish People*. Philadelphia: Fortress, 1983.

Sanders, J. A. "Torah and Christ." *Int* 29 (1975): 372–390.

Sanders, J. T. *The New Testament Christological Hymns: Their Historical Religious Background*. SNTSMS 15. Cambridge, U.K.: Cambridge University Press, 1971.

Sandnes, Karl Olav. *Paul – One of the Prophets? A Contribution to the Apostle's Self-Understanding*. WUNT 2.43. Tübingen: J. C. B. Mohr (Paul Siebeck), 1991.

Schmithals, Walter. *Paul and the Gnostics*. Translated by John E. Steely. Nashville: Abingdon, 1972.

Schoeps, H. J. *Paul: The Theology of the Apostle in the Light of Jewish Religious History*. Translated by Harold Knight. Philadelphia: Westminster, 1961.

Schrage, Wolfgang. *The Ethics of the New Testament*. Translated by D. E. Green. Philadelphia: Fortress, 1988.

———. *Die konkreten Einzelgebote in der paulinischen Paränese*. Gütersloh: Gütersloh Verlagshaus (Gerd Mohn), 1961.

Schreiner, T. R. "Is Perfect Obedience to the Law Possible? A Re-examination of Galatians 3:10." *JETS* 27 (1984): 151–160.

———. "Paul and Perfect Obedience to the Law: An Evaluation of the View of E. P. Sanders." *WTJ* 47 (1985): 245–278.

Schweitzer, A. *The Mysticism of Paul the Apostle*. Translated by W. Montgomery. London: A. & C. Black, 1931.

Schweizer, Eduard, Rudolf Meyer, and Friedrich Baumgärtel. "σάρξ, κτλ." Pages 98–151 in *TDNT*. Vol. 7.

Scroggs, Robin. "New Being: Renewed Mind: New Perception: Paul's View of the Source of Ethical Insight." *Chicago Theological Seminary Register* 72:1 (Winter 1982): 1–12.

Seesemann, Heinrich. "οἶδα." Pages 116–19 in *TDNT*. Vol. 5.

Segal, A. F. *Paul the Convert: The Apostolate and Apostasy of Saul the Pharisee*. New Haven, Conn.: Yale University Press, 1990.

Seifrid, M. "Righteousness Language in the Hebrew Scriptures and Early Judaism." Pages 415–42 in *The Complexities of Second Temple Judaism*. Vol. 1 of *Justification and Variegated Nomism*. Edited by D. A. Carson, P. T. O'Brien, and M. A. Seifrid. WUNT 2. Reihe, 140. Tübingen: Mohr Siebeck/Grand Rapids, Mich.: Baker Academic, 2001.

Siegert, Folker. *Argumentation bei Paulus: Gezeigt an Röm 9–11*. WUNT 34. Tübingen: J. C. B. Mohr (Paul Siebeck), 1985.

Silva, Moisés. "The Pauline Style as Lexical Choice: *Ginôskein* and Related Verbs." Pages 184–207 in *Pauline Studies: Essays Presented to F. F. Bruce*. Edited by D. A. Hagner and M. J. Harris. Exeter, UK: Paternoster Press/Grand Rapids, Mich.: Eerdmans, 1980.

Smit, Joop. "The Letter of Paul to the Galatians: A Deliberative Speech." *NTS* 35 (1989): 1–26.

Stacey, W. David. *The Pauline View of Man: In Relation to its Judaic and Hellenistic Background*. London: Macmillan & Co., 1956.

Stanton, Graham. "The Law of Moses and the Law of Christ: Galatians 3:1–6:2." Pages 99–116 in *Paul and the Mosaic Law*. Edited by James D. G. Dunn. Grand Rapids, Mich./Cambridge, U.K.: William B. Eerdmans, 1992.

Steinhauser, M. G. "Gal 4,25a: Evidence of Targumic Tradition in Gal 4,21–31?" *Biblica* 70 (1989): 234–240.

Stendahl, Krister. *Paul among Jews and Gentiles*. Philadelphia: Fortress, 1976.

Stowers, S. K. *The Diatribe and Paul's Letter to the Romans*. SBLDS 57. Chico, Calif.: Society of Biblical Literature, 1981.

———. "Paul on the Use and Abuse of Reason." Pages 253–86 in *Greeks, Romans, and Christians: Essays in Honor of Abraham J. Malherbe*. Edited by David L. Balch, Everett Ferguson, and Mayne A. Meeks. Minneapolis: Fortress Press, 1990.

Strauss, David Friederich. *The life of Jesus, Critically Examined*. Edited by Peter C. Hodgson. Translated by George Eliot. Philadelphia: Fortress Press, 1972.

Strong, L. Thomas III. "The Significance of the 'Knowledge of God' in the Epistles of Paul." Ph.D. diss., New Orleans Baptist Theological Seminary, 1992.

Tanner, Norman P., ed. *Decrees of the Ecumenical Councils*. Vol. 2, *Trent to Vatican II*. London: Sheed & Ward/Washington: Georgetown University Press, 1990.

Taylor, Greer M. "The Function of ΠΙΣΤΙΣ ΧΡΙΣΤΟΥ in Galatians." *JBL* 85 (1966): 58–76.

Theissen, Gerd. *Psychological Aspects of Pauline Theology*. Translated by John P. Galvin. Edinburgh: T. & T. Clark, 1987.

Thrall, Margaret E. "Pauline Use of συνείδησις." *NTS* 14 (1967): 118–25.

Thurén, Lauri. *Derhetorizing Paul: A Dynamic Perspective on Pauline Theology and the Law*. Harrisburg, Penn.: Trinity Press International, 2000.

Toolan, M. J. *Narrative: A Critical Linguistic Approach*. London: Routledge, 1988.

Torrance, T. F. "One Aspect of the Biblical Conception of Faith." *ExpTim* 68 (1956): 111–114.

Trapp, Michael Burney. "Allegory, Greek." Page 64 in *Oxford Classical Dictionary*. 3rd ed. Edited by S. Hornblower and A. Spawforth. Oxford: Oxford University Press, 1996.

Trench, Richard Chenivix. *Synonyms of the New Testament*. 9th ed. Grand Rapids, Mich.: Wm. B. Eerdmans, 1953 (1880).

Via, Dan O., Jr. *Kerygma and Comedy in the New Testament*. Philadelphia: Fortress, 1975.

Vos, J. S. "Die hermeneutische Antinomie bei Paulus (Galater 3,11–12; Römer 10,5–10)." *NTS* 38 (1992): 254–270.

Wakefield, Andrew H. *Where to Live: The Hermeneutical Significance of Paul's Citations from Scripture in Galatians 3:1–14*. Academia Biblica 14. Atlanta: Scholars Press, 2003.

Watson, Francis. "Is There a Story in These Texts?" Pages 231–40 in *Narrative Dynamics in Paul: A Critical Assessment*. Edited by B. W. Longenecker. Louisville & London: Westminster John Knox, 2002.

Wenham, Gordon J. *Story as Torah: Reading the Old Testament Ethically*. Edinburgh: T. & T. Clark, 2000.

Westerholm, S. *Israel's Law and the Church's Faith*. Grand Rapids, Mich.: Eerdmans, 1988.

———. "On Fulfilling the Whole Law (Gal 5:14)." *SEÅ* 51–52 (1986–1987): 229–237.

———. *Perspectives Old and New on Paul: The Lutheran Paul and His Opponents*. Grand Rapids, Mich.: William B. Eerdmans, 2004.

Whiteley, D. E. H. *The Theology of St. Paul*. Philadelphia: Fortress Press, 1964.

Widmann, Martin. "1 Kor. 2:6–16: Ein Einspruch gegen Paulus." *ZNW* 70 (1979): 44–53.

Wilckens, Ulrich. "Was heißt bei Paulus: 'Aus Werken des Gesetzes wird kein Mensch gerecht'?" Pages 77–109 in *Rechtfertigung als Freiheit: Paulusstudien*. Neukirchen-Vluyn: Neukirchener Verlag, 1974.

———. *Weisheit und Torheit: Eine exegetisch-religionsgeschichtliche Untersuchung zu I Kor. 1 und 2*. Tübingen: J. C. B. Mohr, 1959.

———. "Zu 1 Kor 2,1–16." Pages 501–537 in *Theologia Crucis – Signum Crucis: Festschrift für Erich Dinkler zum 70. Geburtstag*. Edited by Carl Andresen and Günther Klein. Tübingen: J. C. B. Mohr (Paul Siebeck), 1979.

Wilder, Amos. *Early Christian Rhetoric: The Language of the Gospel*. 2nd ed. Cambridge, Mass.: Harvard University Press, 1971.

Williams, Sam K. "Again *Pistis Christou*." *CBQ* 49 (1987): 431–447.

———. "The Hearing of Faith: ΑΚΟΗ ΠΙΣΤΕΩΣ in Gal. 3." *NTS* 35 (1989): 82–93.

———. "Justification and the Spirit in Galatians." *JSNT* 29 (1987): 91–100.

Winter, Bruce W. *Philo and Paul among the Sophists: Alexandrian and Corinthian Responses to a Julio-Claudian Movement*. 2nd ed. Grand Rapids, Mich.: Eerdmans, 2002.

Witherington, Ben III. *Paul's Narrative Thought World: The Tapestry of Tragedy and Triumph*. Louisville, Ky.: Westminster/John Knox Press, 1994.

Wright, N. T. *Christian Origins and the Question of God*. Vol. 1, *The New Testament and the People of God*. Minneapolis: Fortress Press, 1992.

———. *The Climax of the Covenant: Christ and the Law in Pauline Theology*. Minneapolis: Fortress Press, 1992.

Yaron, R. *Gifts in Contemplation of Death in Jewish and Roman Law*. Oxford: Clarendon, 1960.

Young, N. H. "Who's Cursed – and Why? (Galatians 3:10–14)." *JBL* 117 (1998): 79–92.

Yu, Seung Won. "Paul's Pneumatic Epistemology: Its Significance in His Letters." Ph.D. diss., Duke University, 1998.

Ziesler, J. A. *The Meaning of Righteousness in Paul: A Linguistic and Theological Inquiry.* SNTSMS 20. Cambridge, U.K.: Cambridge University Press, 1972.

Zimmerman, Heinrich. "Knowledge of God in the New Testament." Pages 474–8 in *Encyclopedia of Biblical Theology.* Edited by J. B. Bauer. London: Sheed & Ward, 1970.

Index of Ancient Sources

1. Old Testament

Where the verse or chapter numbers of the Hebrew MT differ from those in English texts, the numbering of the Hebrew text is used, with the numbering of English Bibles following in parentheses.

2. Apocrypha

3. New Testament

4. Dead Sea Scrolls

Damascus Document (CD)
II 14–16	257
III 2	200

Florilegium (4QFlor)
1 I 10–12	223
1 II 1	182

Hodayot (1QH)
II 8–12	189
IX 23	38
XII 13	38

Milḥamah (1QM)
Passim	171
IV 3	258

Miqṣat Ma'aśê ha-Torah (4QMMT)
C27	182
C20–22 ⸱	182

Pesher Habakkuk (1QpHab)
V 4–8	189

VII 15	38
VII 14–VIII 3	207

Pesher Nahum (4QpNah)
I 7–8	213

Rule of the Community (1QS)
I 16–17	252
II 5–17	165
IV 18	38
IV 22	39
V 5	257
V 21	182
VIII 10–12	39
VIII 15–18	39
VIII 20	255
XI 7, 9, 12	258

Temple Scroll (11QT)
64.6–13	213

5. Jewish Pseudepigrapha

Apocalypse of Abraham (Apoc. Ab.)
1–8	200
7:10	101

Aristobulus
Frag. 2	241–242
Frag. 4.3	241–242
Frag. 5.9–13	241–242

2 Baruch (2 Bar.)
4:2–6	248
14:12–13	224
32:1	255
32:2	248
54:13	101
57:2	224
59:4	248

1 Enoch (1 En.)
5:4–7	189
9:5	101
40:9	219
43:6	248

60:1ff.	226
82:4–5	189
84:3	101
90:19	171
90:28–29	248
93:2–10	255

2 Enoch (2 En.)
33:7	101
47:3–4	101
55:2	248
66:4	101

4 Ezra
3:28–36	190
4:20–22	205
4:28–30	260
5:23–24	255
7:26	248
8:52	248
9:7	189
9:31–32	255
10	246

6. Philo of Alexandria

7. Flavius Josephus

8. Rabbinic Literature

9. Early Christian Writings

10. Other Ancient Works and Papyri

Index of Early Commentators and Modern Authors

Index of Subjects and Key Terms